Once Upon a Highway
Route 66 in Oklahoma

By John Calvin Womack
With a Foreword by Gailard Sartain

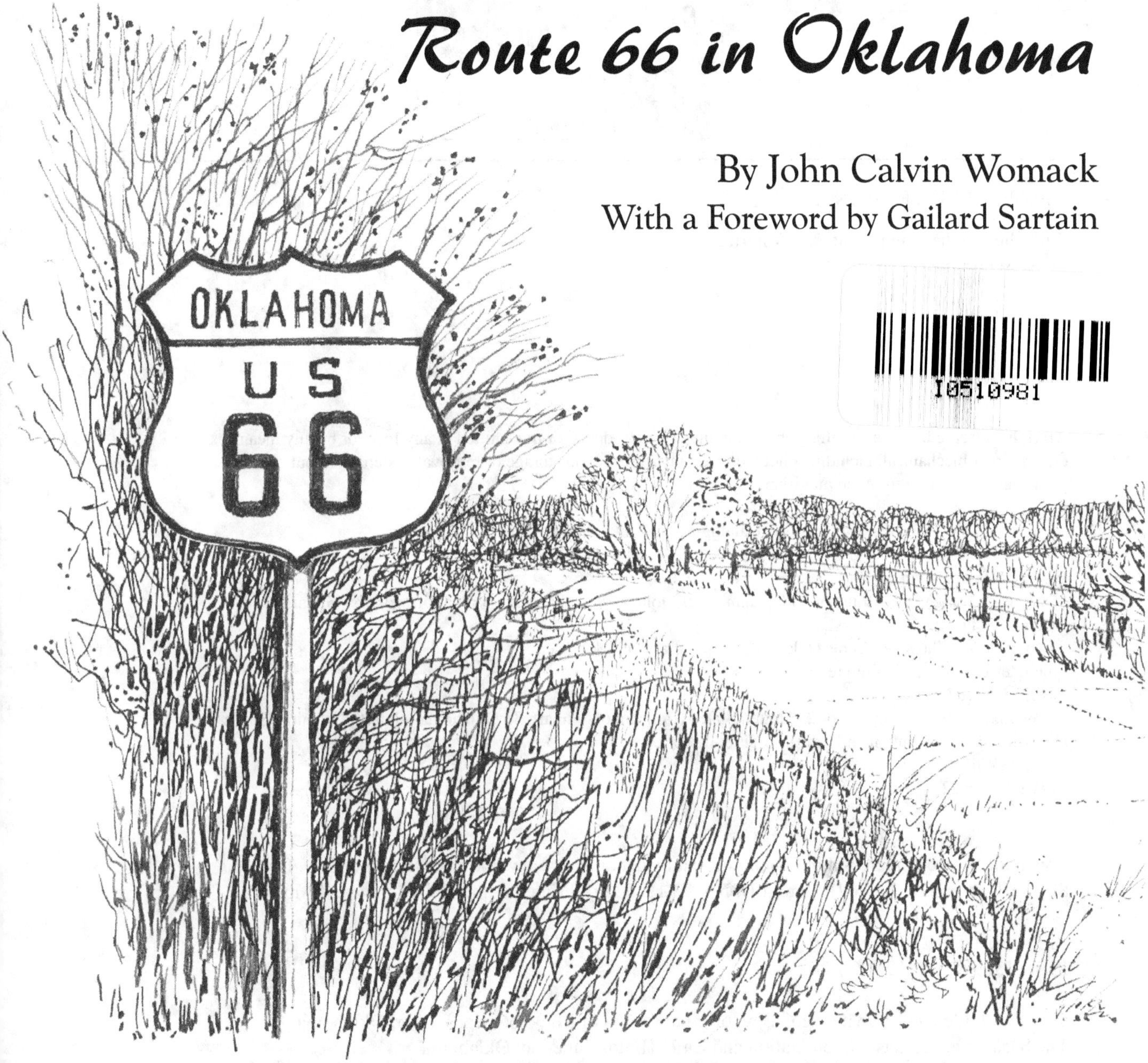

The New Forums Oklahoma Centennial Collectors' Series

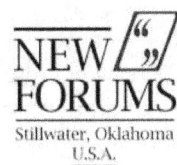

NEW FORUMS
Stillwater, Oklahoma
U.S.A.

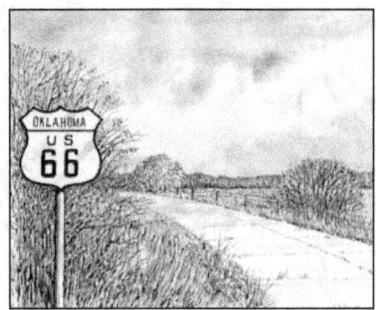

NEW FORUMS PRESS INC.

Published in the United States of America
by New Forums Press, Inc.
1018 S. Lewis Street
Stillwater, OK 74074
www.newforums.com

Library of Congress Cataloging-in-Publication Data

Womack, John Calvin, 1950-
  Once upon a highway : Route 66 in Oklahoma / by John Calvin Womack ; with a foreword by Gailard Sartain.— 2nd ed.
     p. cm. — (The new forums Oklahoma Centennial Collectors' series ; v. 1)
  Includes bibliographical references.
  ISBN 1-58107-138-8
  1. Womack, John Calvin, 1950- 2. United States Highway 66—In art. 3. Oklahoma—In art. 4. United States Highway 66—Description and travel. I. Title. II. Series.
  NC139.W654A4 2005
  741.973—dc22

                                                2005032110

This book may be ordered in bulk quantities at discount from New Forums Press, Inc., P.O. Box 876, Stillwater, OK 74076 [Federal I.D. No. 73 1123239]. Printed in the United States of America.

ISBN 10: 1-58107-138-8
ISBN 13: 978-1-581071-38-2

Cover and title page drawing depicts an original stretch of Route 66 near Luther, Oklahoma. The back cover depicts Hinton Station and Cafe, Hinton Junction, Oklahoma.

Second Edition / 2 3 4 5 6 7 8 9 0

Congratulations!

... upon your acquisition of this first work of the New Forums Oklahoma Centennial Series – *Once Upon a Highway... Route 66 in Oklahoma.* A first edition, case bound, individually numbered and signed by the author, was published as a collectors' work, in 2006.

We are especially proud to make available the excellent works of John Calvin Womack, Oklahoma State University professor of architecture.

For information about other titles in our Oklahoma Centennial Series, visit our web site at www.newforums.com, or call 405-372-6158.

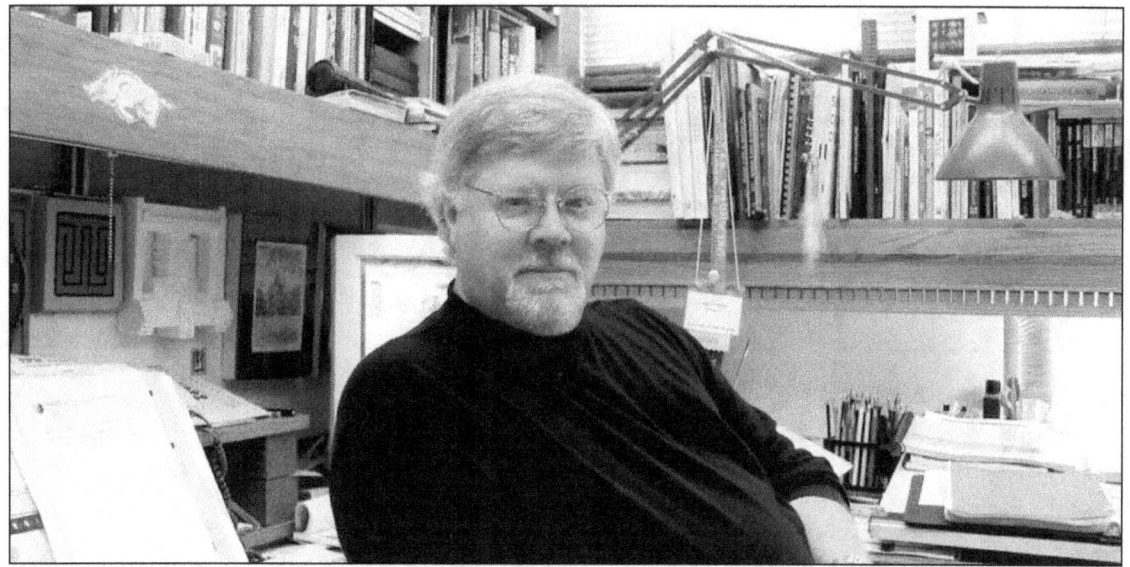

John Calvin Womack

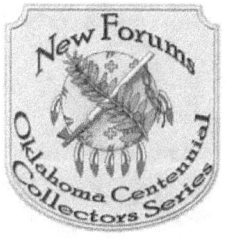

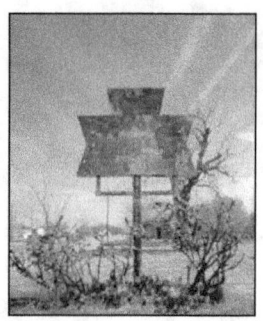

To Becky,
Stuart, Bryan
&
Mary Elizabeth

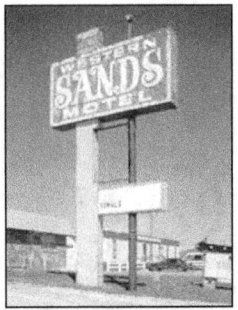

Contents

Foreword

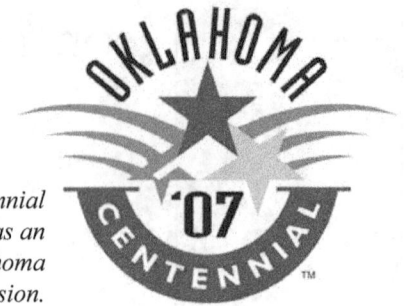

The New Forums Oklahoma Centennial Collectors' Series is recognized as an official project by the Oklahoma Centennial Commission.

I spent my childhood living half a mile from Route 66. I didn't know it was Route 66—it was just 11th Street to me—and I didn't know it was a "highway" or that it was a pulsing artery of our nation; I just knew it went to downtown Tulsa if I turned left and who knows where if I turned right. I did know that it glittered. It glittered with the shiny new paint of exotic cars that I didn't see anywhere else in Tulsa. They traveled fast, usually going west. It seemed like it was my own private new car showroom with license tags from every state in the Union.

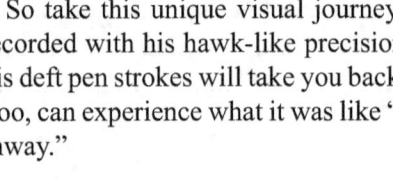

I traveled up and down 11th Street on my black Schwinn bicycle to go to grade school, Boy Scouts, the Will Rogers Theatre and a million other destinations. It seemed as if anything important was on 11th Street. It was an oasis; everything that was vital and life sustaining could be found on either side of it. Although a microcosm, it was the entire world for my buddies and me. As far as we were concerned, nothing else was as exciting.

The neon lights lining Route 66 were inviting and shone like a brightly beaded necklace. At night I could see the blinking lights of the tower on the Will Rogers Theatre (now a parking lot) from my bedroom window. That theatre was seminal for me—I spent so many happy hours there watching good and bad movies with my bicycle waiting for me (un-locked, by the way) on the bike rack outside. When I was very young, my parents and I drove to Los Angeles on Route 66. It felt like it was a trip to another planet—hot and long and scary. My memories of this trek are few, but I still remember the different sounds that the tires made on the different stretches of road and falling asleep only to awaken to a totally different landscape. In the years since, I have traversed the new I-40 many, many times and have reminisced as spots of the old road appear, and fantasies of all the anonymous travelers that went before me are conjured.

In John's magical renderings, he takes us from the neighborhood that I knew to the entire Oklahoma stretch of Route 66, painstakingly exploring the rich textures of the unique structures that punctuate this road.

I'm sure you will enjoy his book as much as I do. Perusing it is like a Twilight Zone episode—the mystery and realism meld together to hauntingly create almost otherworldly images from an era sadly gone. So take this unique visual journey that John has recorded with his hawk-like precision and clarity. His deft pen strokes will take you back in time so you, too, can experience what it was like "once upon a highway."

Gailard Sartain
Tulsa, Oklahoma

Introduction

One Saturday morning in 1971, I was driving east on U.S. Highway 66 from Edmond, Oklahoma, towards the city of Chandler. With no particular destination in mind, and no particular schedule to keep, I was simply enjoying a ride in the country. Driving on Route 66 felt good and brought back memories of the 1960s TV show, "Route 66." This was new territory for me as my parents had only recently moved to Edmond, Oklahoma, from our longtime home in Springdale, Arkansas. But the

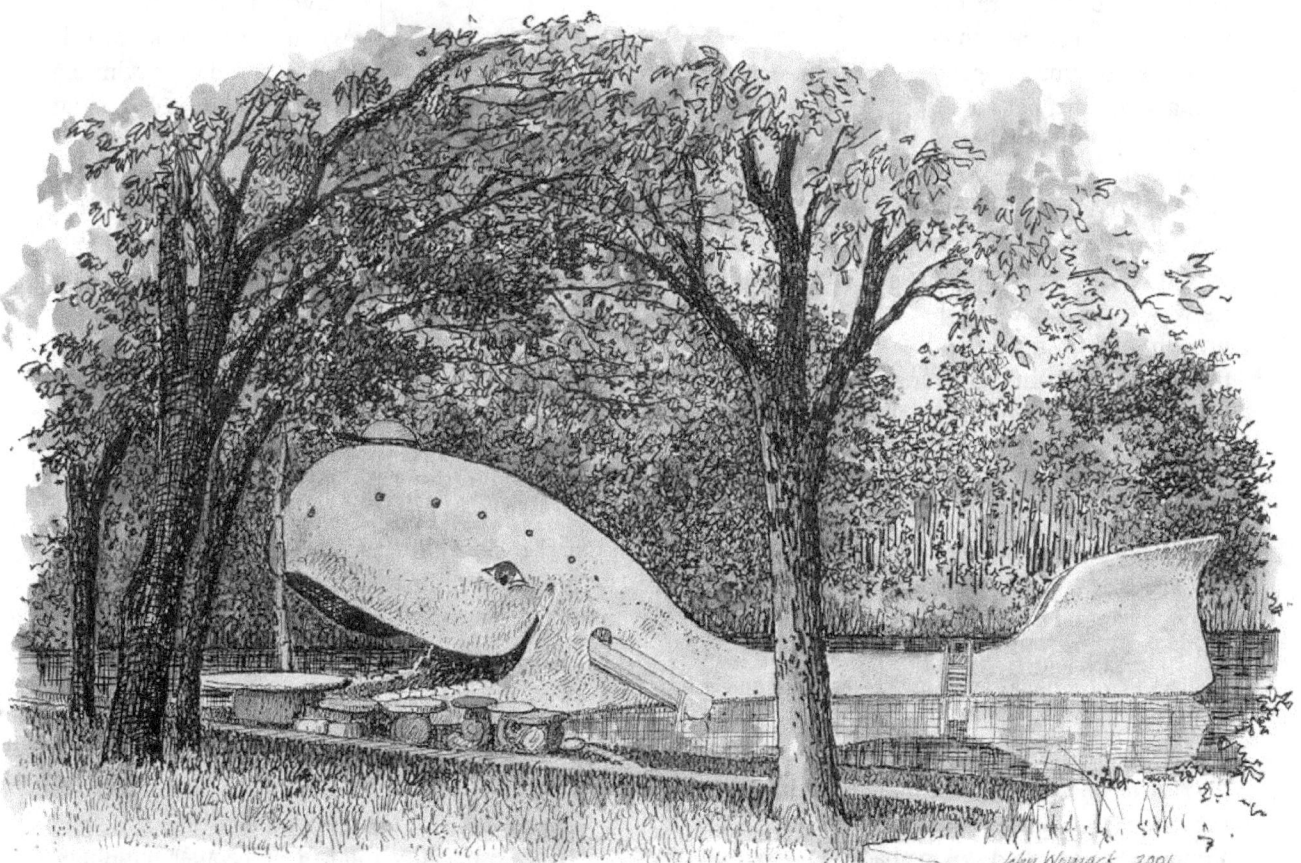

The Blue Whale in Catoosa, Oklahoma, was built in 1972 and remains today as one of the most famous places along the entire length of Route 66 to visit and photograph.

move didn't seem to be so bad after it was all said and done—I found that I liked Oklahoma.

Driving along, enjoying the cool morning air and views of the countryside, I was totally unprepared for the architectural experience waiting up ahead in the little town of Arcadia. As I approached the town, on the left side of the road, a large, red-painted structure with a faded green roof began to emerge through the surrounding trees. The structure appeared to be an old barn, but not like any barn that I had ever seen before—this barn was round!

Pulling over to the shoulder of the road, I parked the car, got out, and for a few minutes stood there looking at the old structure. There was no telling when the barn had last been used, but it appeared to have been years before. The barn obviously had been the center of a sizable farming operation at one time, but now it was empty and abandoned. Weeds and vines seemed to be its only companions now. Here and there remnants of an old wire fence wrinkled its way through the undergrowth, and posted around

the side of the barn were various signs proclaiming "Keep Out" and "No Trespassing."

My curiosity began to get the better of me, and though I certainly don't think it's right to trespass, I had to have a closer look. I walked across the highway, climbed the grassy slope, and stepped through the weeds over to the old relic. The barn was indeed in bad shape and suffering from time and neglect, but it was still something to behold. Though weathered and worn, it was evident that the barn had originally been built with skill and careful attention to detail. I had no idea how old it was.

After spending several minutes walking around the barn and peeking inside where the door was ajar, I returned to my car. Looking back at the barn, I admired its unique form and craftsmanship. Who had built the barn and why had they used the round shape?

I also wondered how long the old barn could remain standing—its roof was starting to cave in, and the sides were beginning to lean.

As I pondered the old barn, I thought how other highway travelers most surely would have noticed it as well. Every highway has its landmarks—places that give substance to location and time, and this barn would surely have been such a landmark. Roadside markers are particularly important to children cooped up inside a car on long trips. My sister and I used to have such points of interest on the way from our house in Arkansas to our grandmother's house in Waverly, Missouri. Such landmarks added interest to the trip, sparked our imaginations, and gave us some indication of when we were going to "get there." If we had traveled Route 66 back when we were kids, this round red barn definitely would have been one of our anticipated landmarks.

Of course, as I later found out, the Round Barn in Arcadia, built in 1898, was indeed a famous landmark on Route 66. In 1988 a group of local citizens, with donated funds from a large number of area people, restored the Round Barn to its original glory. The barn is now open to the public and is listed on the National Register for Historic Places.

The Round Barn is what might be called a "vernacular" building. Vernacular buildings are generally "common" or ordinary structures—not designed by architects. Barns fall into this category. Such buildings are typically designed and constructed by local people using tried and true methods that are well suited to the local climate, available materials, local traditions, economics, etc. Vernacular buildings are born out of common sense and straightforward methodologies—what one might call "honest."

I am especially fond of vernacular buildings, particularly old farm structures, and find it fascinating how such buildings appear so visually comfortable in their settings. I believe this pleasing appearance is, in part, a result of the direct, common-sense problem-solving approach that was required of the pre-modern farmer. Farm making was an incredibly difficult task—there were so many situations to consider. For instance, the farmstead must be carefully oriented to the sun and wind to maximize warmth in the winter and cooling in the summer, the farmhouse should not be downwind of the animals in the summer (unless one revels in barnyard odors while dining or sleeping), getting to and from the barn in a blizzard should be feasible as it can be a matter of life and death, and so on. The wise farmer attempted to take as many things into account as possible when arranging his farmstead. The results of such thinking and planning generally insured a more functional and pleasant working/living environment and, I propose, a more aesthetically pleasing one as well. Individual farms evolved over time, but before changes were made, the overall effect on the whole had to be carefully considered.

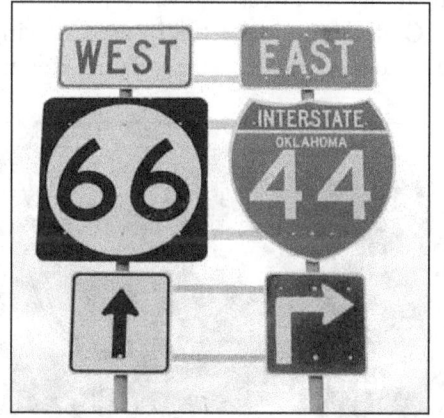

Such environments as mentioned above have a quality that I call "place." A place, whether it is a farm or a city square, is somewhere you like to be because it is comfortable and stimulating. Places beckon to us, welcome us upon our arrival, and reward us as we participate with the circumstances. There are countless aspects to quality places, and each place will differ from the next—no spot on the planet is exactly like another. One important aspect to place, and one which I think all successful places have, is "authenticity." Authenticity reinforces the reality of the experience, making the place more interesting, more tangible, and more enjoyable.

The Round Barn is an example of place, maybe not as strong a place as it once was, but still it evokes a sense of the authentic. It is not a fake. The Round Barn is a true, historical artifact—a direct link to the frontier days of Oklahoma and an immediate roadside witness to the comings and goings along Route 66. The original builders weren't trying to be cute or whimsical in selecting a round form for the barn. The round form was a result of its function as a dairy barn ("form" truly following "function"). When the barn was built in 1898, it was built with the best available tools, the best available technology, and the best available ideas on how it could work best for its anticipated function.

Today when I visit the restored barn I can sense and appreciate the lives of the people that built it, worked in it, danced in it (at one time it was a popular Saturday-night square dance arena), and so on. Standing in the barn and looking out one of its windows to Route 66 below, I find it easy to get lost in an imaginary time warp where history replays itself in front of me. In my mind's eye I can see Model-A Fords chugging along in route to Oklahoma City, or a loaded-down station wagon heading to St. Louis, or maybe a 1960 red Corvette convertible traveling toward some new awaiting adventure. Authentic places trigger my imagination that way.

I experience a great amount of satisfaction and enjoyment whenever I can participate with something that is the genuine thing. In this day and age when so many things are fake or "faux," it is indeed comforting and reassuring to experience things that are real and authentic. For sure, Route 66 had its share of fake facades and funny sideshows ("tourist traps" as my dad called them), but those places became profound parts of the Route 66 experience and were authentic articles of the road. To me, Disneyland is the great fake escape—but then again, Disneyland, in all of its novelty, was very much a part of the Route 66 experience, and was the destination for many a Route 66 traveler.

Today, people drive the old highway for various

reasons, and their emotional reactions to the road vary widely. For some, driving Route 66 is an attempt to retrieve a bit of the "good ol' days." For others, the drive is an attempt to understand a certain period of American history and what interstate travel conditions were once like. Still others drive the road simply to get off the interstate and enjoy a more leisurely drive with more interesting things to see. Whatever their reasons, it is a fact that people come from all over the world to find something on Route 66.

Traveling on Route 66 is not faster, nor is it safer than traveling on the interstate, but it is a lot more interesting. On Route 66 if you want to stop and take a look at something, you simply pull over and park—not so on the interstate. On the interstate if you see something you might want to investigate, you first have to wait for the next exit, find which way to go, then find the right road, and so on. By the time you've figured out how to get back to what interested you in the first place, you've forgotten what was so interesting about it, and the time lost on your unsuccessful venture adds further to the frustration. If I had been driving on Interstate 44 (Oklahoma's Turner Turnpike) on that particular Saturday morning back in 1971, I would never have found the Round Barn—it can't be seen from the interstate.

To sense something of the Route 66 experience you have to drive the road—you can't get it on the interstate. I don't know of anyone who feels like they have been traveling on Route 66 when they have actually been driving on I-44 or I-40—even though those same interstates parallel Route 66 for the most

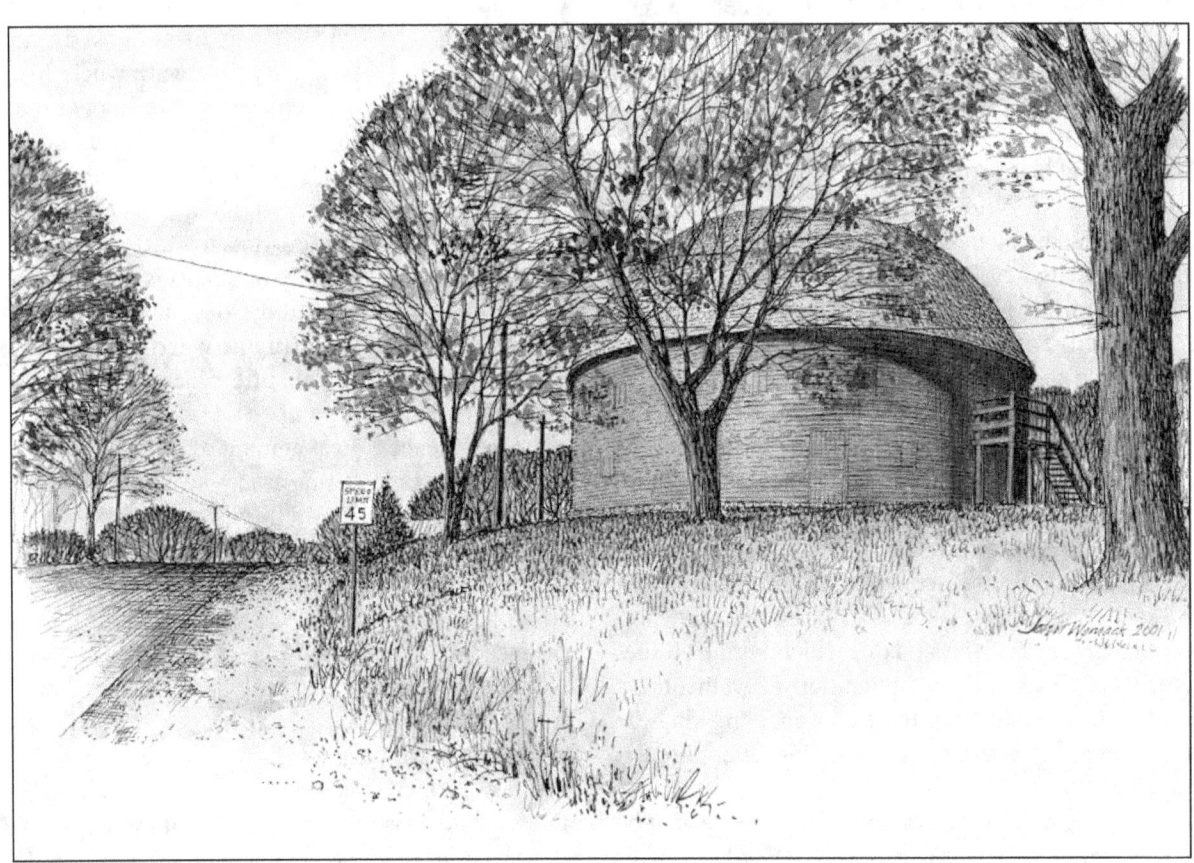

The Round Barn in Arcadia, Oklahoma, offers the Route 66 traveler an opportunity to step back into the historic days of Oklahoma Territory.

part, and travel through the same landscape. You have to be *on* Route 66 to have an authentic experience.

From 1926 when Route 66 began until the 1970s when the interstate system began to dominate, the Route was a thriving, throbbing artery of American transportation and enterprise. Although most of the businesses that eked out a living on Route 66 during its heyday are now long gone, the building shells and sheds are still there in surprising numbers, and these structures have much to do with the Route 66 feeling. You will pass old abandoned gas stations, dilapidated motels, derelict diners, and much more. You will pass old deserted farmhouses, old barns and shacks, and every so often, the dwindling remains of an old drive-in movie theater, bowling alley, or curio shop. There is a sort of ghostly feeling to many of these places, especially in the more rural areas, but then again, maybe these "ghosts" are only the products of my imagination in combination with the desolation and the sound of the wind.

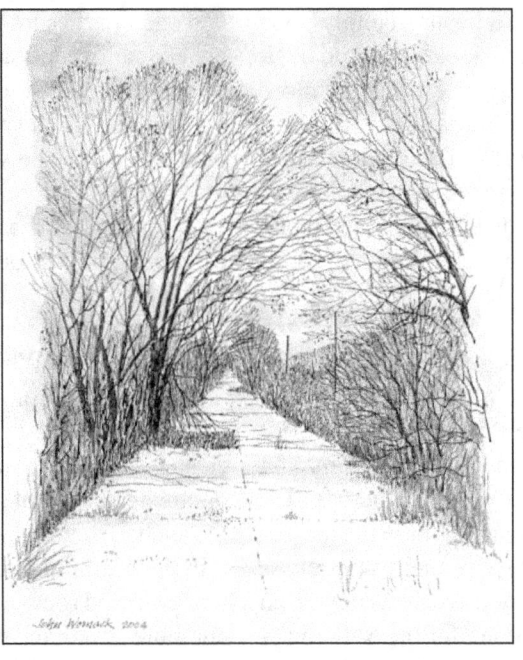

Along the Route, there are a few businesses that are still up and running in their original buildings. A few have been modified a bit, but some remain unchanged. In cities like Tulsa and Oklahoma City, many of the old buildings on Route 66 are still there for your viewing pleasure, but you might have to look a bit harder to find them. Several smaller Oklahoma towns along the Route have many remaining structures that are often in disrepair but still convey a sense of Route 66 in its prime.

Of great significance is the passage by Congress of the National Route 66 Corridor Preservation Act in 1999. Scheduled to terminate in 2009, this act set aside funds for which various sites and locations along Route 66 can apply in an effort to restore and refurbish their properties. This will hopefully save many of the Route's features that might otherwise vanish.

There is a certain sense of permanence that most old buildings (pre-1970) possess that new buildings (post-1970) rarely seem to have. I find that "old" buildings exhibit a greater concern for quality, in both the materials used, and in their manner of construction. These older buildings also usually have more interesting details and ornamentation—especially the old brick commercial buildings found in many Oklahoma communities.

Most of these older buildings were committed to quality and were built to withstand the forces of nature and man. Once upon a time, people couldn't see putting their hard-earned money into something that was going to fall apart in a short amount of time—sustained value was important. Whenever I see an abandoned old building that is still standing after years of neglect and exposure to the weather, I can't help but feel a certain sense of admiration for the building and those that built it. The notion of sustained value makes a lot of sense.

Isn't it interesting how so many old commercial buildings have the original owner's name and date of construction inscribed on the front of the building? Obviously, those original owners took pride in their building and business. Names and dates carved in stone and built into the fabric of the building, not simply bolted on, proclaimed to everyone that the owners appreciated quality and were solid in both finance and in standing with the community. How many buildings built today express this same type of solidity and concern for the well-being of the community? Unfortunately, too many new buildings seem to be more about taking away from the community than giving back. At least these newer, anonymous, and less carefully constructed buildings will fall apart and vanish from our sight at a quicker pace—but what a waste of materials and energy.

Many of the old neon lighted signs are still around. A lot of these signs have seen much better days, but some of them are still in surprisingly good condition. There is a distinctive look to the old business signs on Route 66. The signs that announced the various motel locations and entrances are the most elaborate and eye-catching. Many of these motel signs have certain recurring design features that suggest a single person or company might have designed them. Along with the name of the motel, the most prominent feature of these motel signs is the arrow that points to the motel's entrance. It's fun to note the wide variety of shapes these arrows take.

Another engaging aspect of Route 66 is how so many structures that line the Road continue to bear witness to the individualism and dogged termination of the people who owned and operated them. Often of the "mom and pop" type, many of these businesses made concerted efforts to display their uniqueness and specialties to the highway traveler. Whether an ornate sign, an inventive building form, a gimmicky phrase, or a combination of these, such devices were meant to tweak the curiosity of motoring travelers, entice them to stop for awhile, and hopefully spend a little money. There is an undeniable attraction to these places.

Sometimes the object of interest was not even in the original plans for the business. Take the Blue Whale in Catoosa, for instance. The original attraction was an "ark" where parents could hold birthday and other parties for their children. Later, as the owners added live animals to their attraction, two ponds were constructed—one for swimming at fifty-cents per person. When swimmers remarked that a diving platform would be welcomed, the owners built not just any platform but one whale of a platform! Before long, Catoosa's Blue Whale, like Arcadia's Round Barn, was one of the most famous stops on Route 66.

Such novel roadside statements of individuality like the Blue Whale stand in stark contrast to the rather soulless, corporate owned, franchised establishments of today. At one time motels, along with clean and comfortable accommodations, often offered unique features that made them additionally interesting and fun to visit. Whether it happened to be a swimming pool, miniature golf course, theme restaurant, tepee-shaped rooms, or whatever, staying in a different motel along the way used to be part of the travel adventure. Such is rarely the case today. Today's

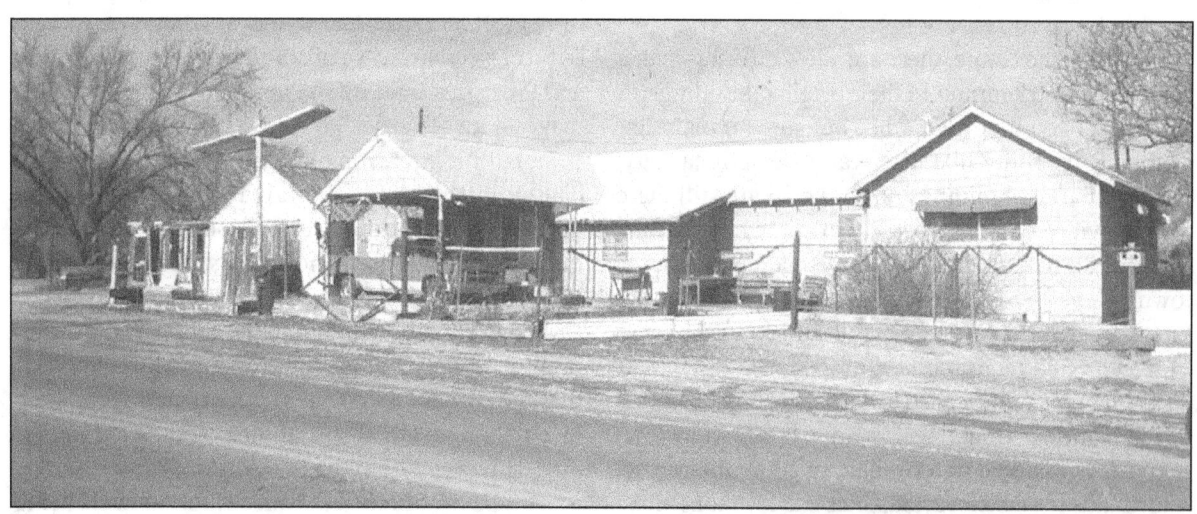

motel chain establishments are basically the same whether they are located in St. Louis, Tulsa, Albuquerque, or Los Angeles. The corporate motel inns of today have taken the idea of sameness to extremes. Some, in fact, promote this generic idea as a plus: "No surprises here" some ads say. Sorry, but life without a surprise every now and then can be pretty dull.

In a way, this book is about relearning, or reconsidering, who we were in an age gone by, and being reminded of whom we are as a people now. These drawings and photographs provide a certain way of looking back by providing glimpses of places along Route 66 in Oklahoma. The drawings depict unique places built by enterprising Oklahomans and utilized by people experiencing a true adventure.

Why create a book that relies primarily on drawings and only minimally on photographs? Photographs certainly provide a more detailed record of a particular scene and that is how they are used here, as details. However, I often find the emotional content of photographs somewhat limiting. Drawings, at least for me, allow my imagination to participate more fully and freely with what is being depicted. Drawings also allow for some visual "editing" when necessary. Another reason is I like to draw.

The scenes depicted here are not historic recreations. With a few exceptions, all of the places shown here appear as they did around the beginning of this millennium. Many scenes are illustrated in detail complete with surrounding weeds, piled up junk, broken windows, etc. In one instance I elected not to show windows that had been boarded up with plywood and instead illustrated the openings with glass and operating window units. I found that I liked the building so much I simply didn't want to repeat what appeared to be an indignity. Maybe I was wrong in doing this, as viewers might have noted how shameful it is to let any beautiful thing deteriorate. But then again, there are several examples within these pages that, hopefully, might motivate people to reconsider the value of refurbishing and restoring potentially useful structures.

Time marches on, and with time comes inevitable change. Some of the scenes contained here no longer exist and more are vanishing daily. The old church in Arcadia was demolished sometime in the late 1970s or early 1980s. Fortunately, I had photographed it before it was torn down. While traveling the highway, I began to notice several curious similarities between the church in Arcadia and others. Notice the similar bell towers, entry vestibules, and window designs on the churches in Chelsea, Davenport, Bridgeport, and Arcadia. I don't know the circumstances behind these similar features (mail order parts, same builder, or stock plans) but I would wager there is a link somewhere.

In one instance, change became startlingly apparent. Within one month of completing the drawing of the Yukon Motel, the sign was gone. Driving through town, and actually preparing my wife for a view of the upcoming sign (which she hadn't seen except in my previously completed drawing), I was totally flabbergasted not to see the sign I was anticipating but rather one of those soulless, generic duds from a national motel chain. Maybe my dismay was fueled by the fact that out of all the Route 66 signs I had viewed and sketched, the Yukon Motel sign had probably been my favorite.

Obviously, not all of the places contained within these pages are of the same landmark status as the Round Barn or the Blue Whale. But, as mentioned earlier, there is a vigor and spirit to all of these places that I find curious and engaging. Whether landmarks or not, you can rest assured that each of the places illustrated within these pages was at one time the most important spot on the entire planet for someone. I have found the Route 66 experience is reliant not only on the icons of the road but on the "in-between"

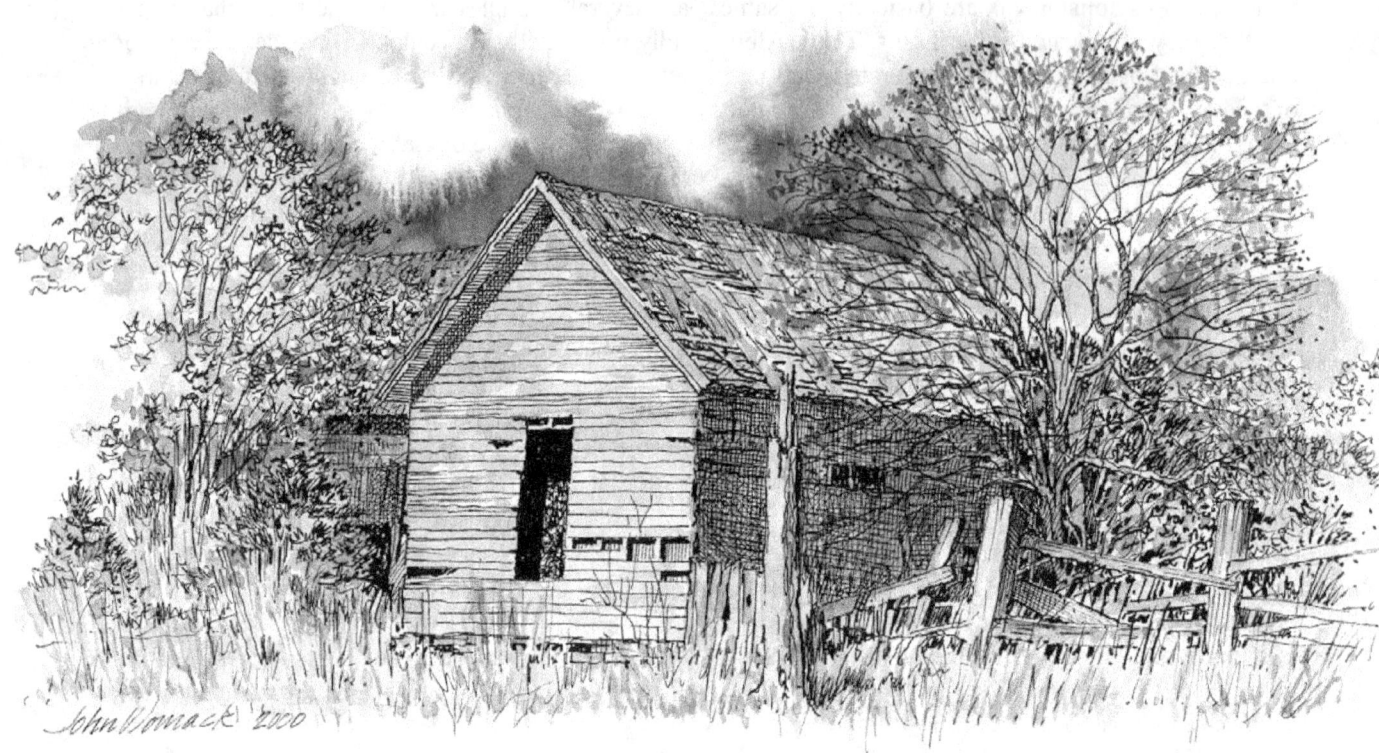

When passing abandoned and crumbling homes along Route 66, one wonders about the families that lived there.

features as well. Sometimes these places are more poignant and provocative than the other more well-known and publicized sights.

This study is not all-inclusive. There are sights and places along the highway that, for various reasons, did not make it into this book, and I apologize to those readers who might feel jilted in not finding one of their favorite sights on or near Route 66 contained here. With a few exceptions, the scenes depicted here are of places located directly along the edge of Route 66. To focus upon these has obviously, yet unfortunately, excluded other examples of Route 66 places in Oklahoma. One could easily argue that any town or city located on Route 66 has many interesting and important structures in the town, but not on Route 66. One structure not included here is the Oklahoma City National Memorial, site of the Murrah Federal Building bombing. The site is of immense significance to Oklahoma City and the nation, but is

it a part of Route 66? I decided not.

Someone once asked me why I thought a highway like Route 66 had so much appeal to so many people, not only Americans but people from all over the world, and I answered, "Freedom." The thought of getting in some sort of vehicle and driving from Chicago to the Pacific Ocean, without going through checkpoints, passport verifications, identification checks, and so on, is quite liberating. You can take as long as you like to make the trip, stop and look at whatever interests you, eat whenever you are hungry, and sleep whenever you are tired—with all of your needs accommodated by various places along Route 66. Freedom of interstate travel is one hallmark of the American idea. Though Americans may take such freedoms for granted, Europeans and Asians find such free and open travel exhilarating. Of course, Americans love the drive, too!

Those discovering the charm of Route 66 for

the first time should know that Oklahoma and Route 66 are so indelibly allied together, you can hardly mention the one without the other. In his book, *Route 66,* author Tim Steil states, "There is a lot of Route 66 in Oklahoma and a lot of Oklahoma in Route 66." And so it is. It was a man from Tulsa, Cyrus Avery, who made sure that Route 66 went through Oklahoma. Avery is considered the "father" of Route 66. It is also significant to note that, after the Federal government decertified the Route in 1985, a few states dropped the "66" highway designation—but not Oklahoma. Following the Federal decertification, Oklahoma designated more than 150 miles of the old U.S. highway as "State Highway 66."

Once upon a highway known as U.S. Route 66, there existed a world of hope and determination, courage and kindness, love and hate, easy-come, easy-go, and hard-come, hard-go. All of these human situations manifested themselves in one way or another into the remnants of the road that we see today. It is my hope the reader and viewer of the things portrayed here will begin to sense some of these human and landscape interactions and make it a goal to get out and experience the Mother Road—especially in Oklahoma.

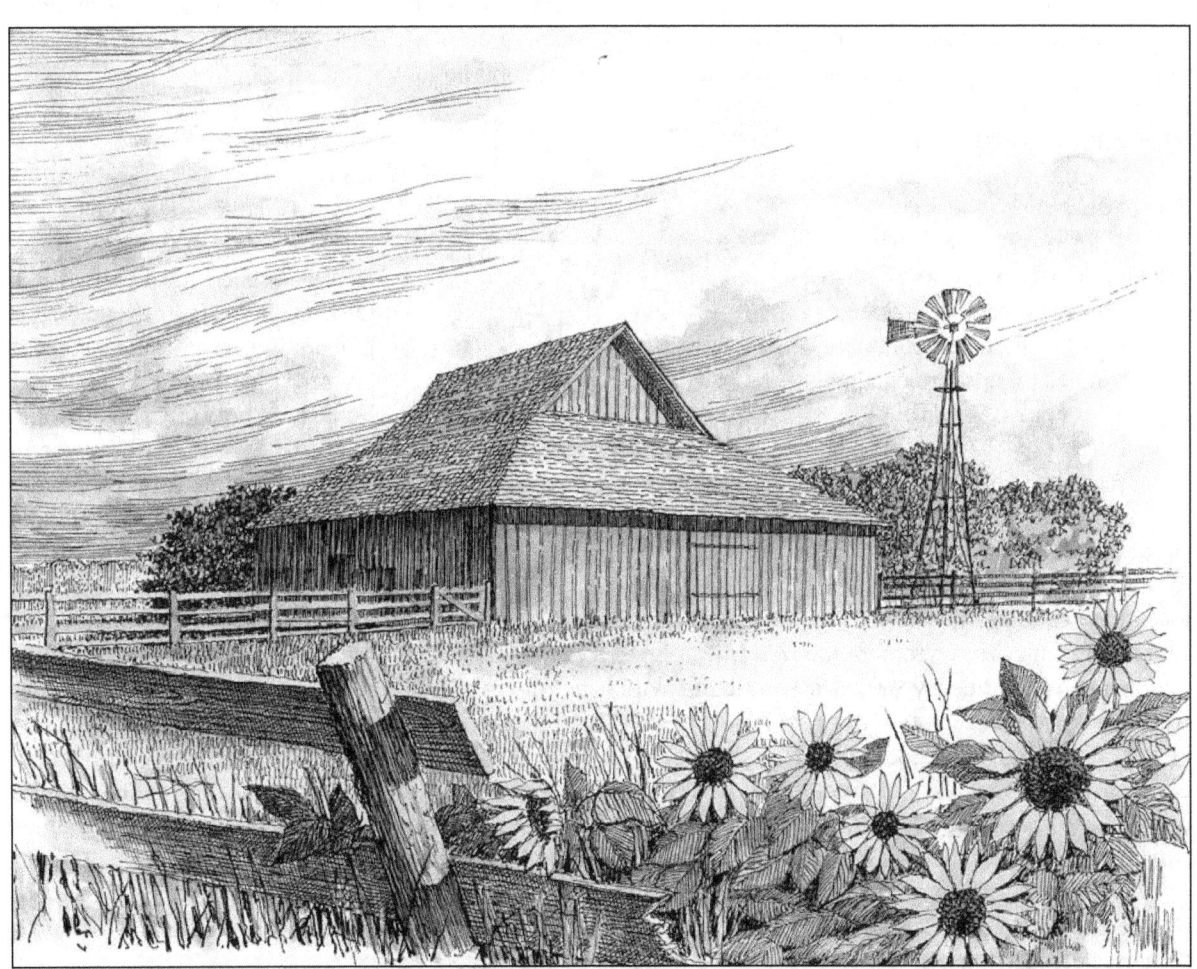

Many handsome barns and windmills occur frequently along the rural reaches of Route 66 in Oklahoma.

Acknowledgements

My initial research on Route 66 led me to the book *Route 66: The Mother Road*, by Michael Wallis. Michael, a resident of Tulsa, Oklahoma, has contributed several outstanding works of history that involve Oklahoma and many of its notable characters. His work has been nominated for the Pulitzer Prize four times. Early in my process of developing the drawings, I sent four or five examples to Michael for his review and comment. He was most kind and enthusiastic with his comments and has continued his encouragement over the years. Thank you, Michael.

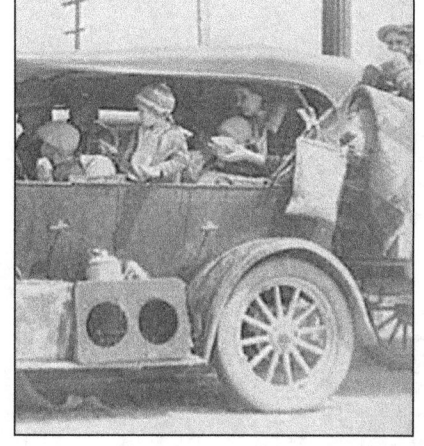

When considering a title for this project, nothing seemed right. It finally dawned upon me to pick up the telephone and pose the title question to my dear friend of almost thirty years, Tom Lutz. Tom wrote for the *Hee Haw* television show for thirteen years, is a whiz-bang with words, and is one of the funniest people I have ever known. Tom is also the godfather to all three of my children. Thirty minutes after my call to him he called me back and said, "How about, *Once Upon a Highway*"? And that was that. Thanks, Tom.

Gailard Sartain is one of the most talented people I know. A gifted actor and artist with more than sixty films to his credit and several paintings for album covers, Gailard grew up in Tulsa and knew the environs of Route 66 intimately. He became an enthusiastic supporter of the work when I first shared it with him, and when I asked him if he would consider writing the foreword for the book, he responded immediately with a "yes," saying further that he would be honored. I am the honored one, Gailard. Thank you for your insight, advice, and most of all, your friendship.

My colleagues and friends at Oklahoma State University have also been most supportive. OSU Dean of the College of Engineering, Architecture and Technology, Karl Reid and his wife, Verna Lou, both grew up on Route 66 and have been enthusiastic supporters of my project. Several mounted drawings from this collection appear on the wall in the Dean's office reception area. Emeritus Professor of Architecture Alan Brunken also grew up on Route 66 in Oklahoma City and was most helpful in providing encouragement and stories from his memories of many of the scenes depicted here. Emeritus Professor of Architecture Bob Wright also greatly assisted me with his warm, friendly enthusiasm and always sound advice. To all of my colleagues and students in the School of Architecture at Oklahoma State University, I extend a heartfelt thank you. I know of no finer or more dedicated group of people on the planet.

My former teacher and Emeritus Professor of Architecture from the University of Arkansas, John

"Gibby" Williams, has always been a source of inspiration and encouragement for my efforts since I was a 12-year-old kid hoping to someday become an architect. John is truly one of the great teachers of all time. John taught me very early in my education the importance of learning to know the difference between "the curious and the beautiful." In so many ways I wish I could be more like him. Thank you, John.

Much of what I am and who I am is due to the guidance and nurturing of my former teacher, mentor, and friend, Fay Jones. Truly one of the great architects of the twentieth century, it was my great privilege and joy to have Fay as one of my college professors and, following graduation, to work with him for ten years in his office. Fay was always appreciative of the many renderings I did for his projects, guiding me, and teaching me all the while. The education I received from Fay Jones is immeasurable in any known terms. My friendship with Fay, and his wife Mary Elizabeth ("Gus") has bolstered and encouraged me beyond belief. I cannot begin to adequately express my gratitude and affection for them. On August 30, 2004, the day before my fifty-fourth birthday, Fay died of natural causes at the age of eighty-three at his home in Fayetteville, Arkansas. He had been so encouraging of my efforts on this project and I had been looking forward to giving him a copy when it was finally published. I suppose that will have to wait till another time and place.

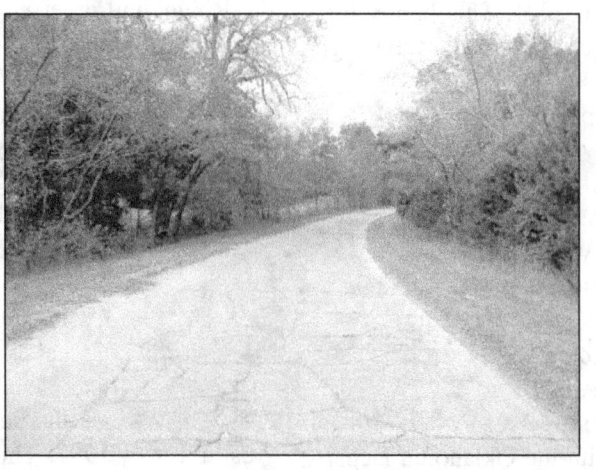

Don Goucher of El Reno has been a close friend since the early 1970s when we began sharing our interests in American history, muzzle loading rifles, and American Indian cultures. In my opinion, he is a true genius and can make or manufacture anything he tackles. His handmade muzzle loading rifles are incredible works of art and have become collector pieces all over America. Growing up on Route 66, Don had many memories of the highway when it prospered and when it began losing business to the interstate. Driving around El Reno, sometimes with our friend Deal Bowman, he would point out certain locations to me and add his memories of their significance—we've always had great fun together. Thanks, Don.

A note of thanks is due to the Route 66 Museum in Clinton, Oklahoma, especially Pat Smith, curator of the museum. Pat displayed a series of twenty of my drawings in the museum as part of its seventy-fifth anniversary of Route 66 festivities. The museum is a must see for any Route 66 enthusiast. The exhibits are fantastic and you won't find a group of people more friendly, dedicated, and helpful than the people that staff this museum.

My wife and I spent many enjoyable afternoon and overnight trips together seeking out these various sites. One night was spent in the Western Motel's "Elvis Room" in Clinton, Oklahoma, where "the King" himself stayed when traveling on Route 66. Ever the supportive and loving partner, she is simply the greatest. My children, now grown-ups, have become knowledgeable and trusted critics. I suppose it is normal, yet still probably rude, for a father to brag about his kids, but I can't seem to help it. My children are wonderful, and I am incredibly proud of them. Thank you always!

Finally, I would like to extend a huge amount of thanks to Major General (U.S. Army, retired) Doug Dollar of New Forums Press, Inc. Doug became an enthusiastic believer in this project from the moment I first mentioned it to him. His assistance and advice in all aspects of this book have been immeasurable and most appreciated. Thank you, Doug!

More Resources on Oklahoma's Route 66

For additional information on Route 66 in Oklahoma, five publications are immediately helpful to the traveler. These are:

Oklahoma Route 66, by Jim Ross, Ghost Town Press, Arcadia, Oklahoma, 2001. This handy little book gives history as well as maps to all of the alignments of Route 66 in Oklahoma. A large number of photographs provide views of various buildings and features of the Route as seen today and as they were in their heyday. A must have book for the serious road warrior.

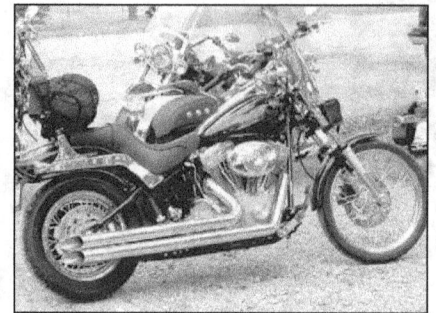

Official Oklahoma Route 66 Association Trip Guide, by the Oklahoma Route 66 Association (in cooperation with the Oklahoma Department of Tourism and Recreation). Printed in newsprint and free to tourists, this helpful 84-page publication offers maps, trivia, and photographs of various sights along Route 66 in Oklahoma. The guide is periodically updated by the association, and copies can generally be found at various business establishments along the Route. The association also mails out to its members a quarterly newsletter, *On the Road,* which provides information about upcoming events and noteworthy news about Route 66 in Oklahoma.

Just for Kicks, Oklahoma Route 66 Music Guide, by Hugh W. Foley, Jr., New Forums, Press, Inc., Stillwater, Oklahoma, 2004. Professor Foley has put together a delightful little book about notable music histories and musicians that are closely tied to Route 66 in Oklahoma. The book also notes annual music events, powwows, museums, side trips off of the Route, and other enjoyable tidbits of Route 66 music and Oklahoma.

Roadside History of Oklahoma, by Francis L. and Roberta B. Fugate, Mountain Press Publishing Company, Missoula, Montana, 1998. Covering much more than just Route 66, this book provides a lot of interesting insight into Oklahoma places and historical events.

The Roads of Oklahoma, by the Shearer Publishing Company, Austin Texas, 1997. This map atlas contains all of the roads and highways in the state of Oklahoma. Various landscape features, creeks and rivers, as well as topographical information is provided.

Additional Reading on Route 66

Route 66: The Mother Road, by Michael Wallis, St. Martin's Griffin, 2001. One of the best histories of Route 66 by one of the best writers anywhere.

Route 66, by Tim Steil, Motor Books International, 2000. Insightful and nicely illustrated with photographs by Jim Luning.

Along Route 66, by Quinta Scott, University of Oklahoma Press, 2000. Photographic essay on Route 66.

Route 66: The Highway and its People, by Quinta Scott, University of Oklahoma Press, 1998. Another photographic essay by Scott with text by Susan Croce Kelly.

Route 66, The Empires of Amusement, by Thomas Arthur Repp, Mock Turtle Press, 1999. Repp gives a fascinating and humorous look at those fun and funky places along Route 66 known to some as "tourist traps." It is a great read with many illustrations that date to the glory days of Route 66. Its chapters on Oklahoma sights include the Buffalo Ranch, Totem Pole Park, Claremore's baths, Blue Whale, Crystal City Amusement Park, Dixieland Park, Frontier City, Queenan's, and Reptile Village.

Route 66 Remembered, by Michael Karl Witzel, Motorbooks International, 1996. This book provides another look back in time with some 200 high quality photographs and illustrations.

Pump and Circumstance, Glory Days of The Gas Station, by John Margolies, Bulfinch Press, 1993. Although not specifically about Route 66, Margolies's book brings the gas station up close and personal through photographs, architect drawings, postcards, road maps, other types of illustrations, and an insightful text. This book is a must-have for all those dedicated road warriors who traversed America's highways during the "glory days" of the gas station.

Route 66 Magazine, published by Paul and Sandi Taylor, Laughlin, Nevada. This magazine offers a fantastic array of Route 66 sights and stories. Many of the larger bookstores sell this magazine.

About the Drawings

Each of the scenes illustrated here were originally drawn on acid free, smooth finish Bristol board, $8^{1/2}$ by 11 inches (landscape format). I used a Mont Blanc fountain pen purchased in the early 1980s but, unfortunately, no longer manufactured by the company. It has a fine-line gold nib that allows bold (or broad) line weights, or when used upside down, a very fine line. The ink in the pen is the same brand of ink I have relied upon for over thirty years, Pelican's 4001 black fountain pen ink.

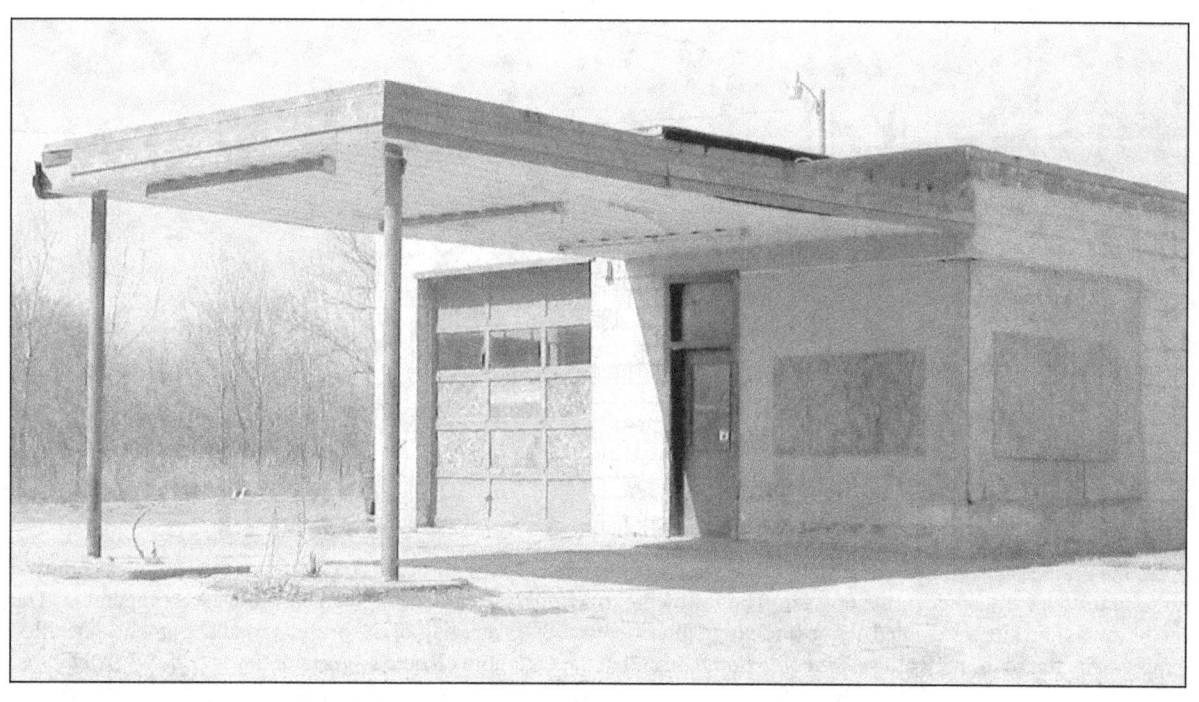

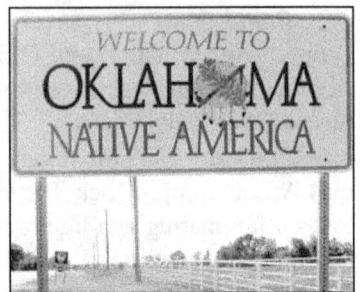

Leaving Baxter Springs, Kansas, heading west, the Route 66 traveler crosses into the great state of Oklahoma, "Native America."

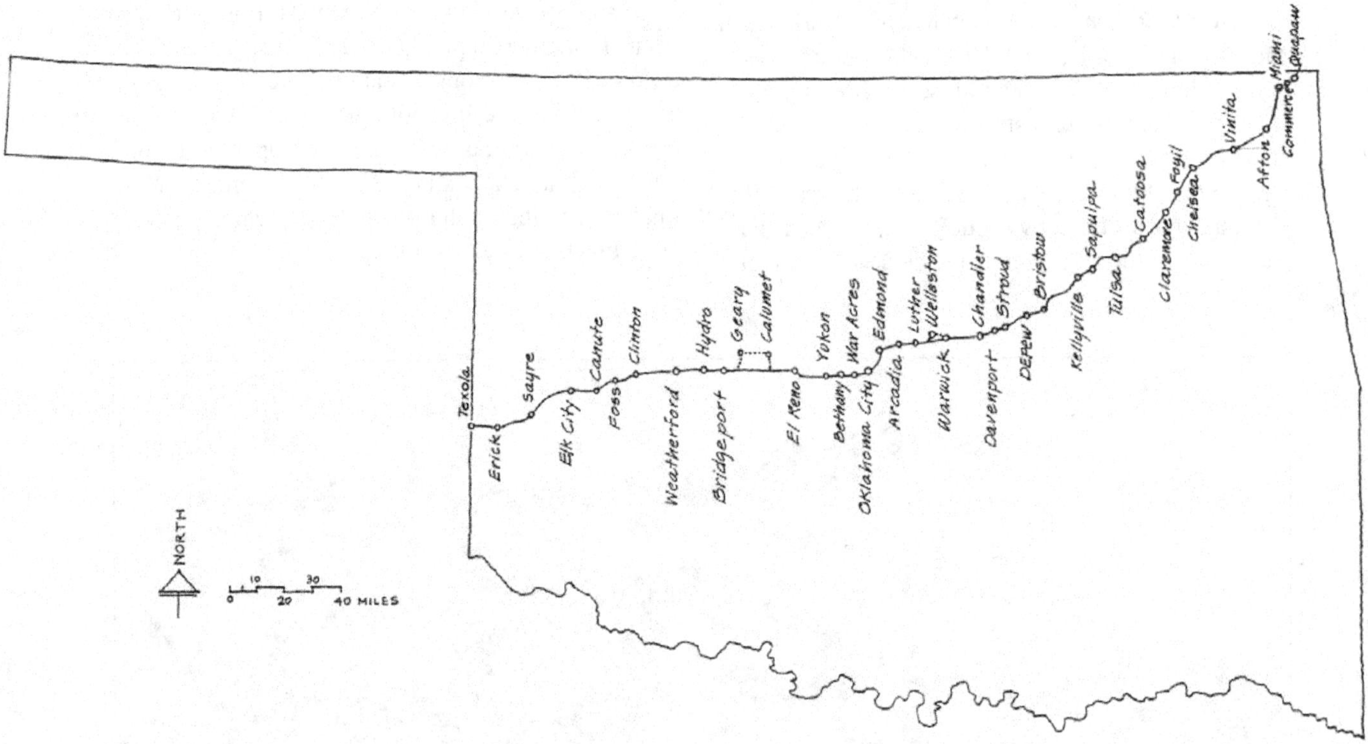

Map of Route 66 in Oklahoma

From the northeastern corner of the state to the western Oklahoma-Texas border, Route 66 traversed some 395 miles—more miles than any other Route 66 state. The following drawings are sequenced in an east to west arrangement. The major towns and cities are noted above (including those "spurs" that were part of the original road alignment). Detailed maps can be found in Jim Ross's *Oklahoma Route 66* and in the Oklahoma Route 66 Association's *Official Trip Guide*.

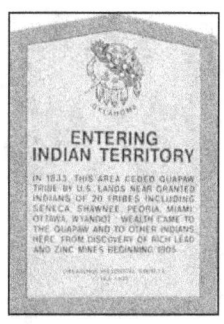

The Oklahoma Historical Society has marked many historical sites along Route 66 with engraved granite markers.

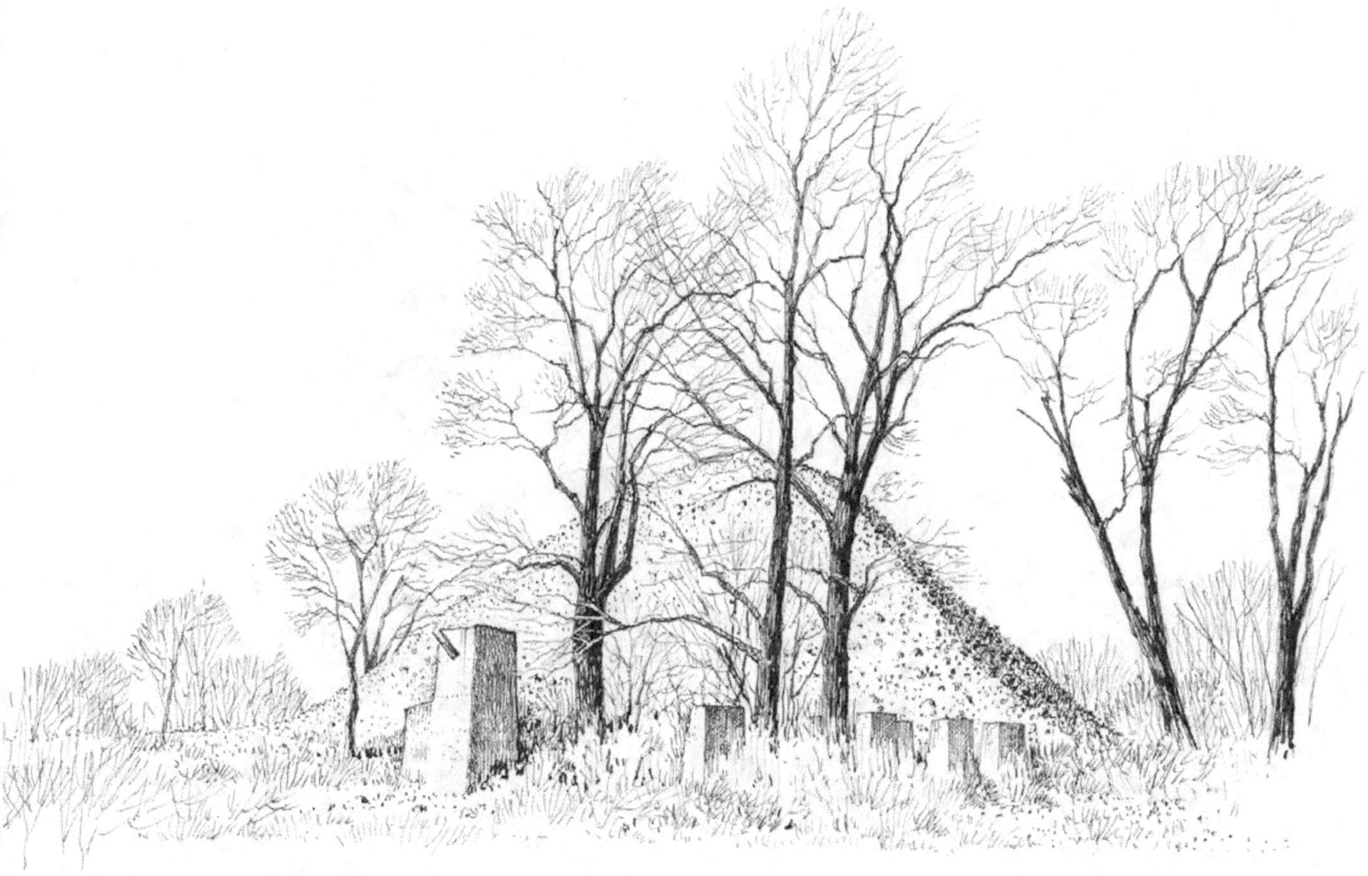

"Chat" Mound, Quapaw, Oklahoma

Quapaw, named after the Quapaw Indians (originally from Arkansas), became one of the centers of lead and zinc mining in the Tri-State Mining Area, which included southeast Kansas and southwest Missouri. These mounds of debris, or "waste rock," serve as ugly reminders of how such mining efforts of the past still impact the quality of our environment today. The *Official Trip Guide* notes that Quapaw marked the point where 66 East became 66 West.

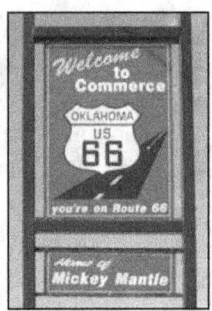

Route 66 originally passed through the middle of many downtown business districts, contributing to the highway's title, "America's Mainstreet."

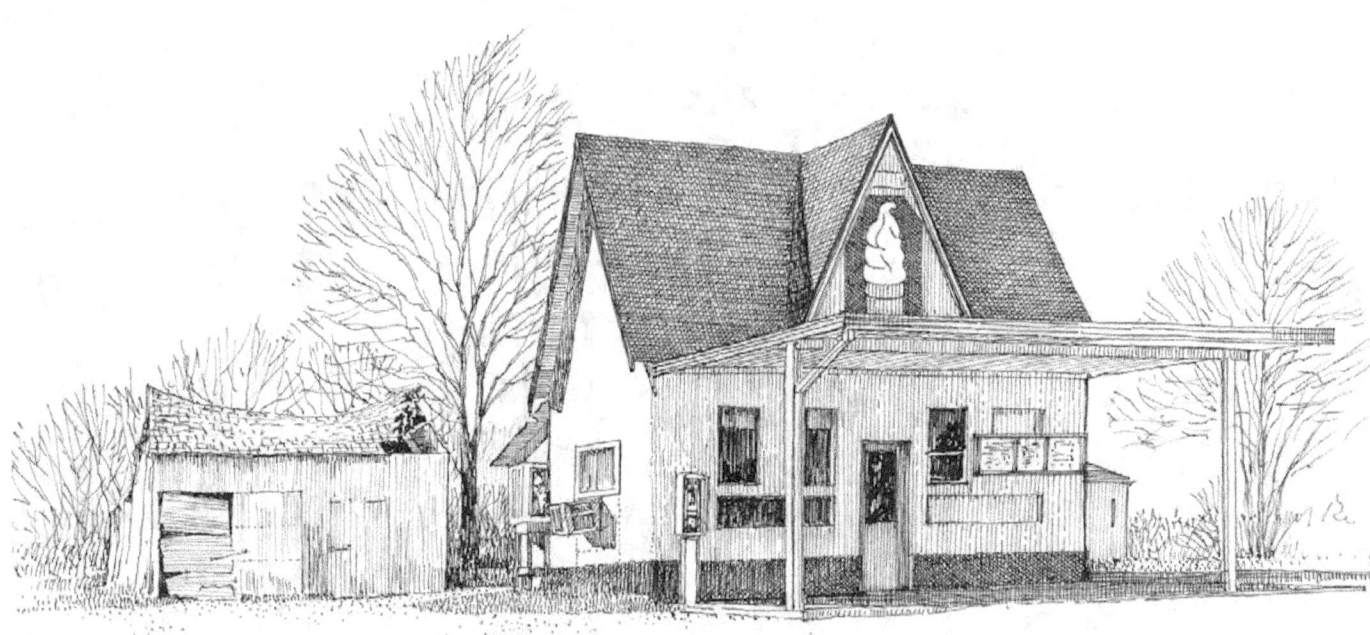

"Dairy King," Commerce, Oklahoma

Commerce is the home of baseball legend Mickey Mantle. When I was a kid, Mickey was in his prime playing for the New York Yankees and was one of my heroes. All my fellow ball players back then hoped to get "Number 7," Mickey's number, when Little League uniforms were distributed. This dairy stand appears to have originally been a service station as its gable-roofed form resembles so many stations along Route 66.

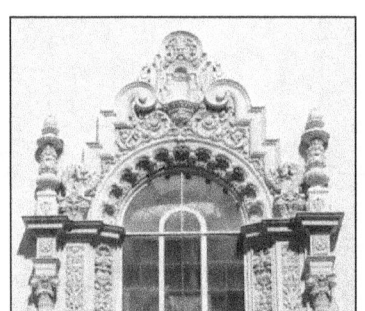

The Coleman Theater's exterior surfaces offer a dazzling display of Spanish Rocco-styled ornamental detail.

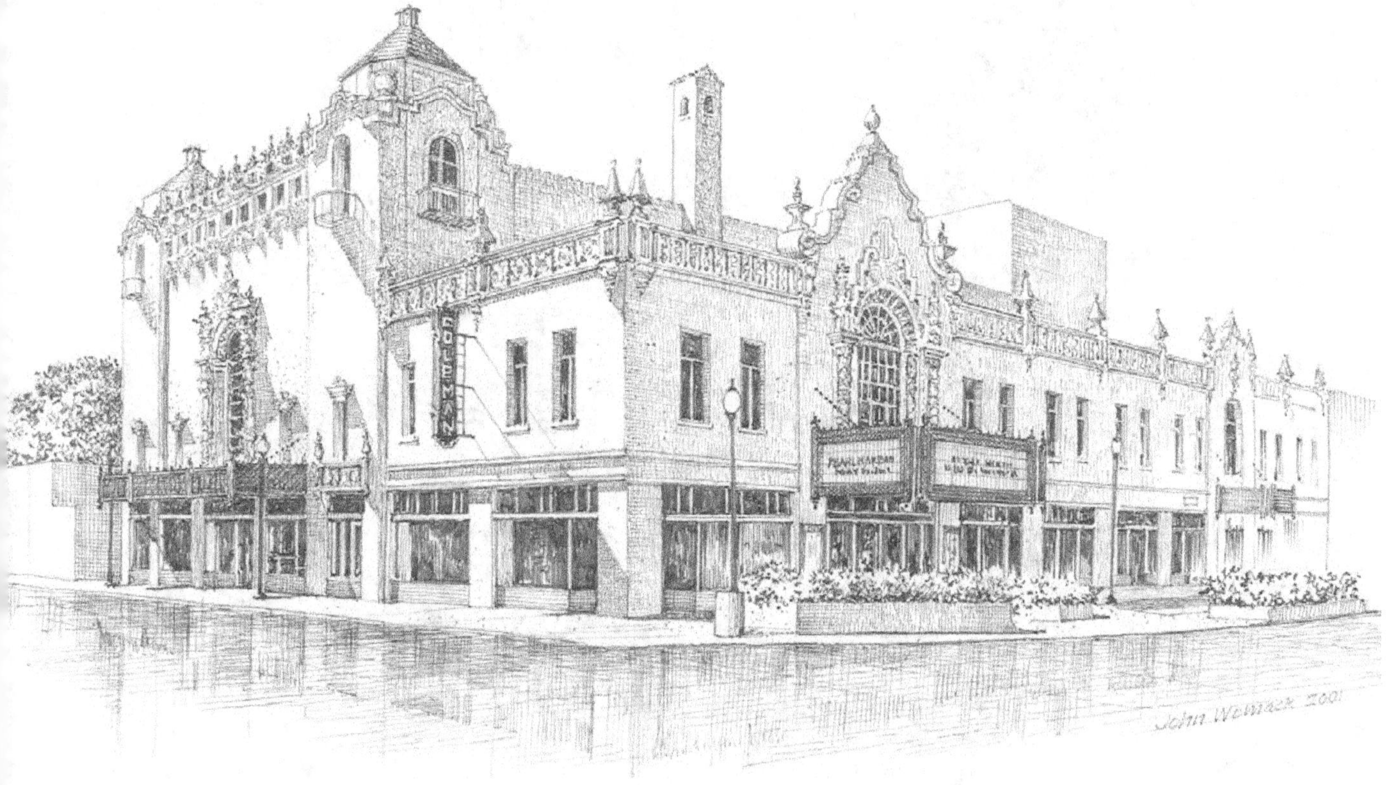

Coleman Theater (1929), Miami, Oklahoma

The Coleman, once the crown jewel of Miami, gradually fell into disuse and was eventually given to the city by the Coleman family in 1989. Unbelievably, at one point in time, a group of people discussed tearing down the old theater in order to create a parking lot. But, the rest of the citizens of Miami came to the fore and embarked upon a restoration program that brought the aging structure back to its original glory. The theater is now open to the public and is prospering.

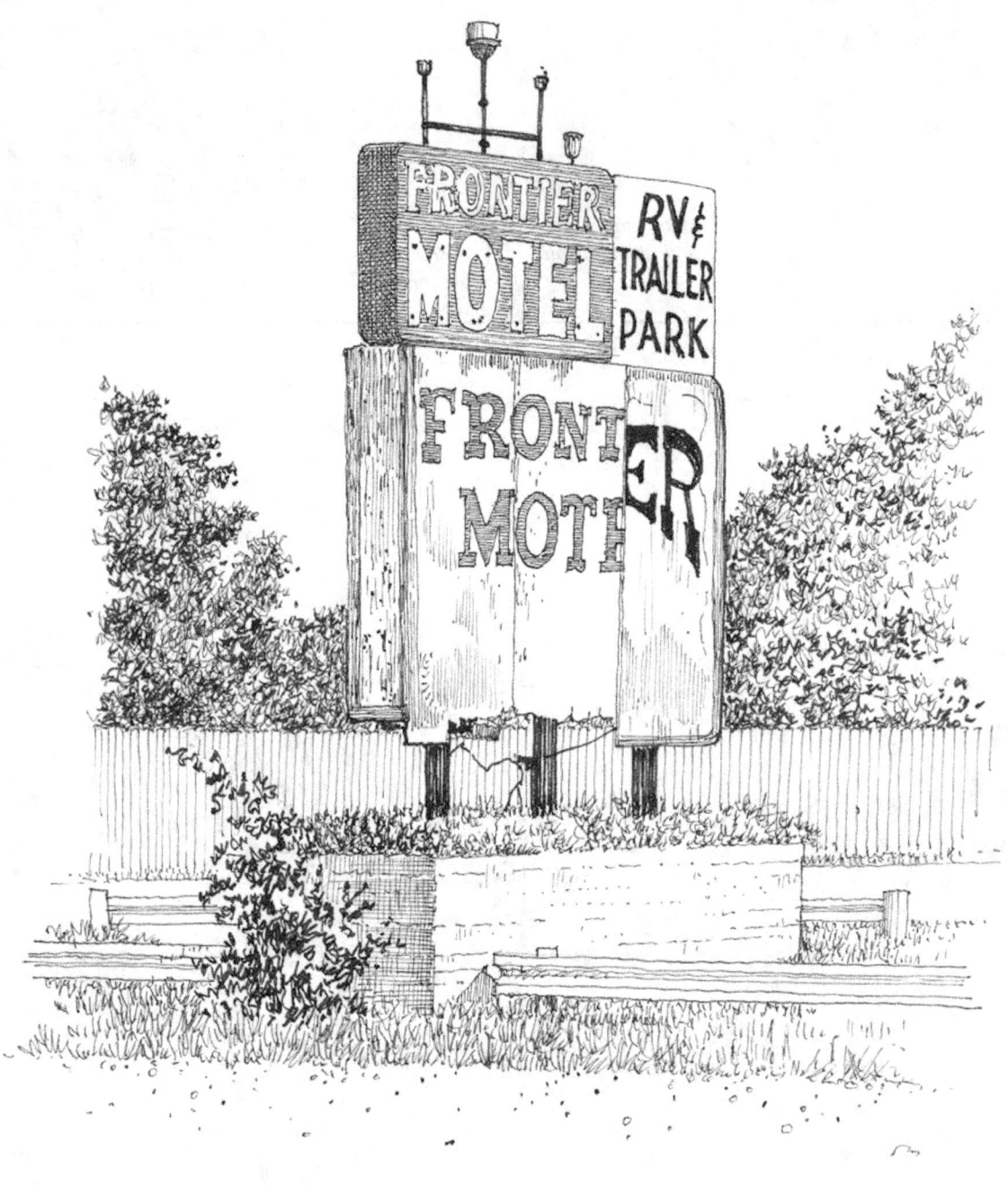

John Womack 2004

Frontier Motel Sign, Miami, Oklahoma

Signage along Route 66 played an important role in both the economic outlook of the various businesses advertised and in the "look" of the Route. The Frontier Motel sign, seen here, has gone through a series of changes through the years, as viewed in the different surface layers, lettering, and the addition of "extra" signage. The Frontier Motel serves now as a low cost apartment complex—at least that was its status in January of 2005.

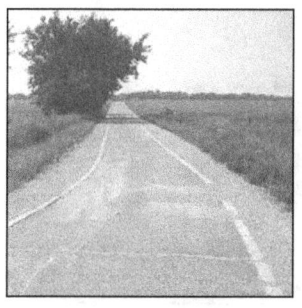

Original sections of Route 66's nine-foot-wide "sidewalk" or "ribbon" highway can still be found around Narcissa and Afton.

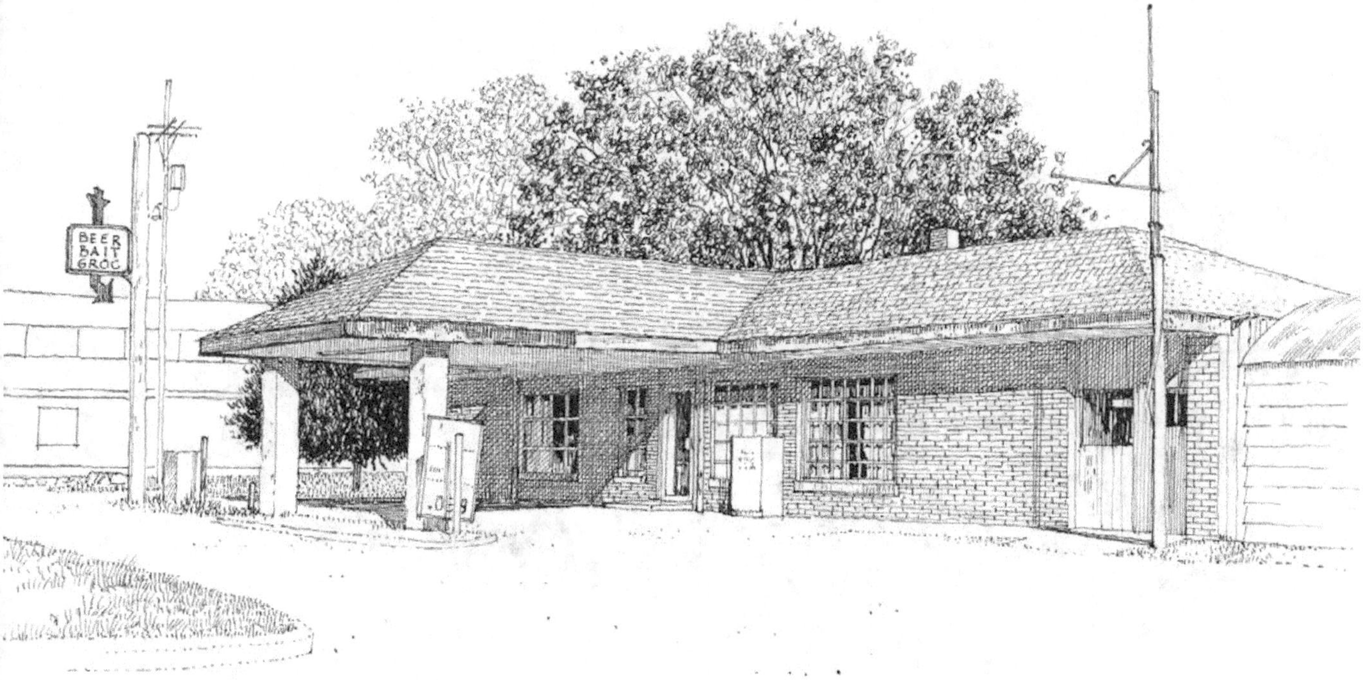

"Beer, Bait, and Grocery" Store and Station (destroyed), Narcissa, Oklahoma

The town of Narcissa is located at the junction of State Highway 25 and Route 66 (now Highway 69) and, as Jim Ross notes, is the only town with the distinction of being on the old original nine-foot wide section of pavement. This store and station, once named to the National Register of Historic Places, was destroyed by fire in 2005.

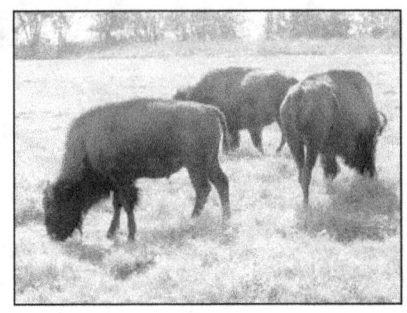

Although the original buildings of the Buffalo Ranch are no longer with us, the buffalo have returned.

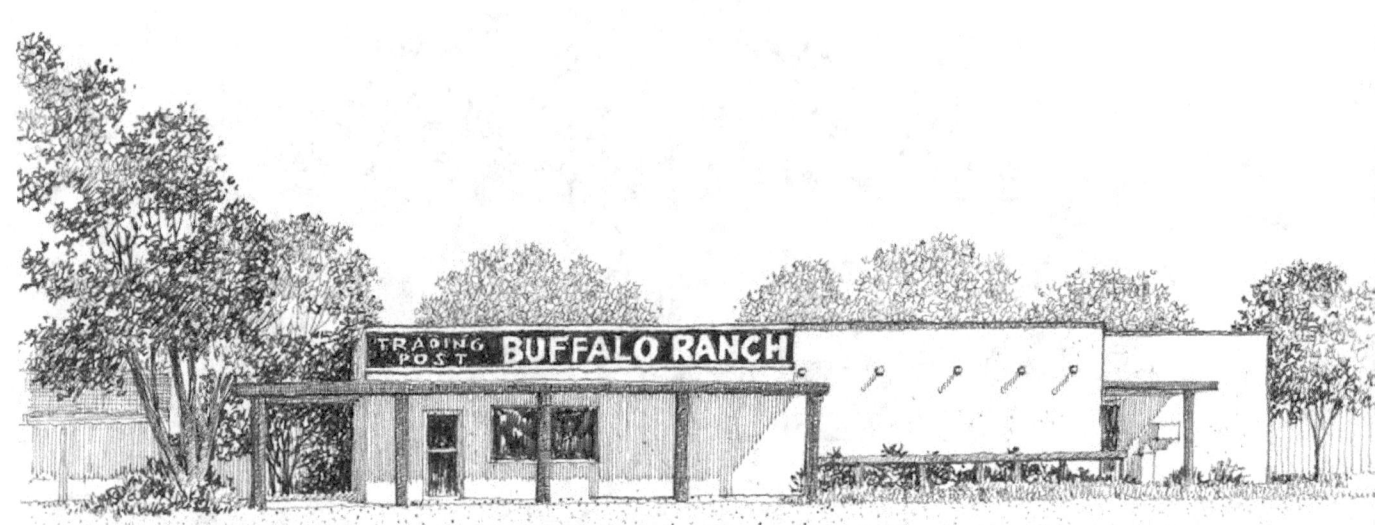

Buffalo Ranch (demolished), north of Afton, Oklahoma

Russell and Aleene Kay founded the Buffalo Ranch in 1953, and it quickly became a favorite spot on Route 66. Along with buffalo, or bison, a menagerie of other animals were on display. There was also a restaurant and a western-wear store on the grounds. The business stayed open until 1997 when Aleene died. The building seen here and the Dairy Ranch were both torn down sometime around 2003.

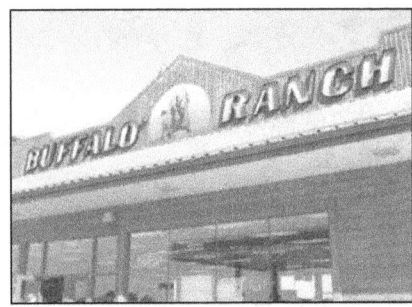

The new Buffalo Ranch has no connection to the original ranch other than in name and location, but it does provide a good clean place to stop, refresh, and gas up.

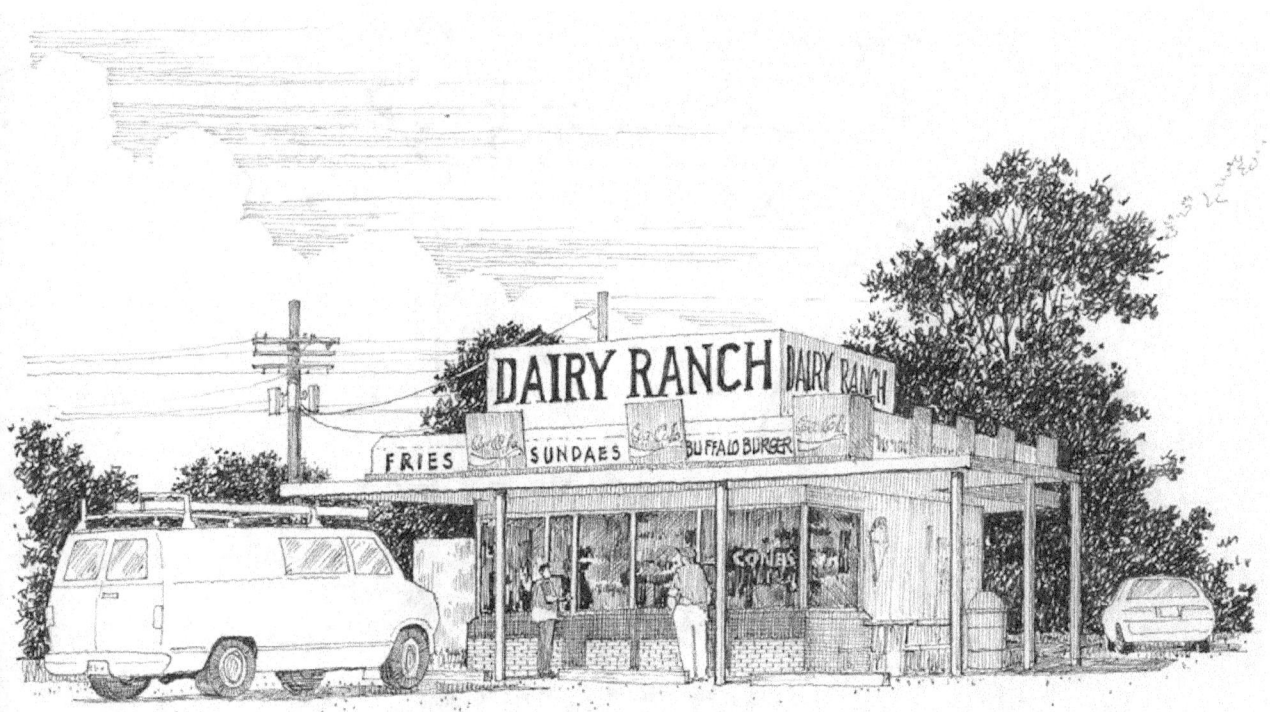

Dairy Ranch (demolished), north of Afton, Oklahoma

This restaurant, one of the original Buffalo Ranch buildings, was torn down in 2003. The structure was in the classic style of drive-in restaurants that began to appear in the 1950s and brings to mind tons of memories from those bygone days. The burgers, shakes, chili-dogs, and sundaes, somehow always tasted better at these places than those made at home. Of course, the food was made to order and the soft ice cream was always freshly made.

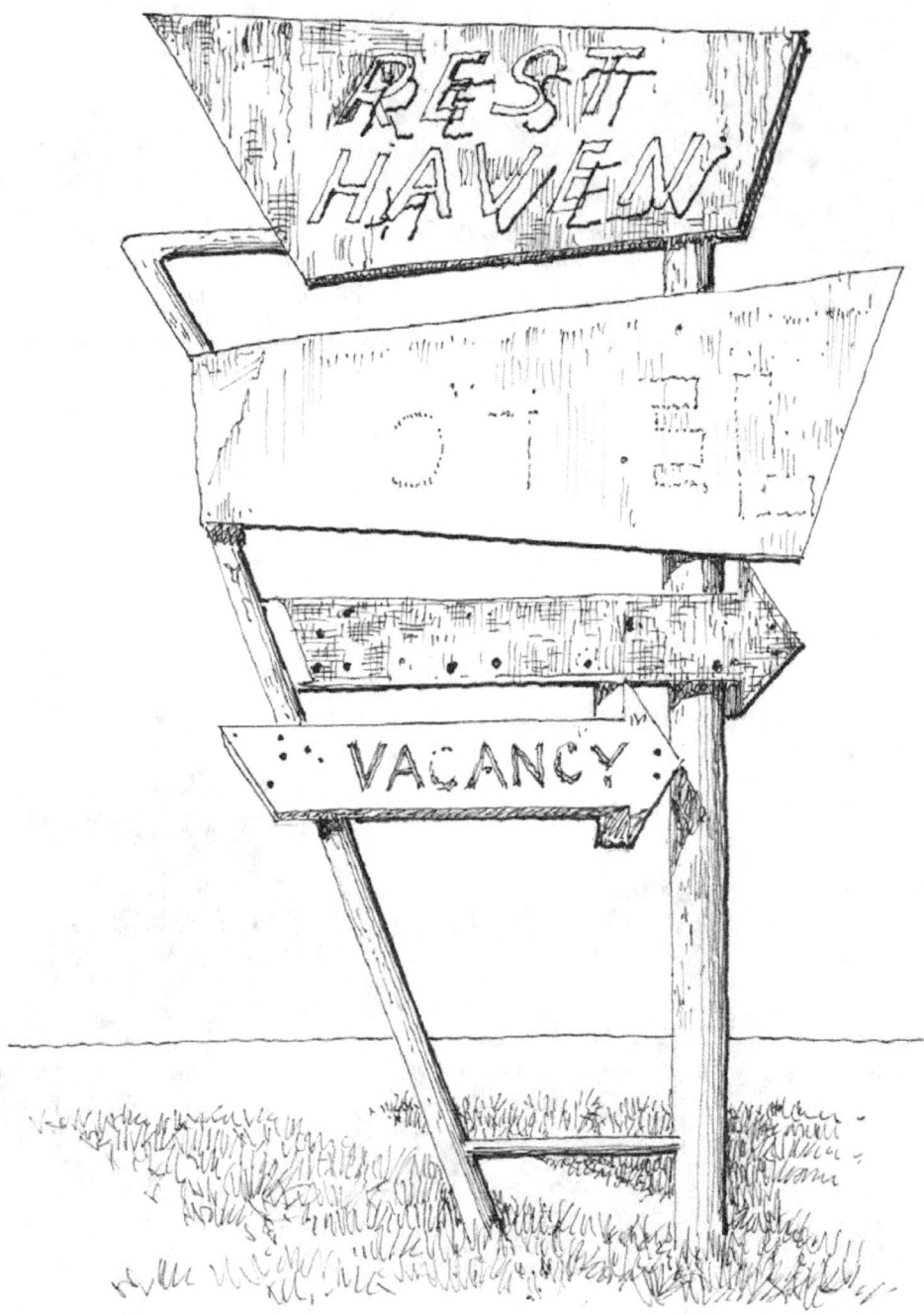

Rest Haven Motel Sign, Afton, Oklahoma

This sign remains a favorite photo stop for many Route 66 travelers today. There is a certain poignancy to its broken neon, faded paint, and rusted metal. Such is the case with many deteriorating Route 66 artifacts. The truncated shapes of the various parts of the sign are curious, yet such shapes are common in motel signage. There seems to be little rhyme or reason to the composition. The arrows are the same size and shape—and point in the same direction!

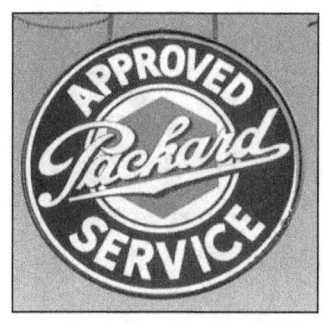

A number of interesting Route 66 relics can be viewed within this restored Eagle-DX station, including the original "Dairy Ranch" sign seen in the drawing on page 21.

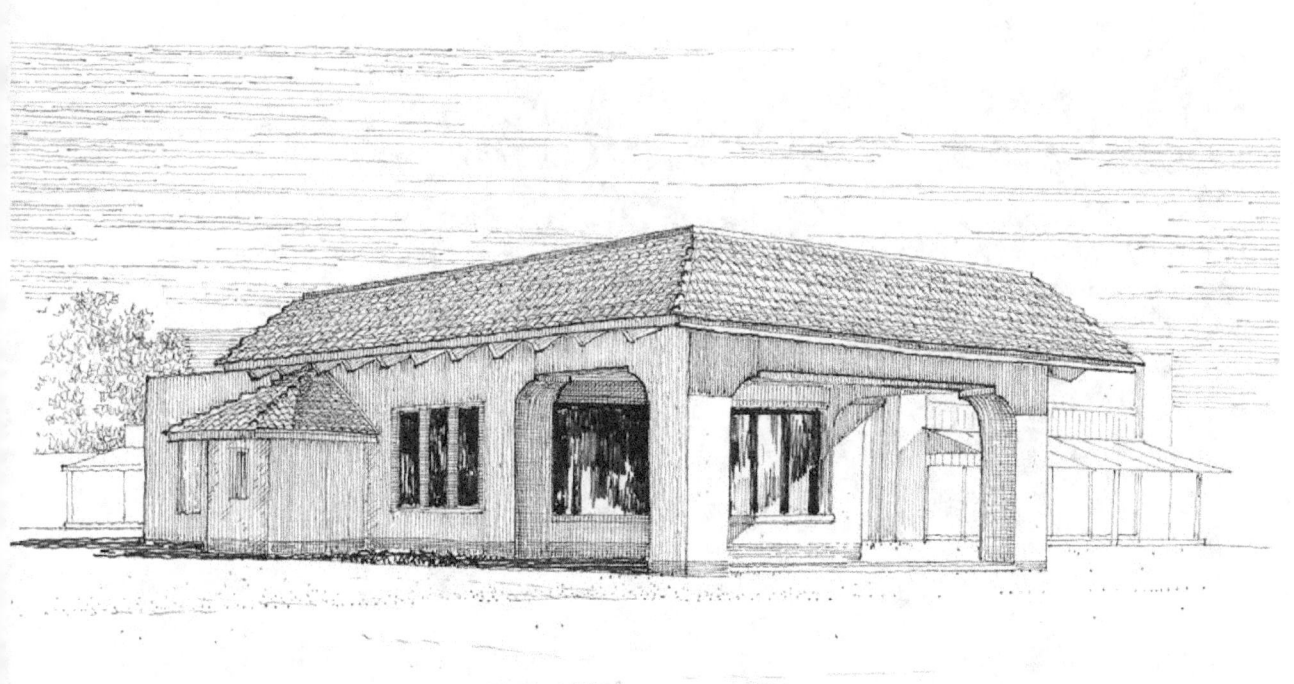

Afton Station, Afton, Oklahoma

This former DX station is one of the more famous gas stations on Route 66 and dates originally to the 1930s. As with many such stations, it fell into disuse and was eventually left vacant following the opening of Interstate 44. The station owners, at the time of this writing, bring an interesting story of how they moved to Afton from Connecticut, restored the building and its side garage, which now houses the owner's collection of vintage Packards.

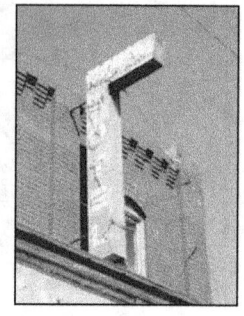

Afton's Palmer Hotel is now closed, but its sign still looks down upon the Mother Road.

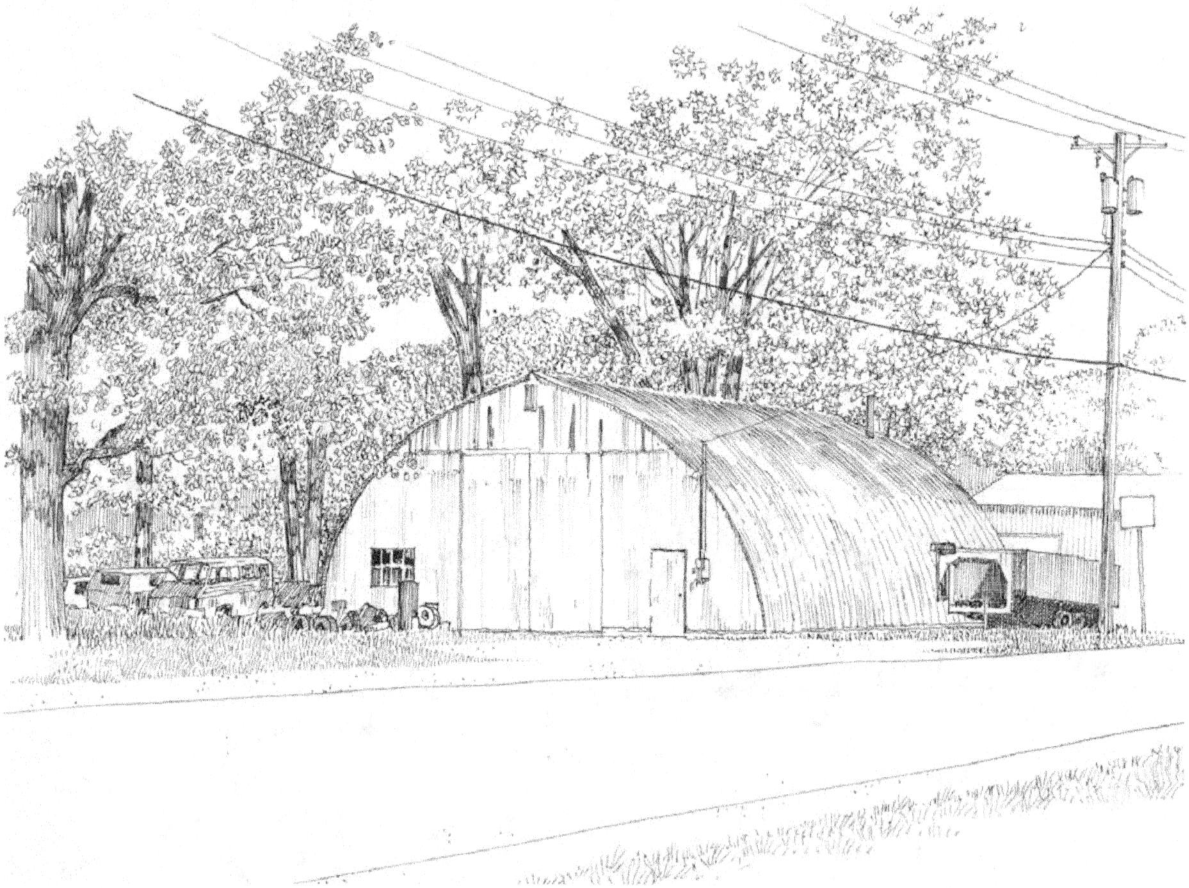

Quonset Hut Garage, Afton, Oklahoma

Quonset huts were developed during World War II and followed an earlier British design known as the "Nissen hut." The birthplace of these incredibly efficient shelters was near Quonset, Rhode Island—hence the name. An estimated 170,000 quonset huts were built during the war. After the war, quonset huts were sold by the government for $1,000 apiece. At one time just about every town in the U.S. had a quonset hut somewhere in its environs.

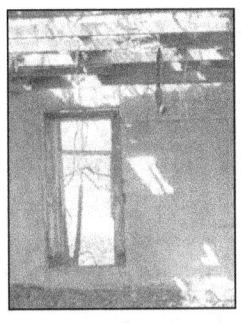

With roof and walls open to the weather, the old Avon Motel is gradually fading away.

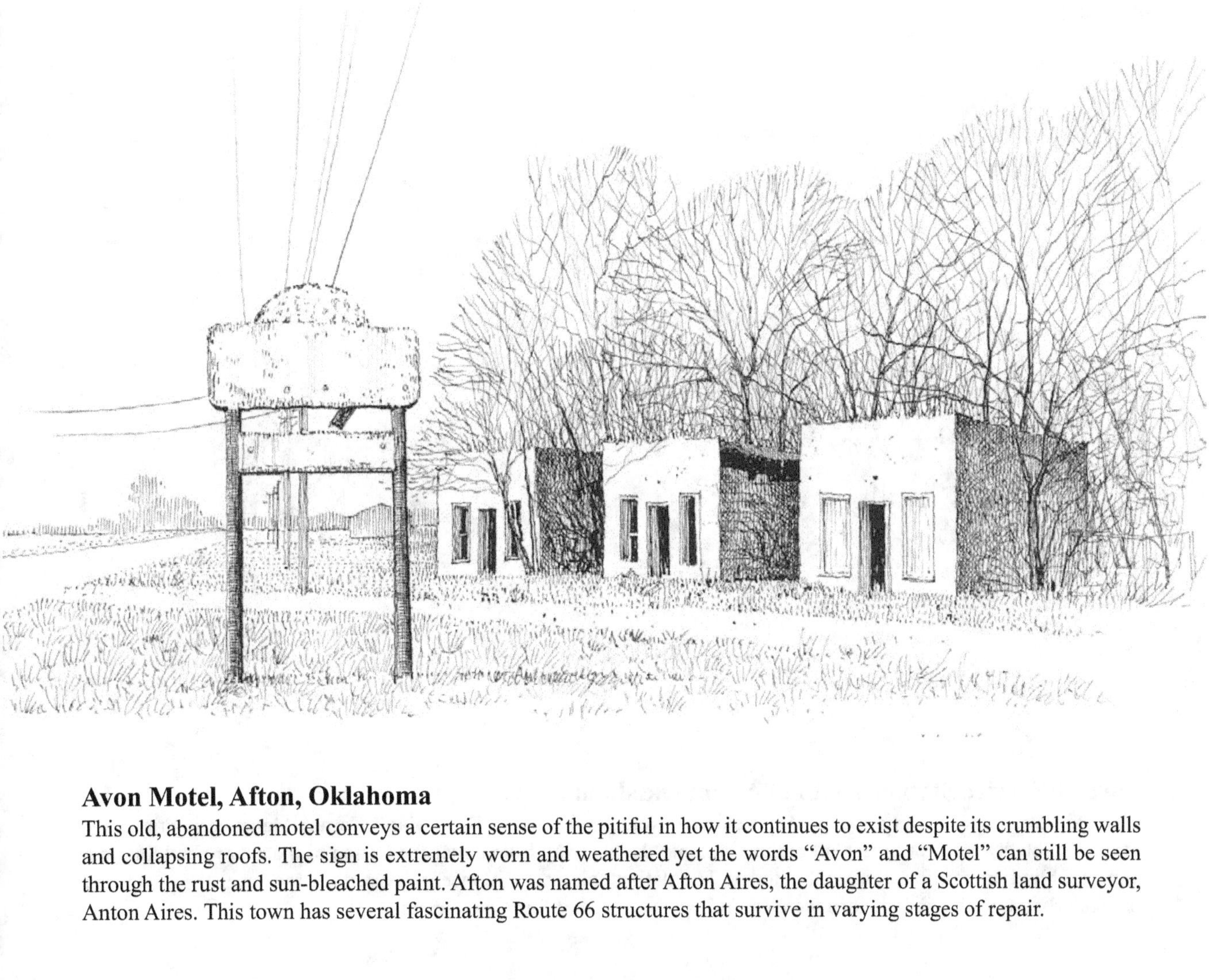

Avon Motel, Afton, Oklahoma

This old, abandoned motel conveys a certain sense of the pitiful in how it continues to exist despite its crumbling walls and collapsing roofs. The sign is extremely worn and weathered yet the words "Avon" and "Motel" can still be seen through the rust and sun-bleached paint. Afton was named after Afton Aires, the daughter of a Scottish land surveyor, Anton Aires. This town has several fascinating Route 66 structures that survive in varying stages of repair.

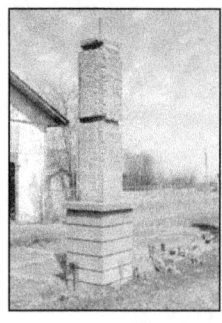

This station, like so many other Route 66 sites, is gradually succumbing to time—even the concrete is slowly eroding away.

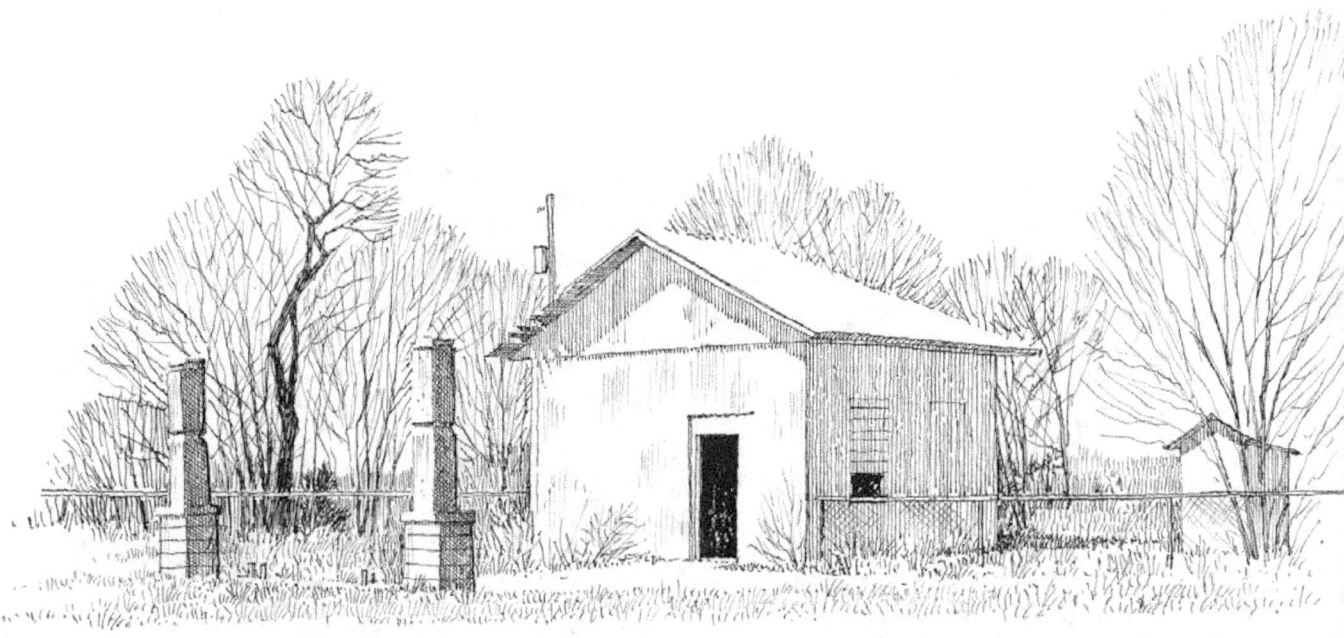

John Womack 2005

Former Service Station, south of Afton, Oklahoma

This old station sits near a right-angled curve on old Route 66 known as Dead Man's Corner. Maneuvering the curve was undoubtedly tricky at times, but pulling out onto the highway from either the station or the nearby building was almost a blind proposition—and still is today. The station columns that once supported the roof over the pumps are particularly interesting in how they were carefully constructed of formed concrete.

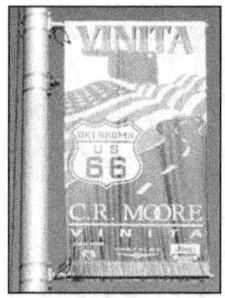

Today Route 66 still plays a significant role in the economic well-being of its many communities, with tourists traveling the old highway, an ever steady presence.

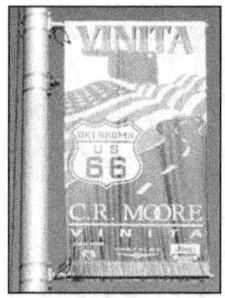

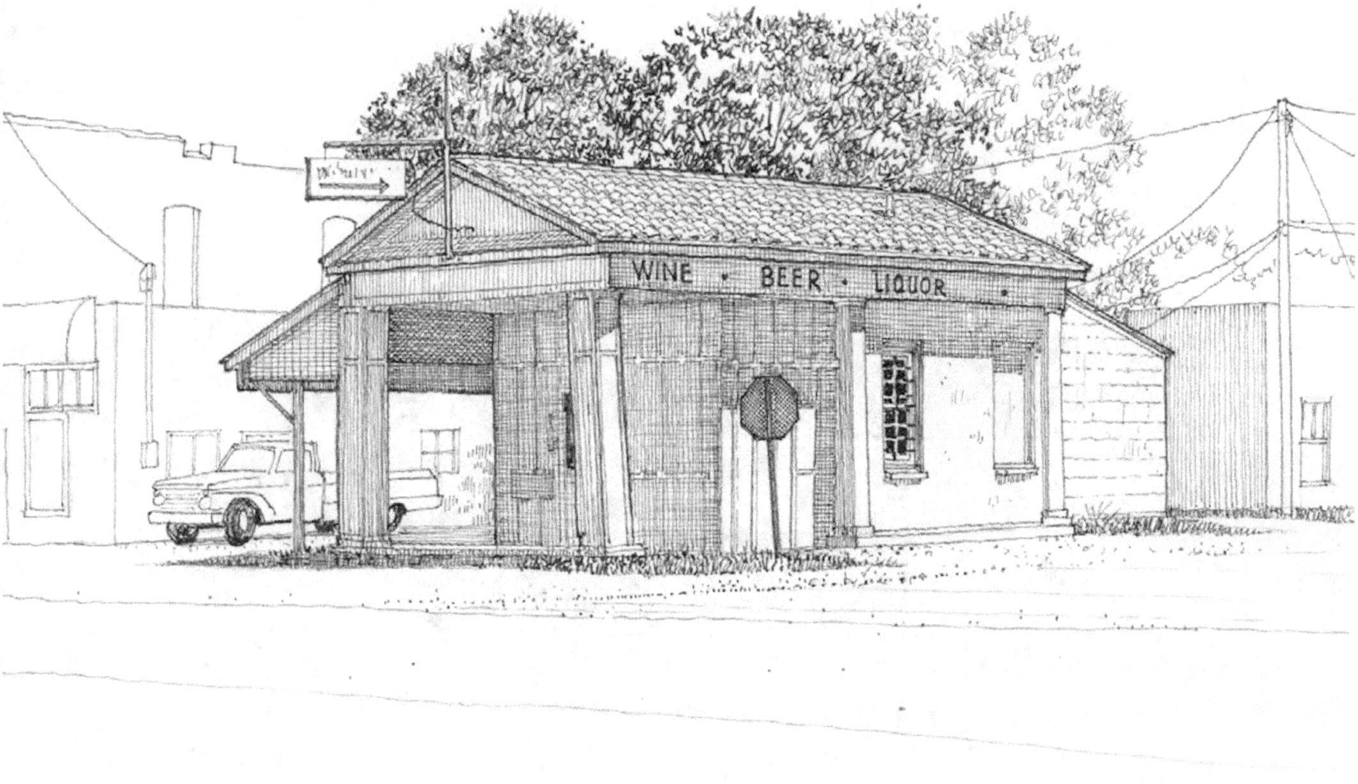

Liquor Store (demolished), Vinita, Oklahoma

This liquor store appears to have once been a service station. There are many examples of such stations along Route 66 that share the covered portico and double column arrangement. This particular example is interesting in how it has interpreted some elements of classical Greek architecture into its facade. At least two additions have occurred through the years (the rear shed and the side-shed covering) leaving the result rather confused.

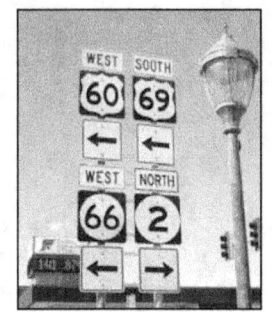

The original road alignment around Vinita can be confusing, so carry along a good map or guidebook to assist your Route 66 travel.

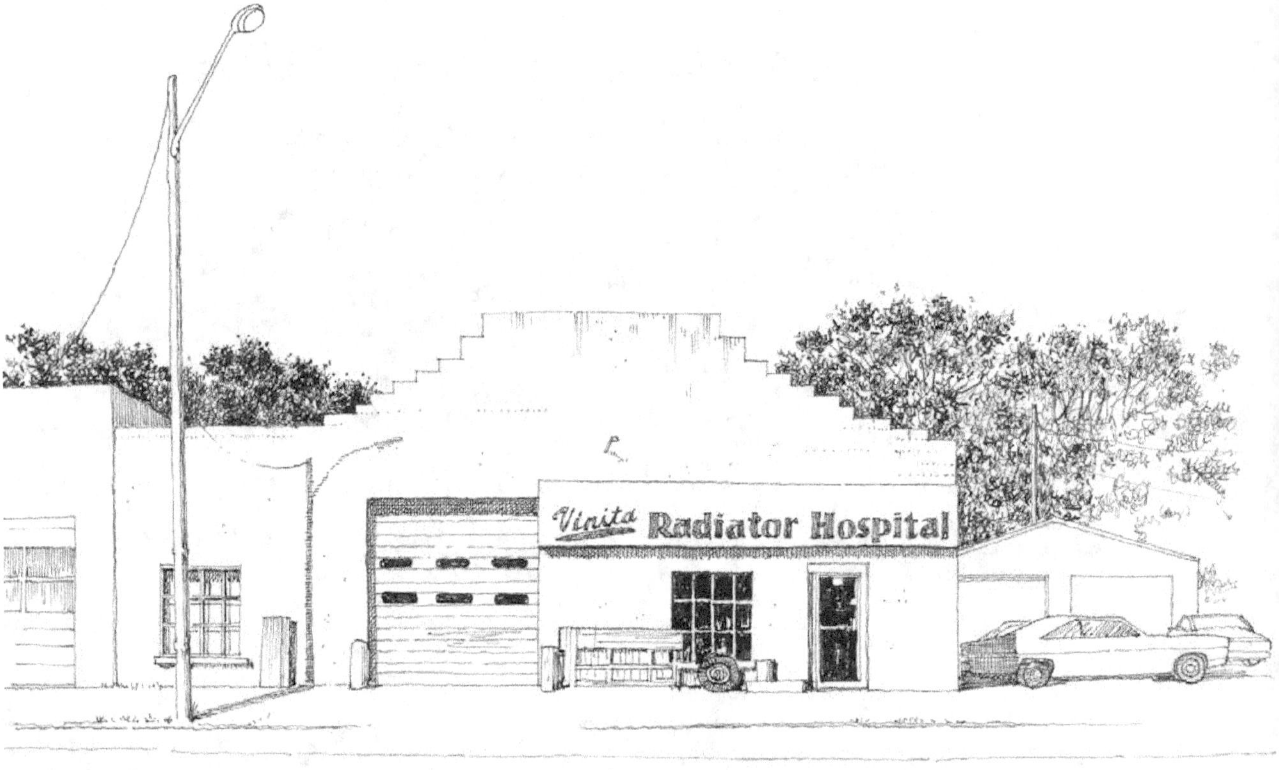

Vinita Radiator Hospital, Vinita, Oklahoma

There is no telling how long this building has been occupied by a radiator repair shop, but because of its rolling overhead door, the building has certainly been associated with automobiles since its beginning. Built of concrete block, the structure's stepped cornice is reminiscent of many roadside building facades from the 1930s through the 1950s. The "fastback" Ford Galaxy parked to the side of the building is one of the classic 1960s "muscle" cars.

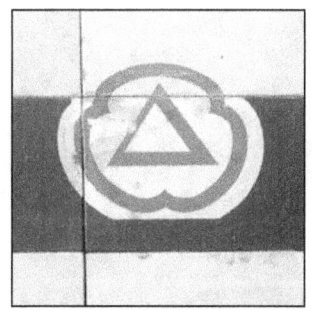

The original Cities Services logo painted on the side of the old station can still be seen today. The station now houses a used-car business.

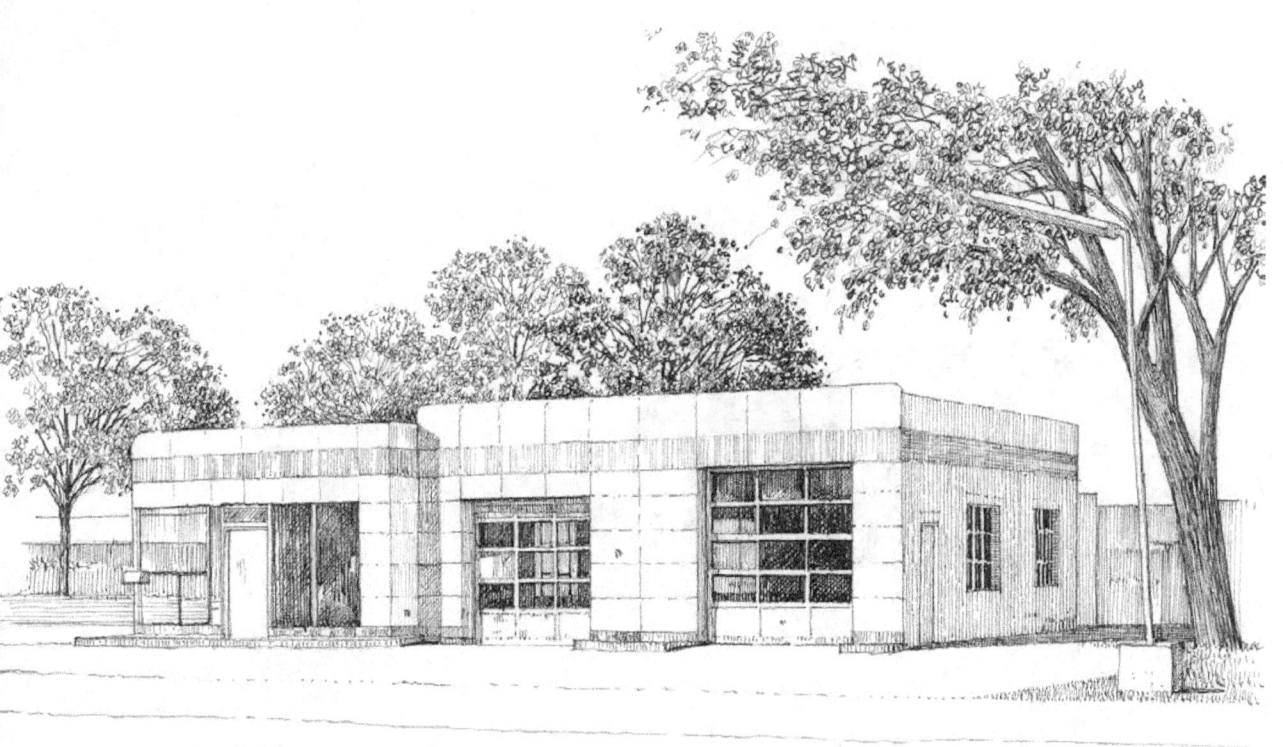

Former Cities Services Station, Vinita, Oklahoma

This old station's exterior is covered in porcelain enameled steel panels, a type of material used often for service stations from the 1930s through the 1950s. These steel panels were ideal for service stations. They were durable and almost maintenance free, requiring little more than a simple washing in order to return the surfaces back to a clean, sparkling white. These paneled stations are gradually going by the wayside with few still in existence today.

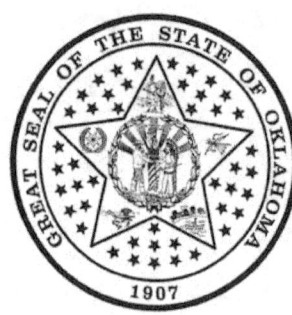

The origin of the name "Oklahoma" is from the Choctaw Indian words OKLA ("people") and HOMMA ("red").

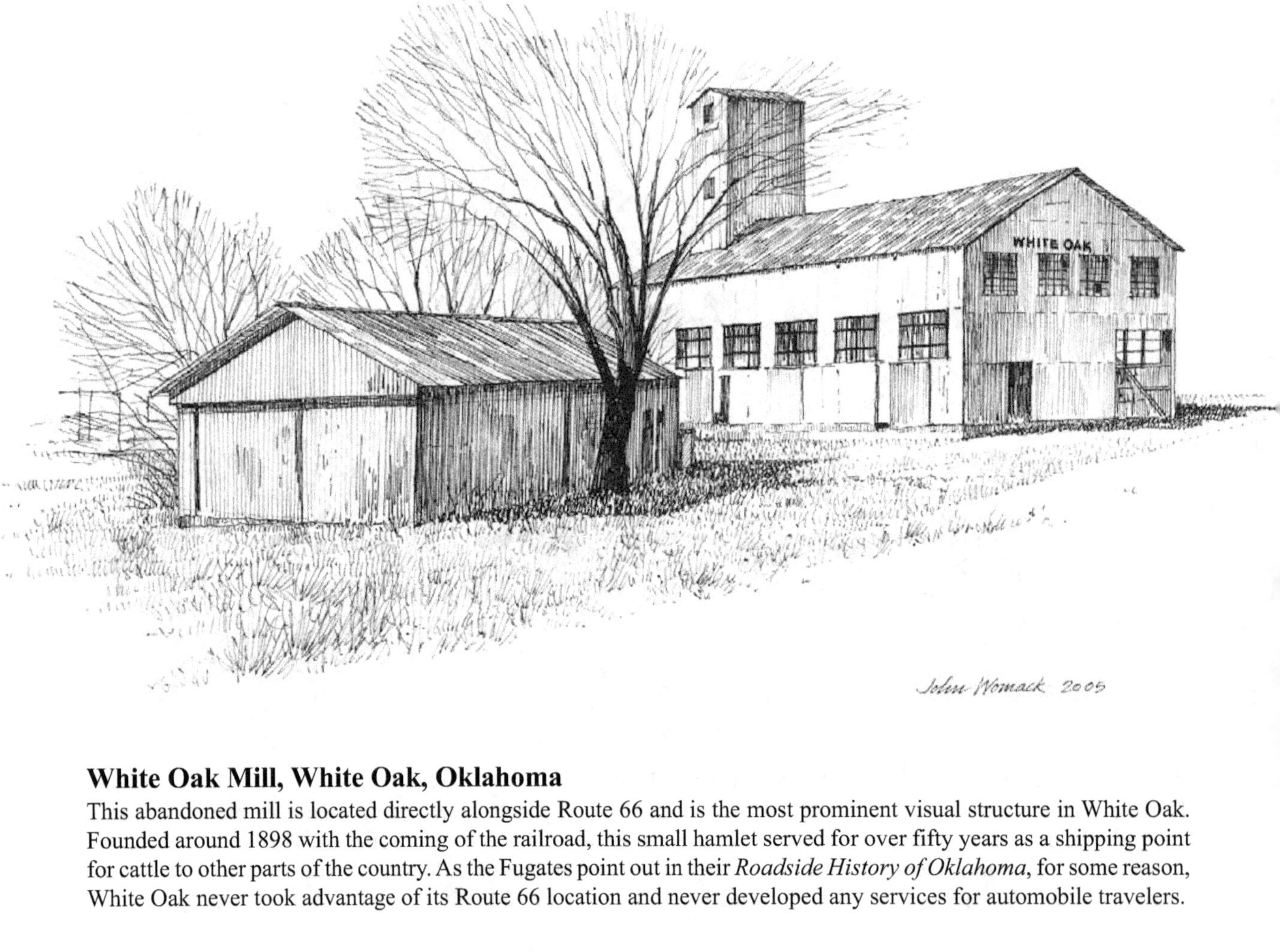

John Womack 2005

White Oak Mill, White Oak, Oklahoma

This abandoned mill is located directly alongside Route 66 and is the most prominent visual structure in White Oak. Founded around 1898 with the coming of the railroad, this small hamlet served for over fifty years as a shipping point for cattle to other parts of the country. As the Fugates point out in their *Roadside History of Oklahoma*, for some reason, White Oak never took advantage of its Route 66 location and never developed any services for automobile travelers.

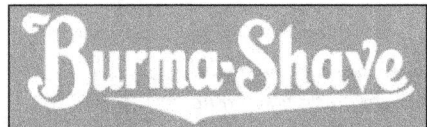

Burma-Shave slogans printed on a series of signs along the side of the road were always a fun experience for kids and adults to read.

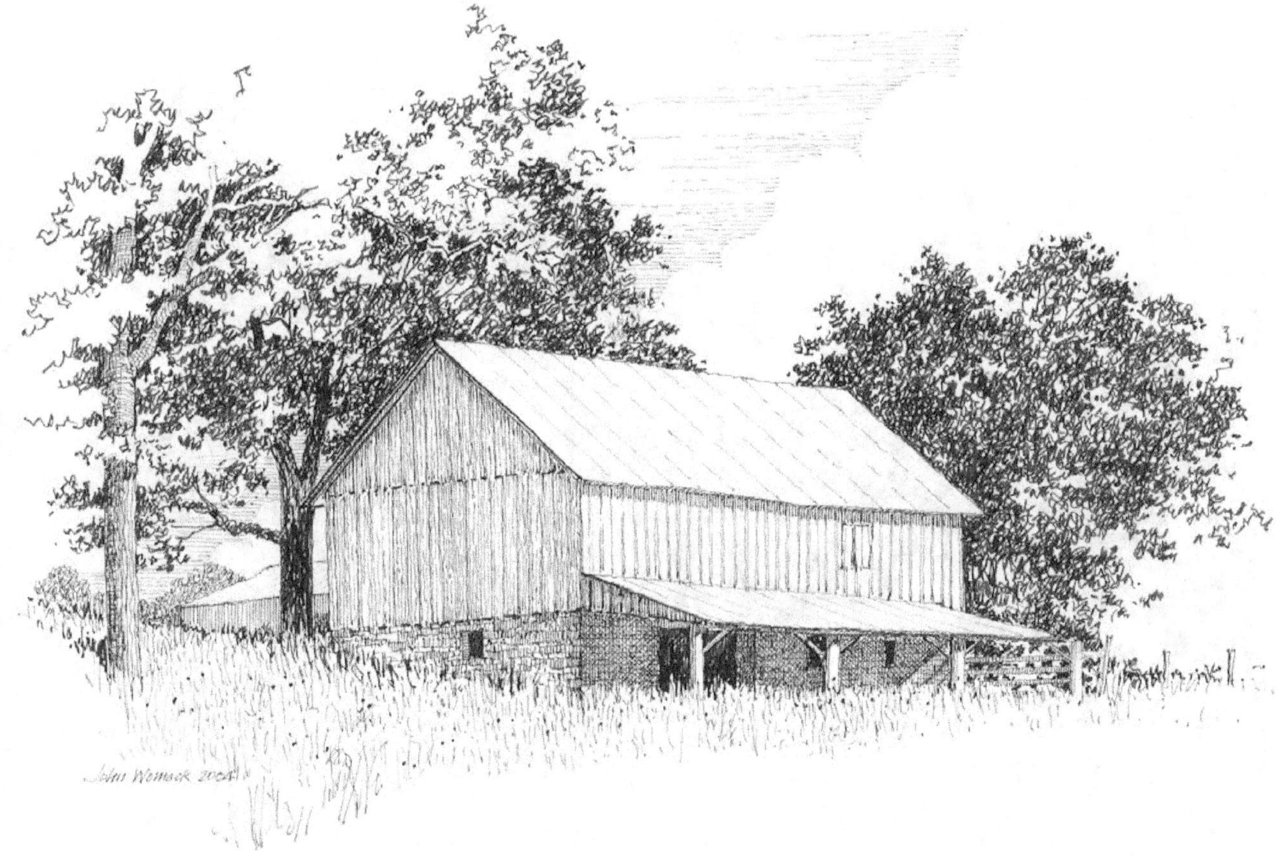

Barn, north of Chelsea, Oklahoma

This simple gabled barn is often referred to as a "bank barn" because it was constructed into the side, or bank, of the sloping terrain. This allows direct ground access to the upper level as well as direct access to the lower level, which is also at ground level. Northeast Oklahoma's sloping prairie terrain is quite conducive for this type of arrangement. Flat fieldstone is readily found in this part of the state and is often used for building foundations, as seen here.

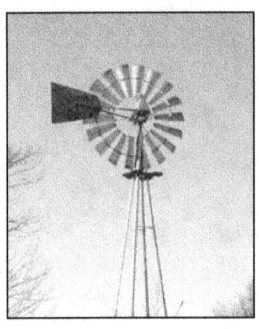

Counting windmills was once a way to occupy kids' minds and time while confined to the inside of the car in travel. My sister counted those on her side of the road, and I counted those on my side of the road.

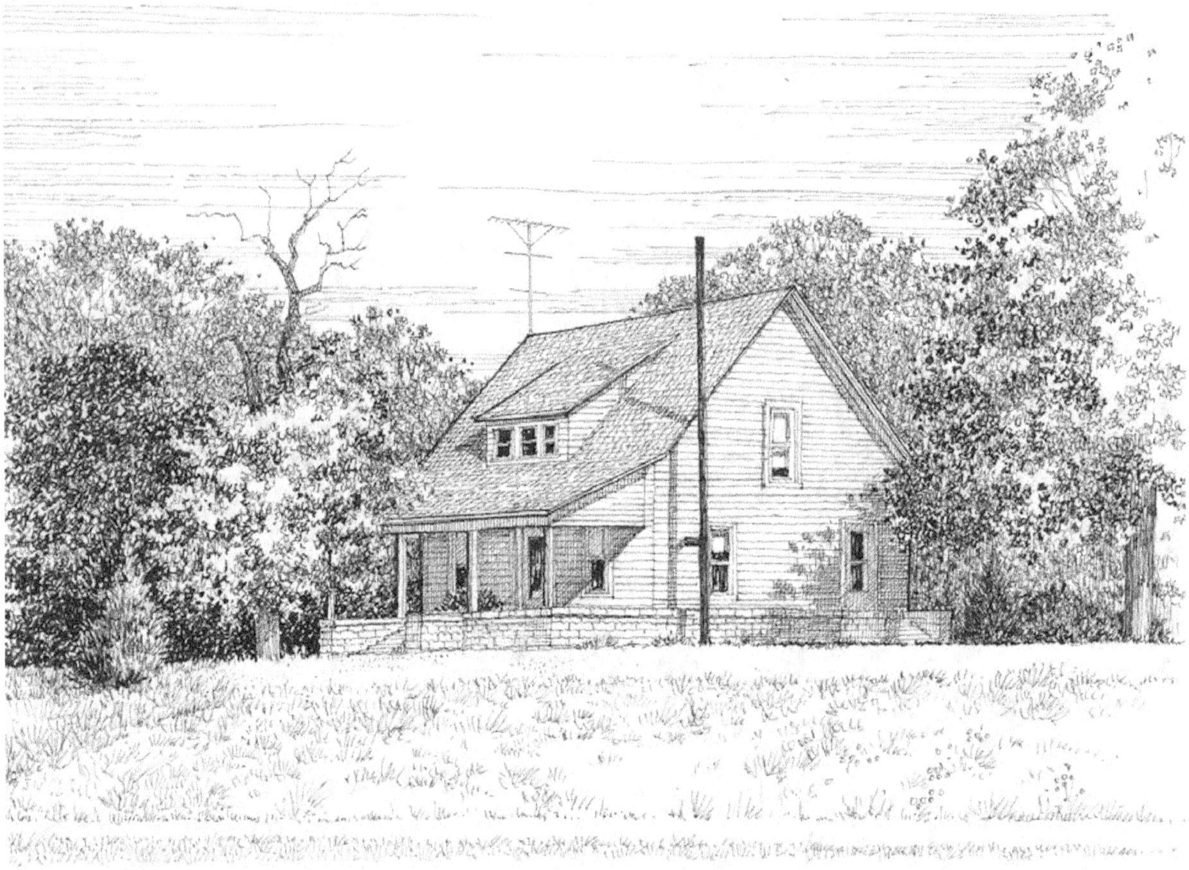

House, north of Chelsea, Oklahoma

This house might be a Sears & Roebuck house from the 1920s. The mail-order firm shipped by rail everything the home owner needed—lumber, nails, hardware—everything. This house closely resembles my grandmother's house in Waverly, Missouri (which also fronted another famous highway, U.S. 65). Built by my grandfather in 1921, it was also a Sears & Roebuck house and had the same type of front-porch and second-story arrangement seen here.

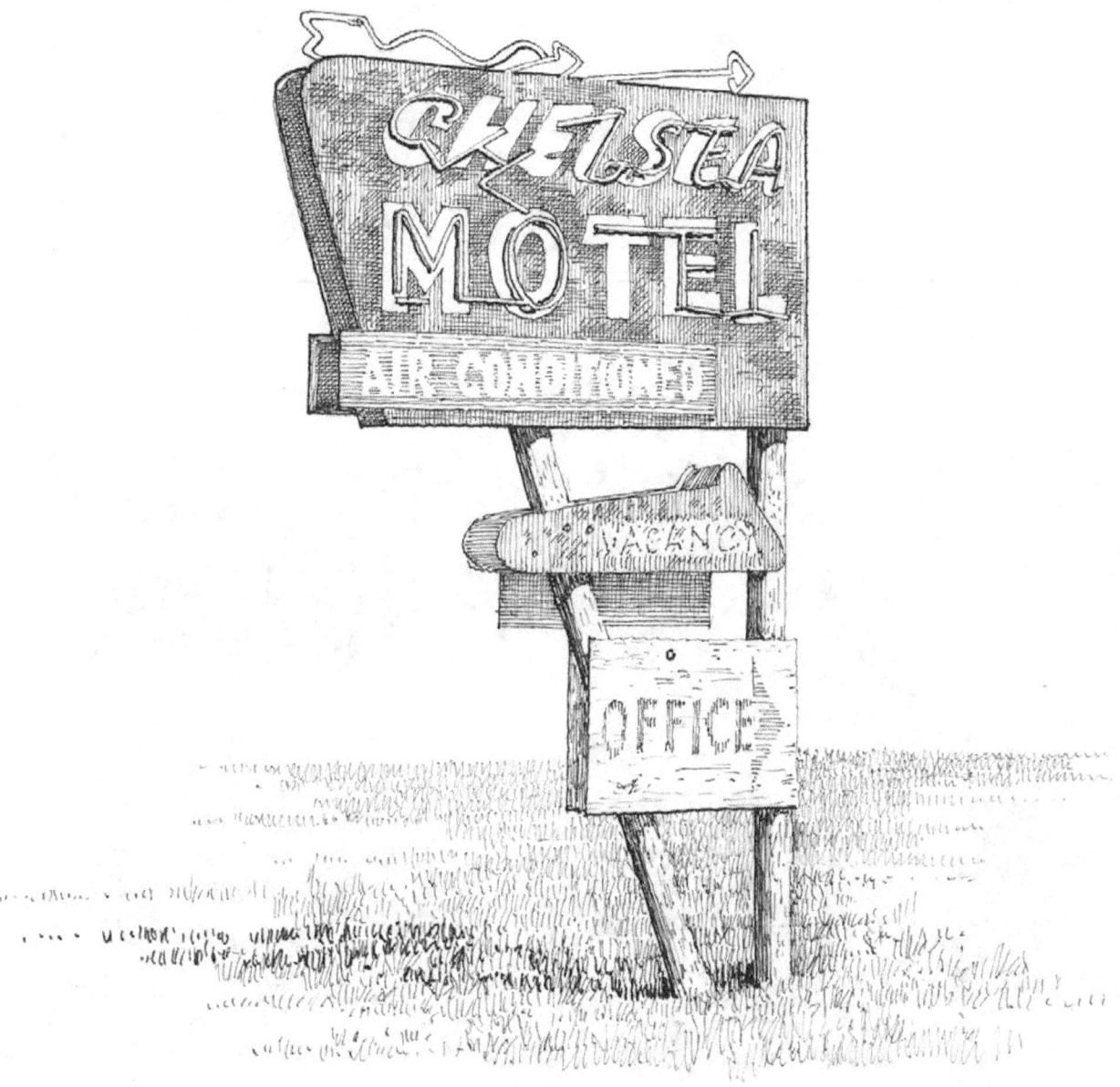

Chelsea Motel Sign, Chelsea, Oklahoma

Named in 1882 by Charles Peach for his former home in England, Chelsea was home of the first oil well drilled in Indian Territory. The oil well hit pay dirt on August 15, 1889, at a depth of only thirty-nine feet. Edward Byrd, the man who drilled the well, was married to a Cherokee woman, which allowed him to lease 94,000 acres from the Cherokee Nation. Gene Autry lived for a while in Chelsea. Will Rogers' sister, Sallie McSpadden, also lived in Chelsea.

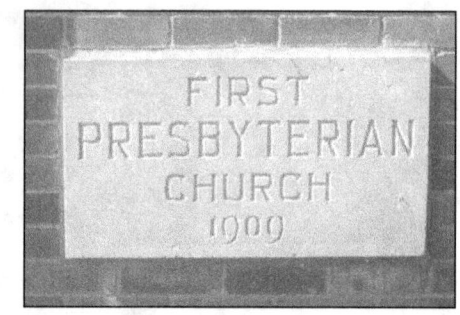

Cornerstones are true historical artifacts that date to a building's beginning and bring us directly into contact with the hopes and dreams of the original builders.

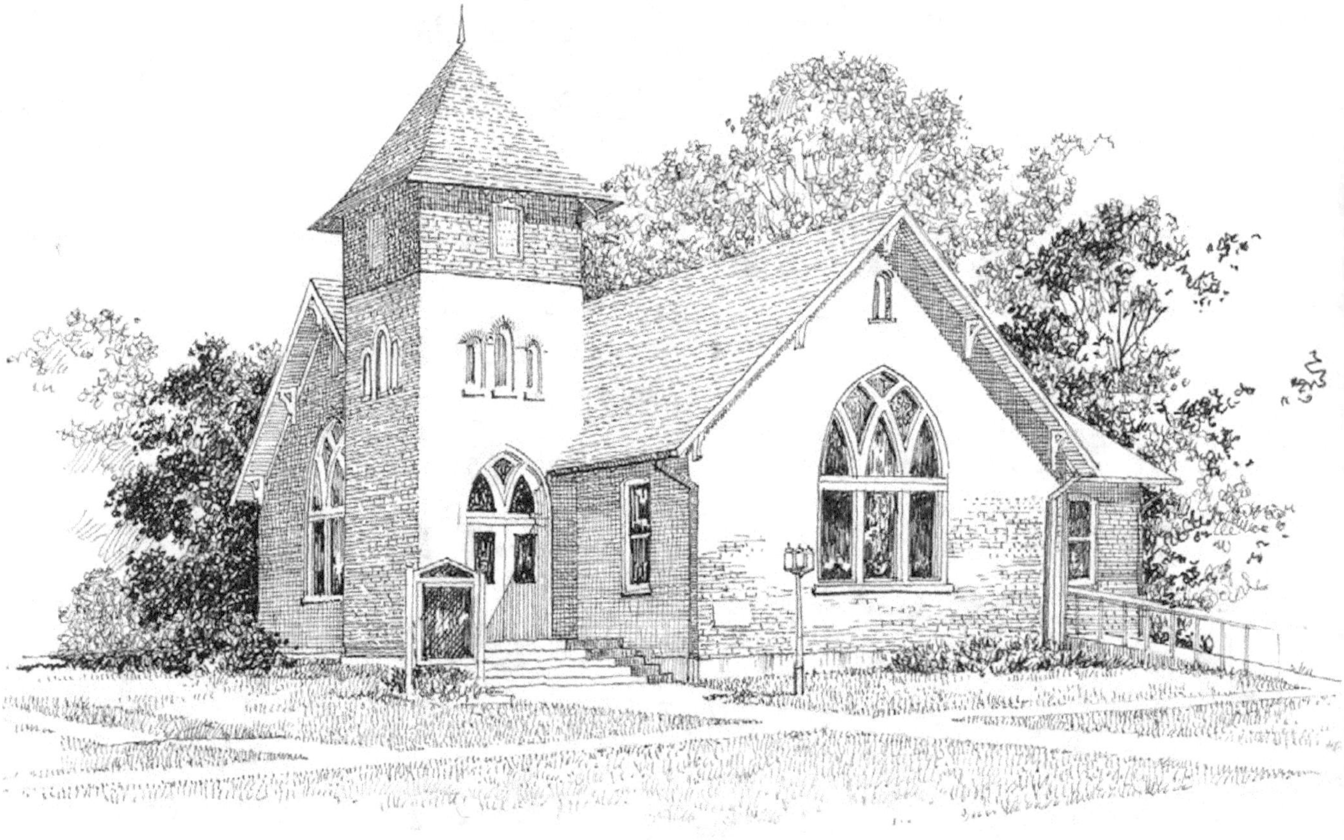

First Presbyterian Church (1909), Chelsea, Oklahoma

Chelsea, population of around 2,000, is a delightful little town with several impressive buildings that date to the early part of the twentieth century. This small brick church is one example of Chelsea's notable buildings. This form of church, with its double-sloped peaked bell tower, appears in similar versions elsewhere in this study. This Presbyterian version is distinctive in that it is made of durable brick and utilizes Gothic arched windows with stained-glass panels.

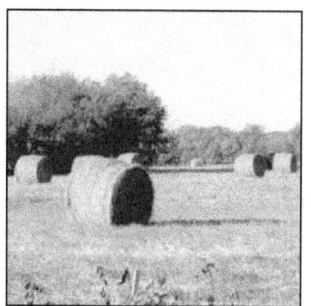

Cutting and bailing prairie grass is an important farm task in preparing for the winter season. Round bales, as seen here, started appearing in the 1970s and '80s.

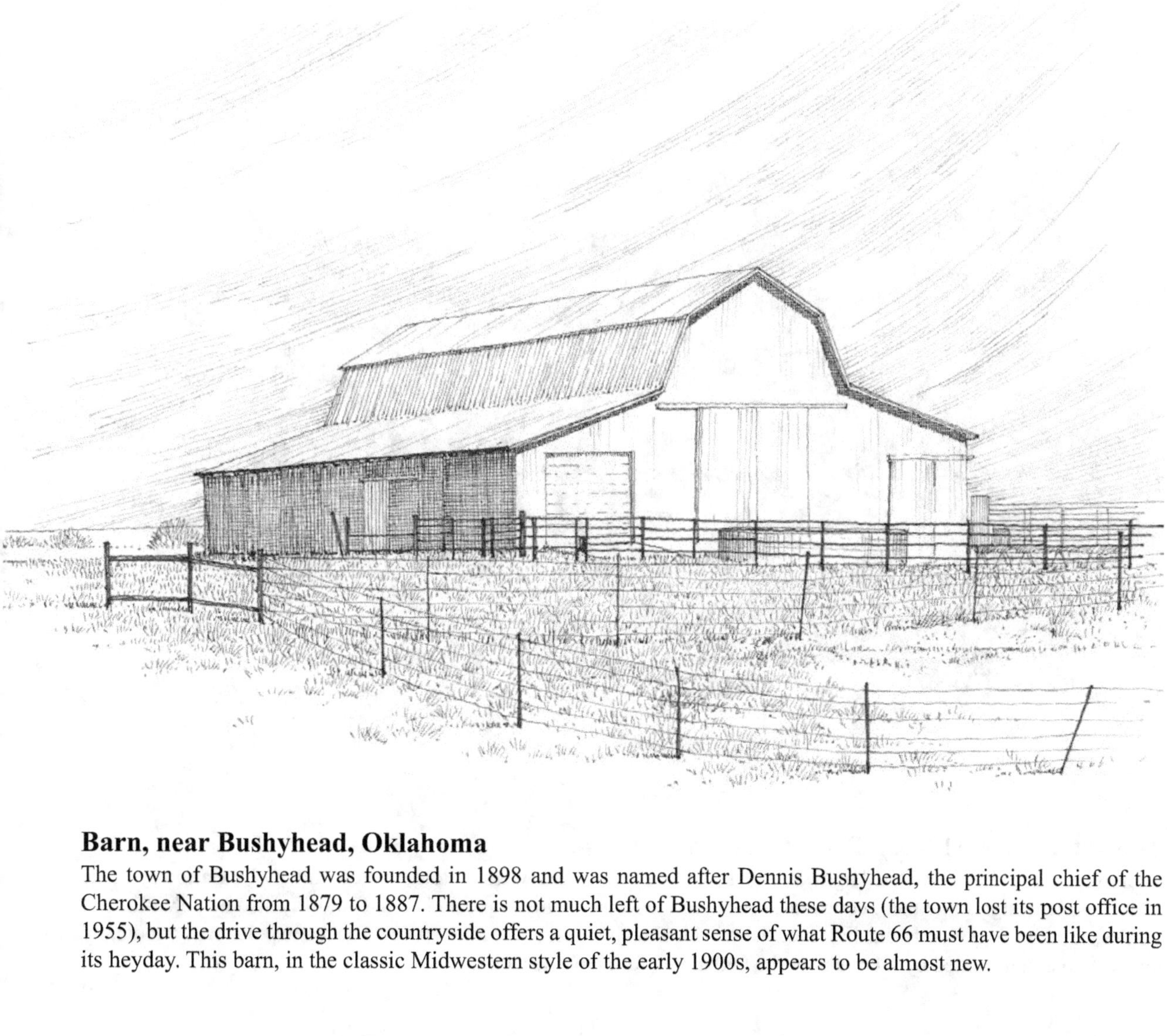

Barn, near Bushyhead, Oklahoma

The town of Bushyhead was founded in 1898 and was named after Dennis Bushyhead, the principal chief of the Cherokee Nation from 1879 to 1887. There is not much left of Bushyhead these days (the town lost its post office in 1955), but the drive through the countryside offers a quiet, pleasant sense of what Route 66 must have been like during its heyday. This barn, in the classic Midwestern style of the early 1900s, appears to be almost new.

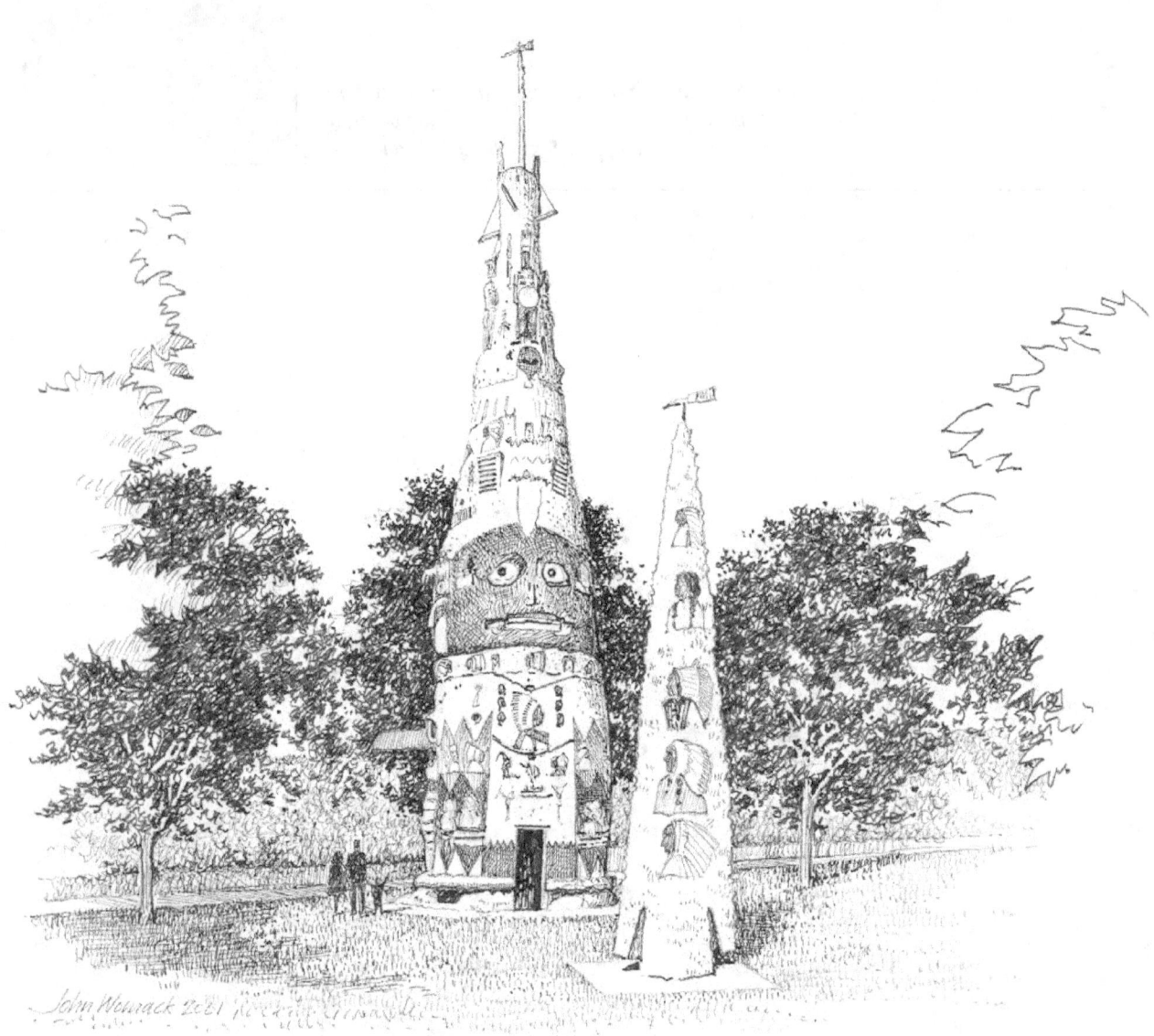

The Totem Poles (1940s), Foyil, Oklahoma

Four miles east of Foyil on State Highway 28A stand these concrete towers, or totem poles, built by Ed Galloway in the 1940s. Novelty sights like these contributed much to the Route 66 mystique and aura. Galloway also made violins, or fiddles, out of various woods and displayed them in his shop just east of the totem poles. The totem poles are periodically touched up and repainted by members of the Oklahoma Route 66 Association.

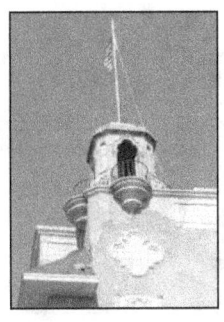

The Spanish-flavored detail and decoration of the Will Rogers Hotel is said to emanate from the decor of Will Rogers' home in Santa Monica, California.

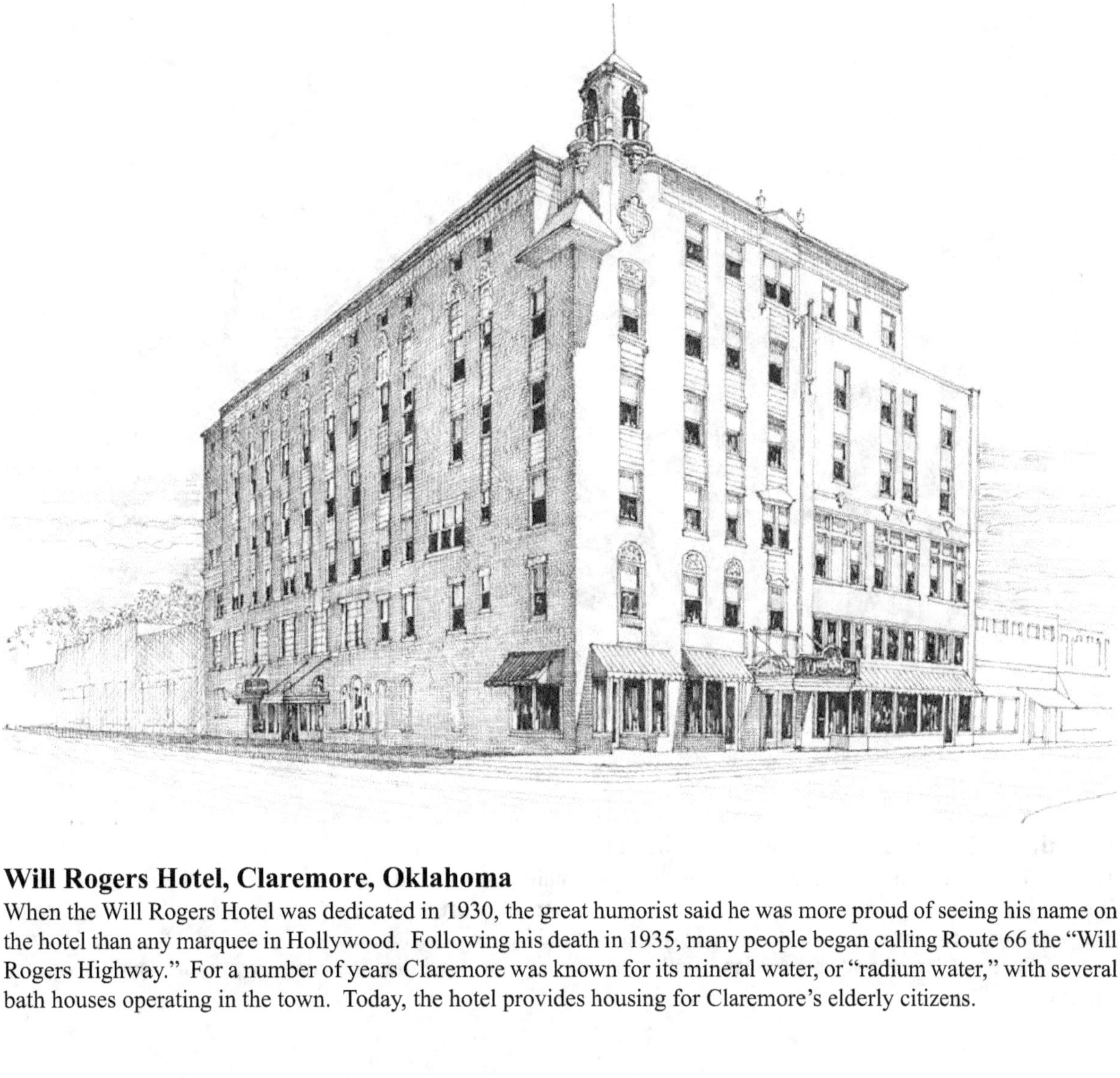

Will Rogers Hotel, Claremore, Oklahoma

When the Will Rogers Hotel was dedicated in 1930, the great humorist said he was more proud of seeing his name on the hotel than any marquee in Hollywood. Following his death in 1935, many people began calling Route 66 the "Will Rogers Highway." For a number of years Claremore was known for its mineral water, or "radium water," with several bath houses operating in the town. Today, the hotel provides housing for Claremore's elderly citizens.

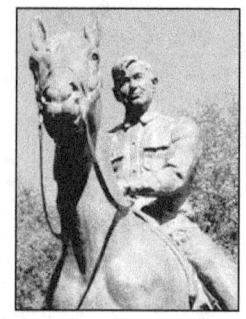

Claremore has several interesting museums including the J. M. Davis Gun Museum and the Will Rogers Memorial Museum.

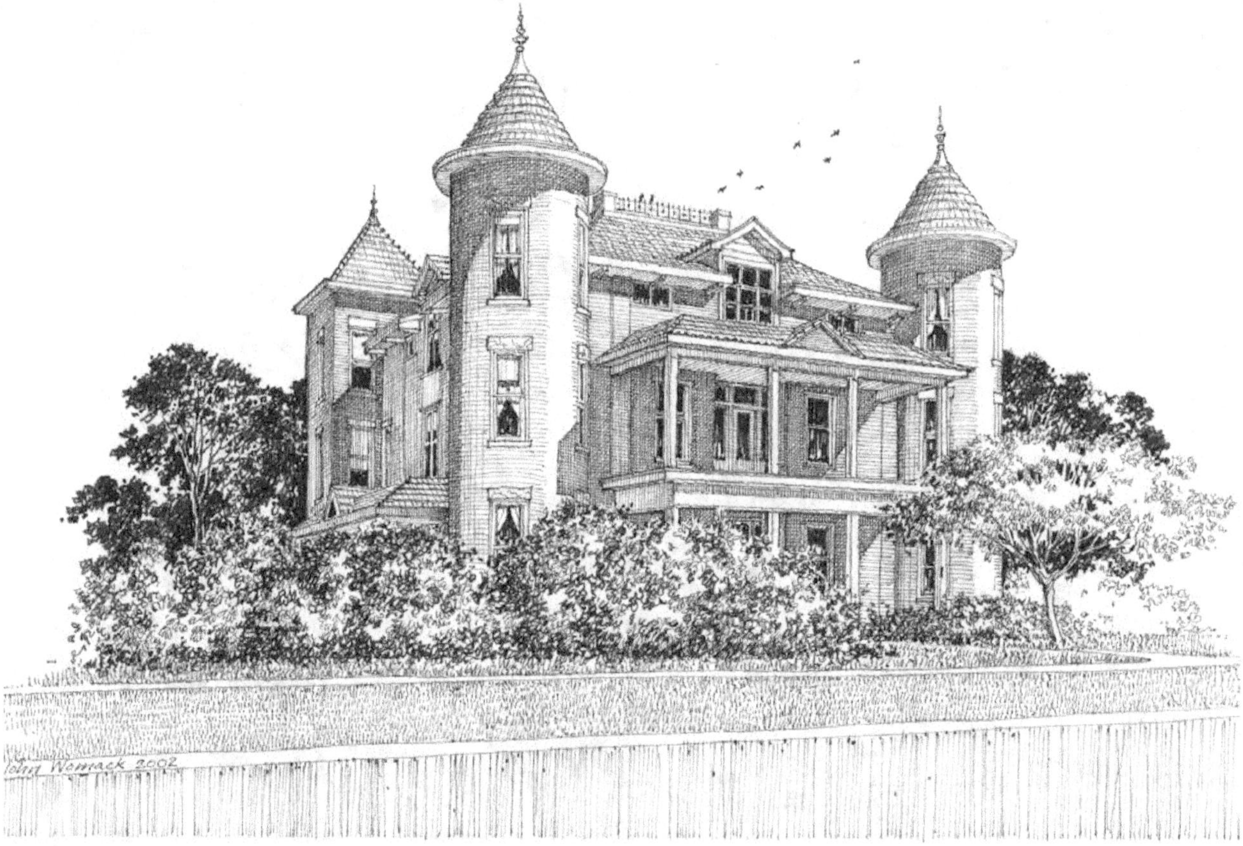

Belvidere Mansion, Claremore, Oklahoma

The Belvidere Mansion, one block east of Route 66, was built around 1910 and is listed on the National Register of Historic Places. The mansion is now home to the Rogers County Historical Society. Claremore was also home to Lynn Riggs, author of *Green Grow the Lilacs*, the play that inspired Rogers and Hammerstein's musical, *Oklahoma!* Rogers State College in Claremore displays a large collection of Riggs memorabilia, including the original "surrey with the fringe on top."

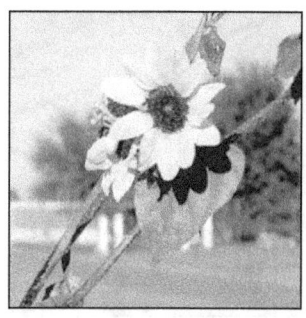

Hugh and Zelta Davis created "Nature's Acres" in the 1960s displaying alligators, snakes, and other wildlife before building the famous Blue Whale.

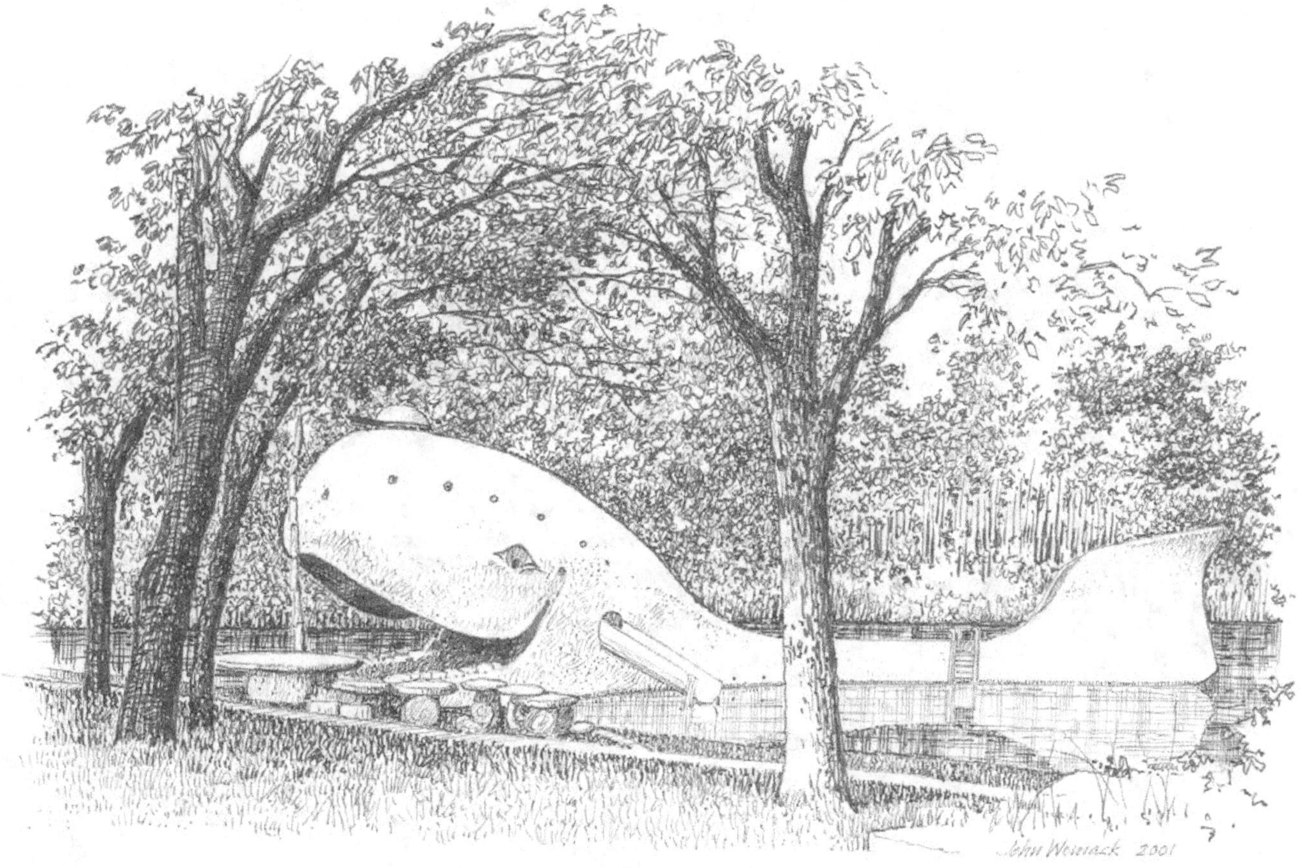

The Blue Whale, Catoosa, Oklahoma

Certainly one of the most loved and well known sights along the entire Route, the Blue Whale began as an anniversary gift from Hugh Davis to his wife, Zelta. Hugh had built the pond as a swimming hole for highway travelers and locals. In 1970 he began building the whale, completing it in 1972. When the attraction closed in 1988, the whale and grounds began to fall into disrepair, but in 1997 area residents restored the whale and continue to perform periodic repairs.

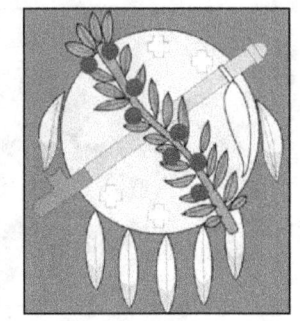

The emblem on the Oklahoma State Flag honors the state's Indian heritage, featuring an Osage shield, a peace pipe, and an olive branch.

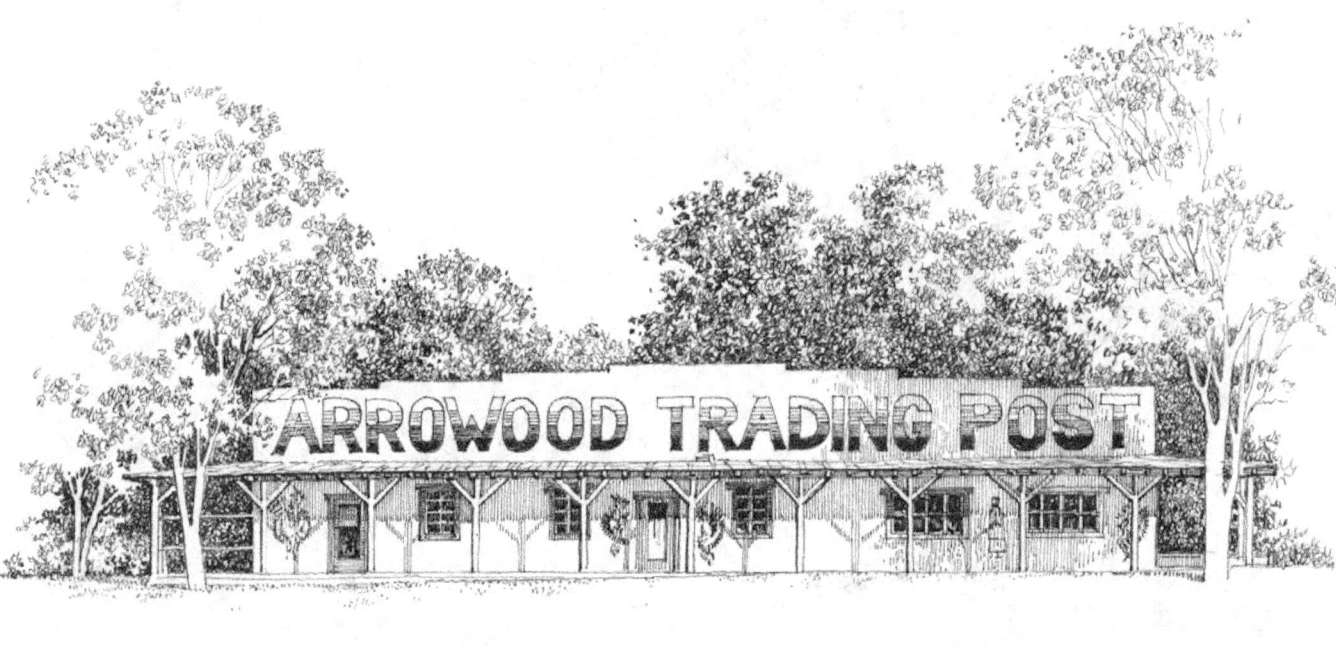

Arrowood Trading Post, Catoosa, Oklahoma

Directly across the highway from the Blue Whale is the Arrowood Indian Trading Post. It is still in business today selling a wide variety of American Indian arts and crafts. Oklahoma contains the largest contingent of American Indian nationalities in the United States and prior to statehood in 1907 was often referred to as "The Nations." Highway travelers were curious about the native tribes, and many businesses along Route 66 utilized an Indian theme.

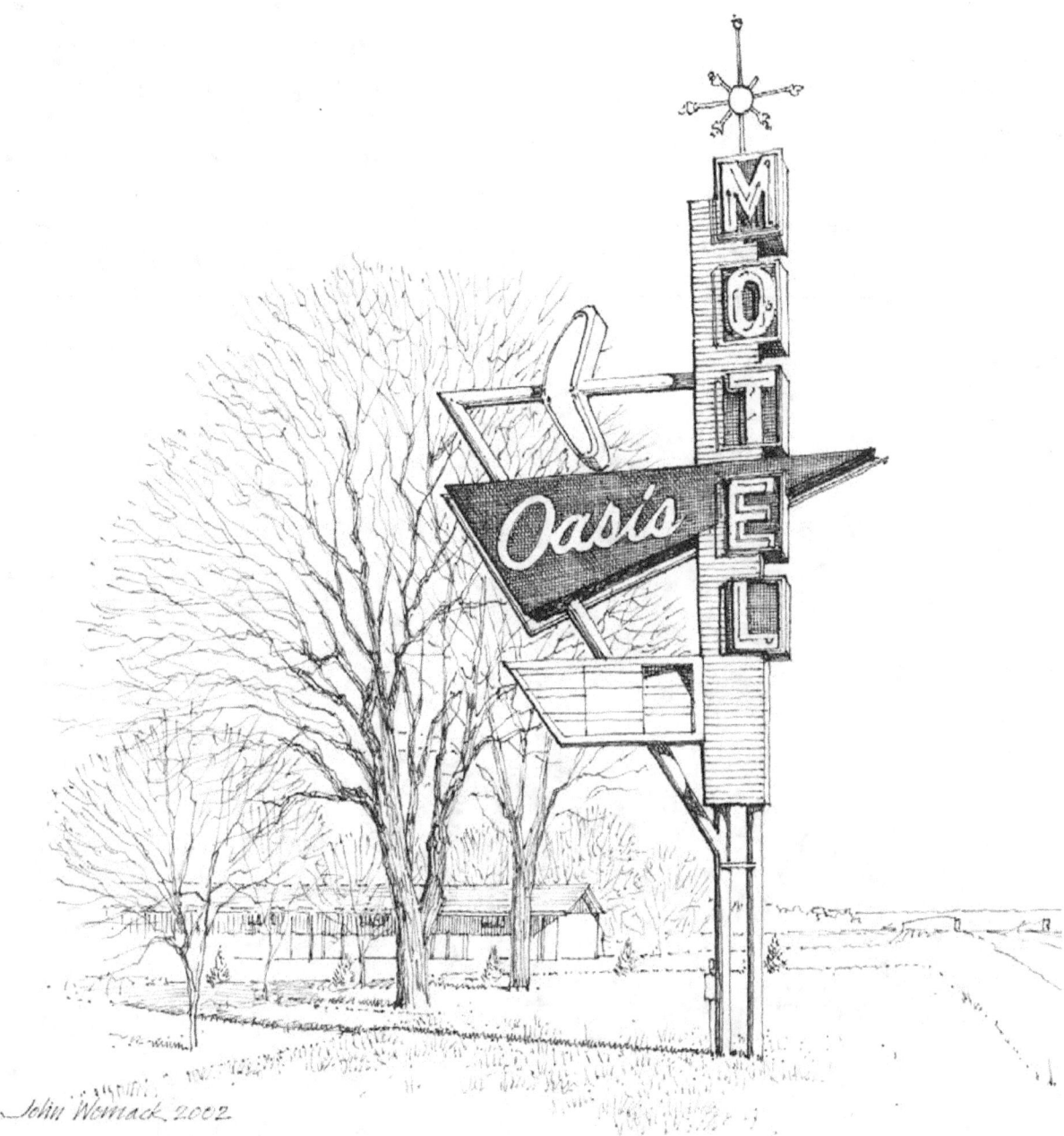

John Womack 2002

Oasis Motel Sign, East Tulsa, Oklahoma

Motel signs along Route 66 are fascinating in their wide variety of neon-lighted shapes and messages. Most of these signs date from the 1950s and 1960s when Americans began traveling and vacationing in earnest. This sign proclaims the motel to be an "oasis" for all weary travelers. The various arrow shapes on Route 66 signs are particularly fun to observe. Here—at least to me—the arrow looks more like a banana than an arrowhead.

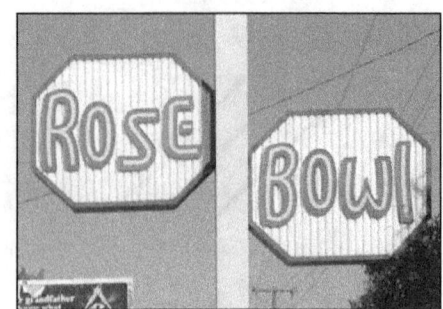

Closing in 2004, the Rose Bowl subsequently endured three deliberately set fires. The building is another Route 66 structure with a doubtful future.

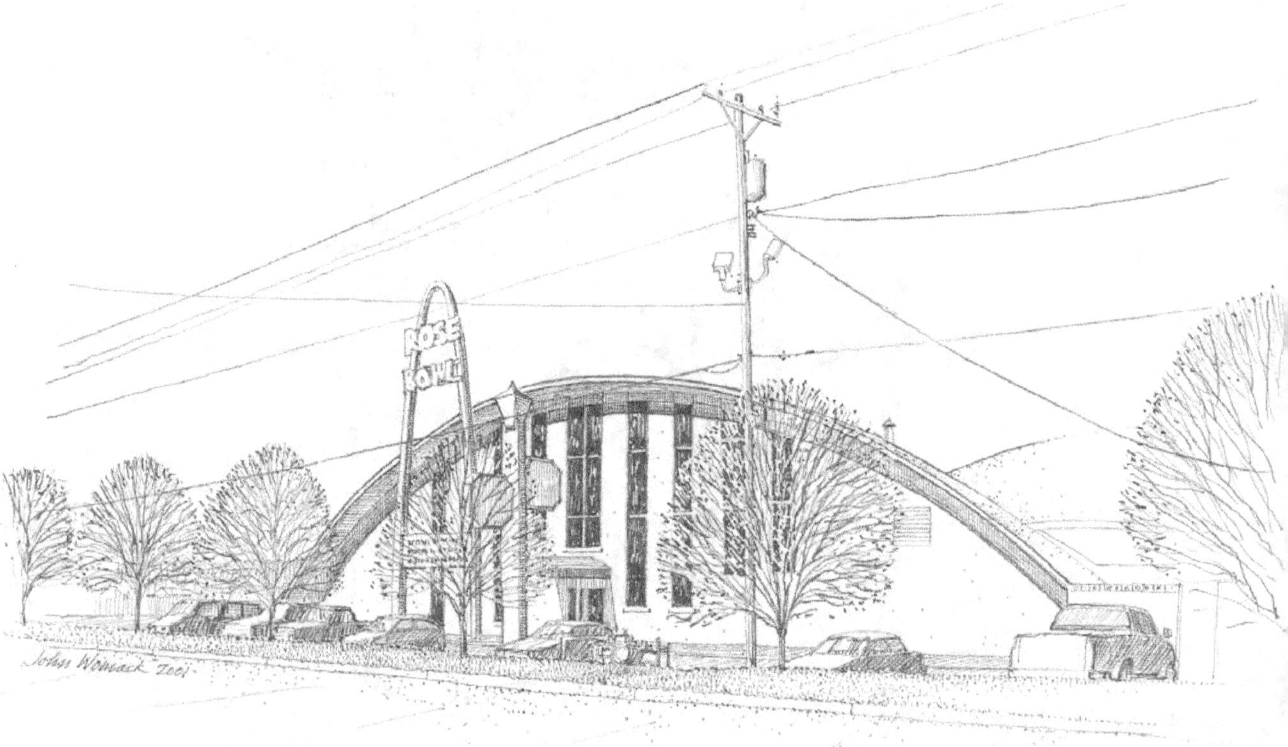

Rose Bowl Bowling Alley, East Tulsa, Oklahoma

Bowling became a national pastime during the 1950s and continues today as a popular indoor form of recreation. The structures or alleyways that housed these activities often became popular gathering spots and often adapted certain design features or themes that gave the buildings a distinctive or novel appearance. Many bowling alleys utilized catch phrases that sought to establish a particular image. The Rose Bowl was once painted a bright rosey pink.

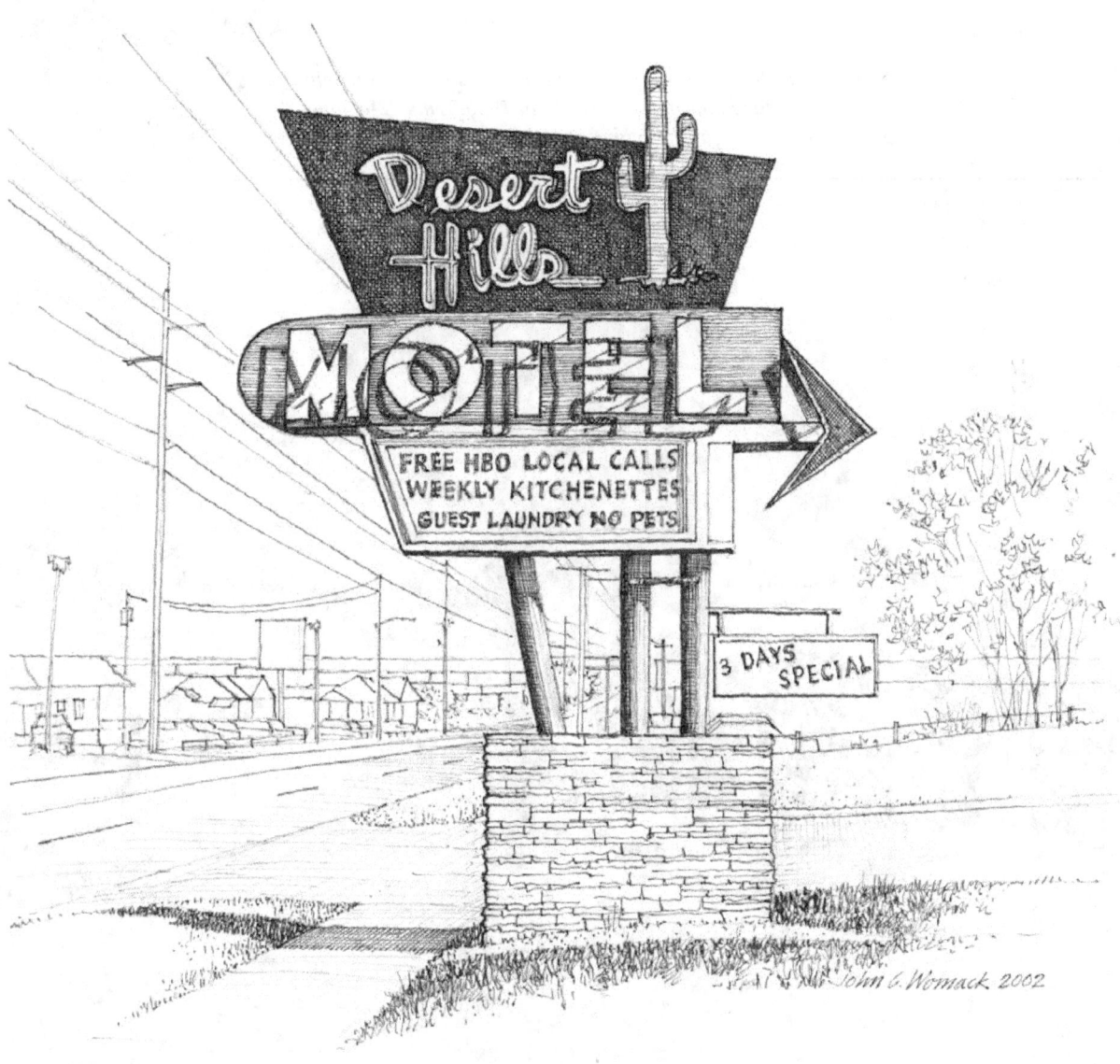

Desert Hills Motel Sign, East Tulsa, Oklahoma

Motel names, so prominently displayed on entrance signs, were carefully created to help highway travelers make up their minds as to what appeared safe and comfortable for an overnight stay. On page 41, the sign's catch phrase was "oasis." Here, just down the road, is a motel that seems perfectly comfortable in making associations with the desert—with cactus from the Sonoran Desert in Arizona depicted on the sign!

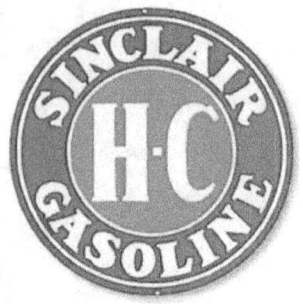

Unable to acquire a franchise for "ethyl," an anit-knock additive, Sinclair Oil developed its high-octane alternative, "H-C,"in 1926. This 72-octane automobile gasoline was the highest available octane at the time.

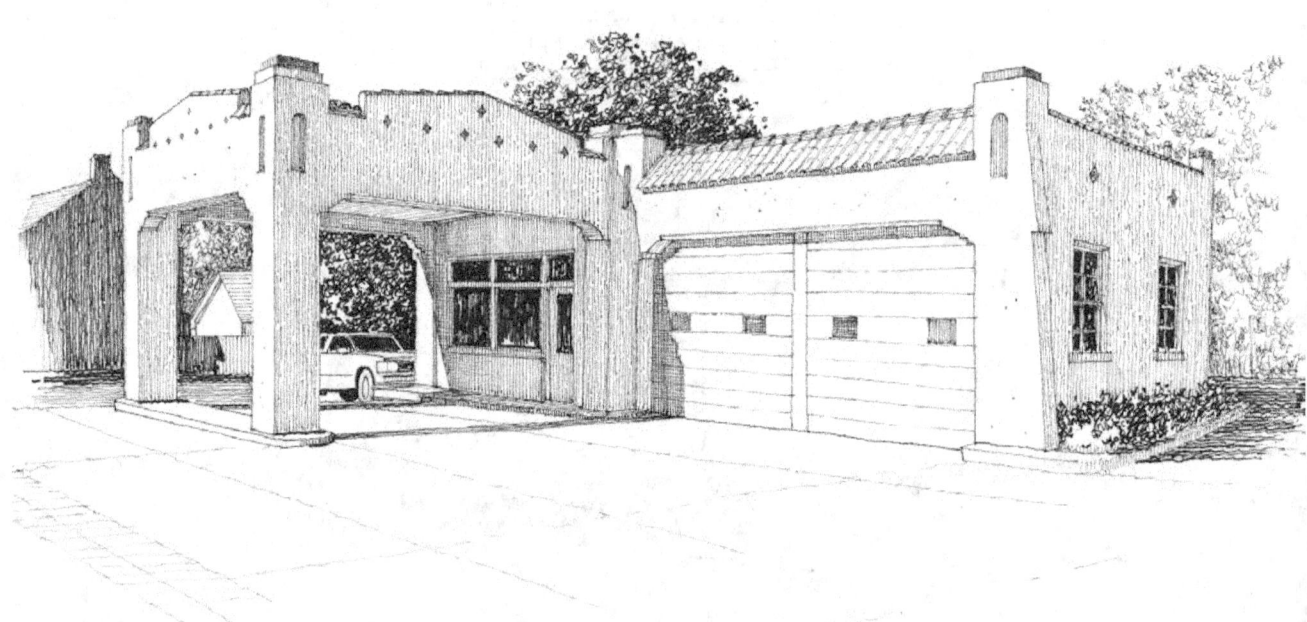

Former Sinclair Station, Tulsa, Oklahoma

In his book, *Pump and Circumstance*, John Margolies illustrates three road maps issued by Sinclair Refining Company. The maps illustrate Sinclair stations with the same styling and detailing seen above. Margolies offers an interesting discussion on the importance of free road maps, stating that by 1964, some five billion road maps had been given out by oil companies to highway travelers. Free road maps gradually became a thing of the past by the mid 1970s.

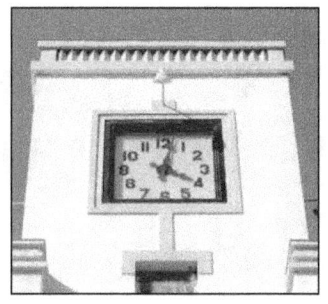

The clock tower and clock of the Tulsa Monument Company display the geometric forms and cubistic details of Art Deco.

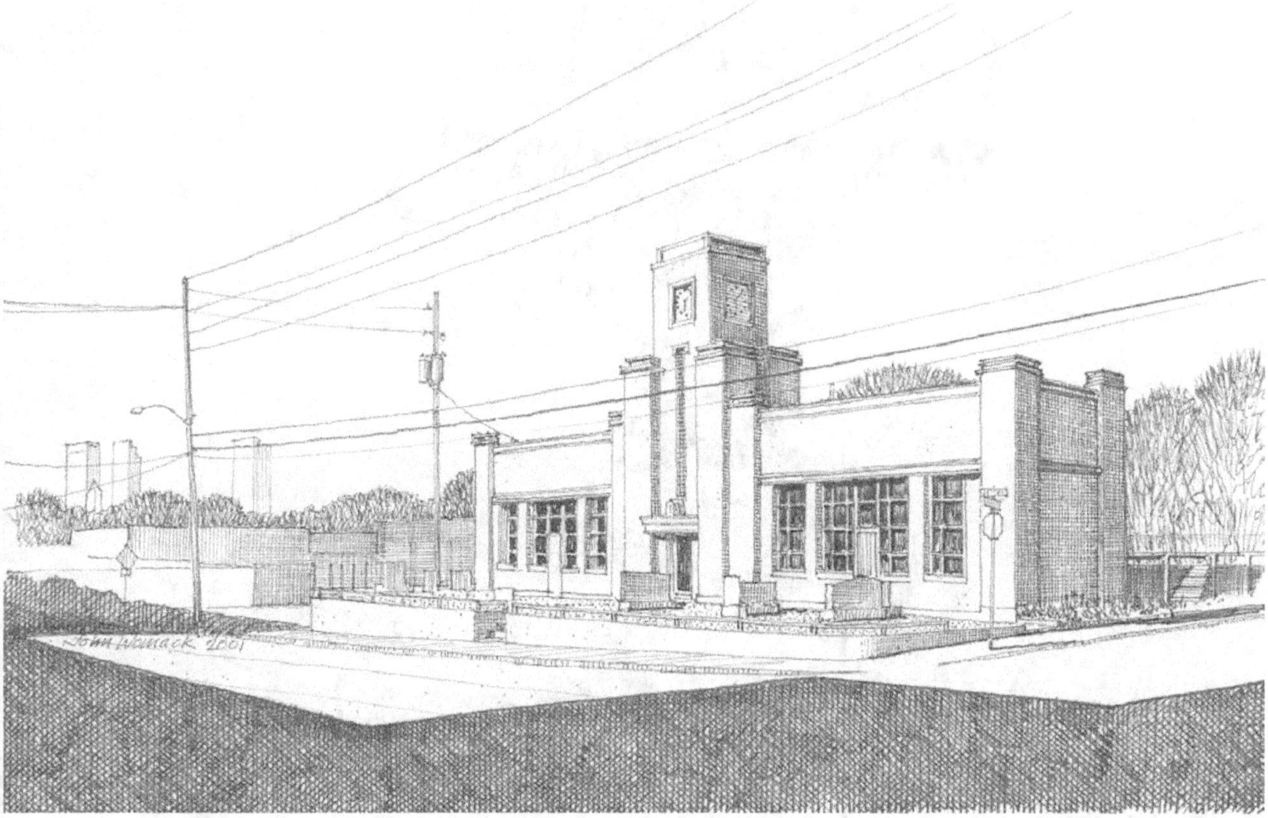

Tulsa Monument Company, Tulsa, Oklahoma

Still in operation, the Tulsa Monument Company is an outstanding example of Art Deco design. It is interesting how the progressive citizens of Tulsa embraced this architectural style during the 1920s. Tulsa has become a place of pilgrimage for people who love Art Deco, and touring maps are available for those interested in seeing Tulsa's sights. Several examples of this style of architecture occur along Route 66 in Tulsa and in other towns along the route.

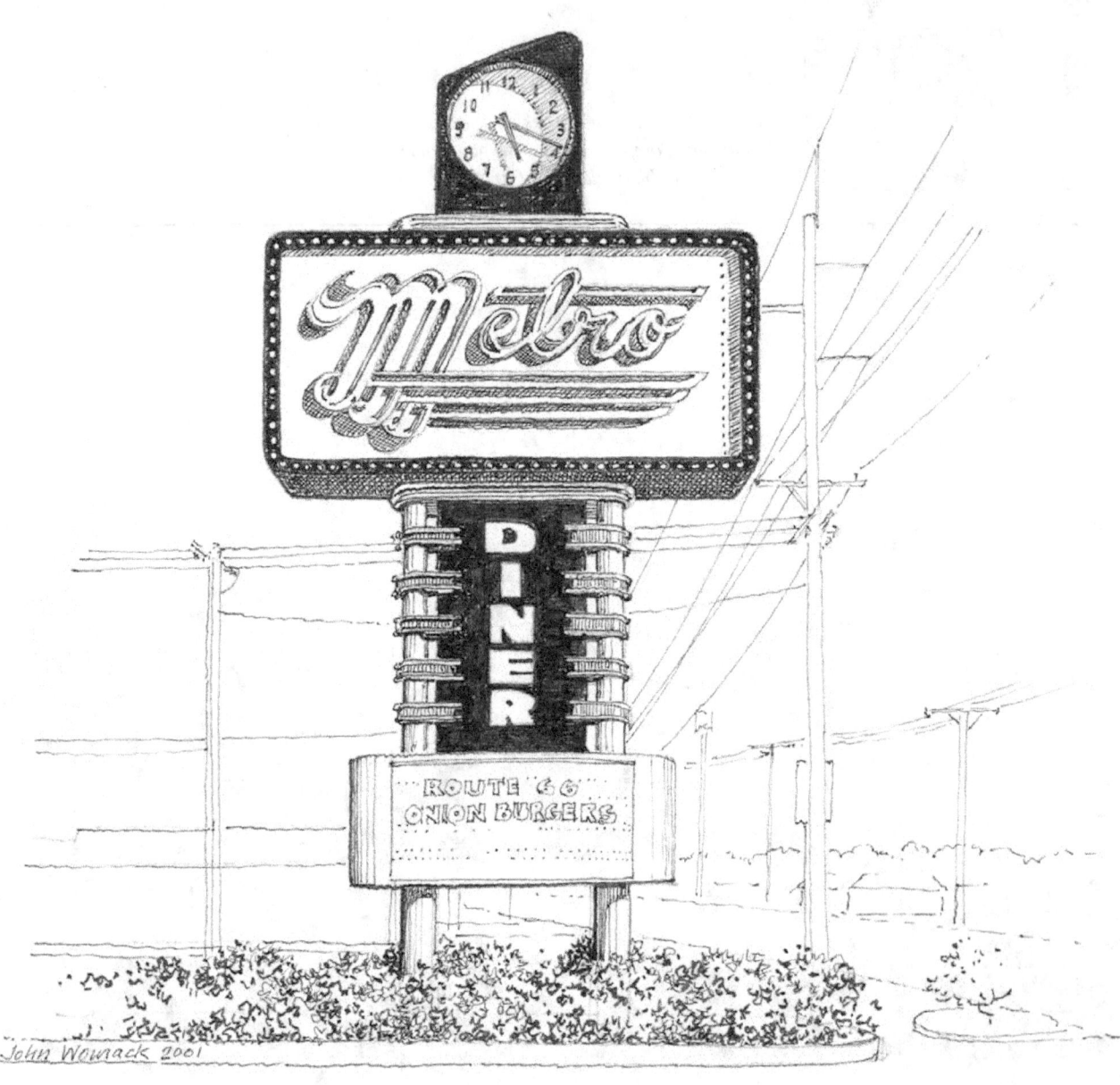

John Womack 2001

Metro Diner Sign, Tulsa, Oklahoma

Much of Route 66 in Tulsa shares its surface with 11th Street. The Metro Diner is located on 11th Street and does a great job of bringing back to life those hot rod days of the 1950s. While basking in the delights of old time rock and roll, poodle skirts, and chrome plating, you can enjoy a great meal. Order up the old Route 66 staple: an onion burger with curly fries and a coke float. Then, top your meal off with a piece of coconut cream pie and a cup of "joe."

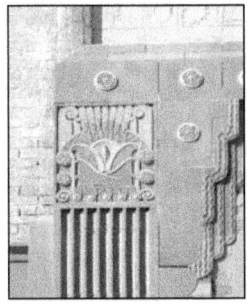

The multicolored terra cotta detail on the Warehouse Market Building (also known as the Farmers' Market) appears as if new.

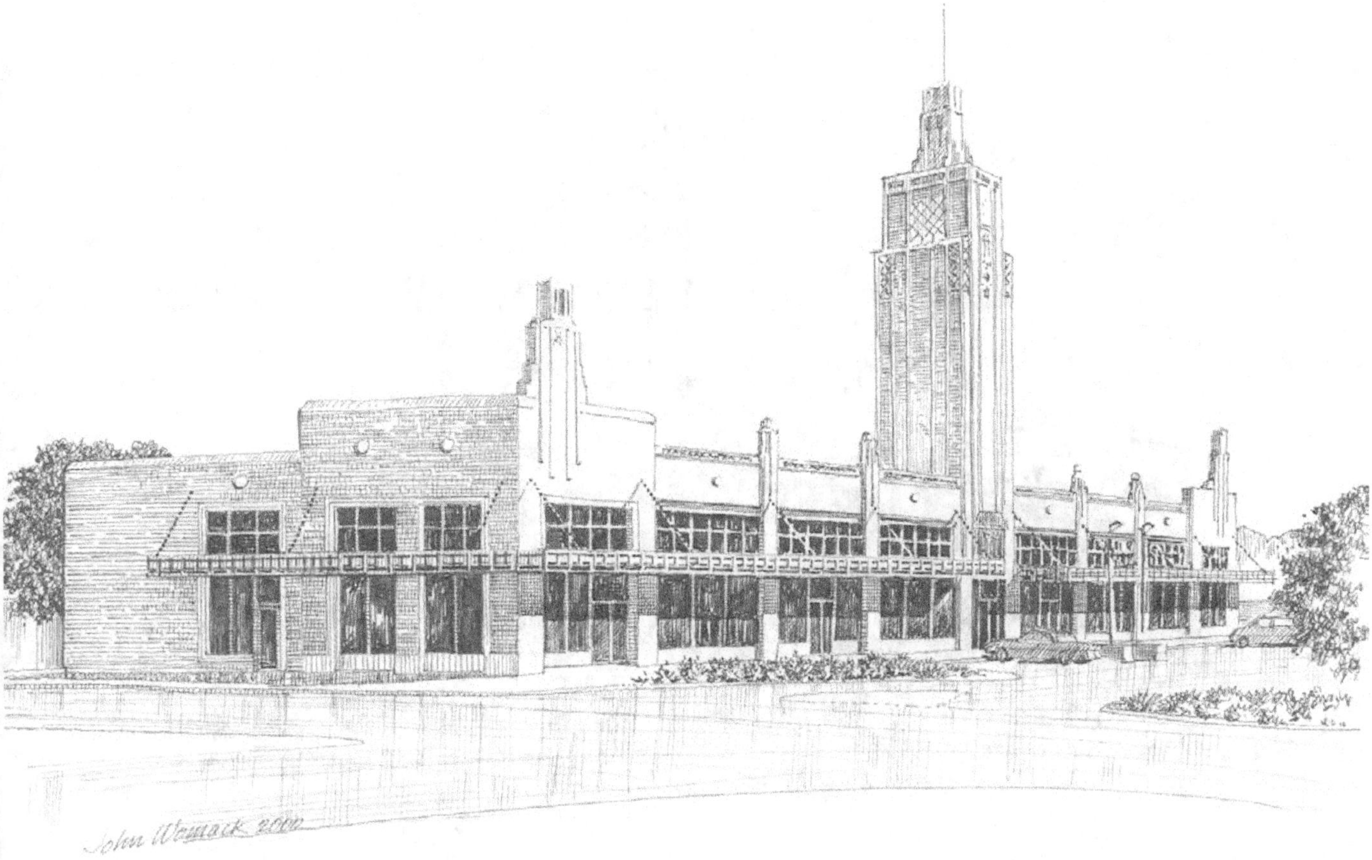

Farmers' Market Building, Tulsa, Oklahoma

Also on 11th Street, this building is another fine example of Art Deco design in Tulsa. Its multicolored ceramic tile and brick work is carefully crafted and coordinated. During the 1990s, the building was almost torn down to make way for a parking lot and a building supply store, but again, concerned citizens and several Tulsa architects rallied to save the structure. Today one of Tulsa's oldest businesses, Lyon's Indian Store, is located in the building.

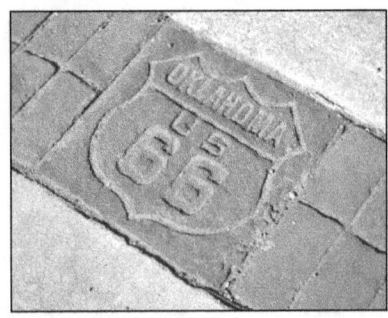

Along the north edge of Tulsa's 11th Street, a brick strip with Route 66 inserts marks the path of the original road.

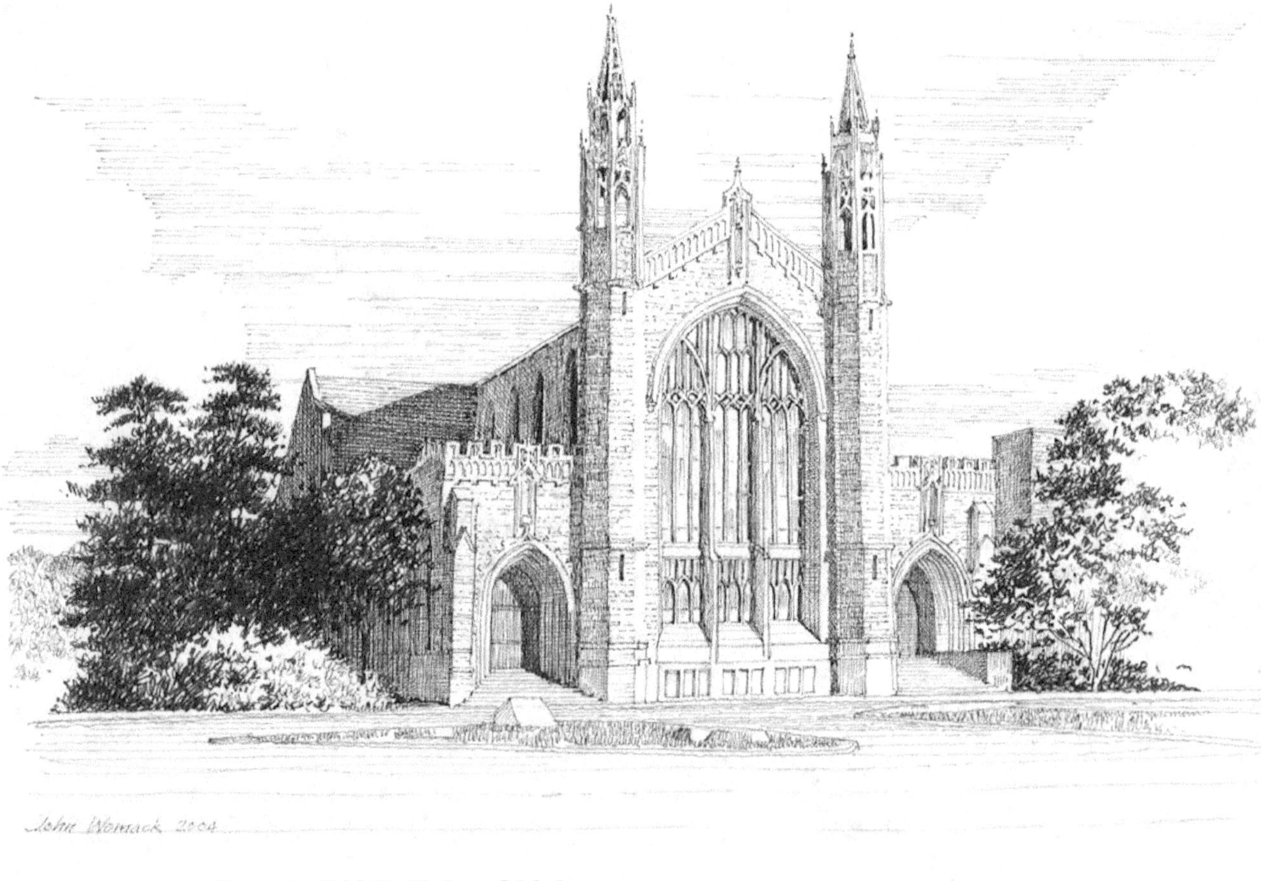

John Womack 2004

First Methodist Church (1921), Tulsa, Oklahoma

This church is a fine example of neo-gothic design, exhibiting beautiful stone masonry as well as stone tracery in the window subdivisions. The church's construction began in 1921 and was completed seven years later. Often called "the Cathedral of the South," it was designed by Charles W. Bolton of Philadelphia. The exterior masonry is made of native sandstone, quarried about 15 miles from Tulsa. The stone trim and tracery is Indiana limestone.

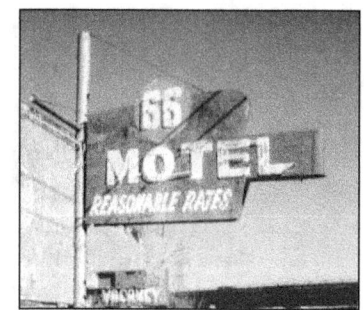

Oklahoma probably has more Route 66 structures in existence than any other Route 66 state, but they are steadily disappearing.

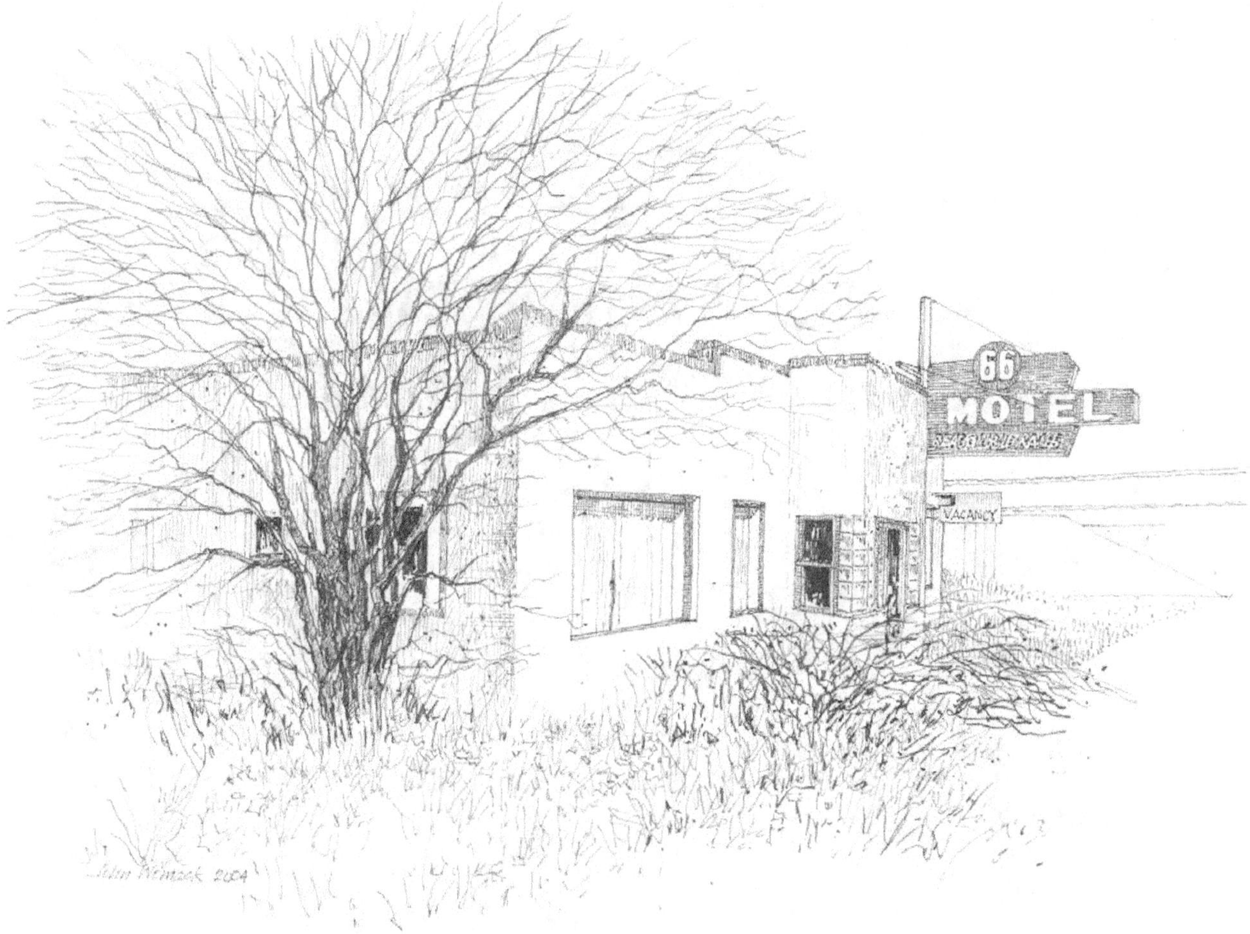

66 Motel (destroyed), West Tulsa, Oklahoma

In *Oklahoma Route 66*, Jim Ross notes how the 66 Motel was one of Tulsa's most recognizable Route 66 landmarks. Unfortunately, it was demolished in 2002. Many abandoned structures along the Route fall victim to the wrecking ball. There are many reasons these buildings don't survive—safety is one of them. When I last visited the abandoned 66 Motel, a portion of it was occupied by a transient family—with no water, no toilets, and no heat.

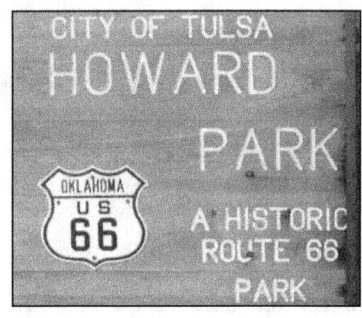

Before air conditioning, traveling in hot weather eventually took its toll on man and machine. Shaded roadside areas became welcomed resting areas—especially if a stream or pond was nearby.

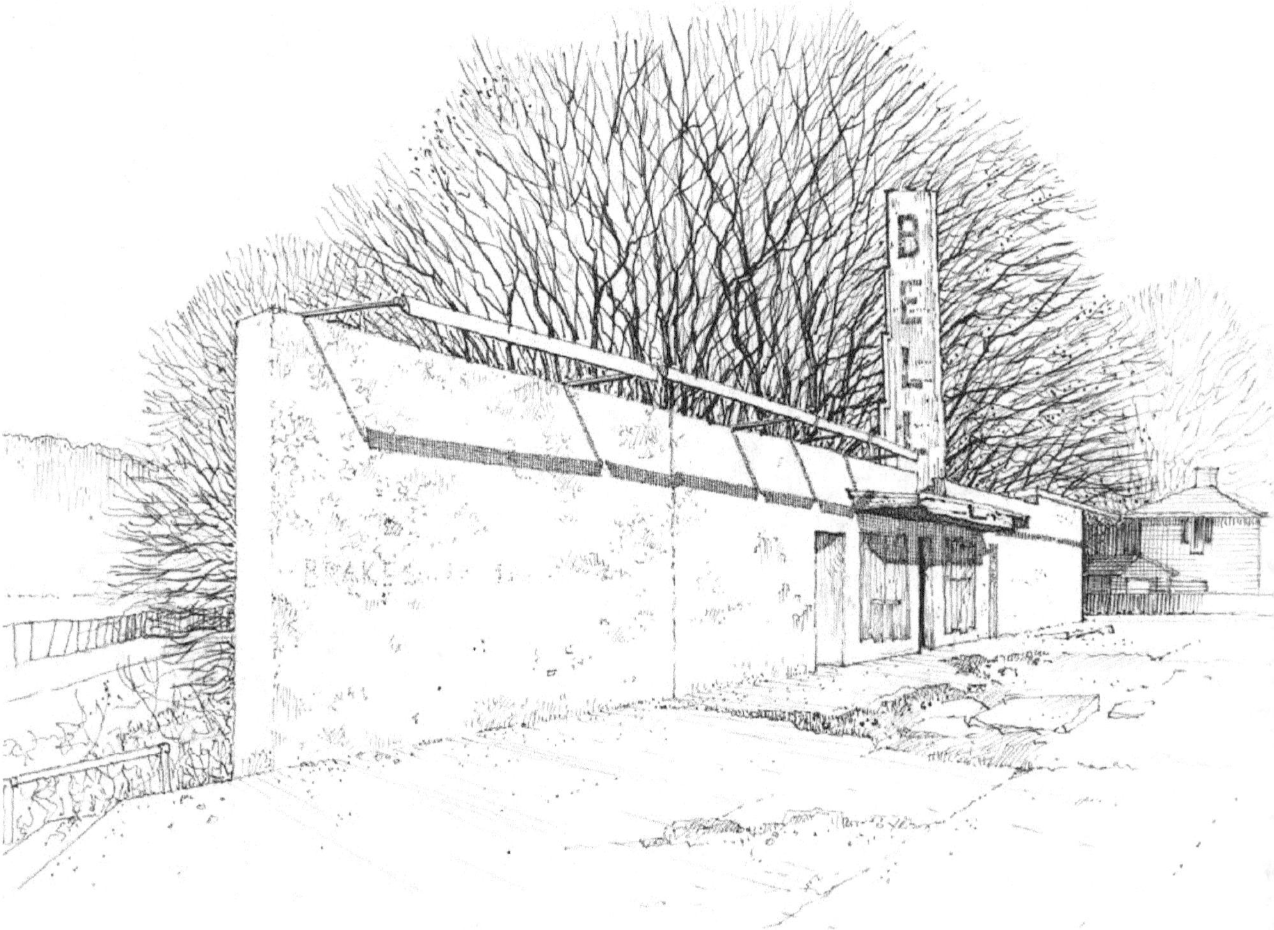

Bell Station and Auto Parts Store, West Tulsa, Oklahoma

Located a short distance west of the Route 66 Motel (now destroyed) is this former gas station and auto parts store. Of interest is how the broad building facade is primarily a billboard that adjoins a rather small interior space (between the two doorways). The painted wall surface advertised various repair services and auto parts. The painted letters on the stucco surface are barely discernible today. The future of this structure, like many others on Route 66, is in doubt.

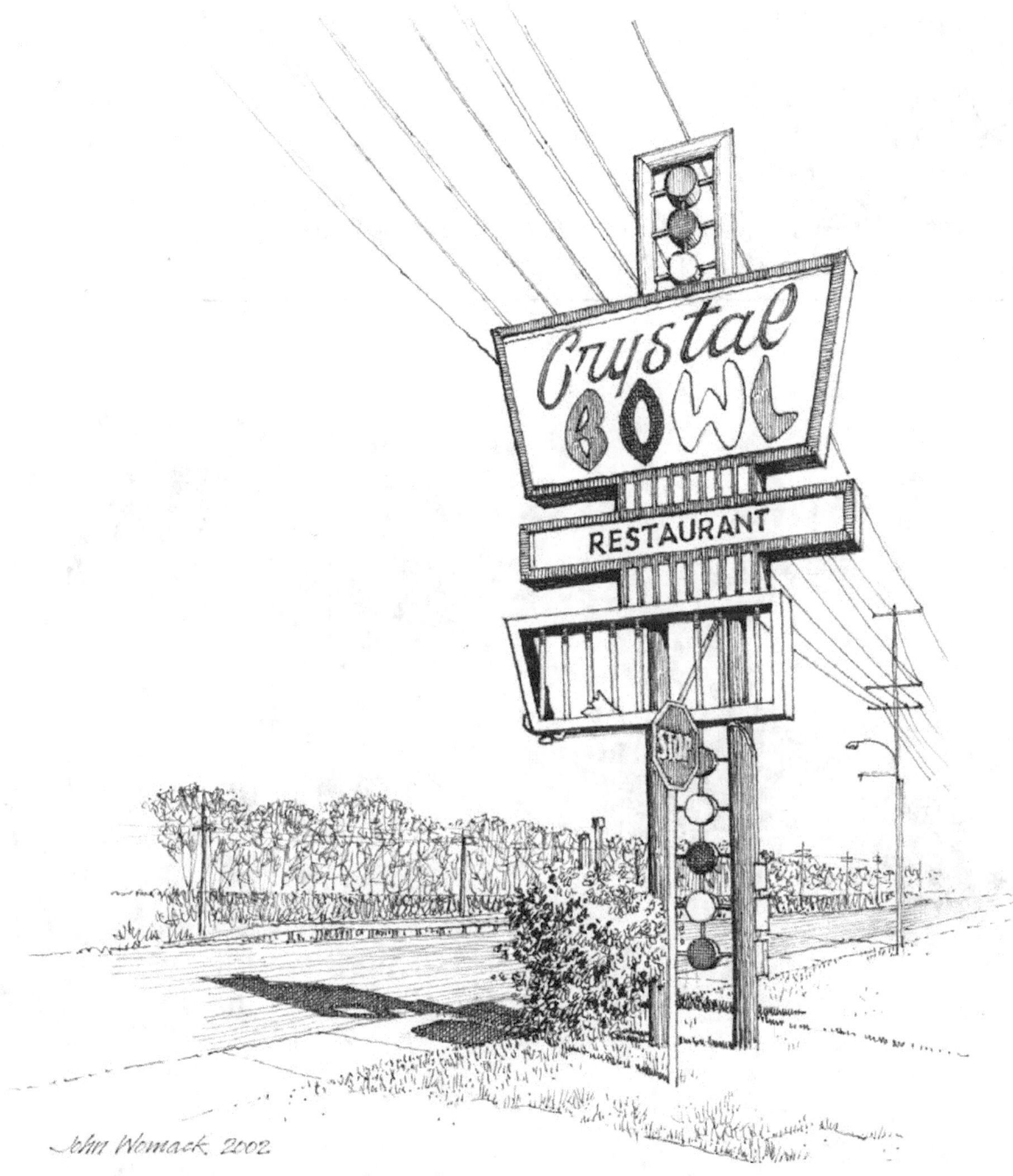

John Womack 2002

Crystal Bowl Bowling Alley sign, West Tulsa, Oklahoma
Catch phrases and novel expressions run the gamut from subtle to sublime along Route 66 and nowhere more than in Oklahoma. Of course, bowling alleys are all about fun, and such lighthearted associations as "crystal bowl" contribute to the atmosphere. Is this sign alluding to a crystal punch bowl or a crystal ball? The railroad was the "blood brother" of Route 66 and ran parallel to the highway for most of the highway's length.

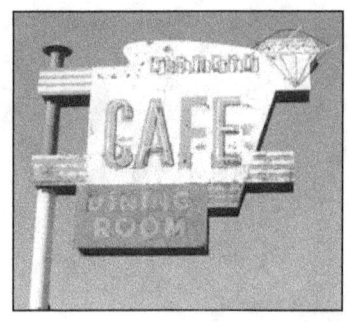

Many businesses along Route 66 have been closed for years but their signs still remain. The Diamond Cafe in Sapulpa no longer exists, but its sign is still present.

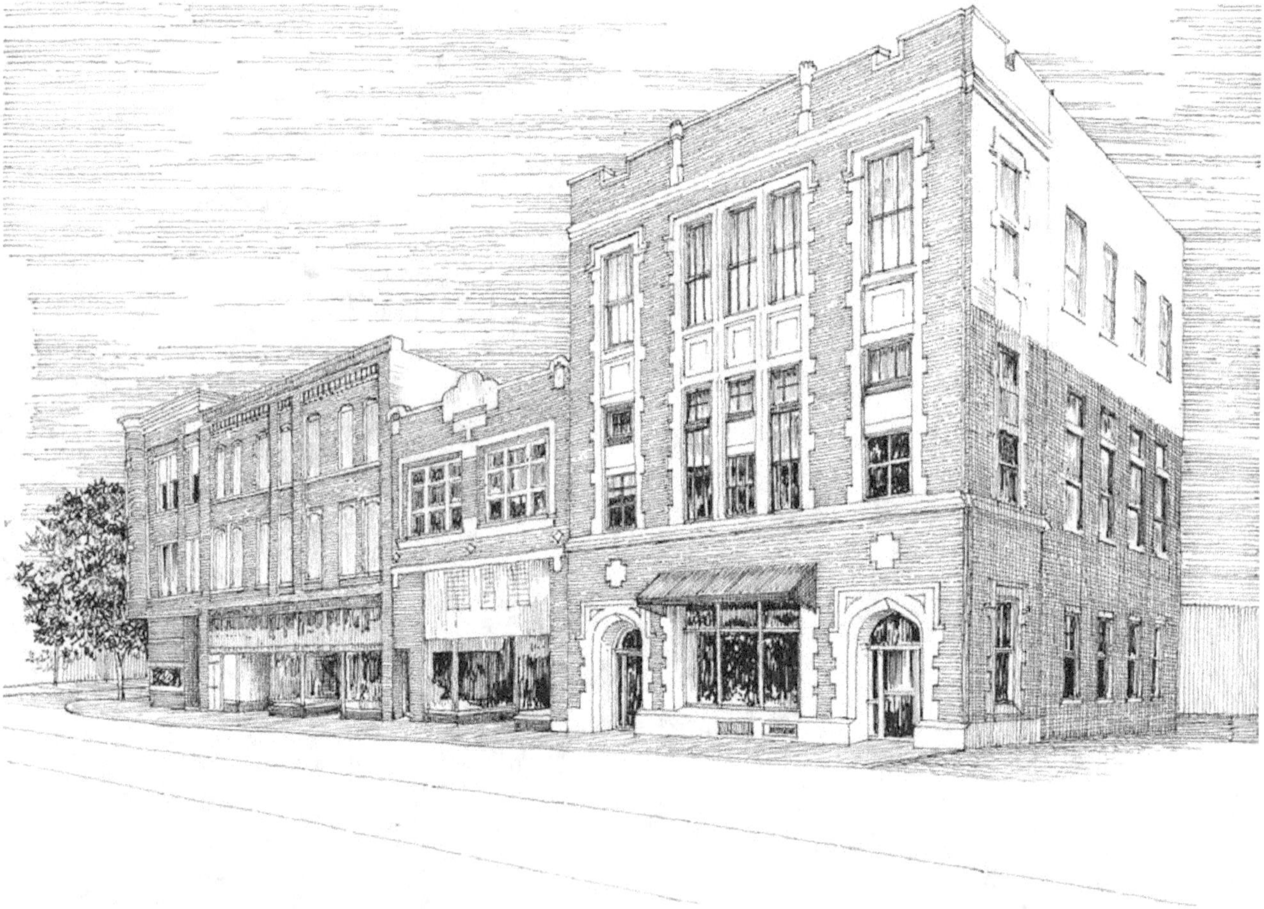

Downtown, Sapulpa, Oklahoma

Sapulpa has many fine buildings that date from the early days of statehood and into the 1920s. The city has endeavored to save as many of these structures as possible. Unfortunately, many of these buildings appear to be no longer in use with most of the upper levels being primarily used for storage. The presence of so many significant structures on both sides of Dewey Avenue (Route 66) lends a pronounced sense of "city" to this town of almost 20,000 people.

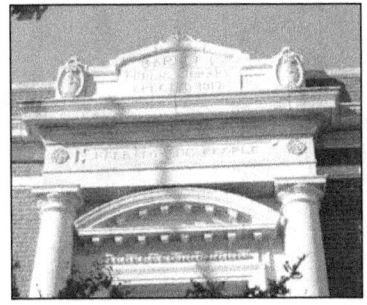

Although no longer the entry to the library, the original portico still displays beautifully-carved limestone details.

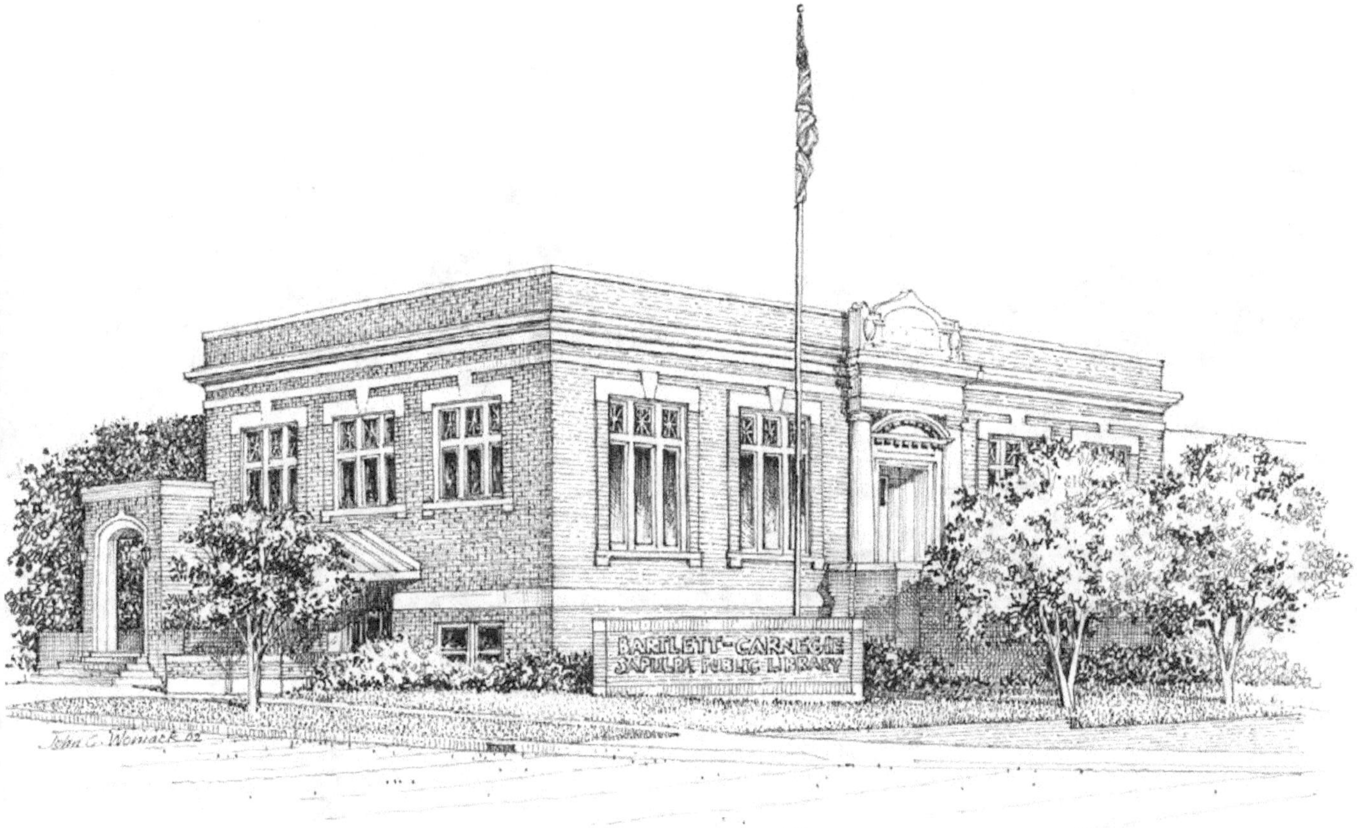

Bartlett-Carnegie Public Library, Sapulpa, Oklahoma

Public libraries are special places that convey much about our most important values and beliefs. Not only do libraries symbolize knowledge and learning, they also symbolize one of the basic tenets of democracy—that an educated people will not be subjugated. This building exhibits carefully proportioned features, finely crafted details, and strong, durable materials. Such attributes contribute to a building's perseverance and preservation and the community's affection for it.

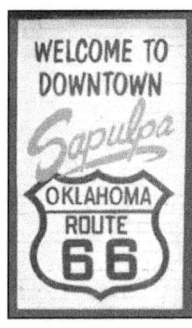

Sapulpa is another Route 66 city that still contains many buildings and places that were once directly tied to the commerce of the highway. Many of these sites, however, are gradually disappearing, too.

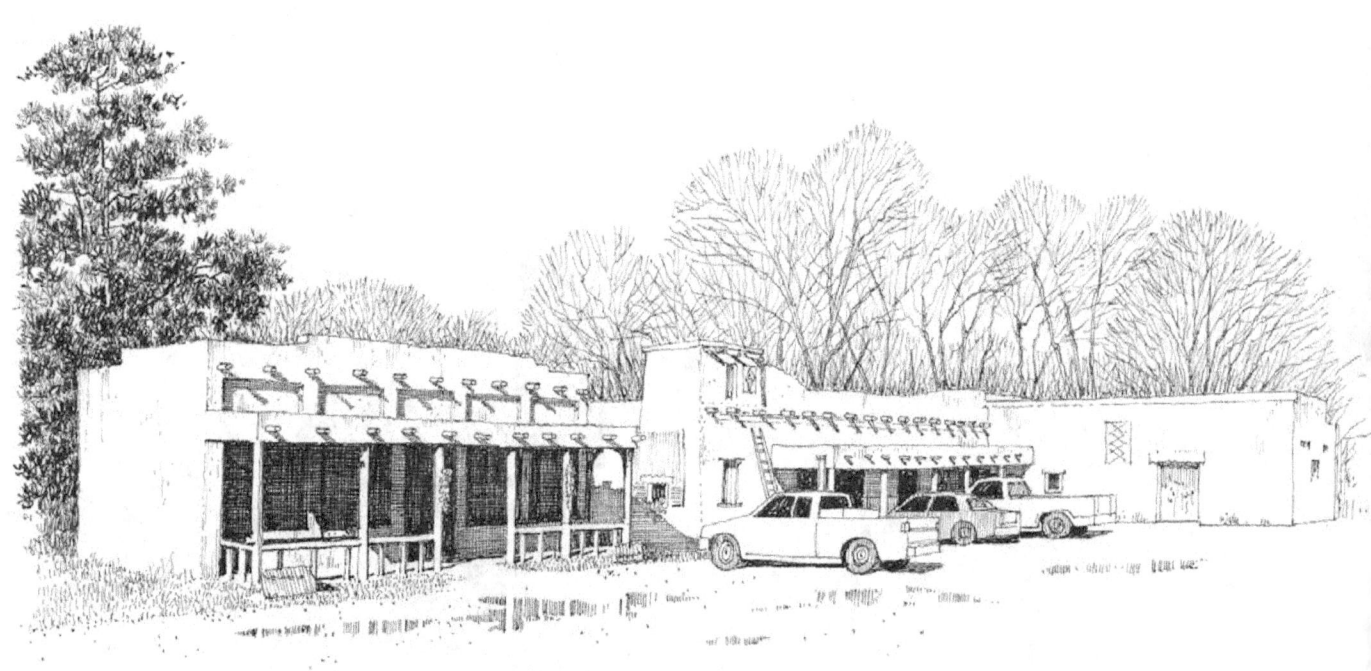

John C. Womack 2004

Mr. Indian's Cowboy Store, Sapulpa, Oklahoma

Sapulpa was named after Jim Sapulpa, a Muscogee (Creek) Indian who settled in the area in 1850. The name means "sweet potato" in the Creek language. Mr. Indian's is located south of Route 66 on Main Street. There are all types of Indian merchandise available here—all handmade by Native Americans. Western clothing, bridles, and saddles are also sold here. Although not genuine adobe, the buildings do convey a sense of the southwest in their design and detailing.

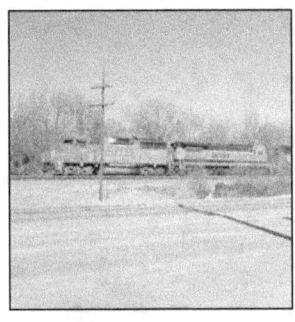

Route 66's surface alignments were altered many times throughout its history, but the trains, which paralleled Route 66, still traverse much of their original rail lines.

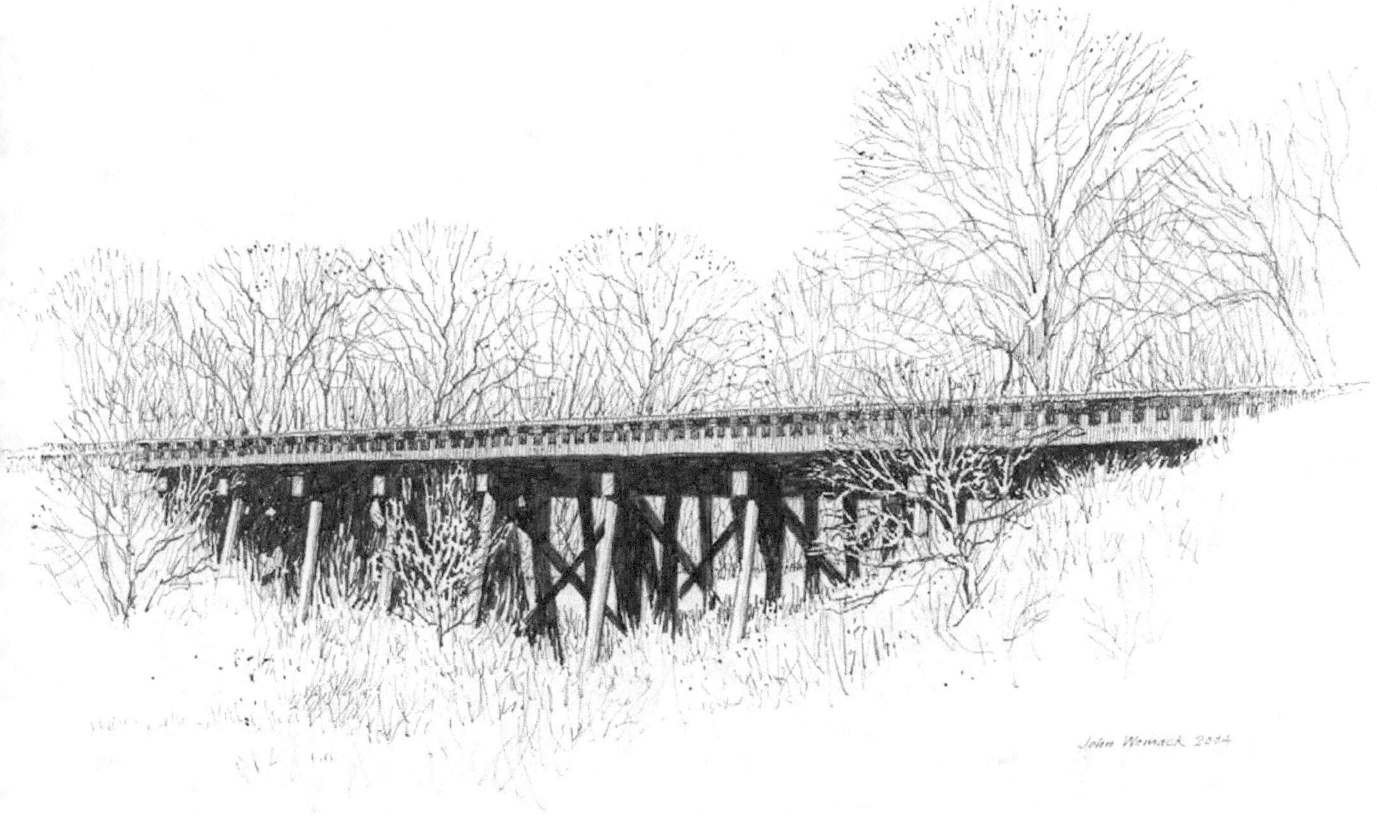

Railroad Trestle, near Sapulpa, Oklahoma

Railroads are always fascinating to kids, and I was no exception. Trains and their environs are inherently dangerous, and my parents made it clear to me that I was never to go near the tracks or cars. Not only can trains be dangerous, but there was also the chance of people "on the bum" being in and around the train yards. Sometimes referred to as "hobos," certainly not all of them were bad; many were simply looking for a free ride to some distant destination.

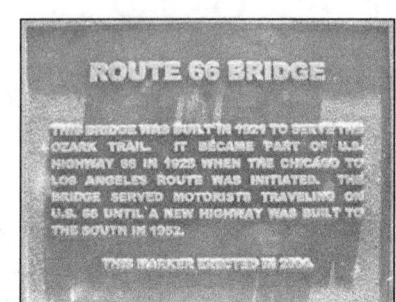

The brick-paved Rock Creek Bridge is a famous Route 66 landmark and was so noted in 2004 with this memorial plaque near the bridge.

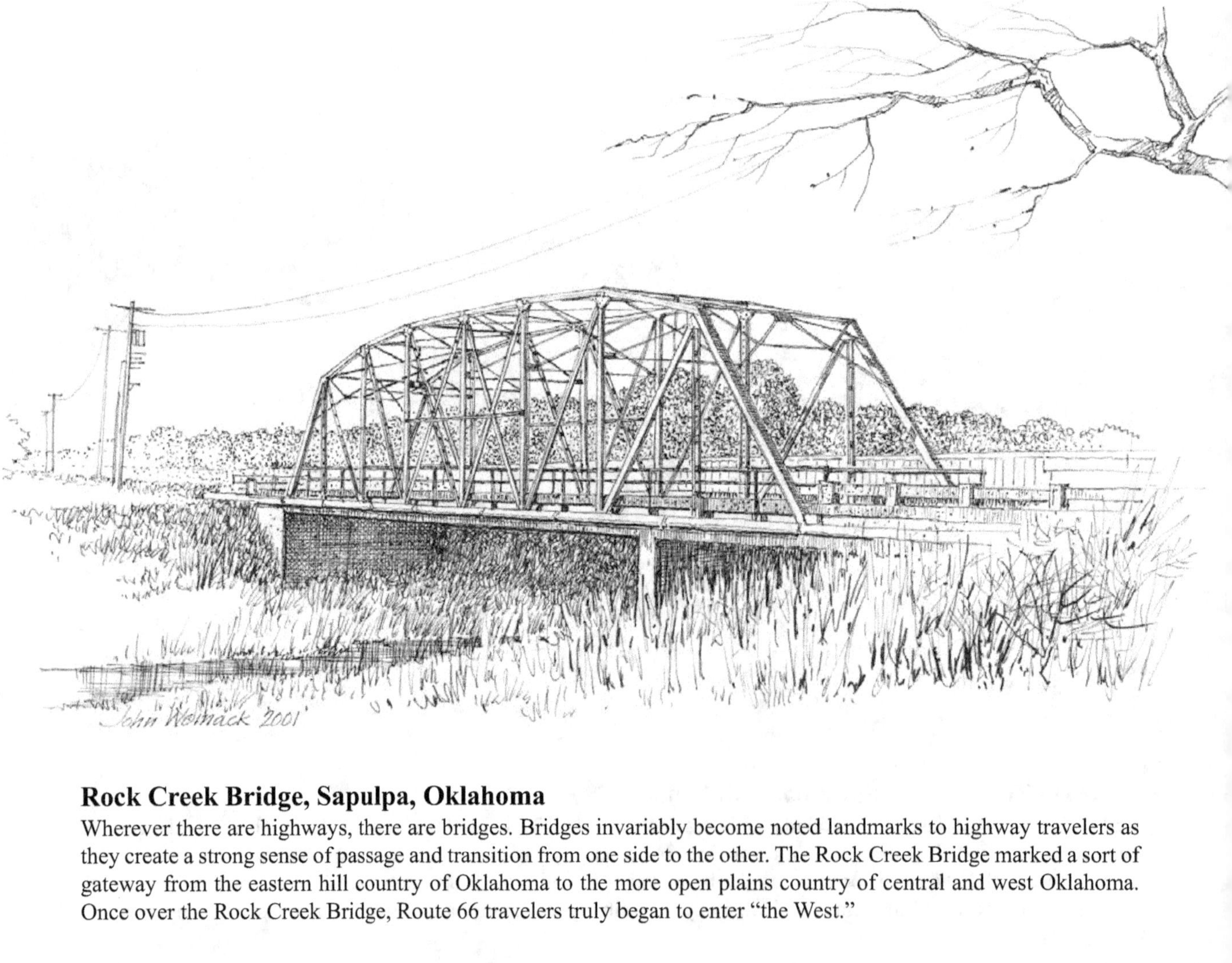

Rock Creek Bridge, Sapulpa, Oklahoma

Wherever there are highways, there are bridges. Bridges invariably become noted landmarks to highway travelers as they create a strong sense of passage and transition from one side to the other. The Rock Creek Bridge marked a sort of gateway from the eastern hill country of Oklahoma to the more open plains country of central and west Oklahoma. Once over the Rock Creek Bridge, Route 66 travelers truly began to enter "the West."

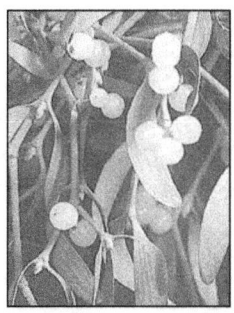

Mistletoe, the State Flower of Oklahoma, is seen only briefly in its flower form. Long associated with the Christmas season, its white berries speak of love and happiness—even if they might be poisonous!

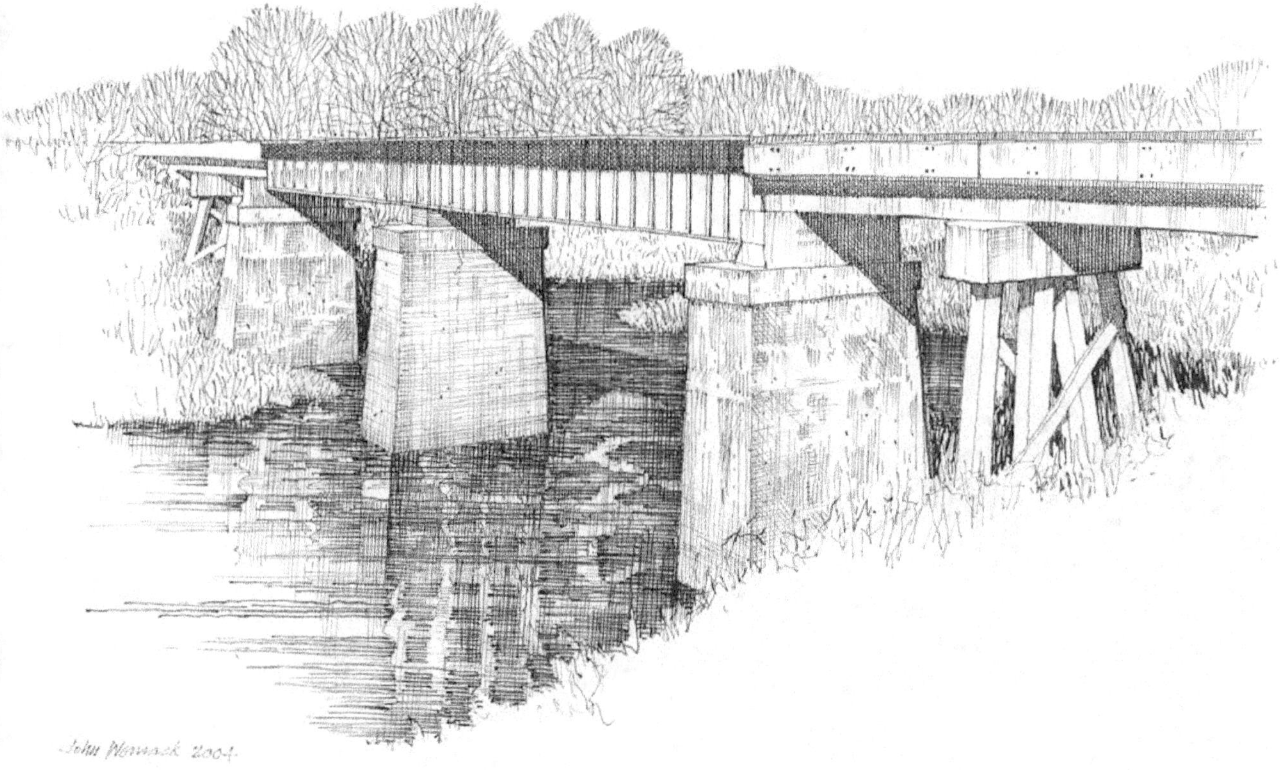

John Womack 2004

Railroad Trestle over Rock Creek, west of Sapulpa, Oklahoma

This trestle is about thirty yards to the north of the Rock Creek Bridge. Route 66 parallels the railroad for almost the entire highway, from Chicago to Los Angeles. For a kid stuck in the back seat of mom and dad's car, especially on long trips, the appearance of a train moving alongside the highway provided an interesting diversion from the tedium and boredom of the back seat world. "Car games" developed as fun traveling pastimes for both kids and adults.

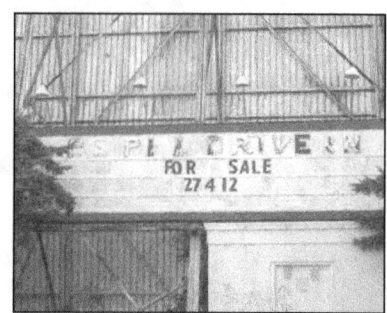

Sapulpa's Teepee Drive-In movie theater is no longer in operation, but its screen, pay-booth, and concession building still exist.

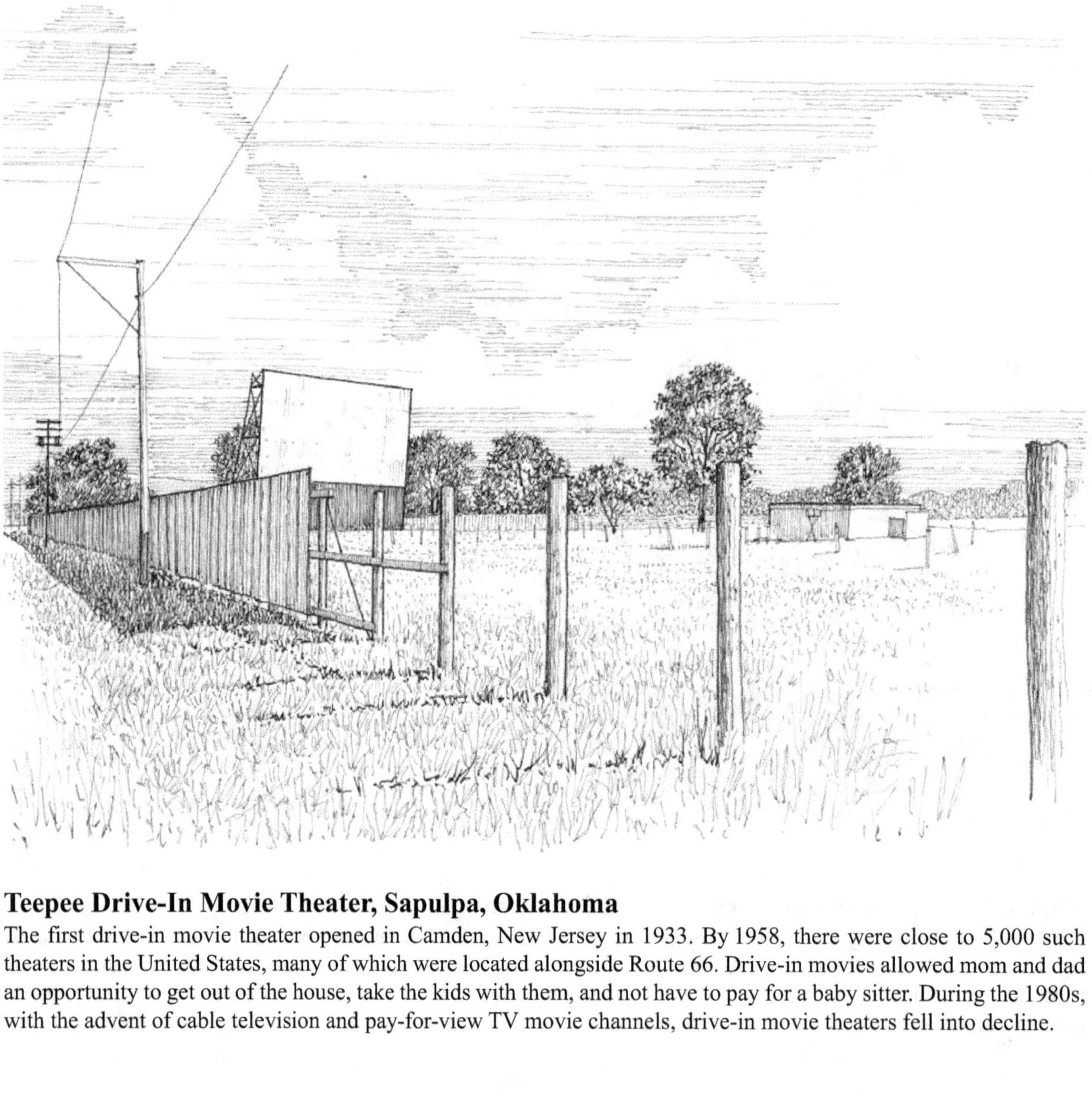

Teepee Drive-In Movie Theater, Sapulpa, Oklahoma

The first drive-in movie theater opened in Camden, New Jersey in 1933. By 1958, there were close to 5,000 such theaters in the United States, many of which were located alongside Route 66. Drive-in movies allowed mom and dad an opportunity to get out of the house, take the kids with them, and not have to pay for a baby sitter. During the 1980s, with the advent of cable television and pay-for-view TV movie channels, drive-in movie theaters fell into decline.

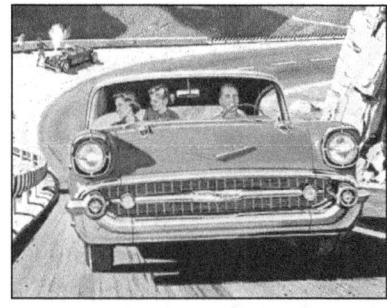

Following World War II, tourism became a major industry in the United States. Many families made summertime trips on Route 66 staying overnight in motels along the way.

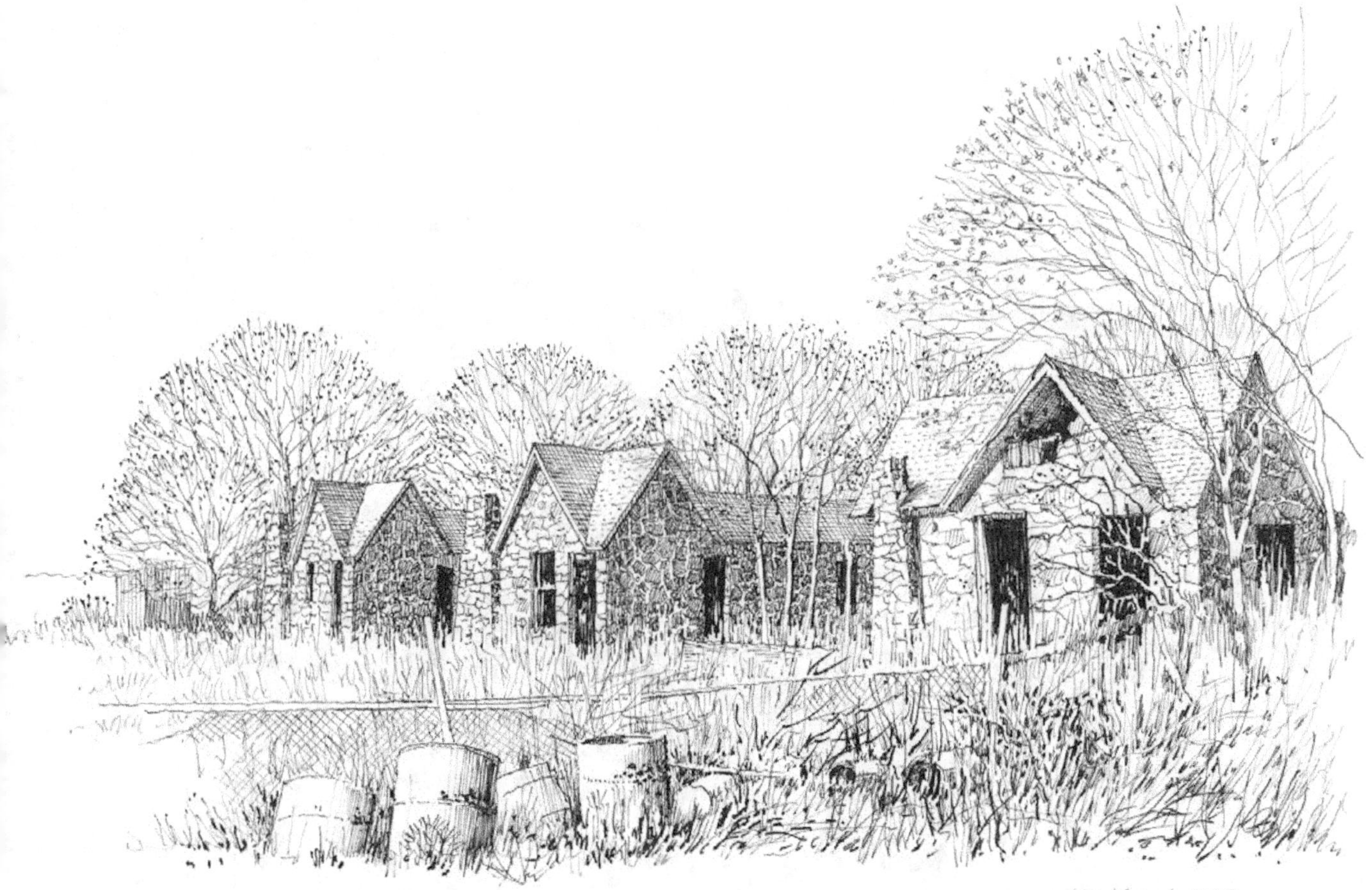

John Womack 2005

Stone-faced Tourist Cabins, east of Kellyville, Oklahoma

This rapidly declining site is located about two miles east of Kellyville. Such tourist cabins, or courts, were once a common sight along Route 66. Overnight places to stay such as this served as a precursor to the later "motel." Stone veneer, applied to the surfaces of wood frame construction, became a much-used exterior in many Oklahoma structures. This stone surfacing was attained locally, was relatively maintenance free, and conveyed a natural or rustic appearance.

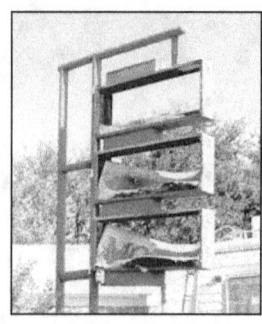

The old Blue Top Motel sign is another Route 66 artifact that is gradually scumming to the forces of time.

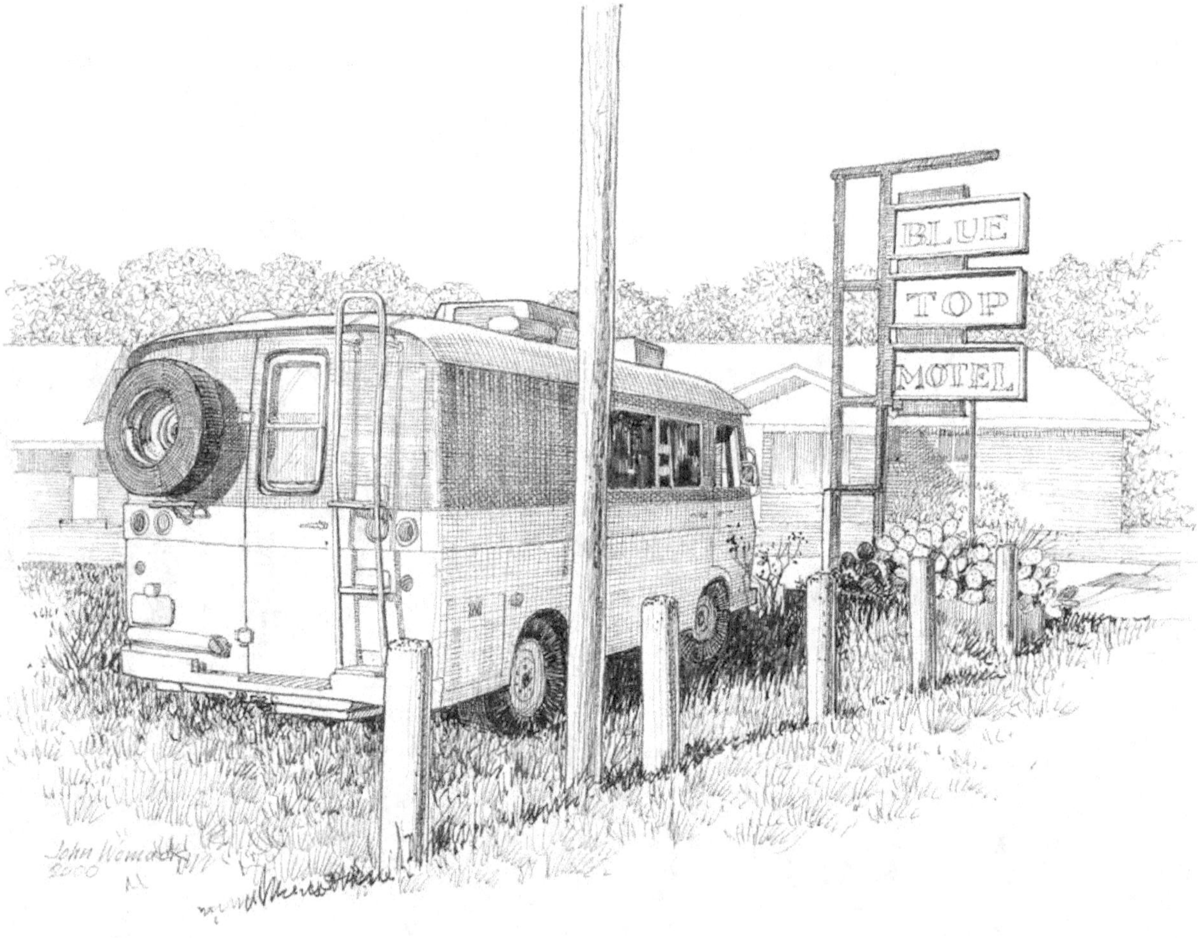

Blue Top Motel, Kellyville, Oklahoma

Now a private residence, the owners continue to display the original Blue Top Motel sign. The sign is interesting in that it has prickly pear cactus in its planting bed—another indicator of entering western lands. The significance of the motel's name, "Blue Top," is unclear. Maybe it alludes to blue skies above—a weather condition that is always welcome in a state where dark forbidding skies can happen all too often. The van appears to be a classic 1968 Cortez.

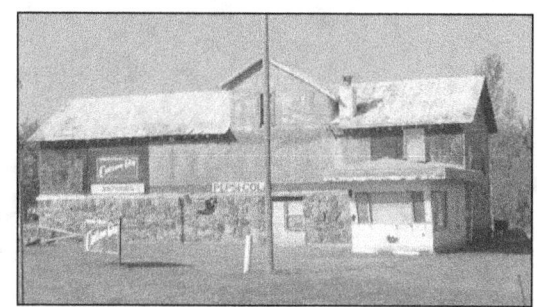

By 2005, the old Cotton Gin Diner had lost most of its painted corrugated metal siding, exposing much of its wooden understructure to the weather.

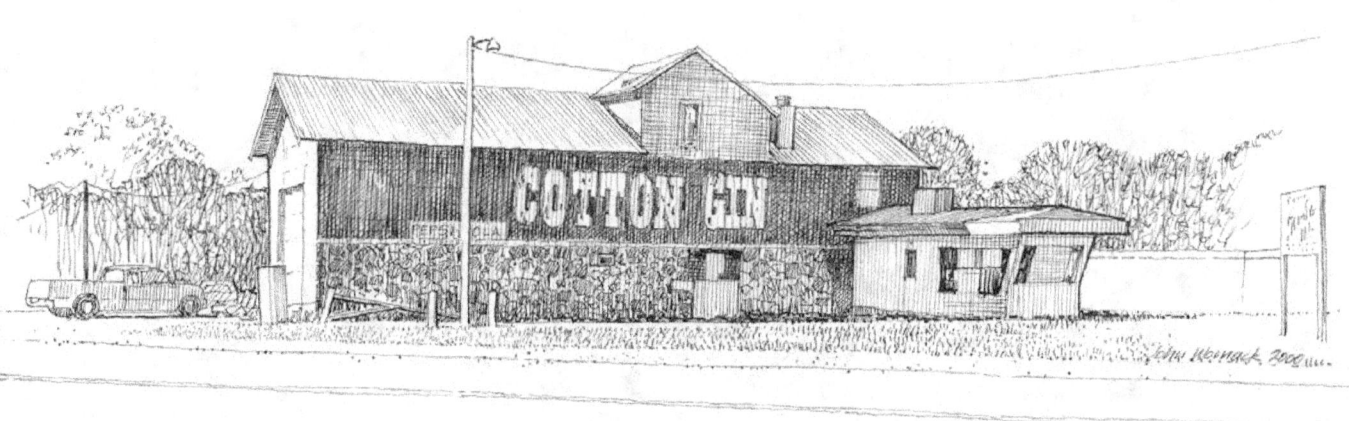

Cotton Gin Diner, Kellyville, Oklahoma

The Cotton Gin Diner was originally a true cotton gin and dates back to the days when cotton was a major cash crop in Oklahoma. The old gin was converted to a restaurant, and the little hamburger stand on its northeast corner was added later. The stand looks very much like the numerous Dairy Queens and other burger joints that I experienced in the 1950s and 1960s. The old diner has since become an antique shop, and the hamburger stand is closed.

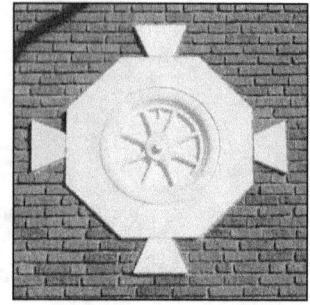

One of the carved limestone wheel insets on the Bristow Motor Company.

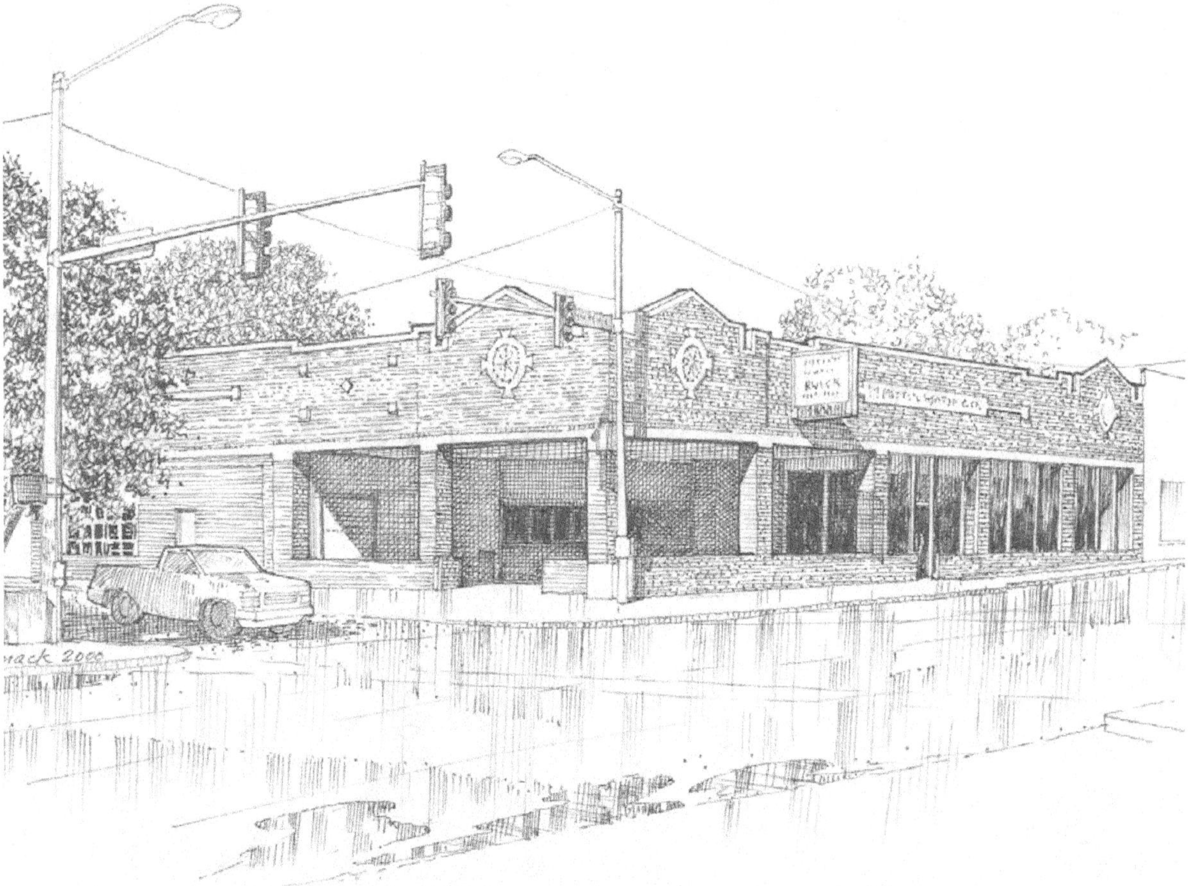

Bristow Motor Company (1923), Bristow, Oklahoma

The circular medallions set in the brick walls above the porch-like areas are carved stone images of the old wooden spoke automobile wheels of the early 1920s. The structure exhibits the same fine craftsmanship in its other details, and the building is still used today as an auto dealership. The Bristow Motor Company, built in 1923, sits directly alongside Route 66 preceding the incorporation of Route 66 by three years.

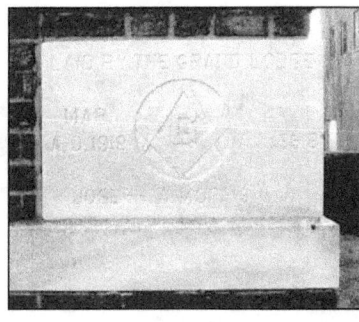

During the first 150 years of building in the United States, many public buildings were dedicated by the Masonic fraternity.

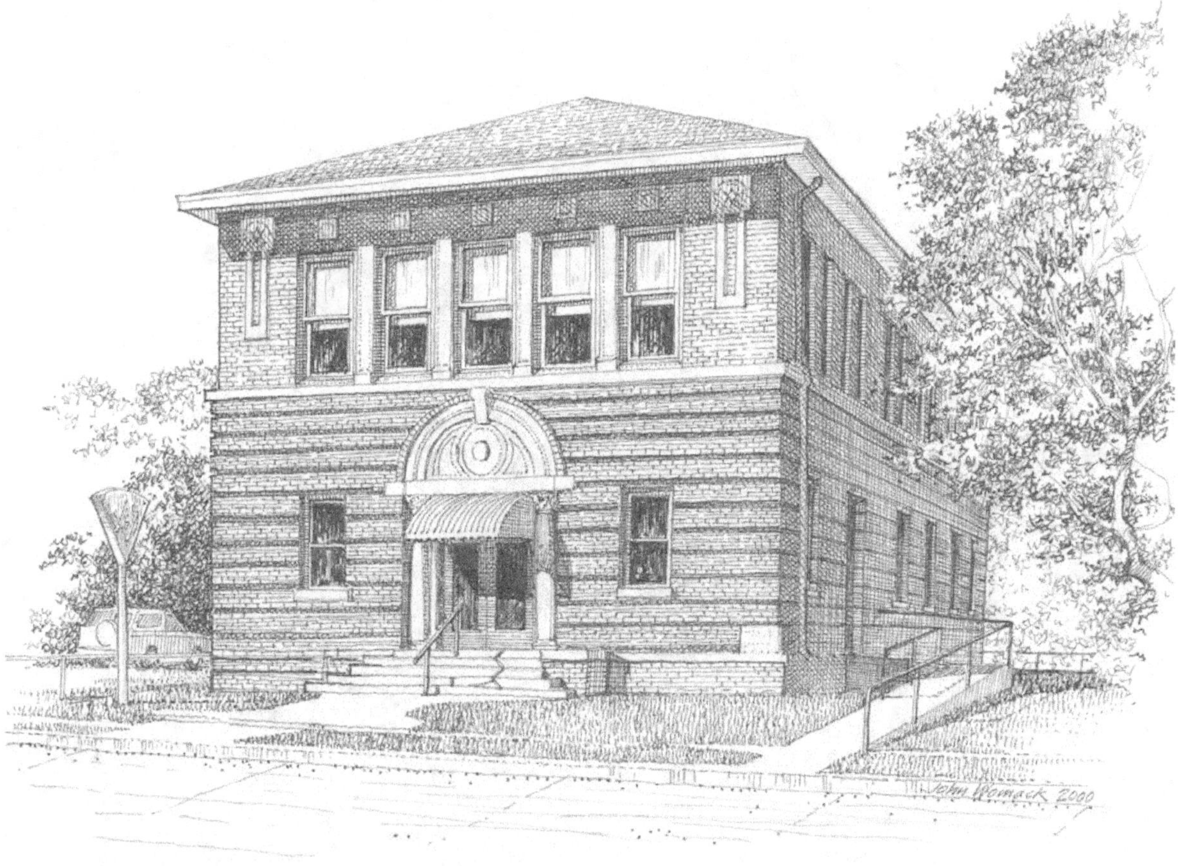

Masonic Lodge, Bristow, Oklahoma

In this drawing, I followed my impulse to "recreate" the building's appearance. In reality, the structure's upper windows were boarded over, which seemed like such an indignity for such a fine building. The structure's alternating recessed brick courses and limestone inserts suggest links to the Prairie Style, first developed in Chicago during the 1890s and early 1900s by the great architect, Frank Lloyd Wright. The stubby roof overhang appears to be from a later alteration.

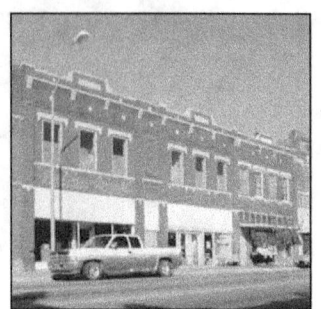

Bristow's Thurman-Wells building continues to gradually return to its original appearance. Note the removal of the metal siding on the far right.

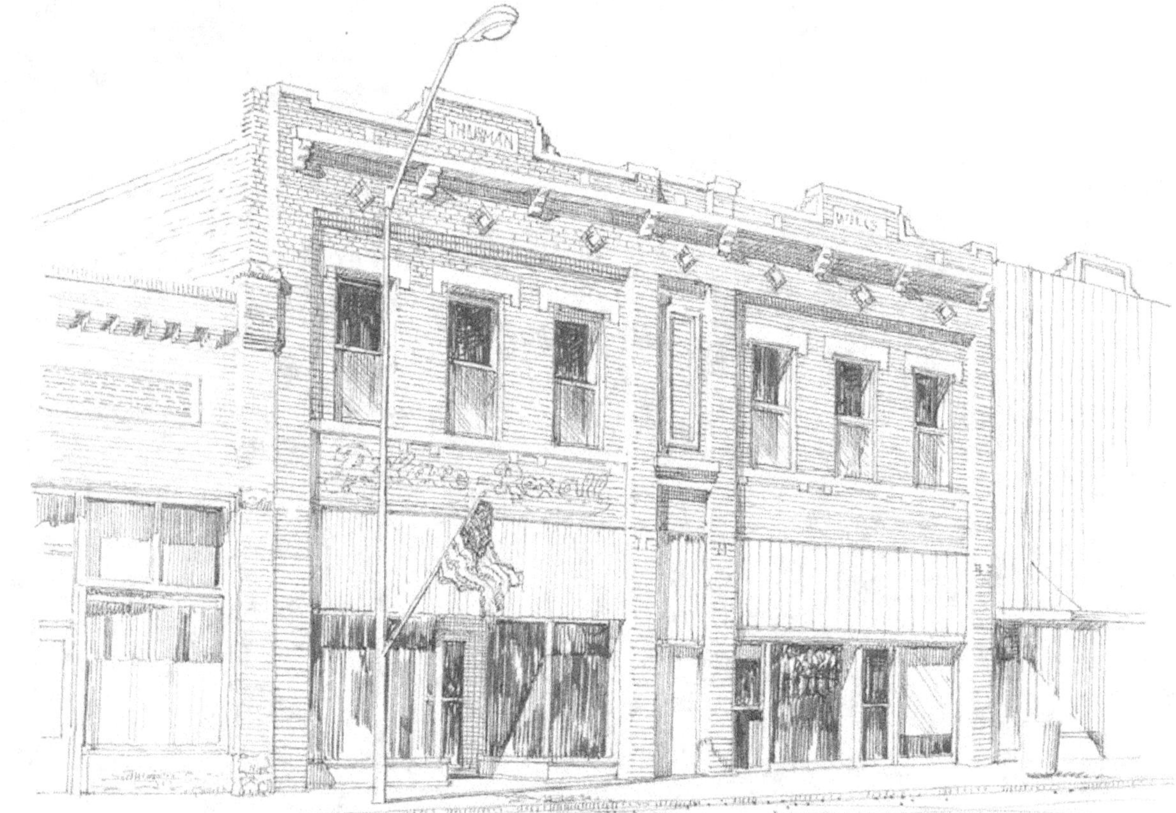

Thurmond and Wells Building, Bristow, Oklahoma

During the 1960s, several communities around the United States implemented a plan of change called "Urban Renewal." Sadly, the approach did more harm than good. Many fine old buildings were destroyed in the name of progress. This structure has retained most of its original features with the exception of the glass transom sections above the sidewalk display windows. The owner's name, inscribed upon the original facade, reflects a sense of pride and accomplishment.

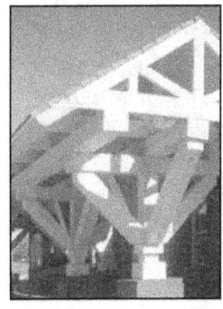

The heavy wood-timber framing of Bristow's old train station is impressive in its design and engineering.

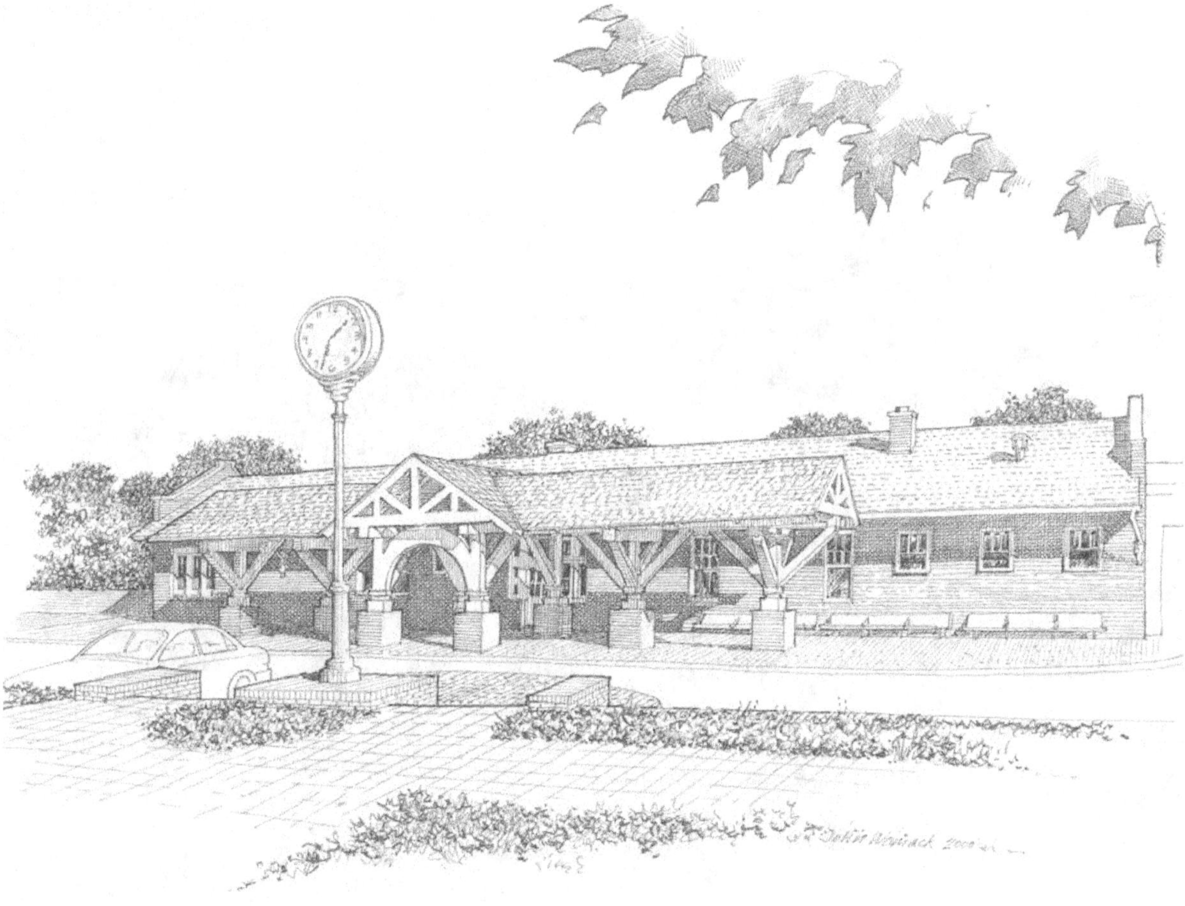

Train Station, Bristow, Oklahoma

The town of Bristow has made several bold gestures toward restoring and retaining much of its history and culture through the restoration of many of its buildings. The old train station has been restored and is now home to the Chamber of Commerce and a museum. Bristow seems to revel in its association with Route 66. All along the sidewalks that border the highway are granite markers set into the concrete with "Route 66" finely engraved in their surface.

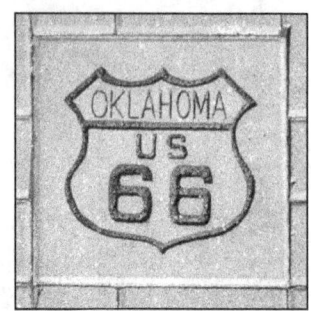

*Bristow has commemorated its length of
Route 66 with engraved granite markers
embedded in the sidewalk.*

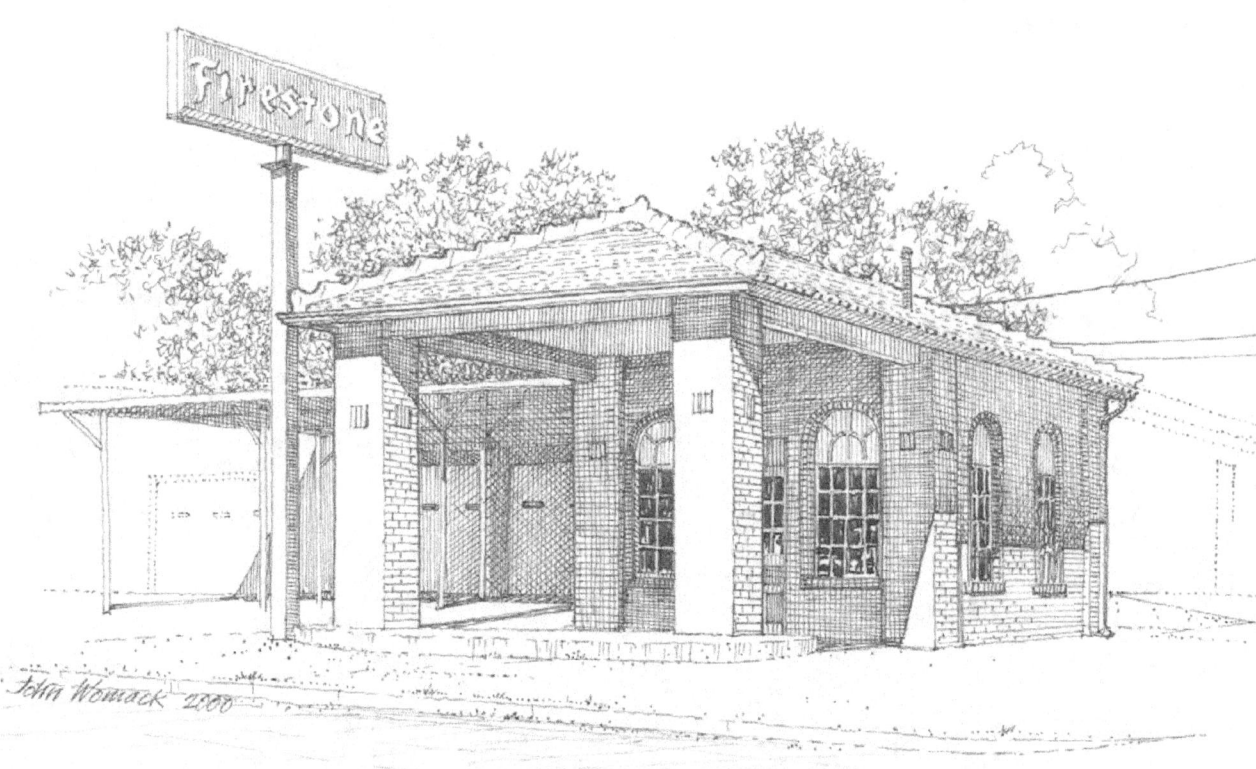

Bristow Tire Company, Bristow, Oklahoma

Service stations of this design (or similar) occurred all along the length of Route 66—especially in Oklahoma. Most of them are long gone now, having succumbed to the more modernized designs of the 1950s and 1960s. This example has survived, however, and operates today as a tire sales and repair store. There is an undeniable quaintness and friendliness to these buildings—a concept that Phillips Petroleum later sought to establish in its "cottage" stations.

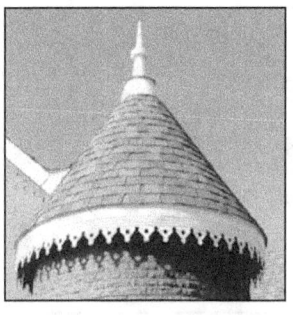

The gingerbread trim on the edge of the turret roofs is made from sheetmetal which was easily bent around the circular form.

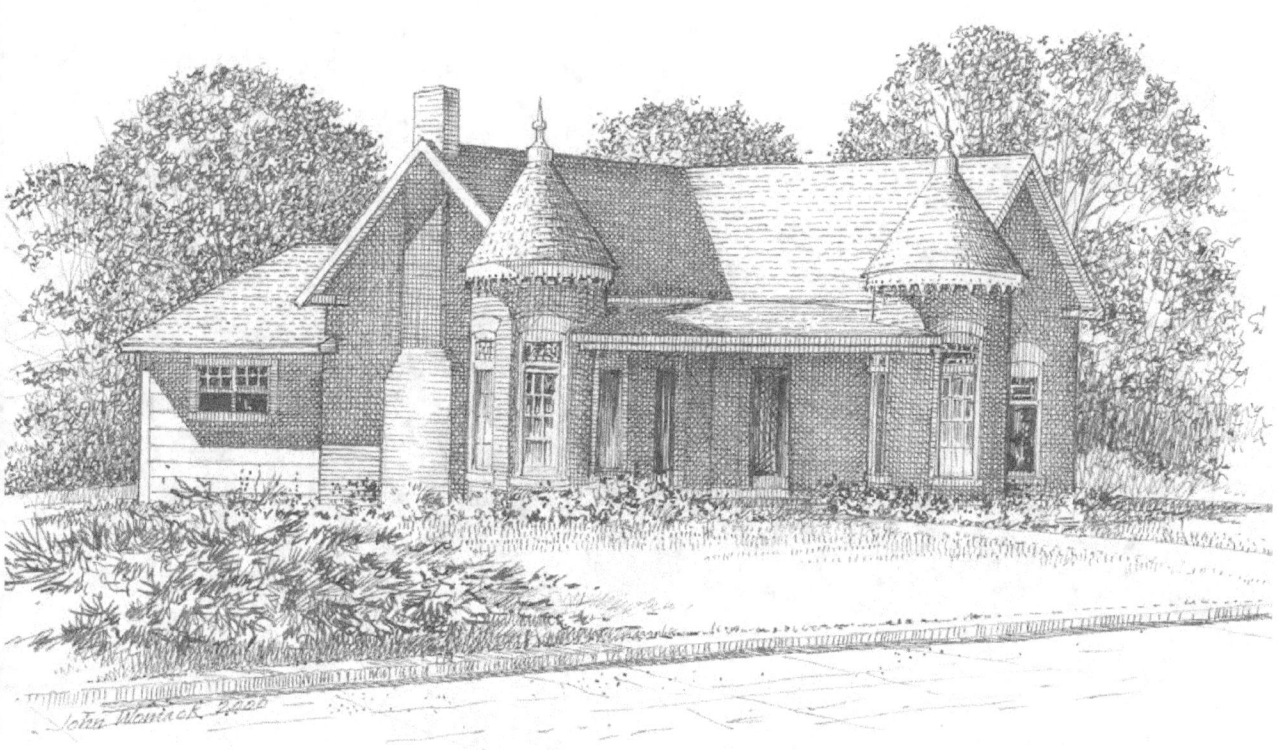

Twin Turrets House, Bristow, Oklahoma

This house (now an office) sits directly across the highway from the Bristow Tire Company. The twin turrets and gingerbread trim lend a distinctive appearance to the house and speak to us of a time when detail, scale, and quality construction were the norm. The addition to the rear of the building is clunky and ungainly and illustrates how a lack of design skill or an absence of care has created a distraction rather than a sympathetic response to the original design.

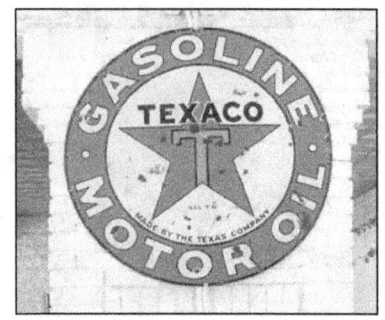

The Texas Fuel Company officially became "Texaco, Inc." in 1959. By that time, the Texaco Star was a familiar sight on Route 66 and all over the country.

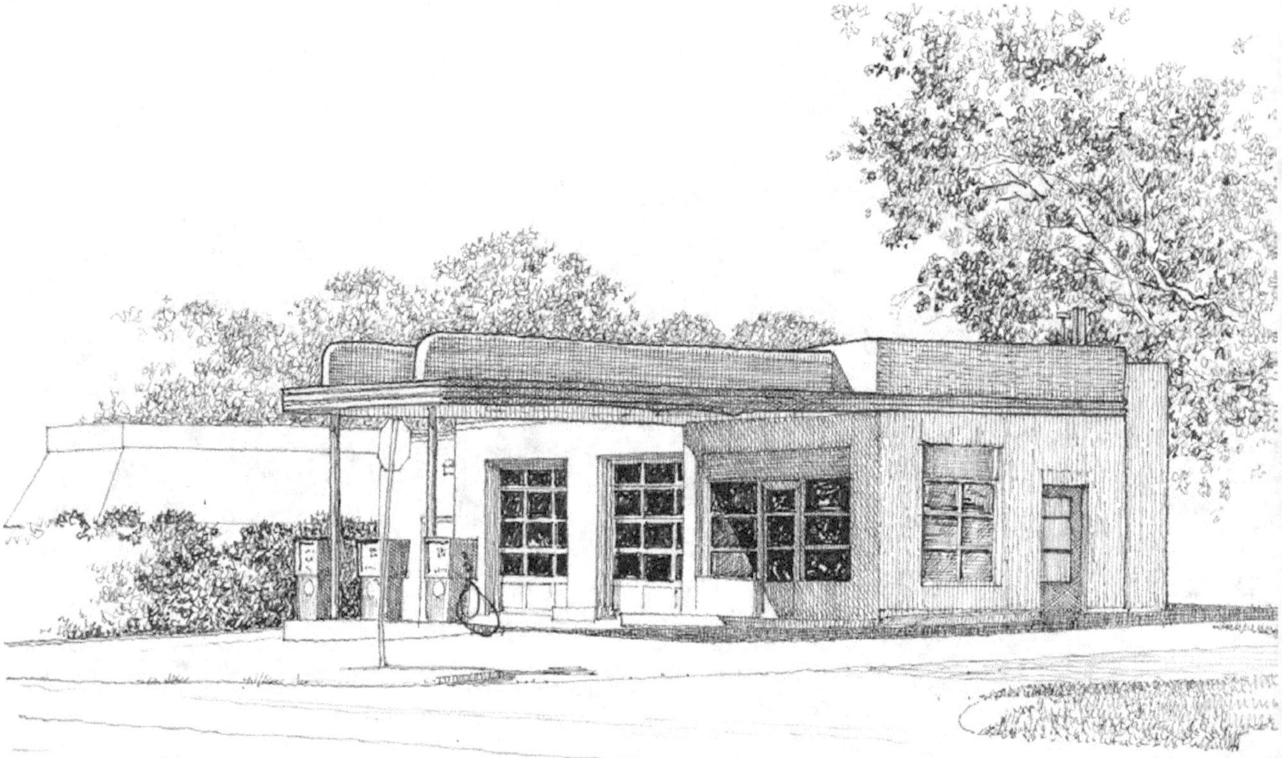

Texaco Service Station (demolished), Bristow, Oklahoma

Oil companies developed their own service station designs as part of their marketing strategies. Certain design features would become easily recognizable as a traveler approached a station. Highway intersections often had a different company's gas station on each of the four corners. Such design elements as the exposed rounded beams above the covered service area, as seen here, announced that up ahead, a Texaco station was ready and waiting to serve.

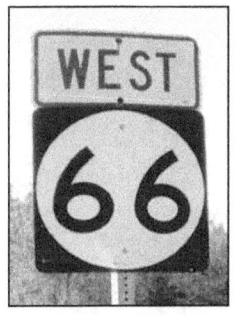

Throughout the course of its history, Route 66's alignment was altered several times. When traveling Oklahoma's State Highway 66, you are, for the most part, on the old U.S. Highway 66.

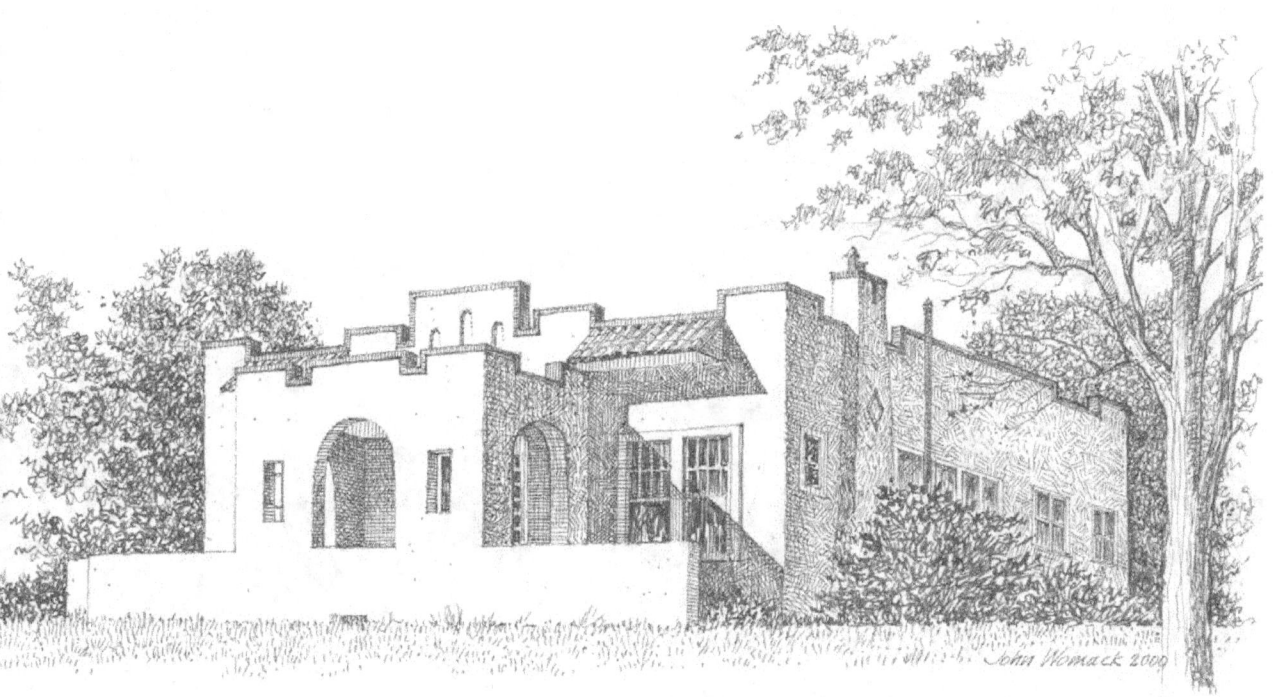

Mission Revival Style House, Bristow, Oklahoma

This house sits upon a rise of land where Route 66 makes a sharp turn to the left (traveling west). It also sits in front of a cemetery, and I originally thought it might have been the cemetery office. About three years after completing this drawing, I gave a presentation on Route 66 to the Oklahoma Historical Society. Afterward a man came up to me, told me it was indeed a house, and mentioned how a friend of his had loved this house so much he waited 25 years to buy it.

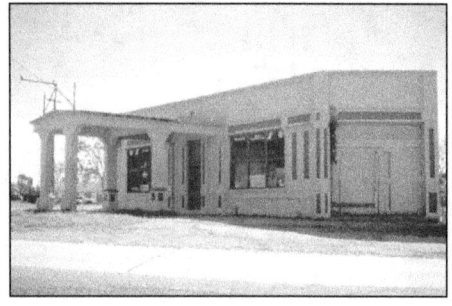

This former service station in downtown Depew is constructed of reinforced concrete—a unique use of material for a service station. Today it houses an auto parts store.

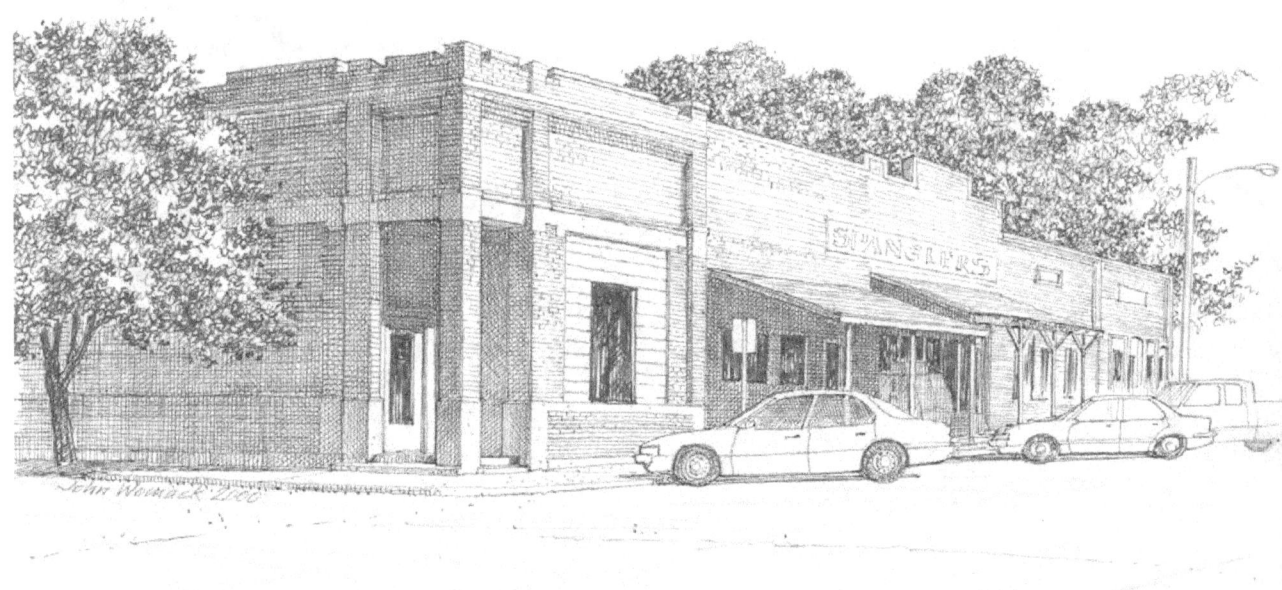

Downtown, Depew, Oklahoma

Today, Depew appears to be almost a ghost town. The building seen on the corner was once a bank. Every frontier town had a bank soon after the town became incorporated. Like many commercial buildings of the early 1900s, most old banks were well-built with durable materials. Some of these little town banks fell prey to the likes of Bonnie and Clyde, Pretty Boy Floyd, and other desperadoes looking for a quick pay off.

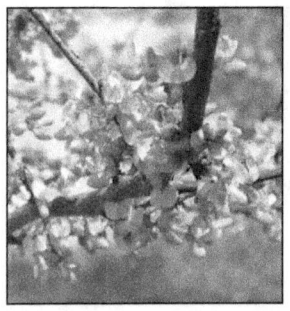

Oklahoma's State Tree, the redbud, brings one of the first hints of spring to the state. Its purple-red color is always a welcomed sight.

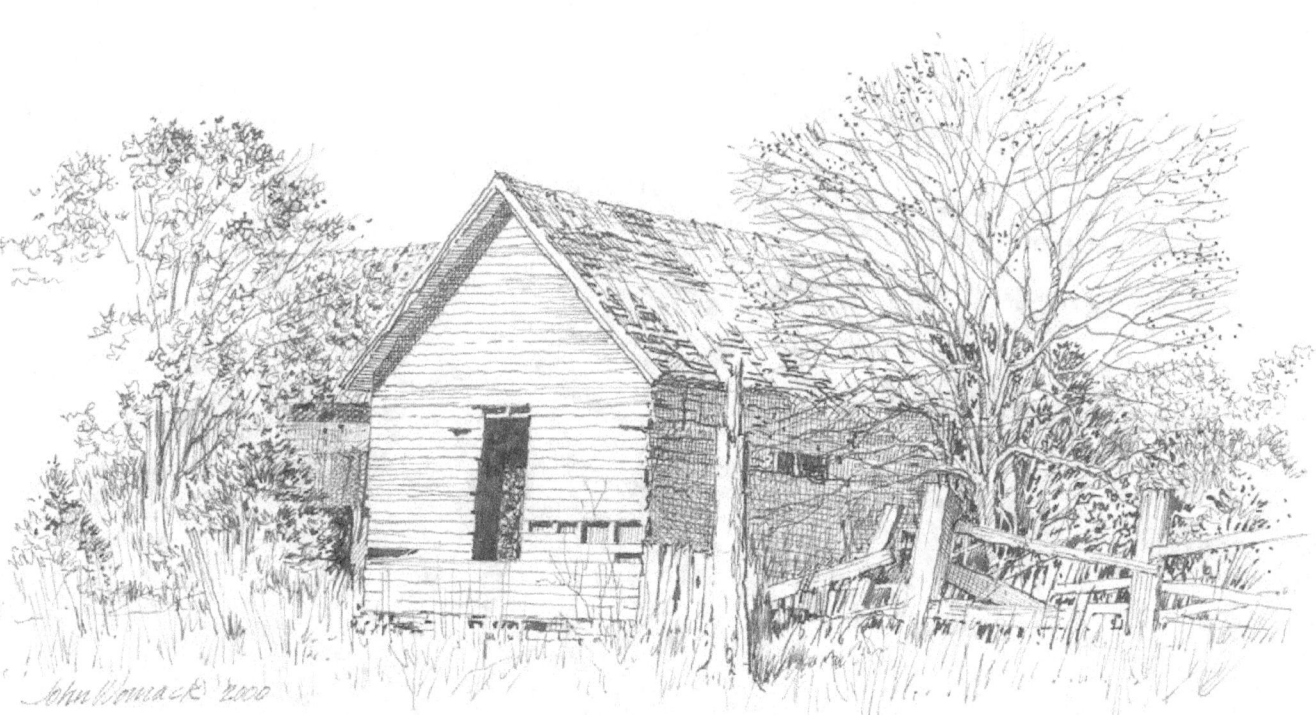

Abandoned Farm House (demolished), east of Stroud, Oklahoma

Ruins fascinate me and none more so than old abandoned farmhouses and barns. Such sights as these create in me a flood of notions about the history of the place and the people who might have lived and died there. I always find it curious why such places become abandoned. Was it the dust bowl, the depression, good times, or bad times that caused the occupants to leave—or did they just die? Was it a happy home or a sad one?

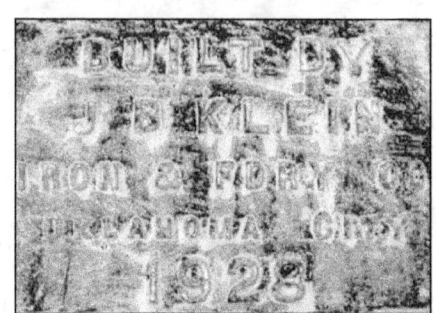

"Built by J.B. Klein Iron & Fdry. Co., Oklahoma City, 1928" can still be read on the plaque attached to the bridge.

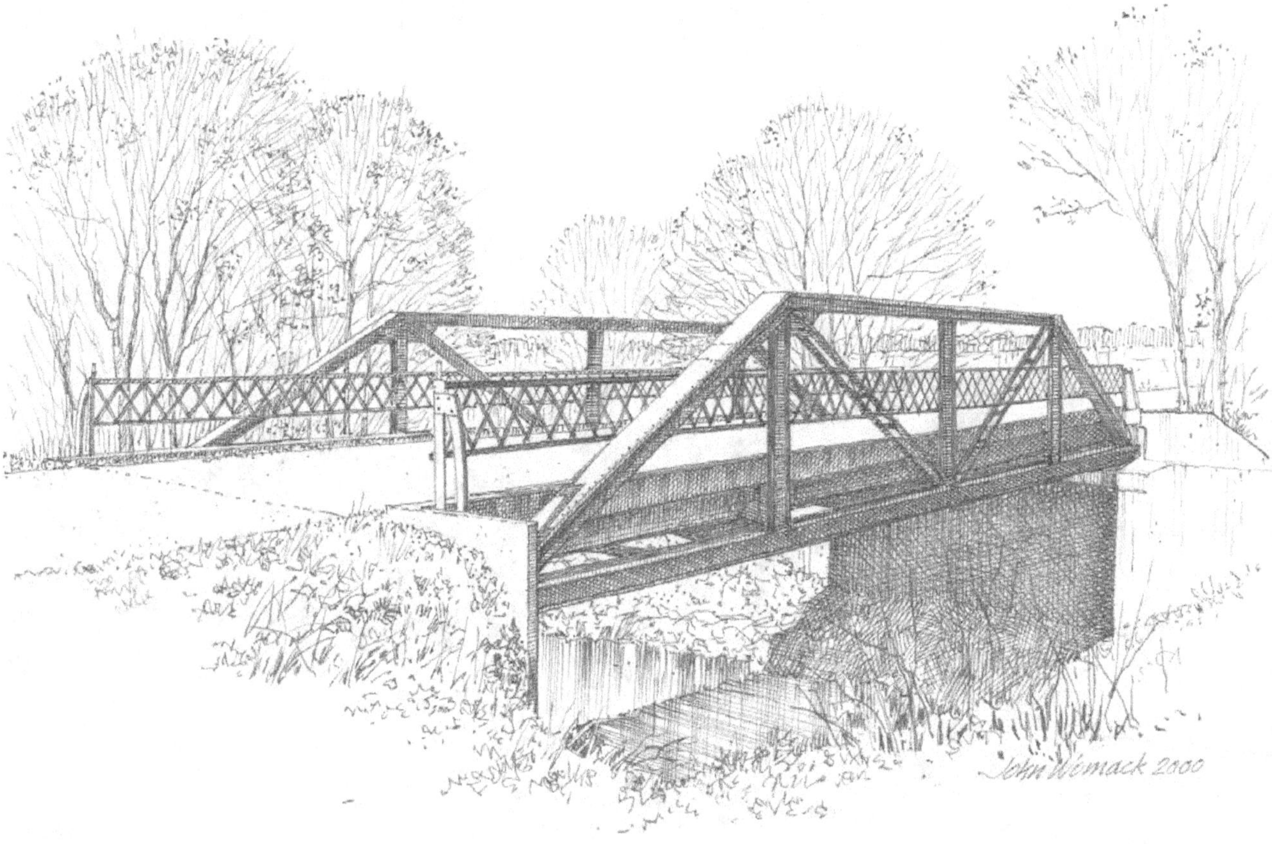

Salt Creek Bridge, east of Stroud, Oklahoma

This steel bridge was built in 1928, and though no longer in service, it still bears testament to the skill and care of its builders. This particular bridge was a standard U.S. highway design and can be found in several locations along Route 66. These bridges date to a time when traffic moved at a slower pace than today; however, even at slower speeds, there is little doubt that such narrow bridges contributed to more than their fair share of accidents.

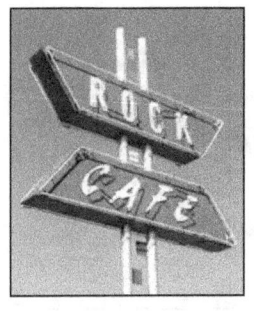

The Rock Cafe's sign, recently restored, beckons to hungry road warriors of home-cooked food and friendly conversation.

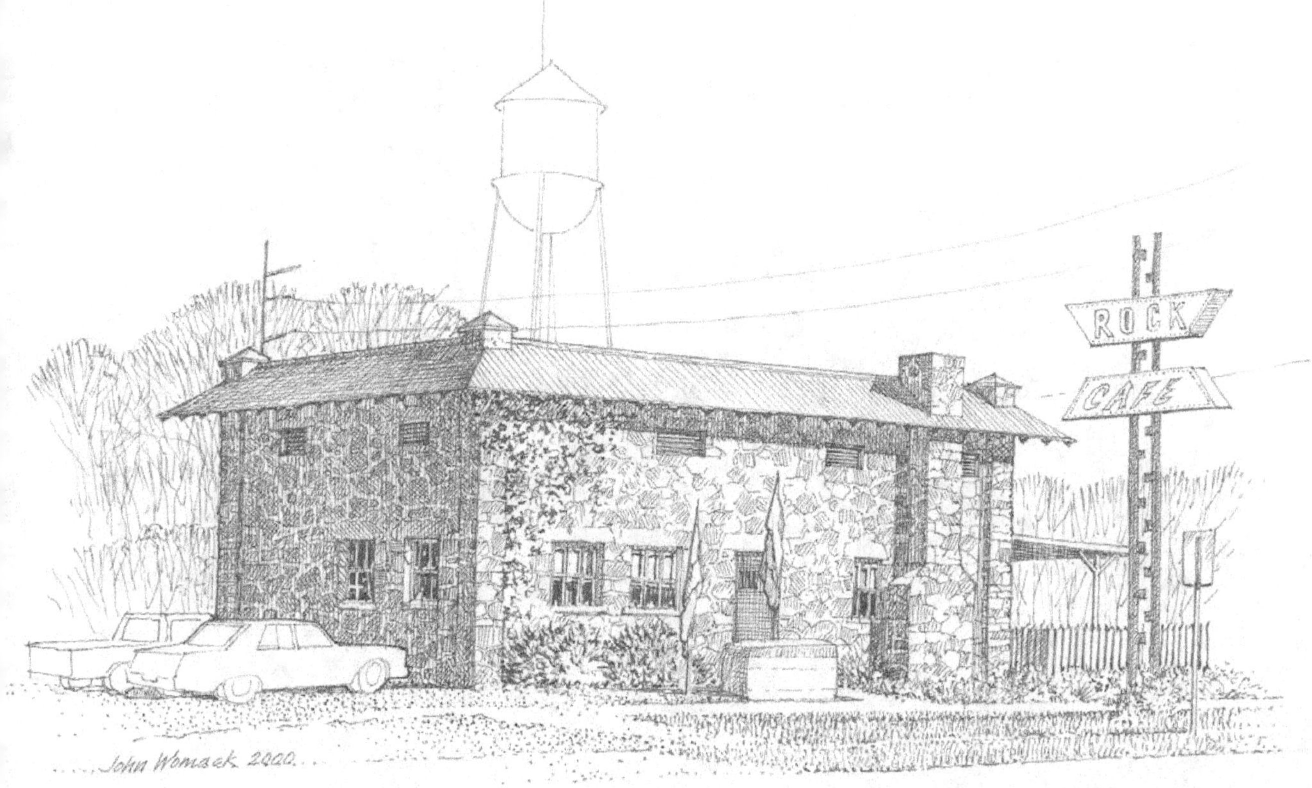

John Womack 2000.

The Rock Cafe, Stroud, Oklahoma

Built in 1939, the Rock Cafe is one of the landmark structures along Route 66. You can still get great food at the Rock (including buffalo burgers), and the guest book is a must see—be sure and sign it, too. The water tower in the background is a standard type used all over the state of Oklahoma. As one travels west, amounts of rainfall diminish, and water becomes more and more valuable—for people, crops, livestock, and wildlife.

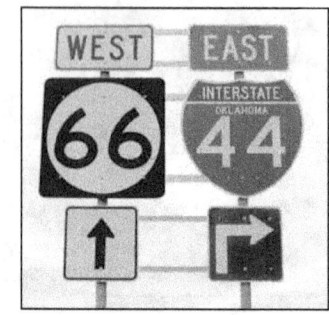

Paralleling Route 66 is Oklahoma's Turner Turnpike, also part of U.S. Interstate Highway 44.

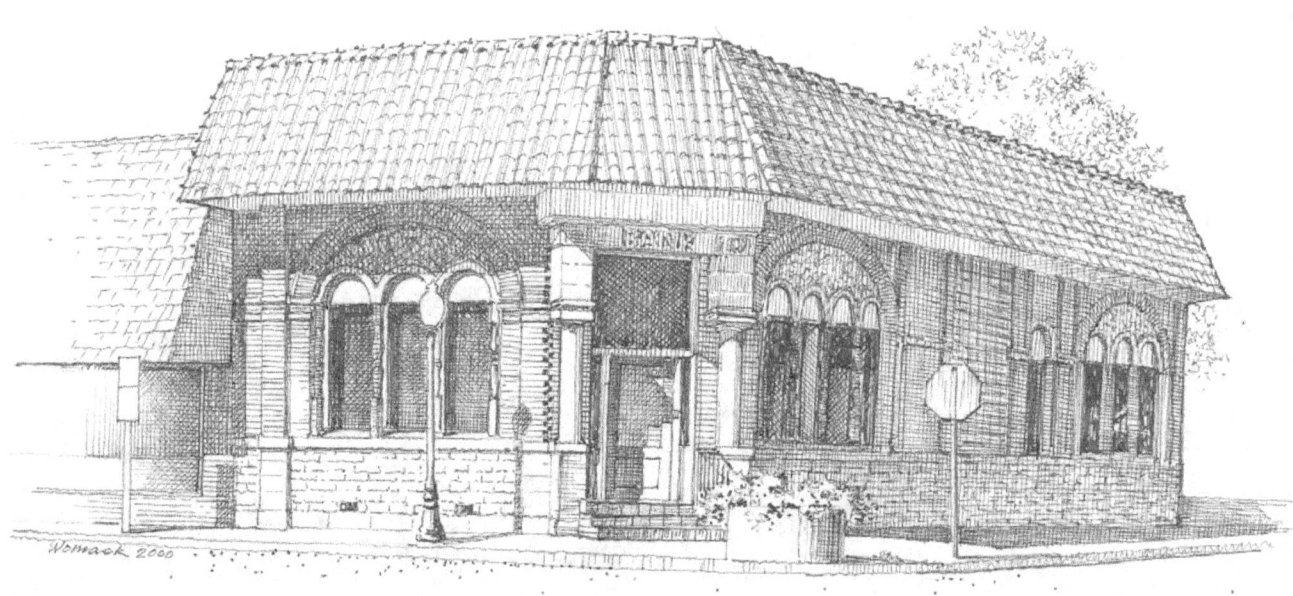

Former Bank, Stroud, Oklahoma

There was a time when probably every bank in Oklahoma gained the eye of some get-rich-quick character who wondered about how he might pull off a robbery. Oklahoma once had a reputation for being home to more than a few bandits and bad guys. Whether toting six-guns, shotguns, or machine guns, these criminals were constantly looking for the quick-haul, and depending upon the available local lawman, banks like this could be an easy mark.

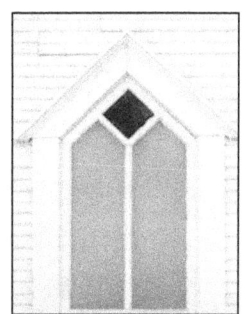

The style of this "Y" motif window is shared by other churches along Route 66, and in other Oklahoma communities as well.

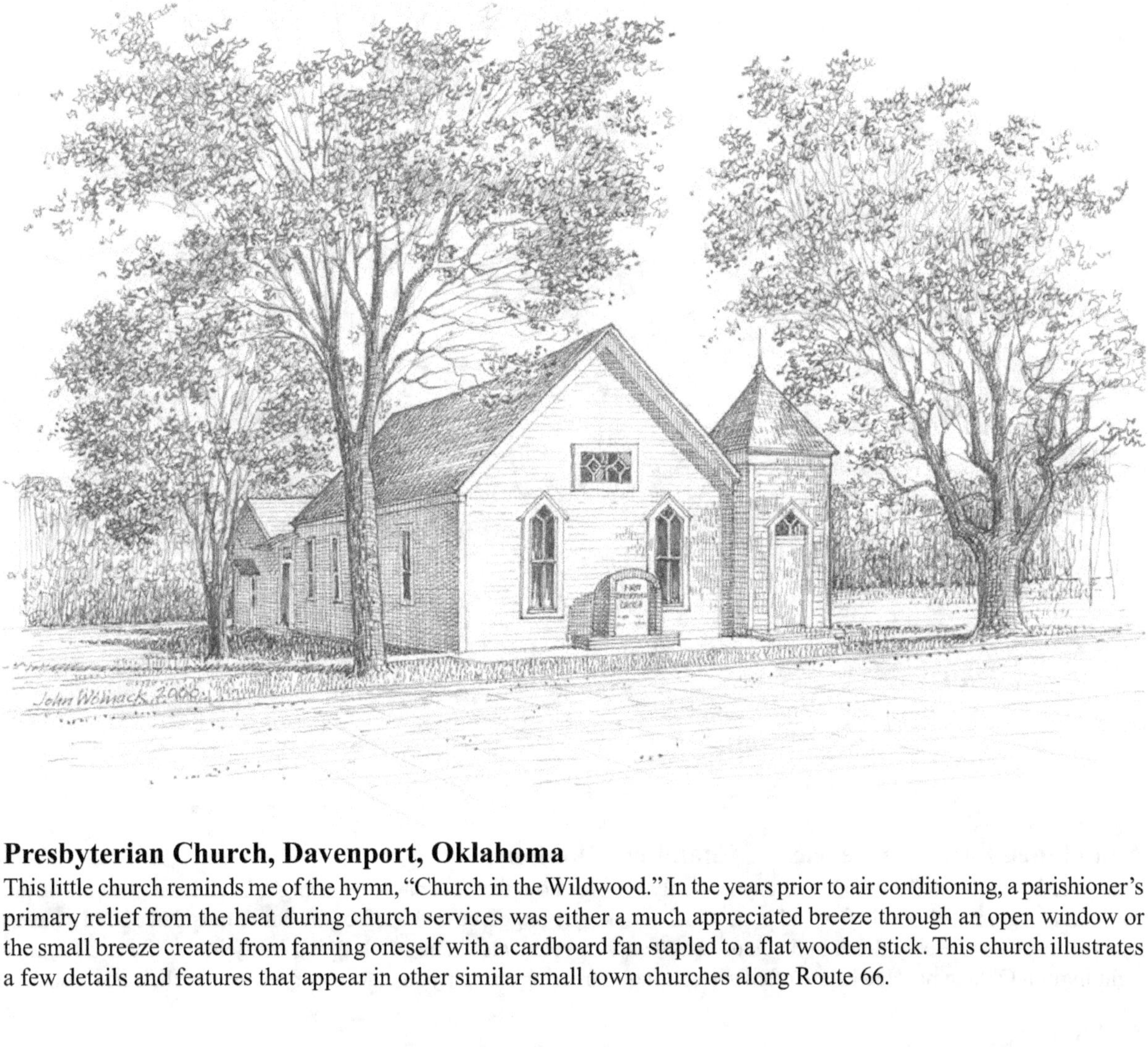

Presbyterian Church, Davenport, Oklahoma

This little church reminds me of the hymn, "Church in the Wildwood." In the years prior to air conditioning, a parishioner's primary relief from the heat during church services was either a much appreciated breeze through an open window or the small breeze created from fanning oneself with a cardboard fan stapled to a flat wooden stick. This church illustrates a few details and features that appear in other similar small town churches along Route 66.

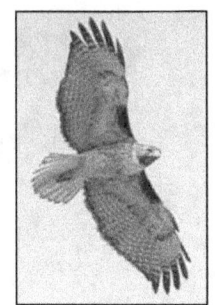

Until the insecticide DDT was banned in the 1970s, raptor populations were on a serious decline. Hawks, owls, and eagles have since returned to healthy populations.

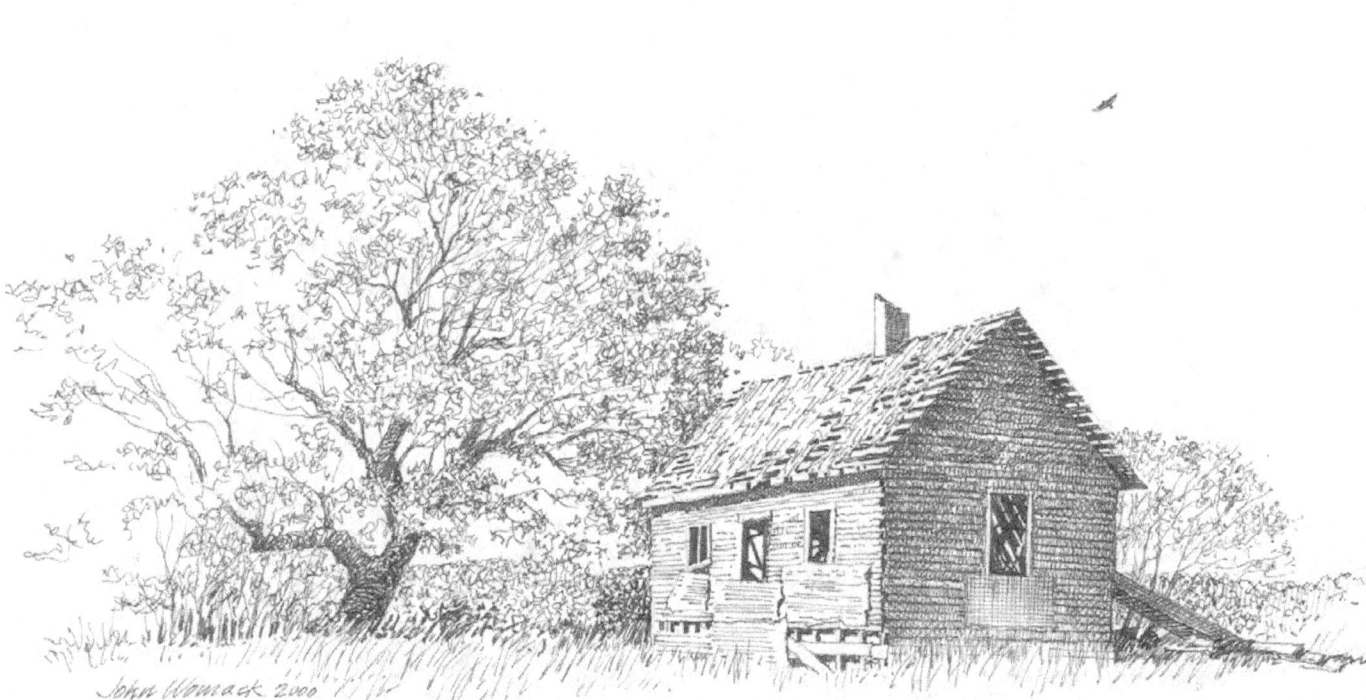

John Womack 2000

Abandoned Farm House, east of Chandler, Oklahoma

This little house faces Route 66, and one can only wonder how the occupants here might have reacted to all of the comings and goings of people from all parts of the nation. The large tree to the left of the house must have been a haven from the heat for not only those in the house but weary travelers also. The hawk flying lazily in the sky is a familiar sight in rural Oklahoma. Hawks are often seen sitting in trees or on utility lines while trying to eye their next meal.

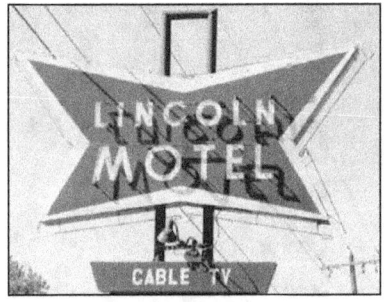

The Lincoln Motel in Chandler, still in business, remains one of the classic motor court motels on Route 66.

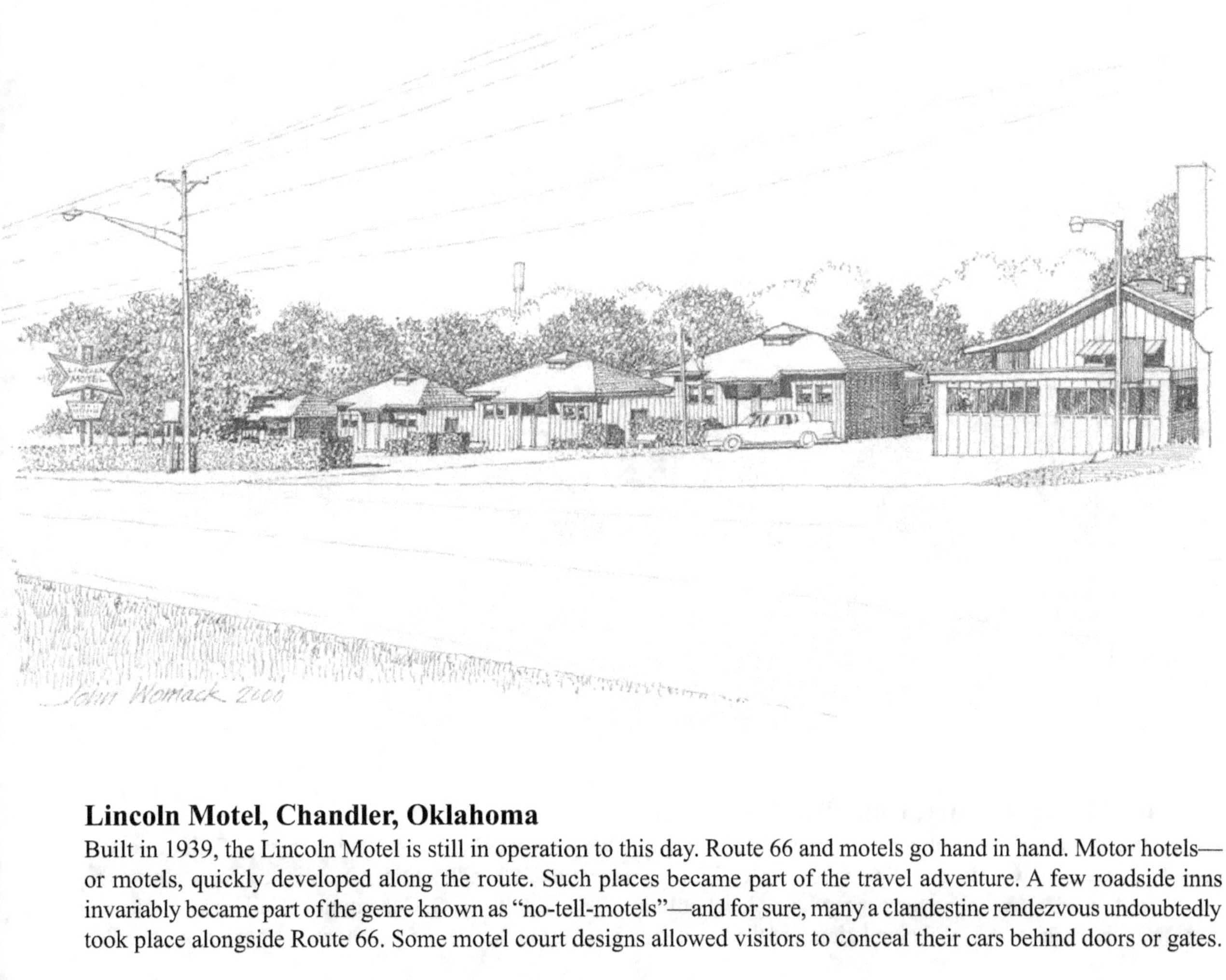

John Womack 2000

Lincoln Motel, Chandler, Oklahoma

Built in 1939, the Lincoln Motel is still in operation to this day. Route 66 and motels go hand in hand. Motor hotels—or motels, quickly developed along the route. Such places became part of the travel adventure. A few roadside inns invariably became part of the genre known as "no-tell-motels"—and for sure, many a clandestine rendezvous undoubtedly took place alongside Route 66. Some motel court designs allowed visitors to conceal their cars behind doors or gates.

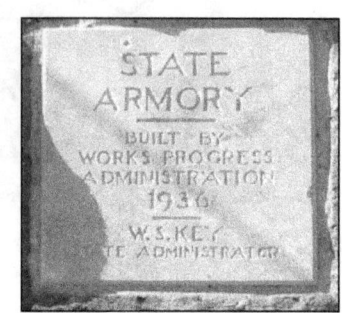

"State Armory, built by the Works Progress Administration, 1936, W. S. Key, State Administrator."

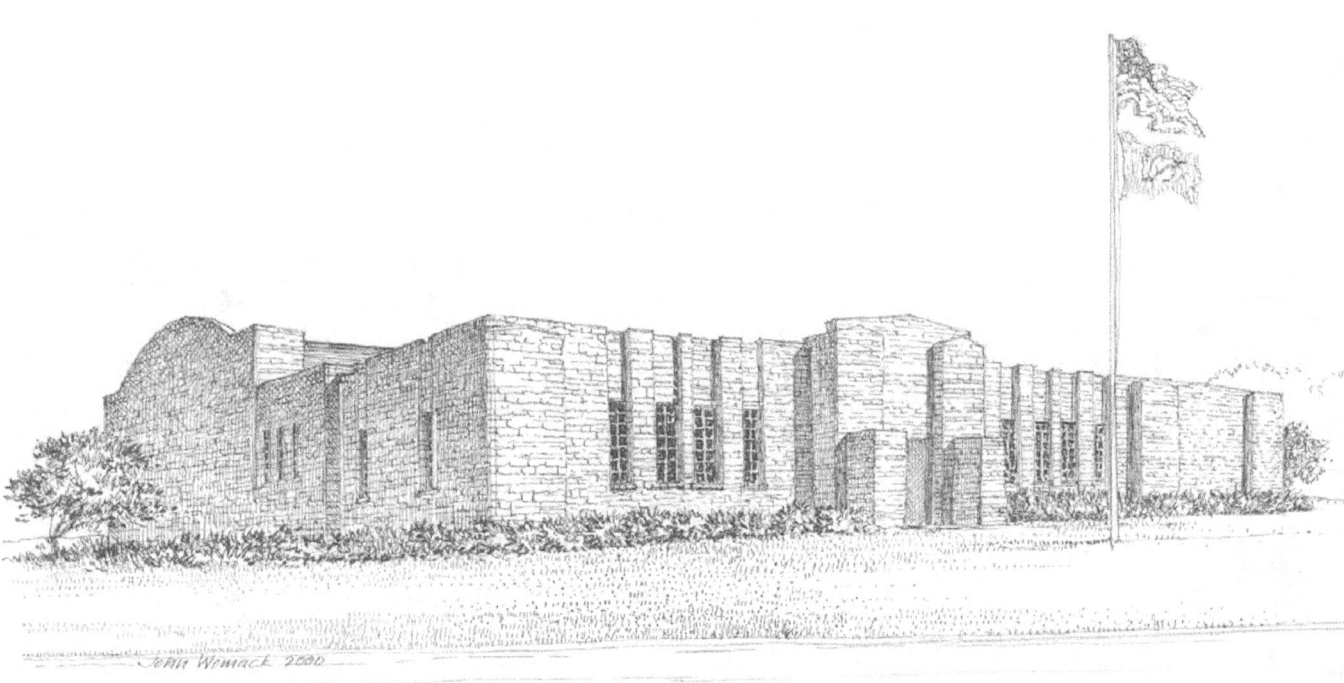

National Guard Armory, Chandler, Oklahoma

During the Depression, a number of armories were built by the WPA (Works Progress Administration). This armory is quite large and is now in danger of being torn down, although a group of Chandler citizens continue efforts to save the structure. Armories symbolize the concept of a "local militia" as stated in the U.S. Constitution. National Guardsmen were from the ranks of the local population, and they drilled and trained in the area of their homes. Not always so today.

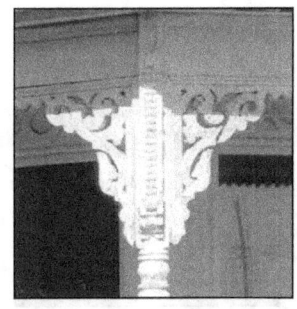

The carved fretwork of "gingerbread" Victorian architecture is admired by many people who appreciate not only the intricate detail but also the carpenter skills necessary to build them.

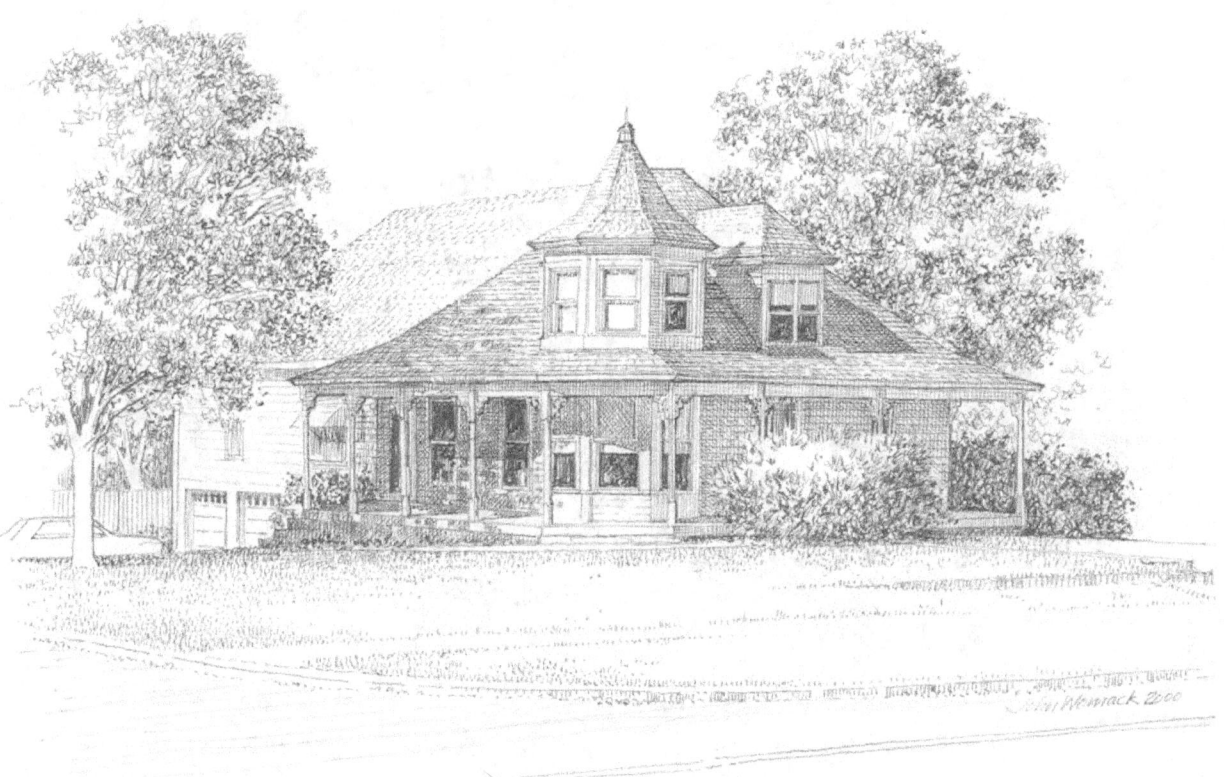

Victorian Style House, Chandler, Oklahoma

Porches are wonderful places. They protect the walls of the house, provide refuge from the rain or snow, create shaded outside spaces for various activities during hot summer months, and provide a comfortable spatial transition from the exterior world to the interior of the house. Before air conditioning, front porches were the norm for most houses. People would gather on the porch and visit or simply sit and watch the world pass by their door.

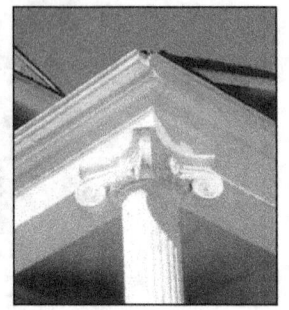

Ionic-styled columns have great appeal to many people. Their graceful capital volutes and fluted shafts are subtle reminders of our inheritance from the ancient Greeks.

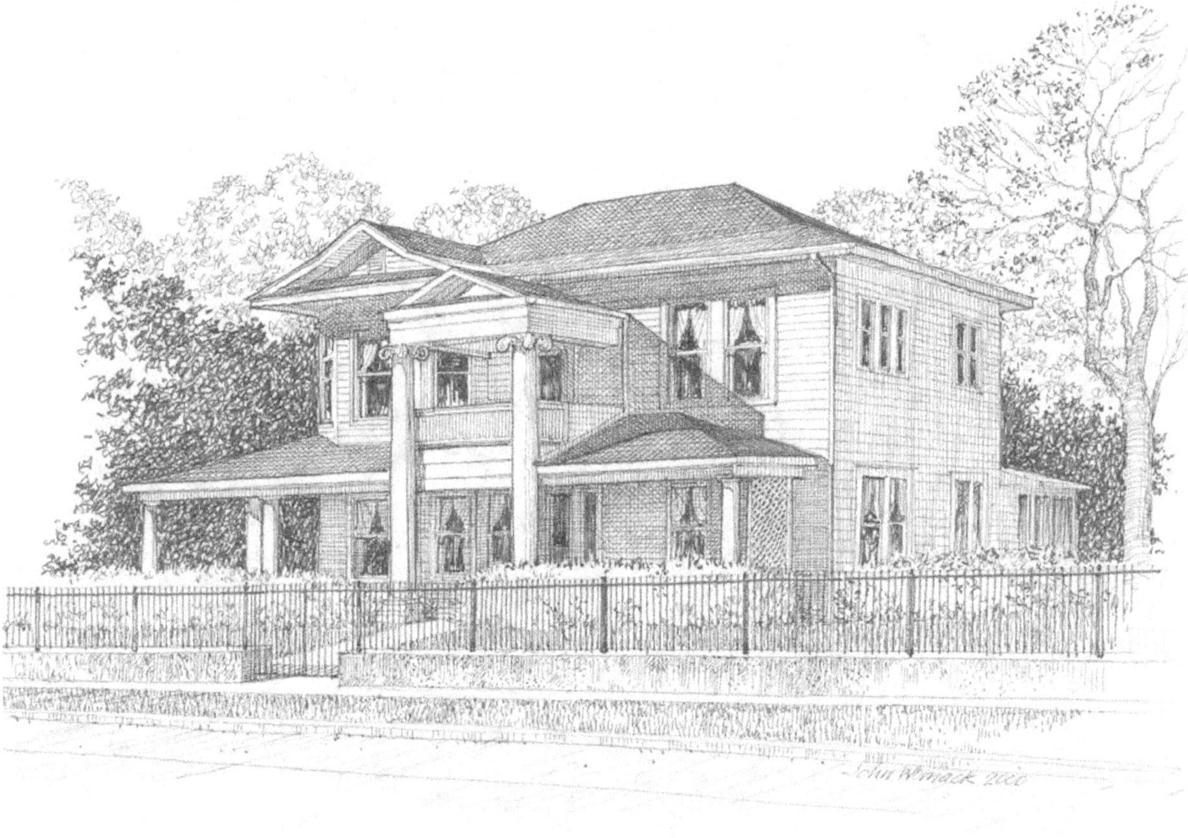

Colonial Revival Style House, Chandler, Oklahoma

This house sits across the street from the Victorian house on the previous page. The front porch on this house, though is a bit more imposing than the example on page 79. In addition, this house has an upper level porch that suggests another level of desired security and privacy. The iron fence and brick wall provide further clues about the original owners. This house, though finely crafted and detailed, doesn't seem as friendly as the example on page 79.

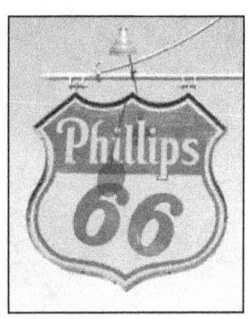

The restored Phillips 66 sign at the old station in Chandler leaves no doubt about the intentional resemblance between the Phillips sign and the Highway 66 shield seen on the next page.

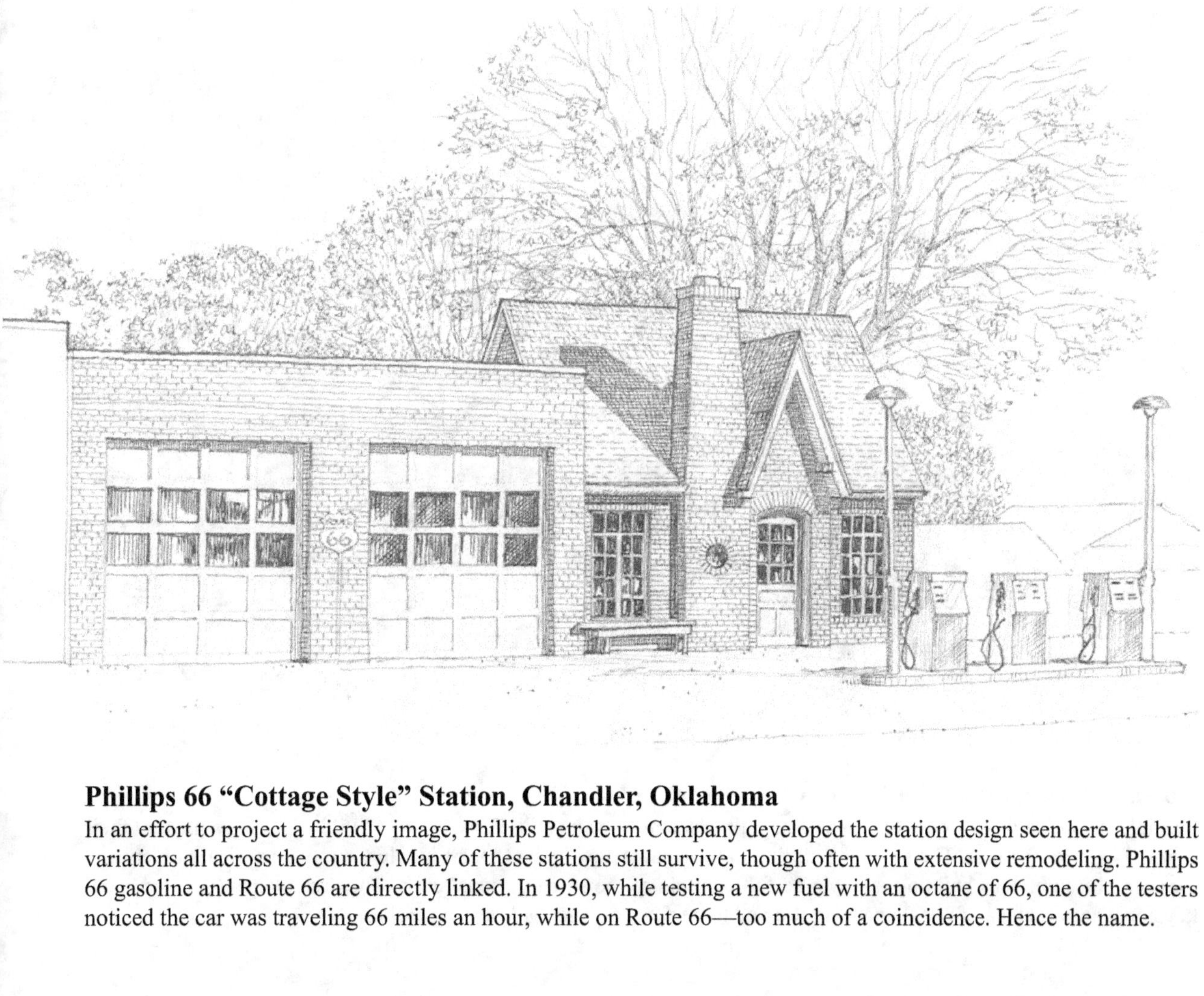

Phillips 66 "Cottage Style" Station, Chandler, Oklahoma

In an effort to project a friendly image, Phillips Petroleum Company developed the station design seen here and built variations all across the country. Many of these stations still survive, though often with extensive remodeling. Phillips 66 gasoline and Route 66 are directly linked. In 1930, while testing a new fuel with an octane of 66, one of the testers noticed the car was traveling 66 miles an hour, while on Route 66—too much of a coincidence. Hence the name.

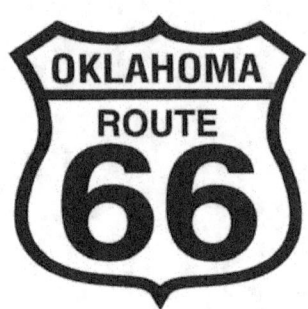

As noted on page 81, the Route 66 highway designation shield was most certainly the inspiration for the Phillips 66 service station sign.

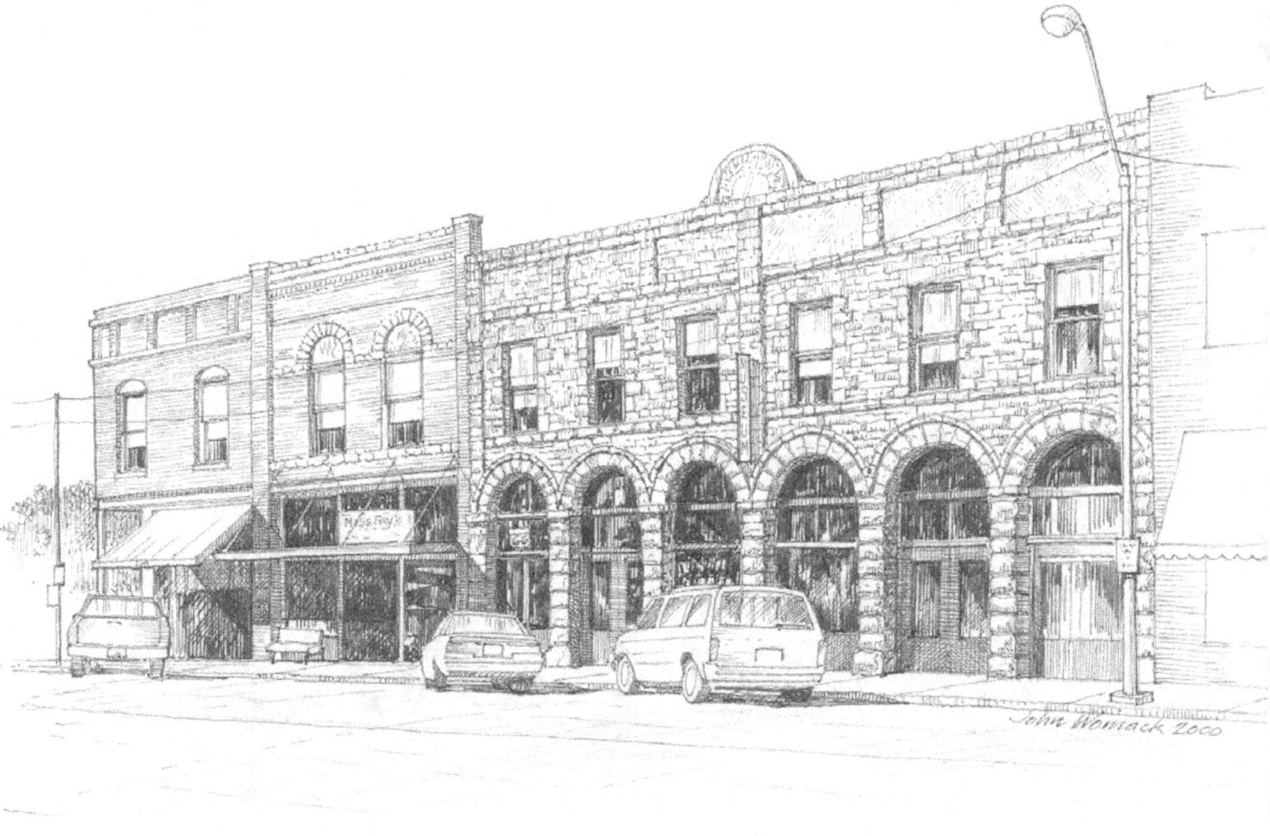

Downtown, Chandler, Oklahoma

Chandler is one of those Route 66 towns where time seems to stand still. This group of buildings retains most of their original exterior features. The arcaded building to the right is now home to the Lincoln County Historical Society and Pioneer Museum. This building is a wonderful example of the stone masons' craft. The arch stones (*voussoirs* and keystones) are each carefully shaped and dressed to perform as true load-bearing arches.

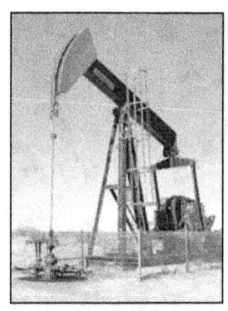

Oil played an important role in the early development of Chandler. Oklahoma remains today one of the major producers of petroleum and natural gas in the United States. Pumping rigs are a common site along Route 66 in Oklahoma.

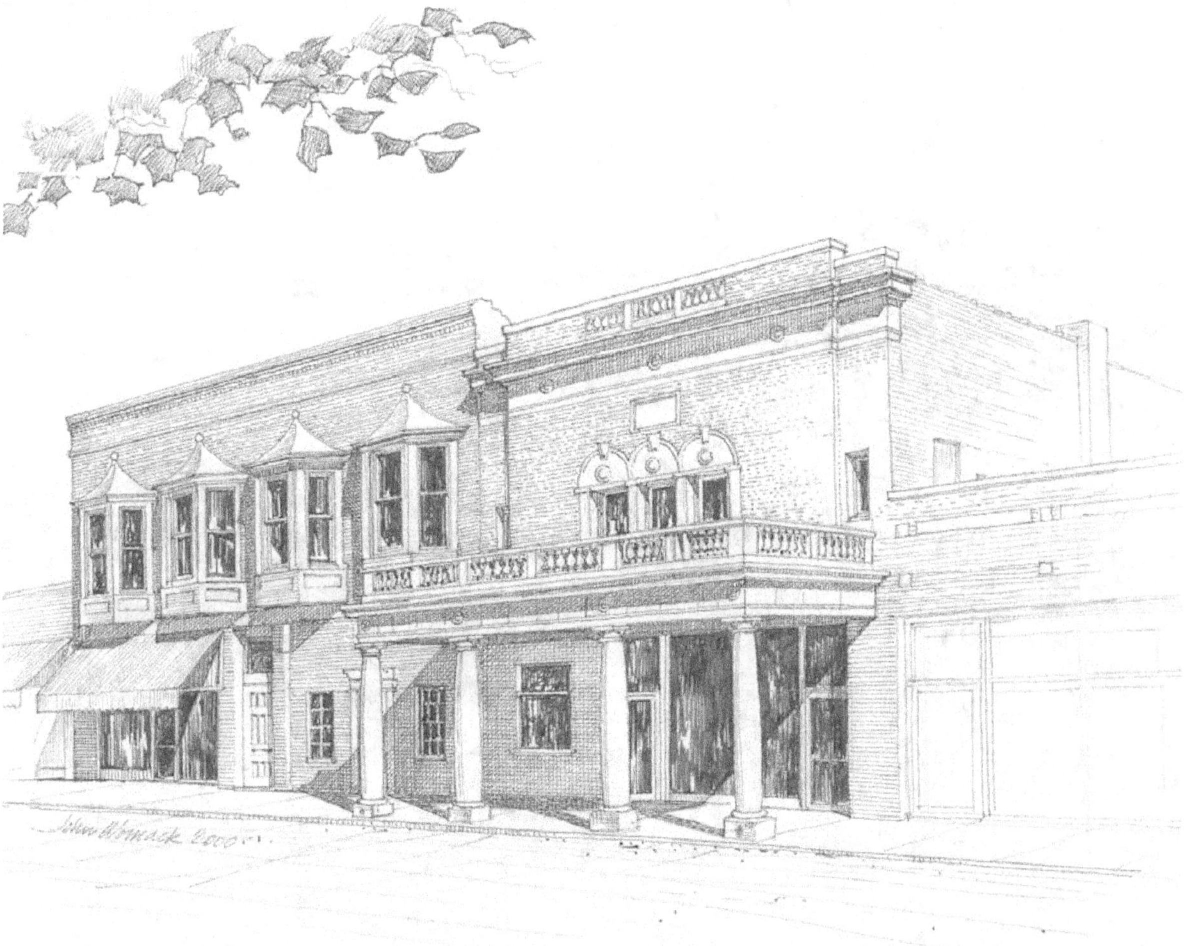

Downtown, Chandler, Oklahoma

This group of buildings obviously dates prior to the construction of Route 66—the portico on the old hotel entrance and its columns sit immediately on the curb edge of the highway—rather precarious for automobile and truck traffic. Chandler was founded in 1891 and was almost wiped off the map by a tornado in 1897. Today, Chandler has a wide array of business types but promotes itself as the "Pecan Capital of the World."

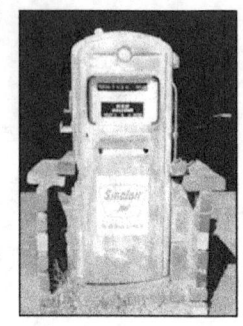

An old gas pump at PJ's has been set in place with a brick masonry base.

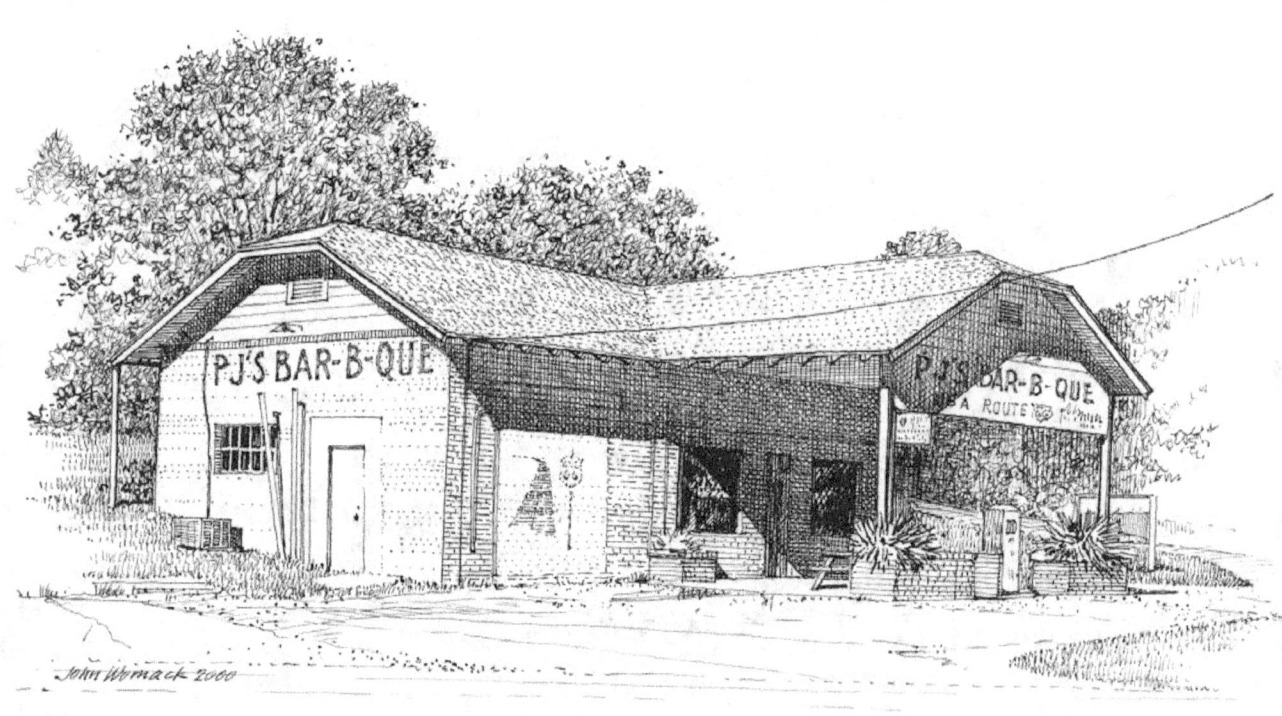

PJ's Bar-B-Que, Chandler, Oklahoma

Some say this place has been a barbecue stand for as long as they can remember. At one time, however, it was a service station. Route 66 and barbecue have something in common that encourages a lot of barbecue stands along the highway—at least in Oklahoma, and I can't say that I know why—but I do love barbeque. The painted Route 66 sign on the wall of PJ's is a typical type of adornment seen on many structures along the old highway.

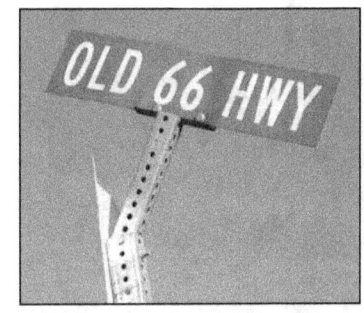

The old highway is noted in many forms along its length.

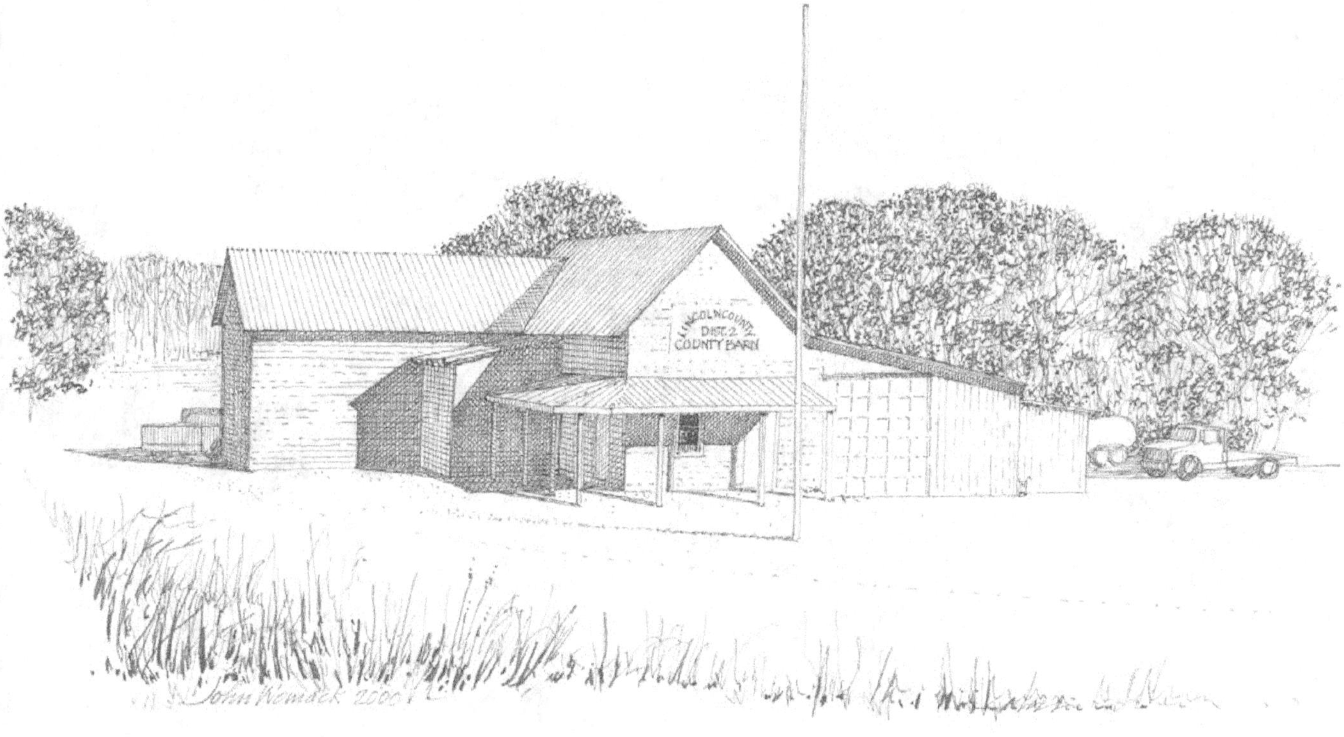

Lincoln County Highway Barn, Chandler, Oklahoma

Sometimes it is easy to forget that every highway demands a tremendous amount of maintenance, care, and tax revenue. Snow, ice, rain, accidents—any number of events—can seriously affect the condition and safety of not only the road surface, but the right of way as well. When one considers the breadth and scope of such maintenance, one has to be impressed—and it is required in all kinds of weather and temperature extremes. Road work can be extremely dangerous.

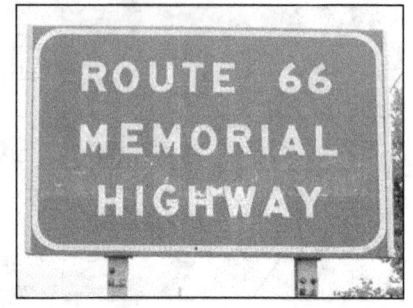

So many people have memories of Route 66! It is fascinating how the old highway continues to capture the imagination of travelers – from all over the world!

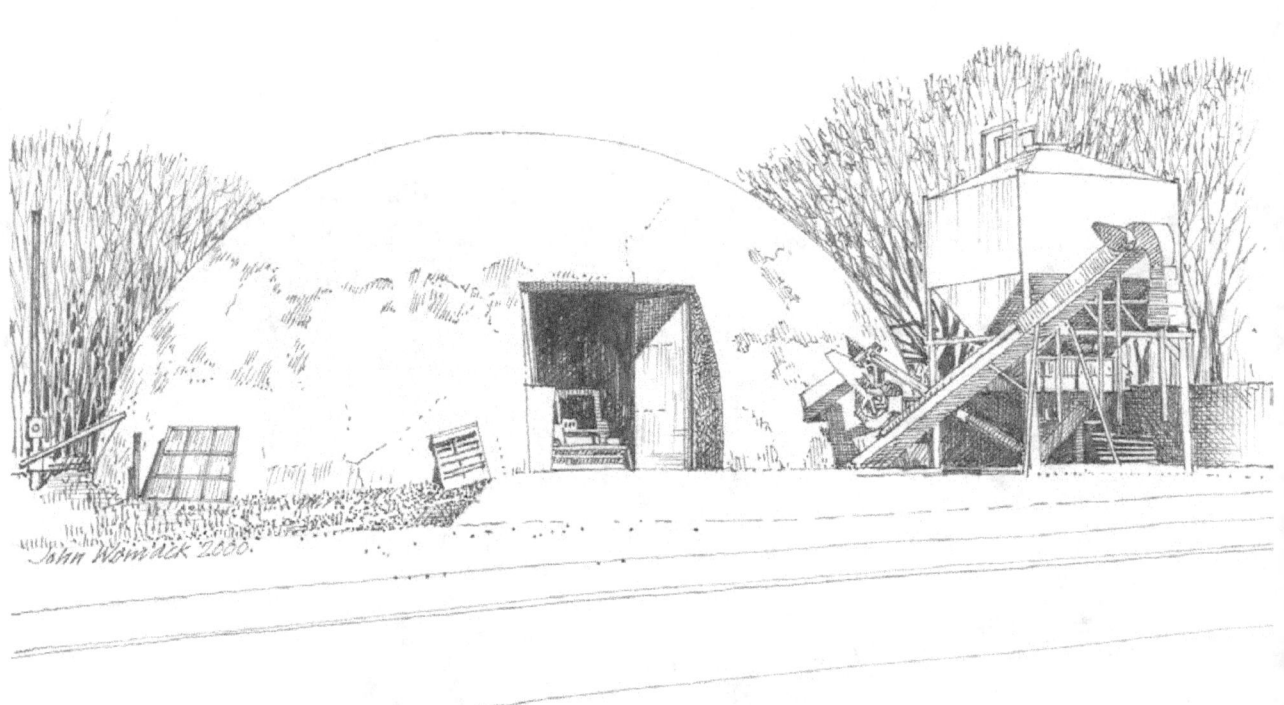

Salt and Gravel Storage Barn (demolished), Chandler, Oklahoma

Roadside landmarks are important features to the highway traveler. Grown-ups use such markers for gauging distances and time left to travel—and so do kids. I am sure that my sister and I would have remembered this barn as "the igloo." Our parents usually helped us name such places. Looking down the road in anticipation of seeing such sights always added to the fun of the trip and detracted from the otherwise cramped environment of the car's interior.

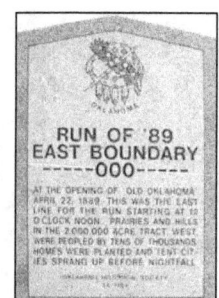

The Oklahoma Land Run is a fascinating story. So many land seekers were killed or injured during these events, the Federal Government finally eliminated "runs" and resorted to lotteries.

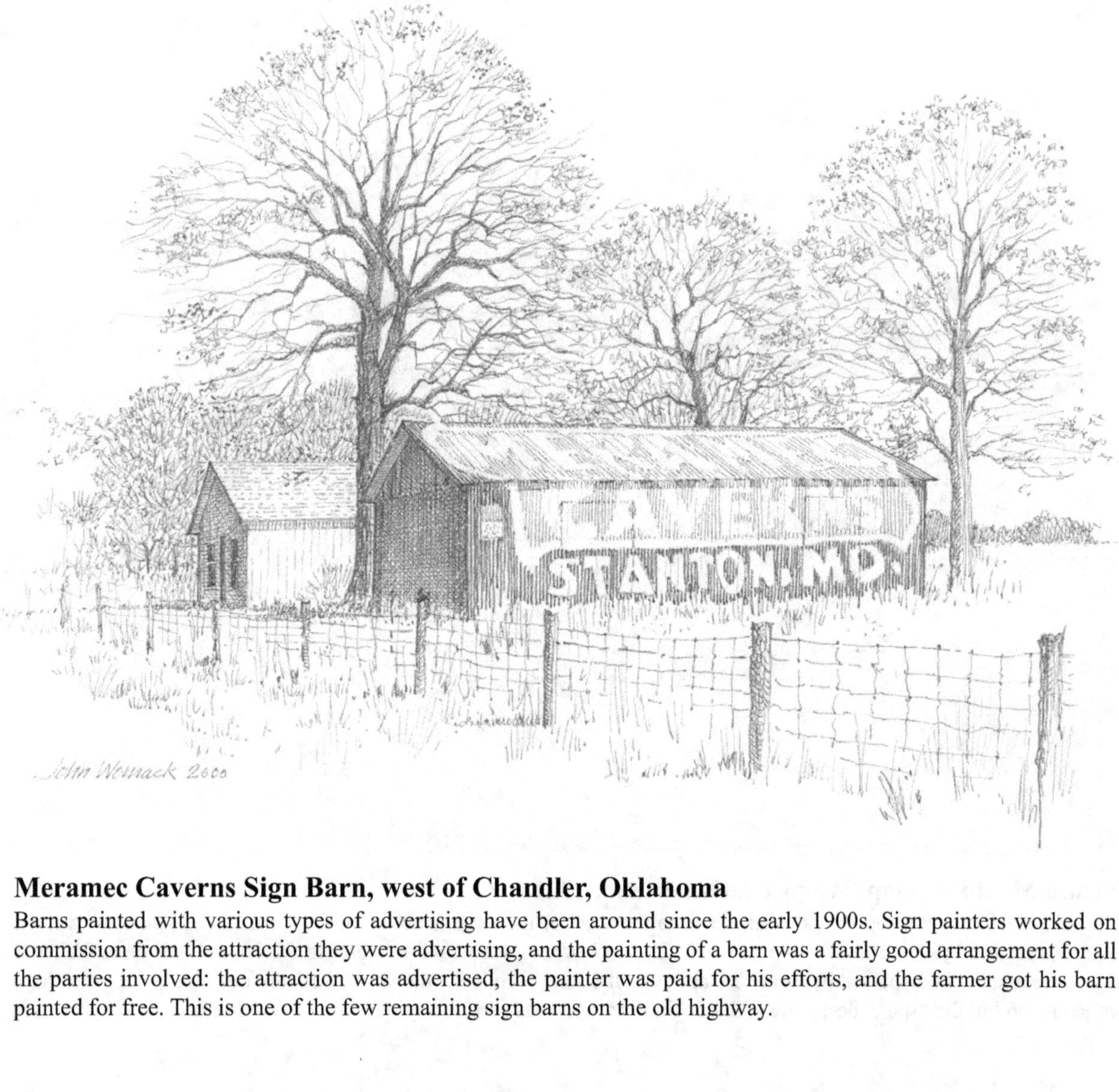

John Womack 2000

Meramec Caverns Sign Barn, west of Chandler, Oklahoma

Barns painted with various types of advertising have been around since the early 1900s. Sign painters worked on commission from the attraction they were advertising, and the painting of a barn was a fairly good arrangement for all the parties involved: the attraction was advertised, the painter was paid for his efforts, and the farmer got his barn painted for free. This is one of the few remaining sign barns on the old highway.

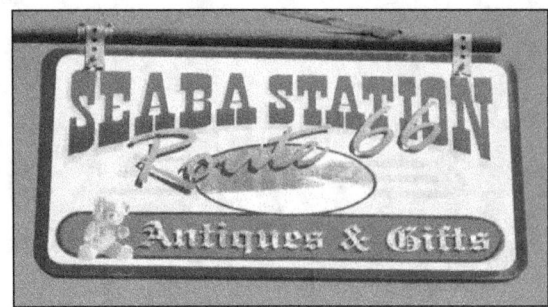

The old Seaba Station is now an antiques and gift store.

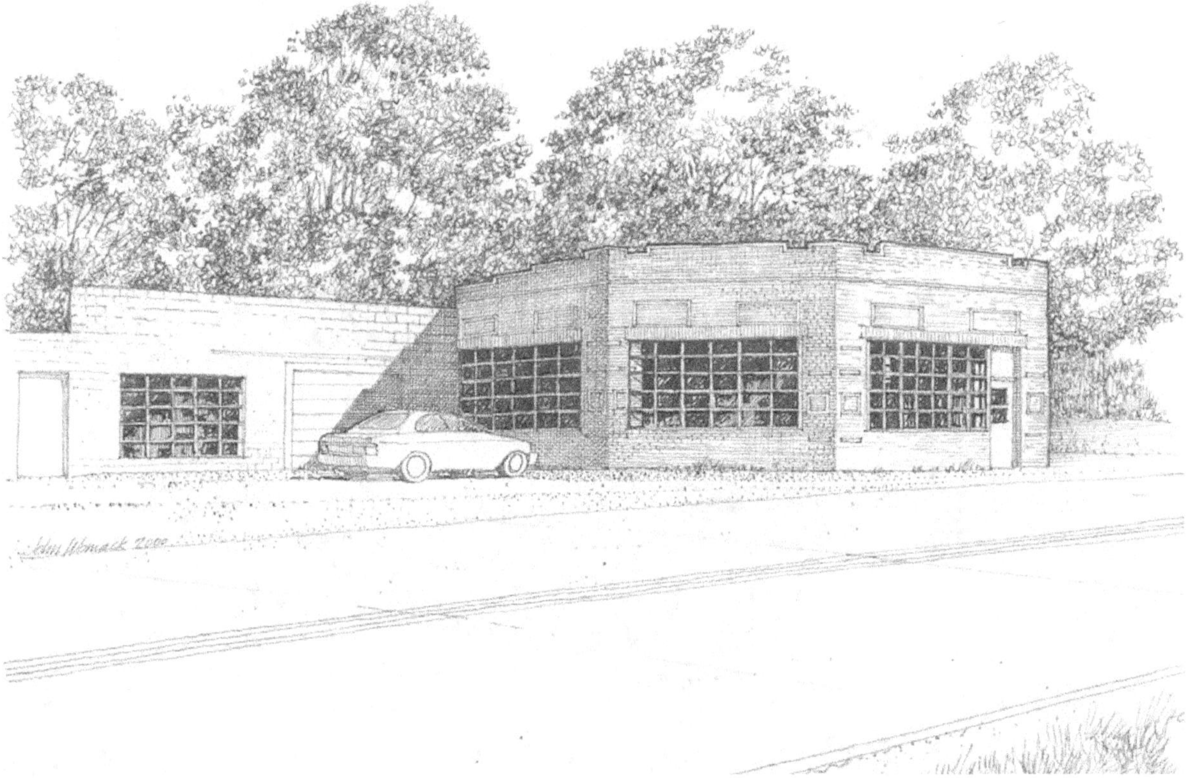

Seaba Machine Shop, Warwick, Oklahoma, 1921

The old machine shop and the railroad trestle to the west of the shop is about all that remains of Warwick, a town founded around 1890 and named after a town in England. Warwick is near the turnoff to Wellston, Oklahoma. Wellston was scheduled to be bypassed by Route 66, although the state promised otherwise. Wellston ultimately did get a share of Route 66 but the "spur," designated "State Highway 66," was paid for by the state of Oklahoma.

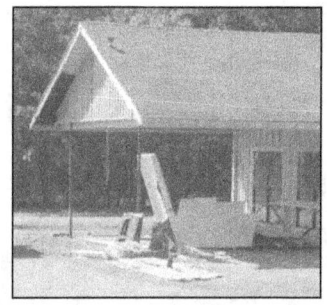

After being razed by an errant automobile, the old barbecue stand was reborn in 2005, with a new building on the old foundations.

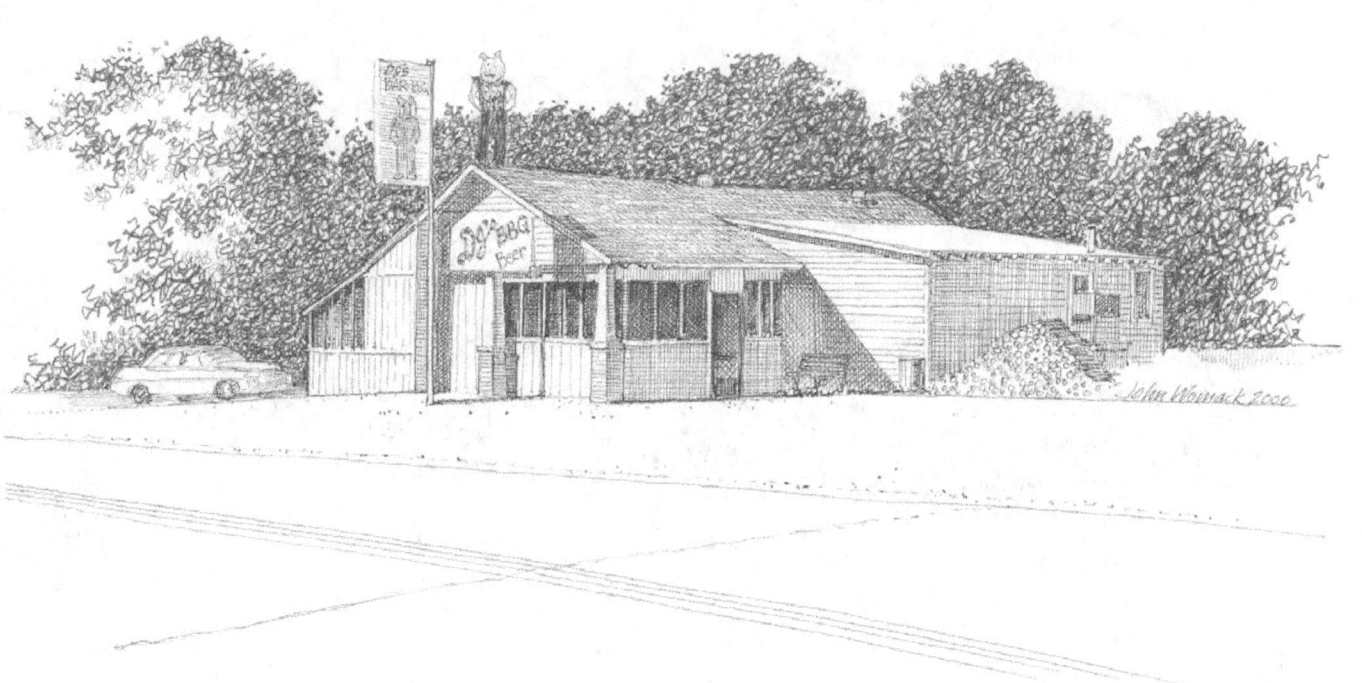

DJ's Barbecue (demolished), near Luther, Oklahoma

It is said this little building was built in 1921 and has a history of housing various functions. It is curious how barbecue places get their name. Down the road from DJ's is PJ's, the barbecue place in Chandler seen previously on page 84. Is one playing off the other's reputation or competing in a face-to-face manner, or both? DJ's is located near a sharp curve and in 2004 a car missed the curve and plowed through the building, destroying most of what is seen in this drawing.

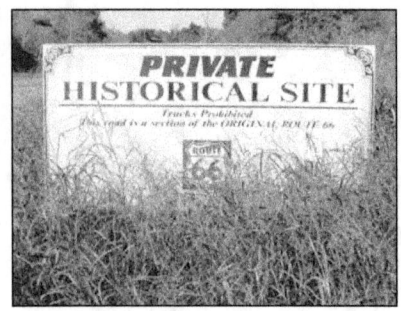

Near Luther, an interested and caring land owner allows people to drive upon an original length of Route 66 pavement (cars only, please).

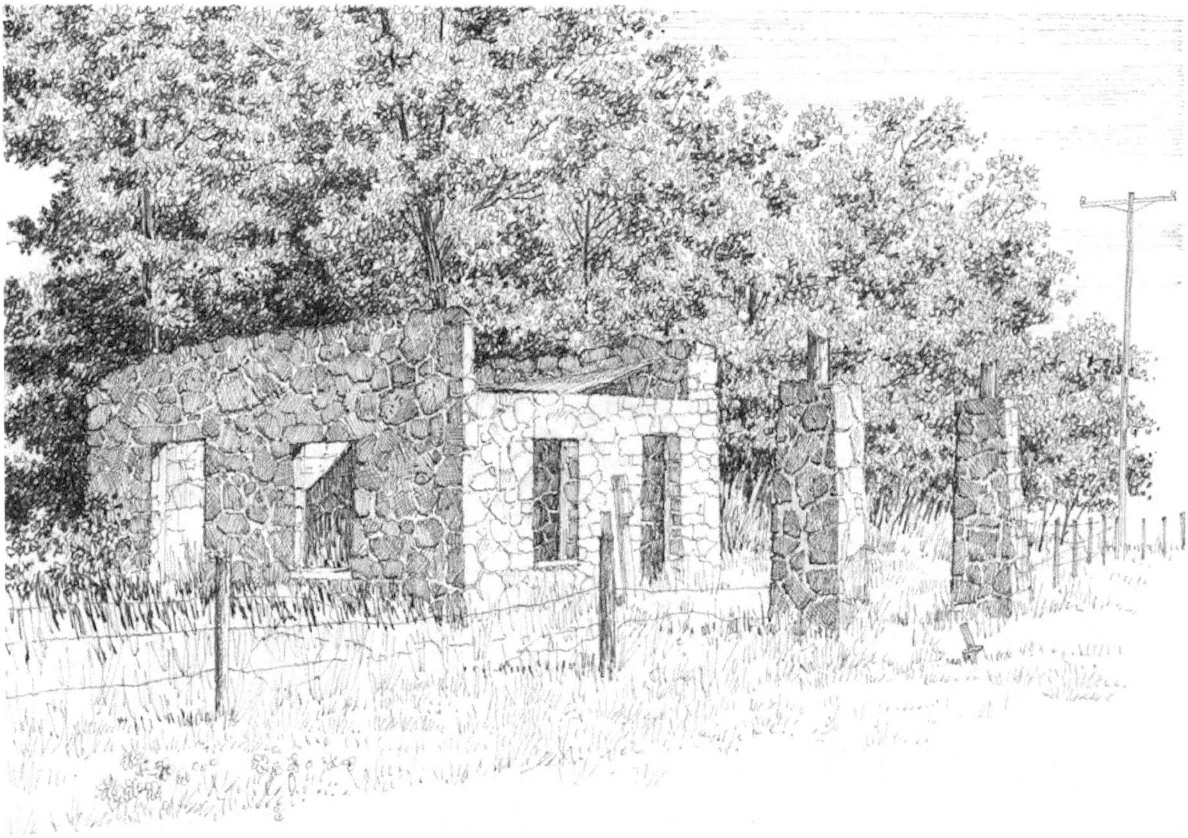

Former Conoco Service Station, west of Luther, Oklahoma

During the 1970s this old station still had its roof and windows, but sometime later various circumstances led to its condition as seen here. A plaque on a post near the original front door relates how onetime owners succumbed to the suggestion of a Chicago gangster and set up a counterfeit printing operation in back of the store. They were caught before a bill was ever passed. Some 50 years later, a dead body was found inside the old ruins.

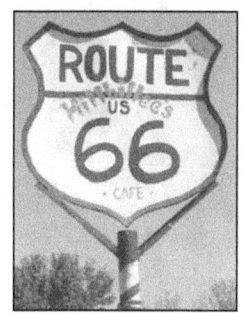

The "old" Hillbillee's Cafe sign in Arcadia still greets tourists and customers.

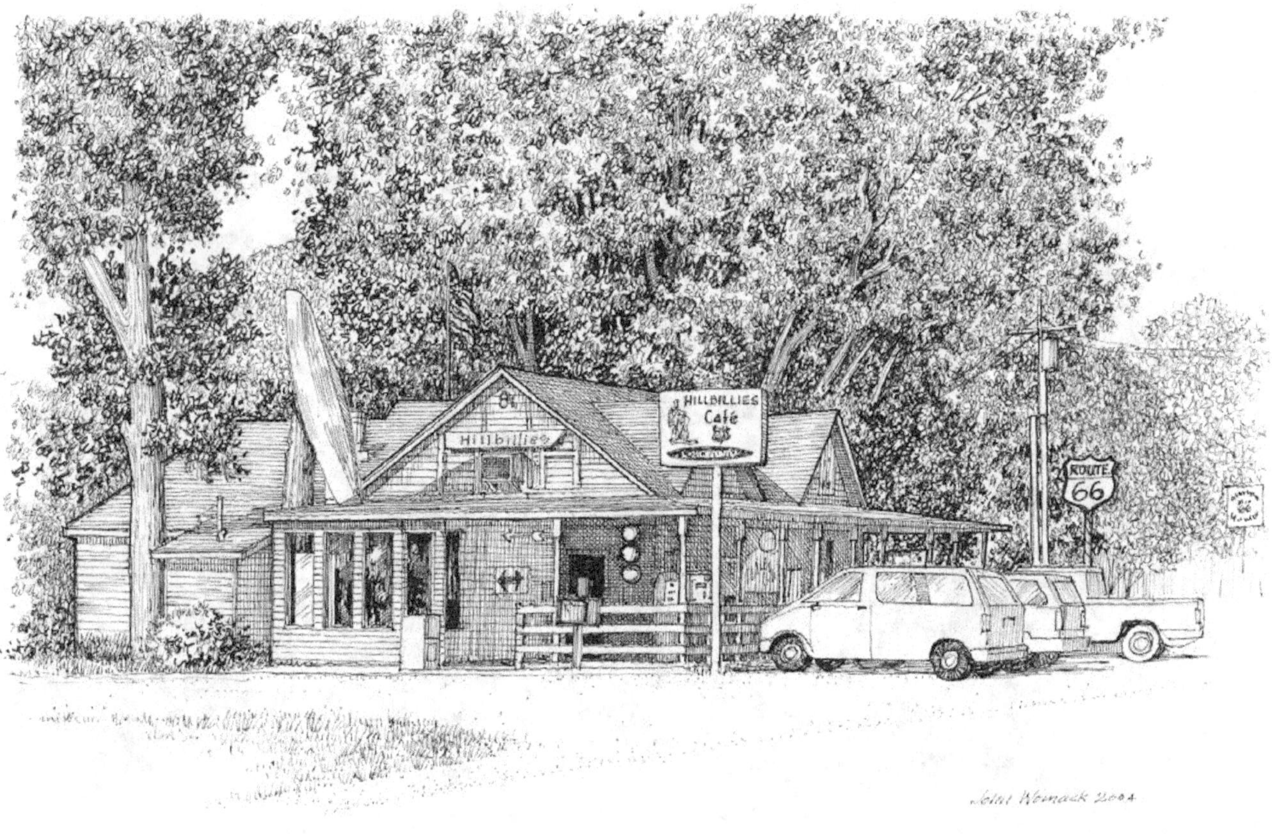

![Pen and ink illustration of Hillbillies Cafe building with vehicles parked outside, surrounded by large trees]

Hillbillie's Cafe, Arcadia, Oklahoma

The buildings that make up Hillbillie's Cafe and Bed and Breakfast are the remains of a former motor court. The restaurant was originally the office for the cabins and later became a Phillips 66 station. Through the years several restaurants have been located here. The former cabins are slowly being renovated. The complex of buildings convey some of the old Route 66 "feeling."

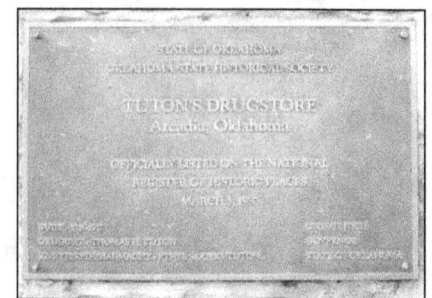

In 1980, Arcadia's Tuton Drugstore was named to the National Register of Historic Places.

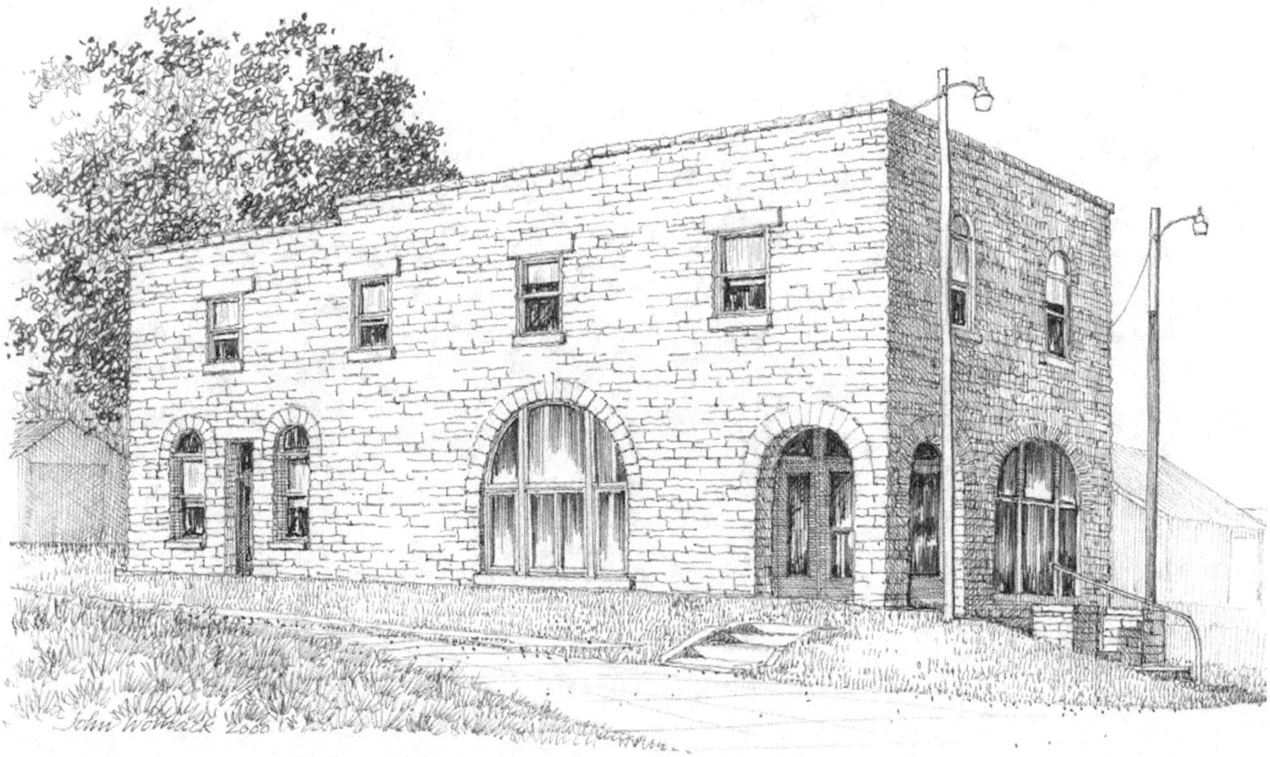

Former Tuton's Drugstore, Arcadia, Oklahoma

This stone building is another outstanding example of the stonemason's craft. The wedge-shaped arch stones are carefully shaped and placed in time-honored fashion. The stone is local and varies in color from buff to red. Arcadia is one of those small towns that has survived in spite of the significant loss of highway traffic to Interstate 44 (Oklahoma's Turner Turnpike). The town today seems to thrive on its Route 66 heritage with visitors stopping in, from near and far.

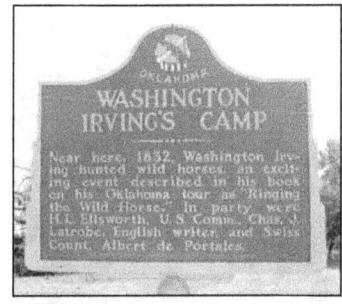

Near Arcadia, American novelist Washington Irving camped with a U.S. Army scouting force in 1832—making him one of the first to travel Route 66 country.

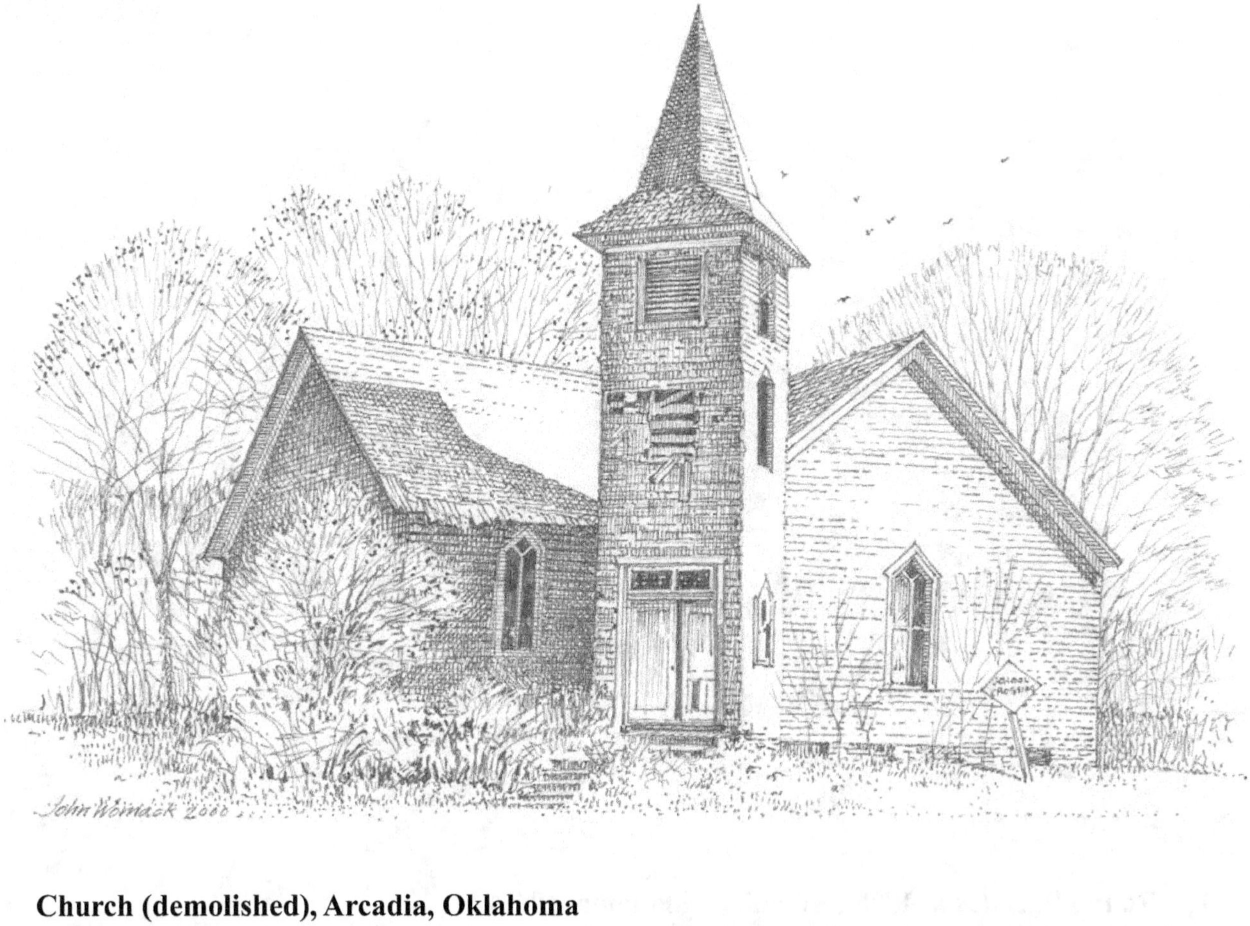

Church (demolished), Arcadia, Oklahoma

Luckily, I had photographed this old abandoned church prior to its being razed sometime in the 1970s or '80s. In an earlier discussion of the church in Davenport on page 75, I alluded to how certain details occur in other churches along Route 66. There are churches in El Reno and Bridgeport that are very similar in appearance to this church. Note the pointed window and "Y" mullioned glazing.

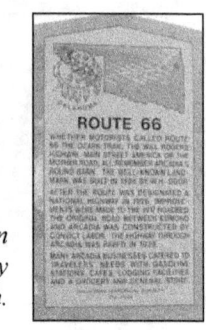
The Round Barn (as in 1978), Arcadia, Oklahoma, 1898

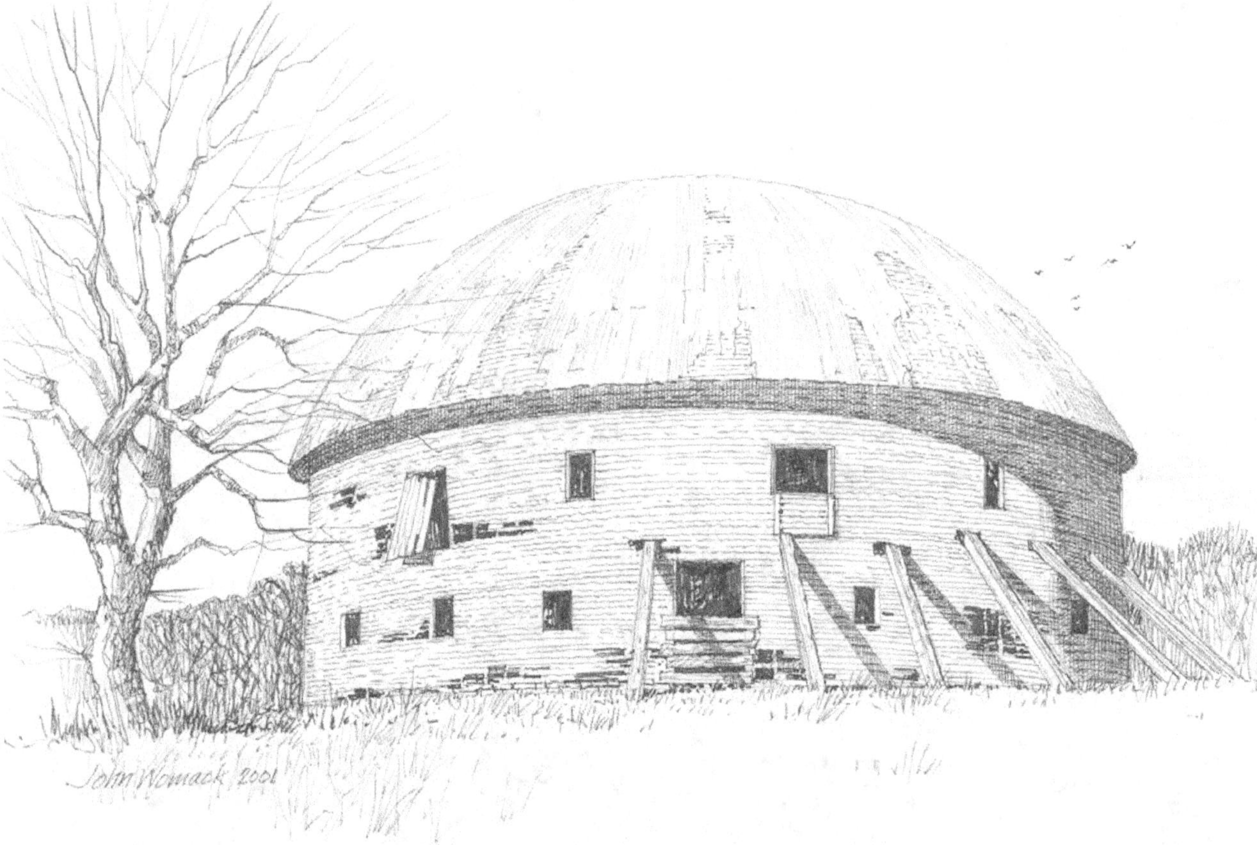

There are few Route 66 landmarks that elicit such affection from travelers as the Round Barn. Barns do speak to us of a much less hectic time, of a time when our days were much more in tune with the cycles of nature and the weather. The Round Barn began as a dairy barn, which accounts for its round shape. This barn sits on an abrupt rise and is quite close to the edge of the highway. There was no overlooking it when traveling this section of Route 66!

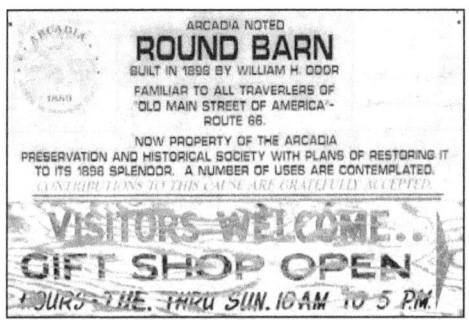

Arcadia, founded in 1891, has a population today of some 280 people. Though few resources are available, the community continues to keep its preservation efforts alive.

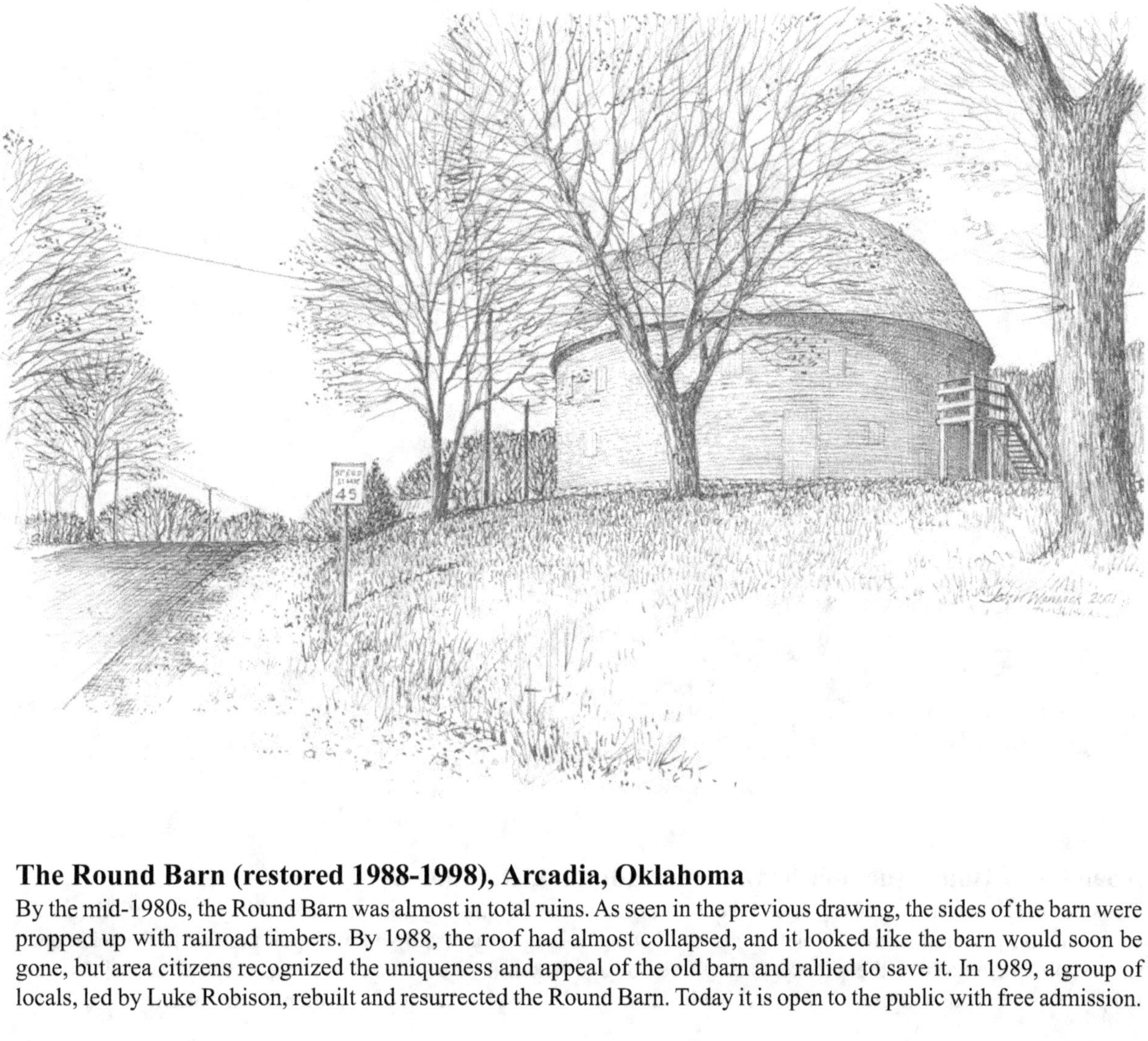

The Round Barn (restored 1988-1998), Arcadia, Oklahoma

By the mid-1980s, the Round Barn was almost in total ruins. As seen in the previous drawing, the sides of the barn were propped up with railroad timbers. By 1988, the roof had almost collapsed, and it looked like the barn would soon be gone, but area citizens recognized the uniqueness and appeal of the old barn and rallied to save it. In 1989, a group of locals, led by Luke Robison, rebuilt and resurrected the Round Barn. Today it is open to the public with free admission.

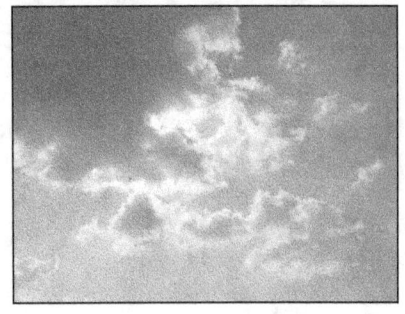

People from Oklahoma learn to keep a sharp eye peeled on the sky at all times of the day. In Oklahoma, weather is a fact of life—and sometimes death.

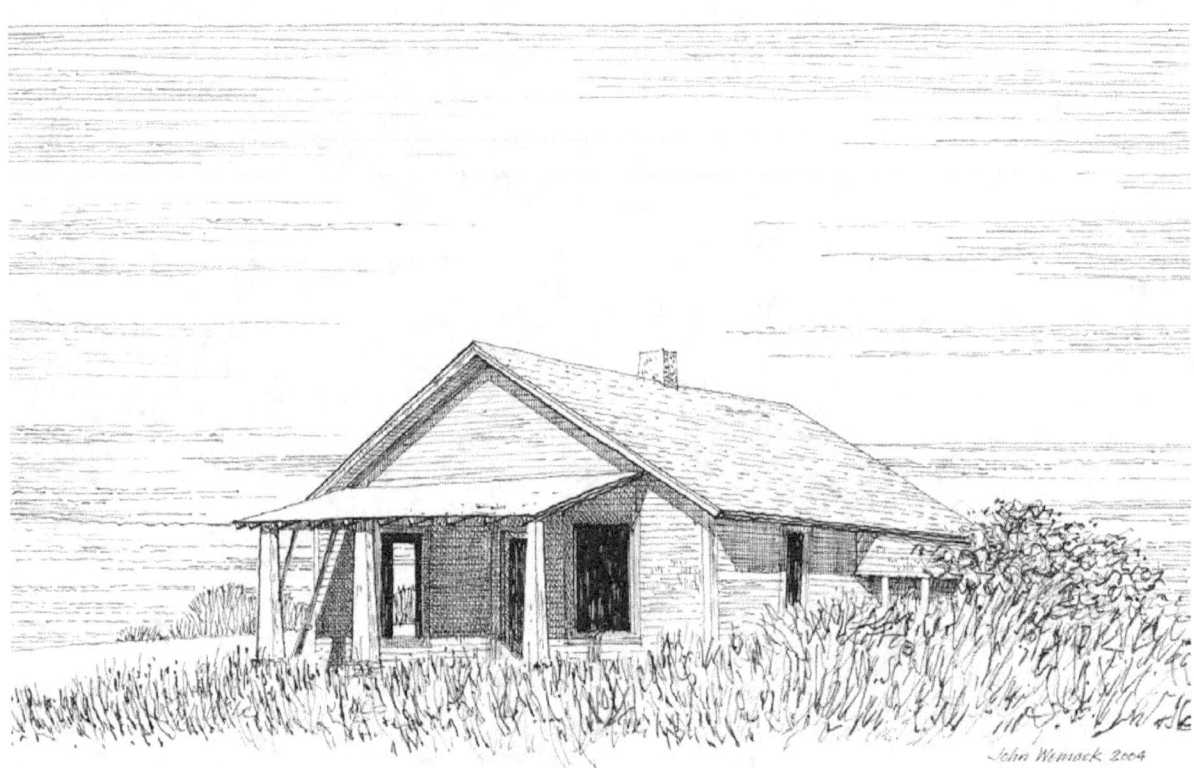

Abandoned House, (demolished), east of Edmond, Oklahoma

The skies of Oklahoma can offer some of the most brilliant, colorful displays one might ever hope to see. Oklahoma's skies can also present the kind of picture that sends one looking for a "fraidy-hole." Upon moving to the wide open spaces of Oklahoma from the hilly regions of tree-covered Arkansas, I became much more weather conscious—not simply because there was more sky to see, but because the sky also held a lot of important information.

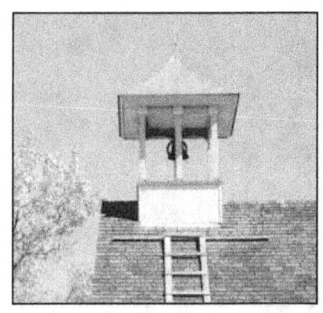

In 2004, the city of Edmond replaced the Saunders Camera Shop with a facsimile of the original first public schoolhouse in Oklahoma Territory.

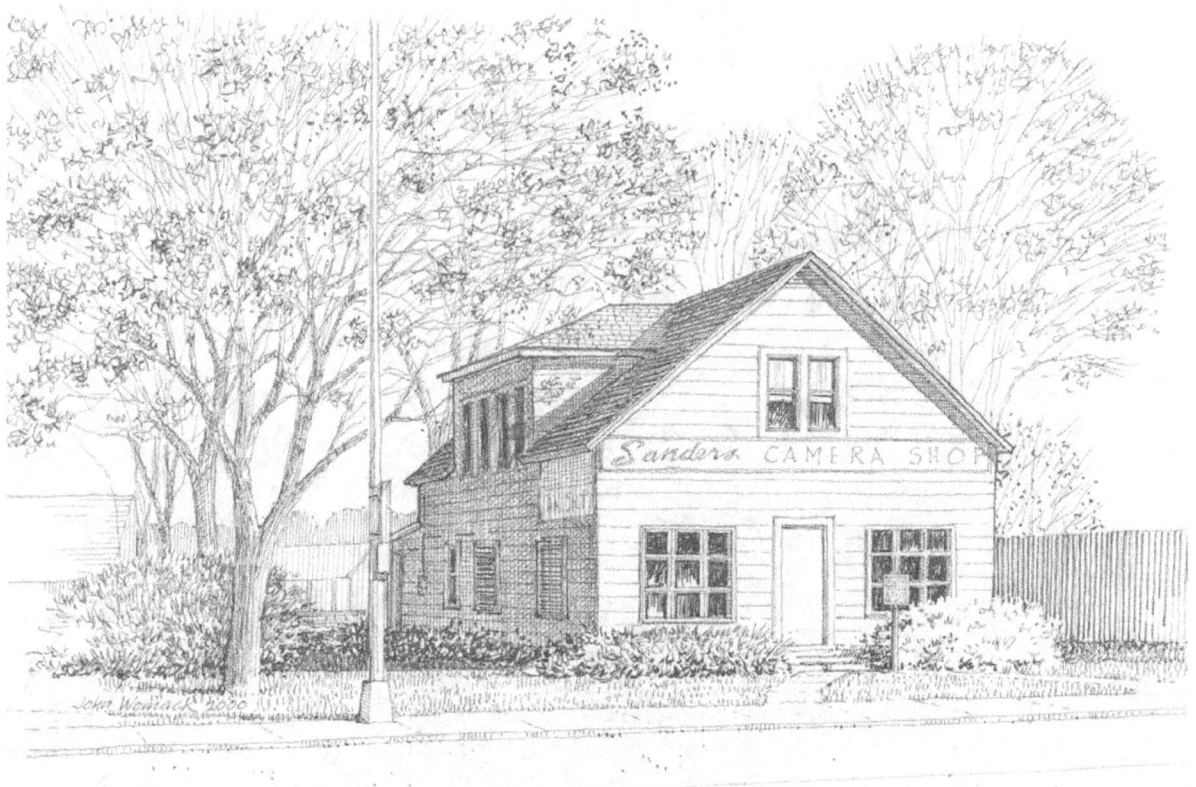

Sanders Camera Shop (demolished), Edmond, Oklahoma

Prior to 1954, Route 66 entered Edmond east of town and became 2nd Street before turning south onto Broadway and then Kelly Road. The Camera Shop on 2nd Street is the site of the first public school building built in Oklahoma Territory. A replica of the original schoolhouse is now located on the site. In 1954, Route 66 bypassed the heart of the town and turned south on what is now I-35.

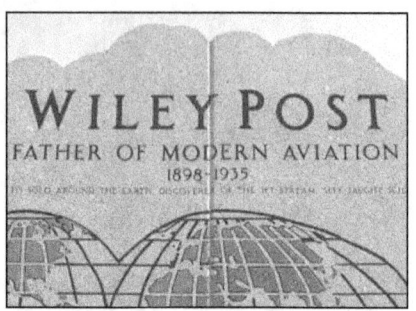

*The Wiley Post monument in Edmond's Memorial
Cemetery is located near the tall Gothic spire in
the center of the cemetery grounds.*

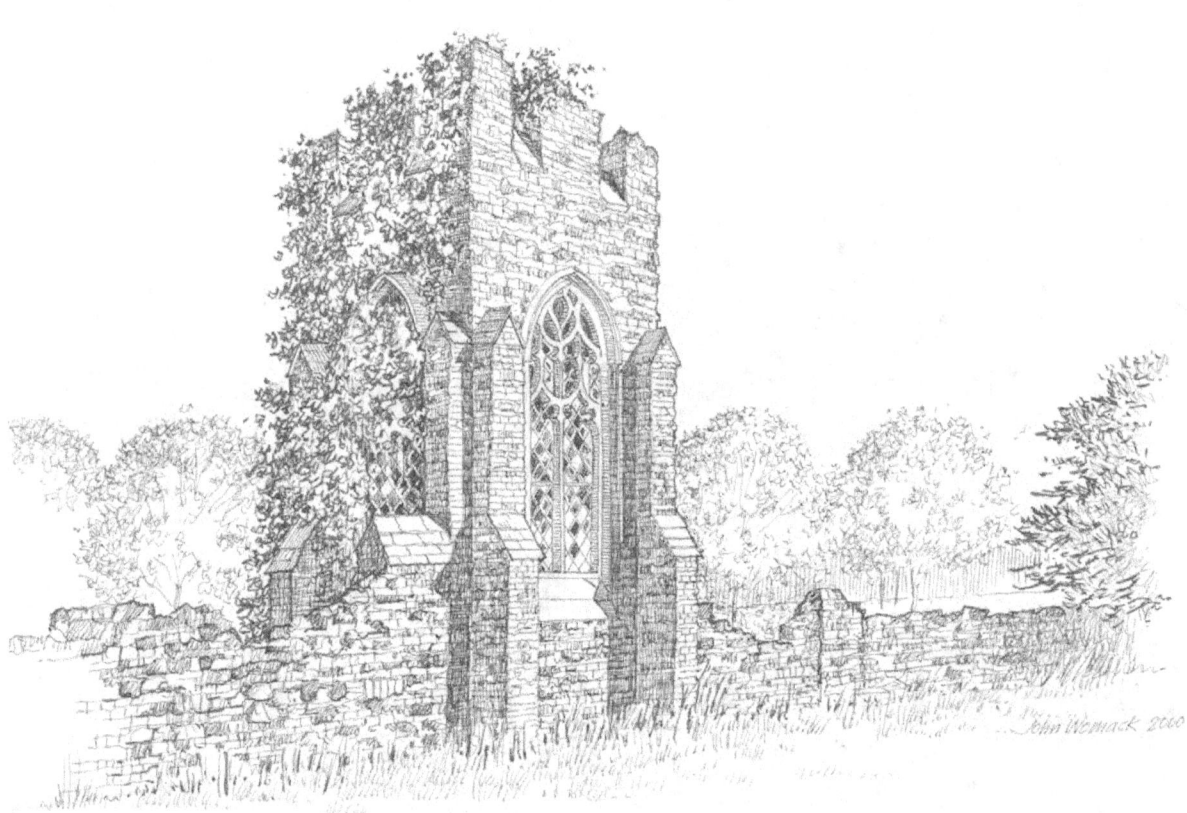

Edmond Memorial Cemetery, Edmond, Oklahoma

Edmond's Memorial Cemetery is the resting place for the great aviator Wiley Post who died with Will Rogers in a 1935 plane crash. The cemetery is bordered by an extremely rustic wall of clinker brick and bits of natural stone. This tower is on the western edge of the cemetery, which fronts Route 66, now known as Kelly Avenue. It is unclear what the function of the tower is, but it recalls many of the romantic follies built in Europe during the 18th and 19th centuries.

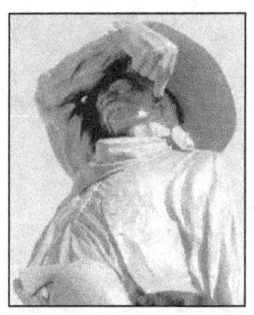

The bronze statue at the entry to the National Cowboy and Western Heritage Museum captures the emotional tension of a lone cowboy in, "Welcome Sundown," by sculptor, Hollis Williford.

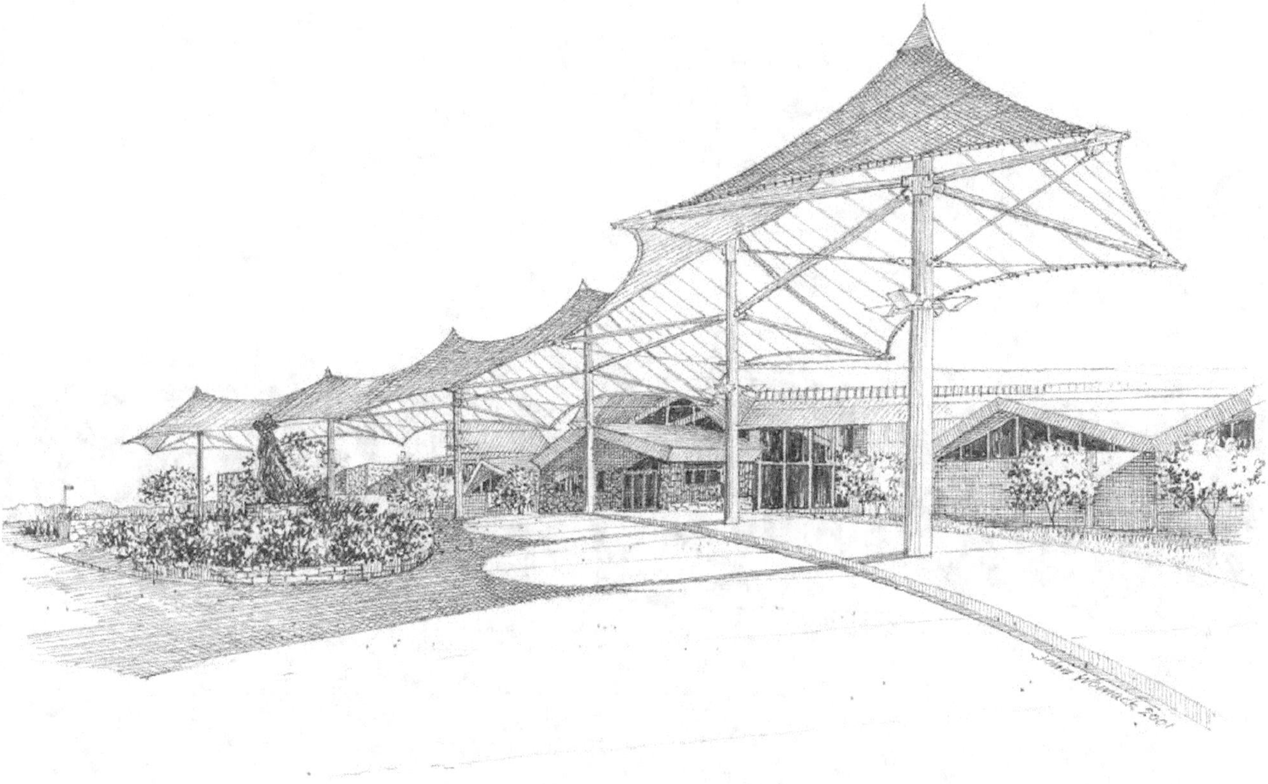

National Cowboy and Western Heritage Museum, Oklahoma City, Oklahoma

Oklahoma is indeed a center of American cowboy culture, and this museum in Oklahoma City is one of the best in the nation with its presentations on cowboys, the Old West, and Western art. Located about a quarter mile east of old Route 66, or Kelly Avenue, the museum has undergone many additions and face-lifts over time. This steel and fabric tensile canopy structure announces the main entry into the building.

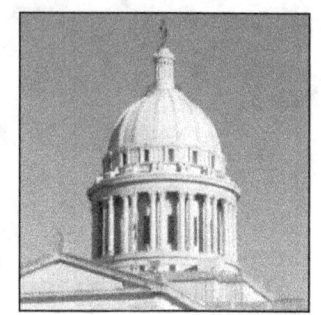

The Oklahoma Capitol dome was added to the existing building in 2002.

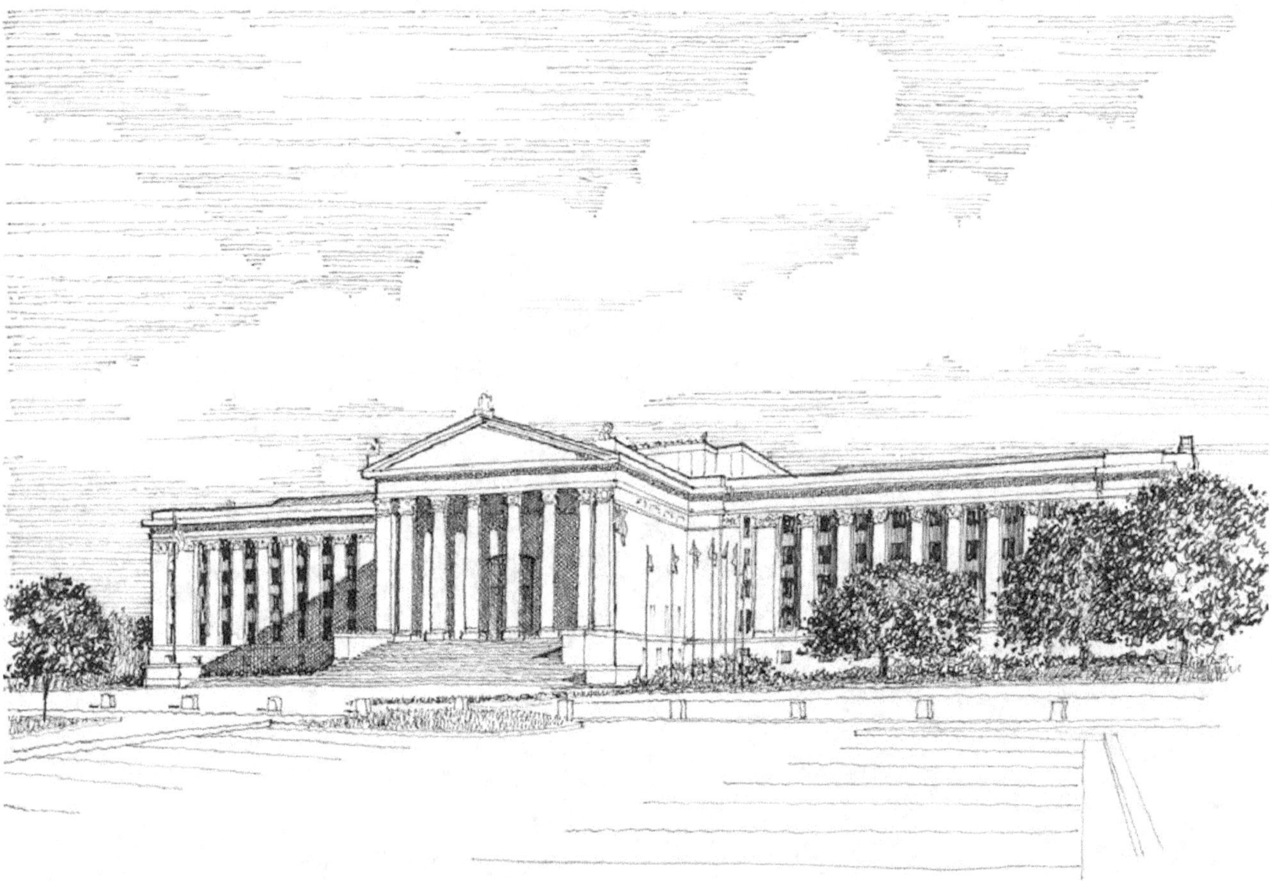

Oklahoma State Capitol Building, South Facade, Oklahoma City, Oklahoma

The state capitol of Oklahoma is located at the intersection of Lincoln and 23rd Streets. When the state capital was moved from the town of Guthrie to Oklahoma City in 1910, the original capitol was in the Lee Huckins Hotel. Construction began on the capitol building, seen here, in 1914. At one time there were twenty-eight oil wells working on the capitol lawns. In 2002, a dome, planned in the original scheme but not built, was finally constructed.

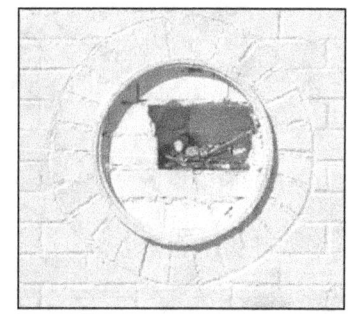

The circular portal set into the "fireplace" was a distinctive design feature on these type of stations.

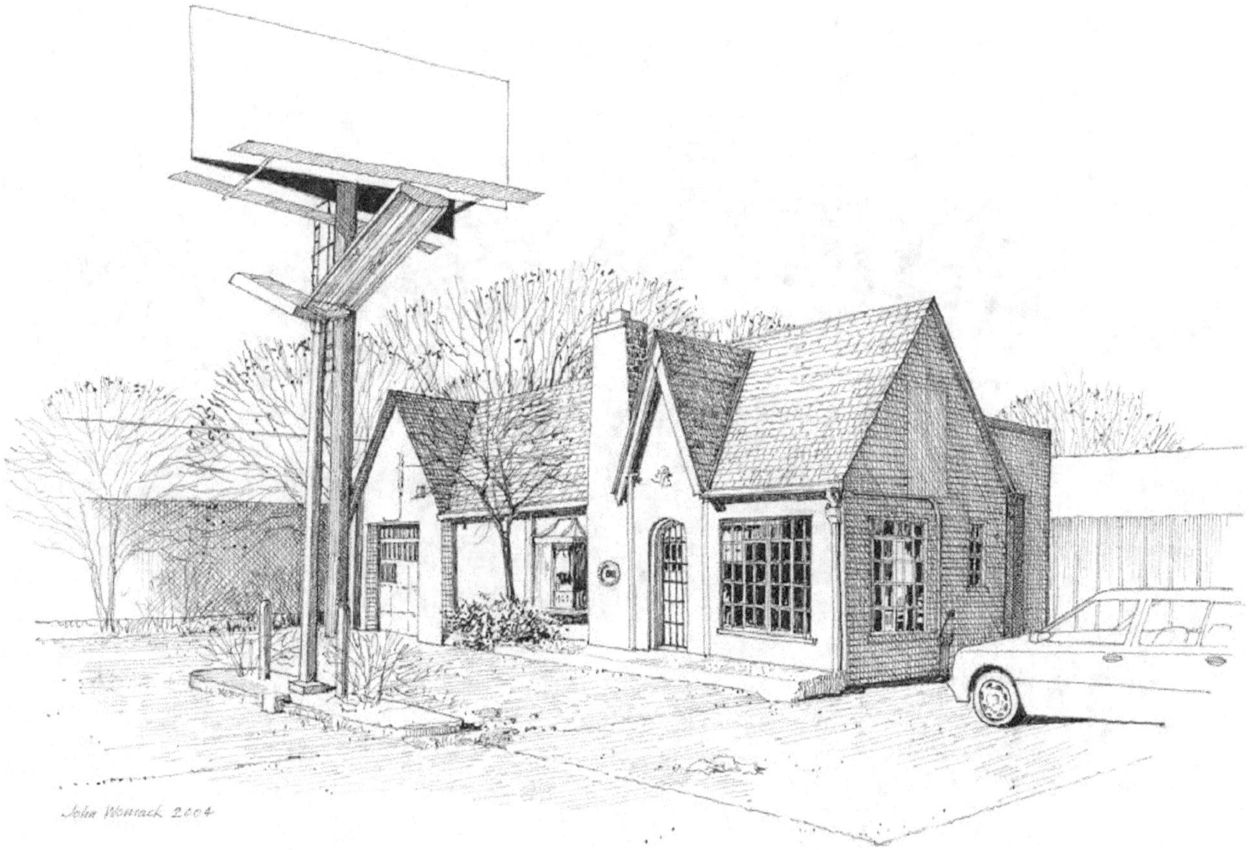

Phillips 66 "Cottage-style" Service Station, Oklahoma City, Oklahoma

This is another well-preserved cottage station. The gabled entry to the garage area is interesting in how it differs from the station in Chandler Oklahoma, seen on page 81. The gabled garage section seen here gives every indication of being the original design, whereas the garage portion of the station in Chandler appears to be either a later addition or a later alteration (taller and wider—and not necessarily in sync with the cottage style).

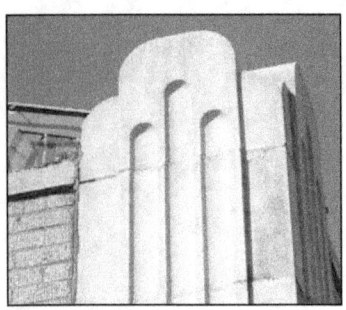

The Art Deco styled pylons at Cheever's are constructed of carefully carved limestone blocks.

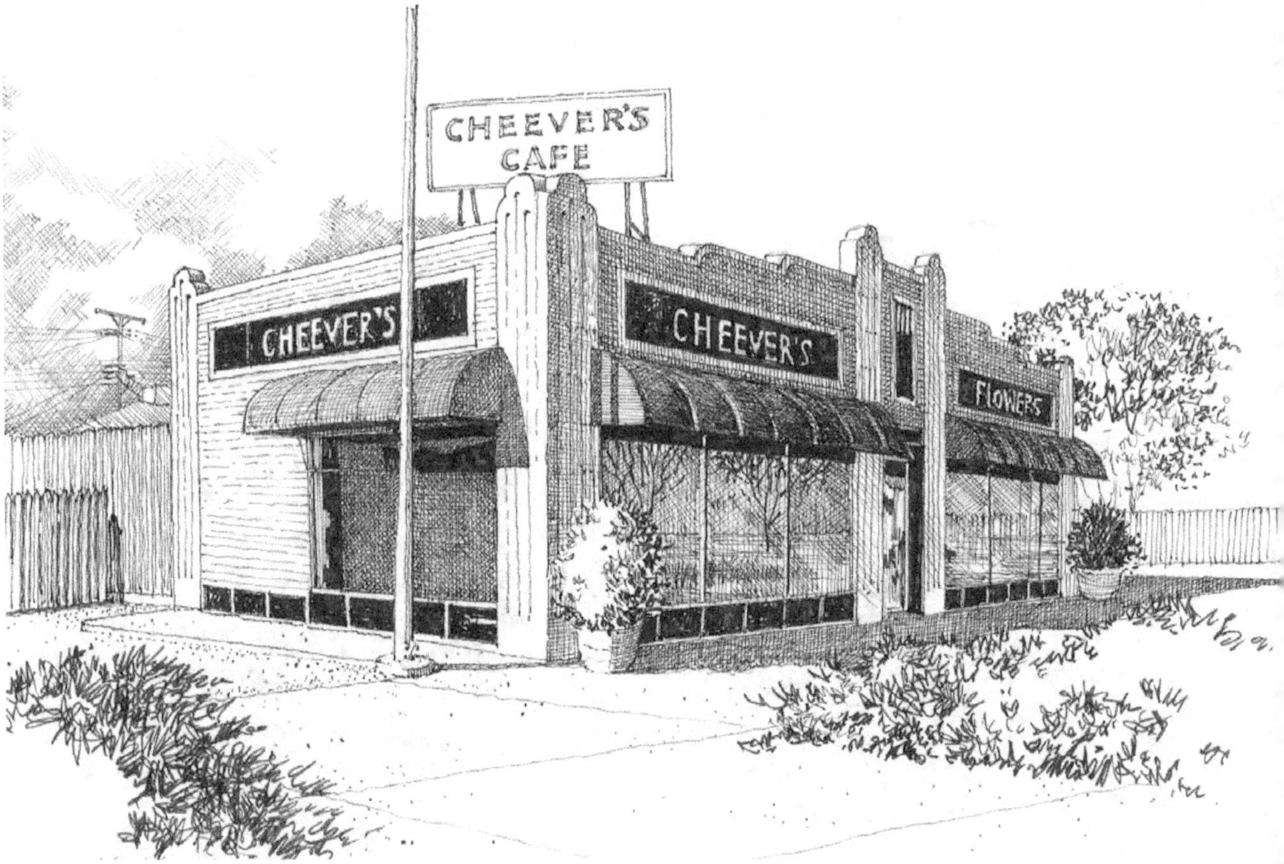

Cheever's Flower Shop, Oklahoma City, Oklahoma

Originally a flower shop, Cheever's, located on 23rd Street, is now a cafe. The building has several distinctive Art Deco, or Moderne, features on the exterior and utilizes panels of black "Vitrolite," a type of colored opaque structural glass that was developed in 1916 by Libby-Owens-Ford. Cheever's sits near the double gabled Phillips 66 cottage station seen on the previous page.

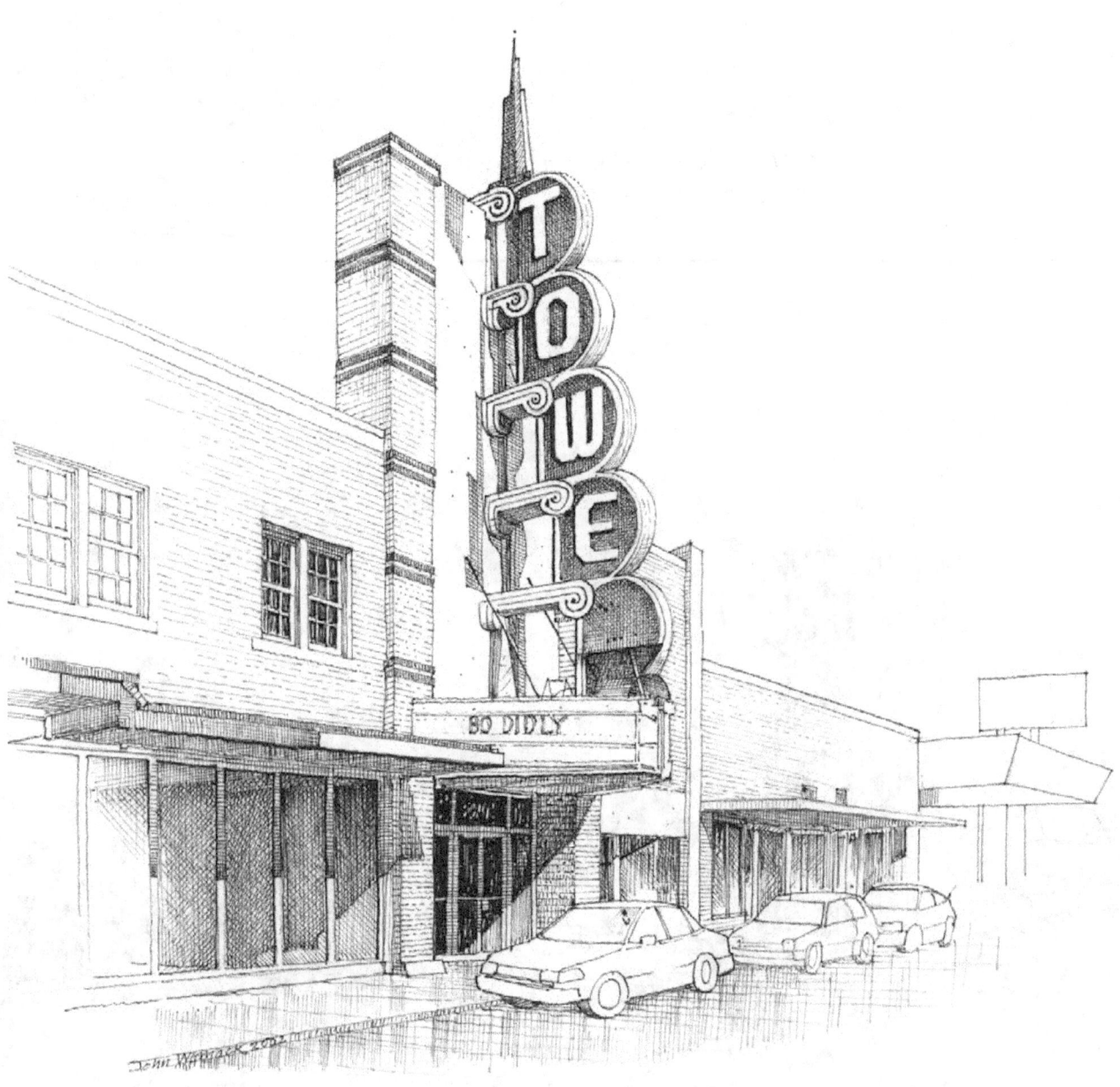

Tower Cinema, Oklahoma City, Oklahoma

From 1926 to 1954, Route 66 shared pavement with Oklahoma City's 23rd Street. This stretch of road is still rich with buildings that relay the spirit of the Mother Road. The Tower Cinema's sign is a proud remnant of the days when neighborhood movie houses had bright neon lights and bold design features that beckoned to all that might be interested in taking in a movie. The Tower Theater is gradually succumbing to age and neglect.

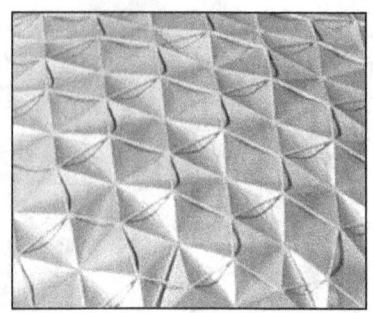

The Gold Dome is a "geodesic" structure, a type of building system advocated in the 1960s by the architect/scientist, Buckminster Fuller.

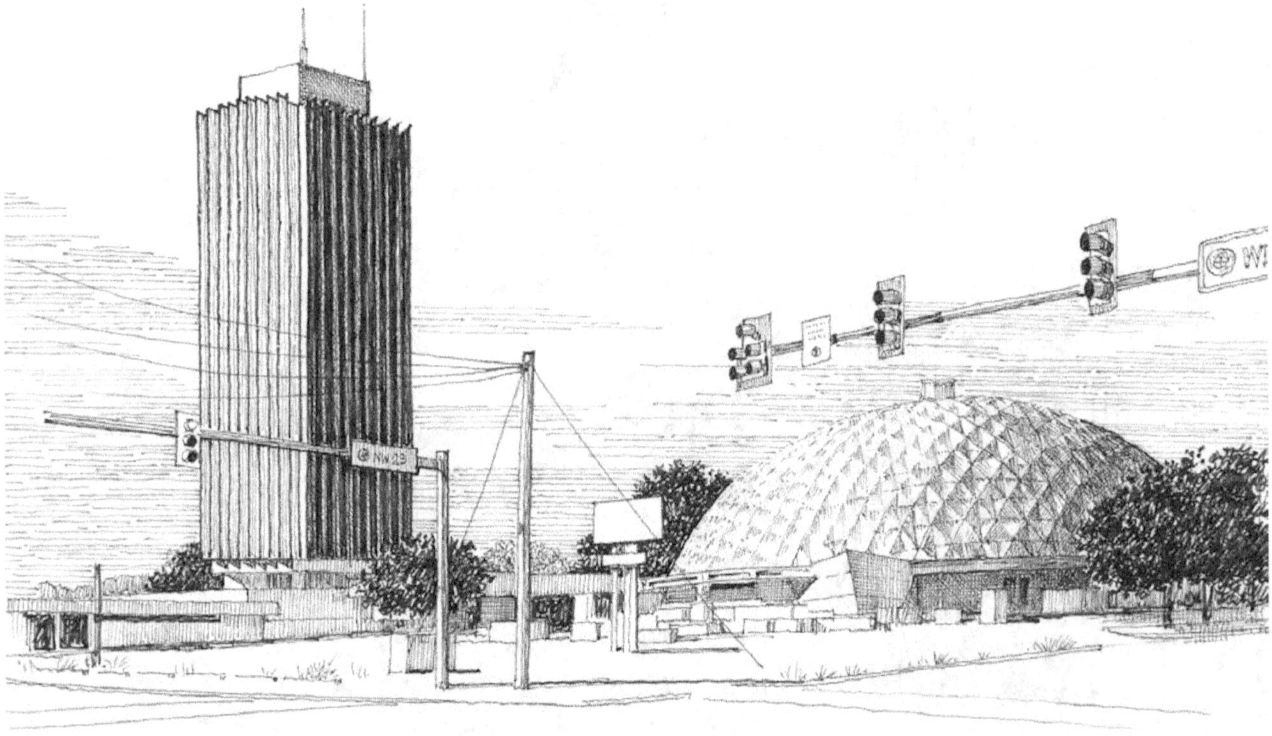

"Gold Dome" Bank Building and Tower, Oklahoma City, Oklahoma

Built in 1958, the domed bank building and neighboring office tower were very much in the "spirit" of Route 66 in their unconventional forms and color schemes. The bank's dome and the tower's vertical sunshade fins were made of gold anodized aluminum which imparted a pronounced golden glow in the landscape. For a number of years, the dome was in danger of being torn down but several concerned people fought and won the battle to save the building.

At the corner of 23rd Street and May Avenue, where Route 66 turns north, stands William H. Taft Junior High School (now a middle school). It is a magnificent example of Art Deco design—and for a school building, no less.

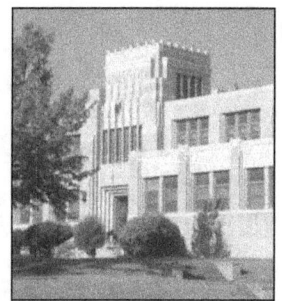

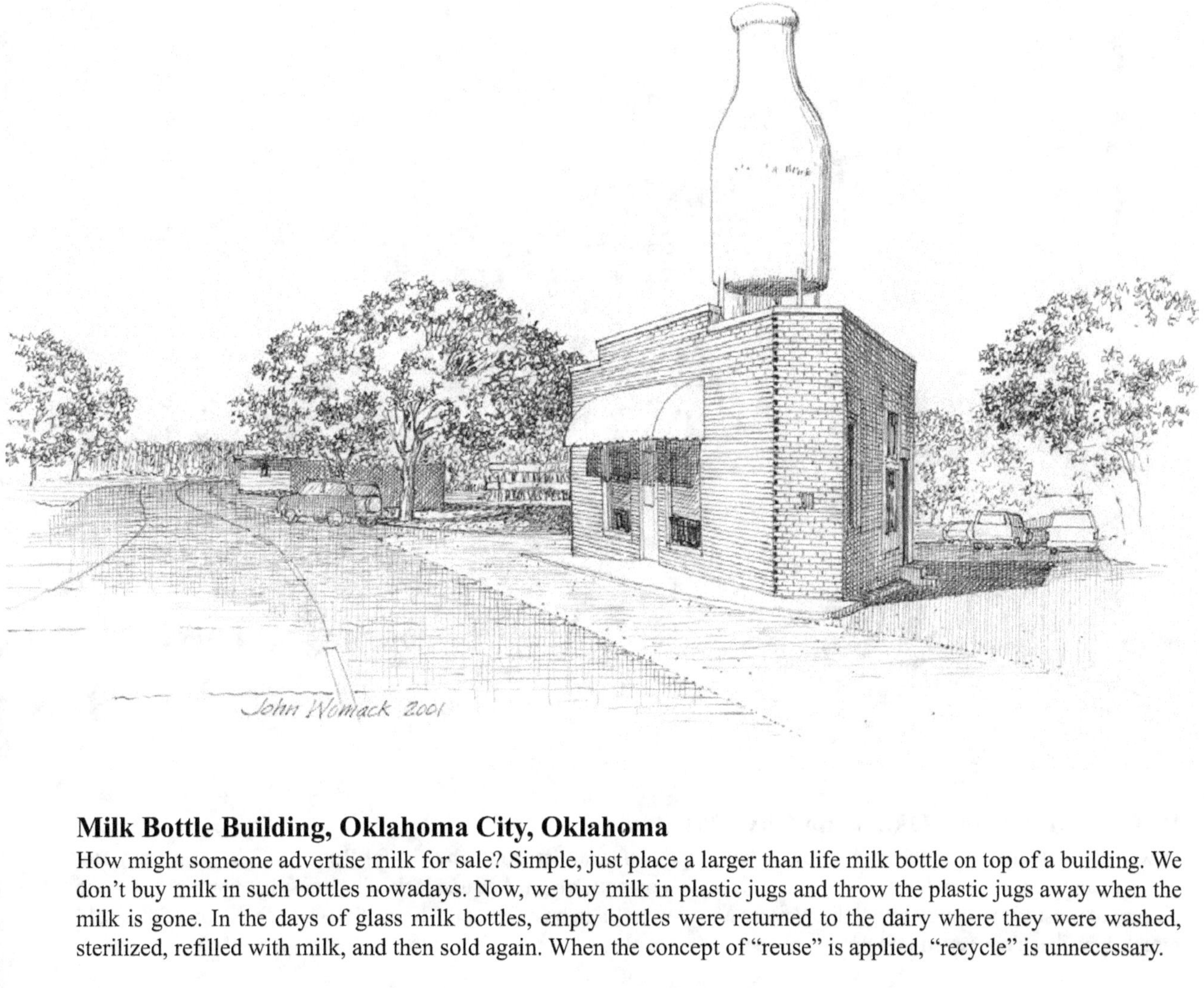

Milk Bottle Building, Oklahoma City, Oklahoma

How might someone advertise milk for sale? Simple, just place a larger than life milk bottle on top of a building. We don't buy milk in such bottles nowadays. Now, we buy milk in plastic jugs and throw the plastic jugs away when the milk is gone. In the days of glass milk bottles, empty bottles were returned to the dairy where they were washed, sterilized, refilled with milk, and then sold again. When the concept of "reuse" is applied, "recycle" is unnecessary.

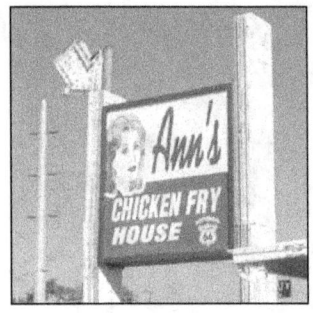

Planning where one would spend the night and locating a favorite restaurant were part of the Route 66 travel adventure.

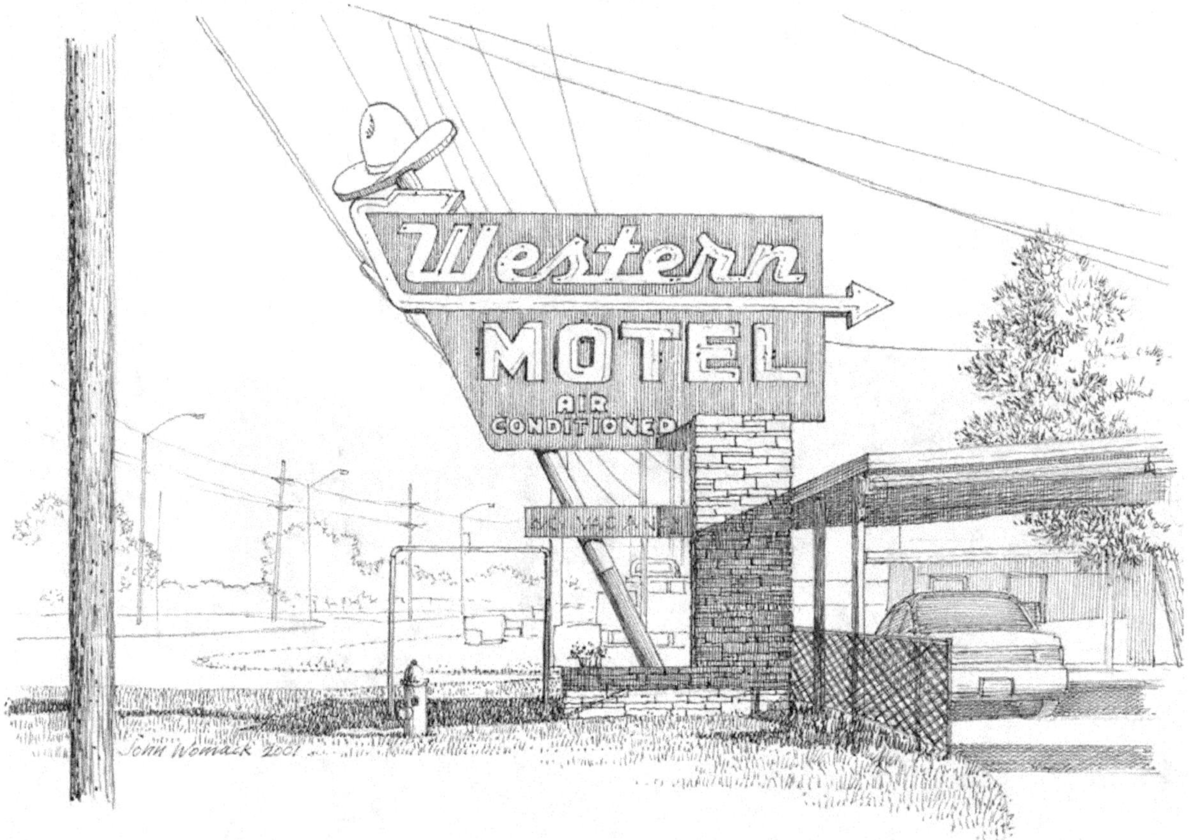

Western Motel Sign, Oklahoma City, Oklahoma

In western Oklahoma City there are a few remaining motels that date to the heyday of Route 66. The Western Motel was remembered by many for its distinctive cowboy hat on a stick sign. Age and lack of business has contributed to the closing of most of these motels, but the Western Motel was still in business at the time of this sketch. Many of these old motels have been converted into private residences—one was even converted into a correctional facility.

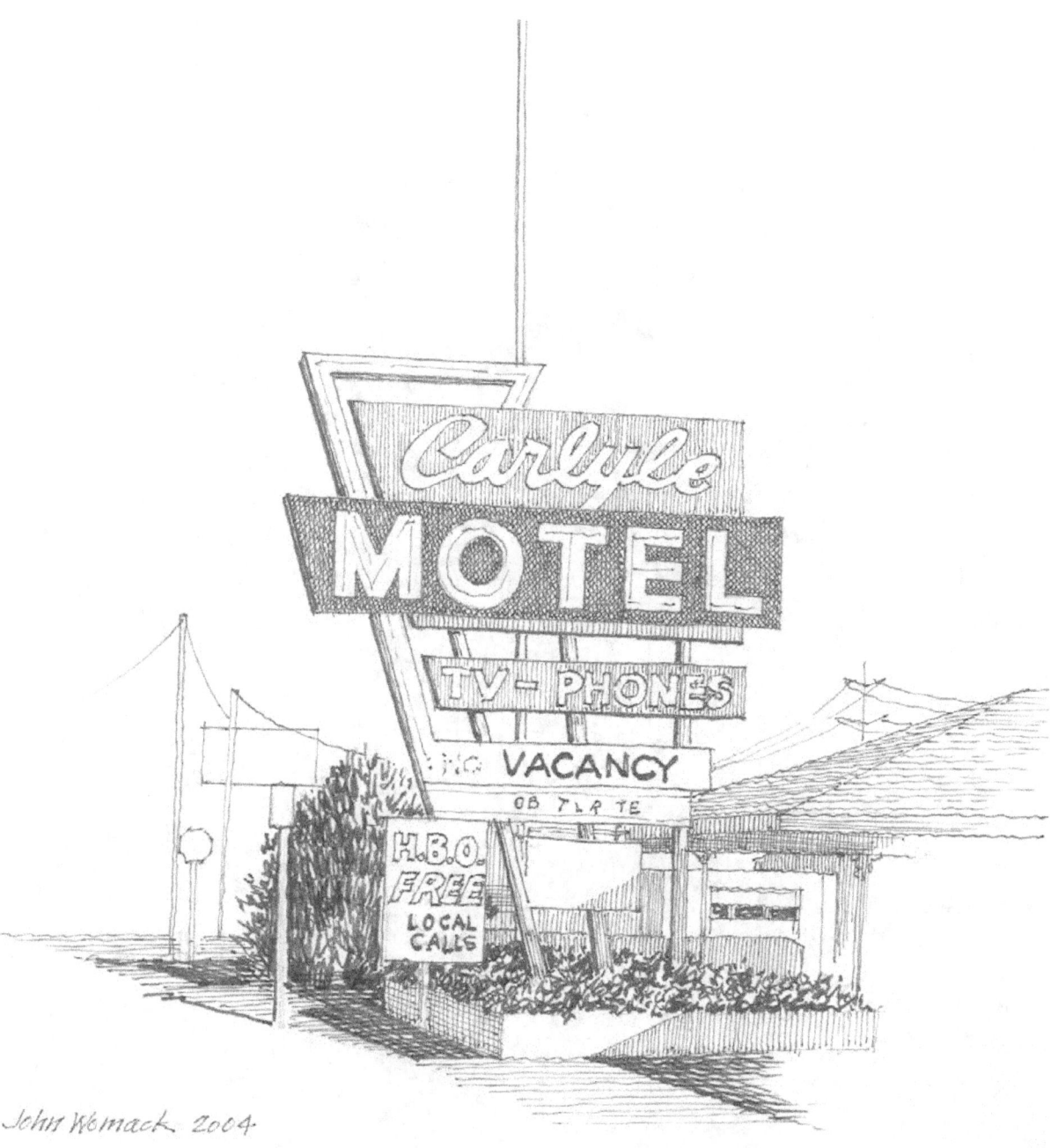

John Womack 2004

Carlyle Motel Sign, Oklahoma City, Oklahoma

Motel signs provide a glimpse into certain technologies that have developed over time and were important to the hospitality business. Here television and telephones were part of the original sign and were advertised for their obvious appeal to the highway traveler. Then came cable television as well as free local phone calls. As business declined motels struggled to keep their heads above the rising tides of financial deep water.

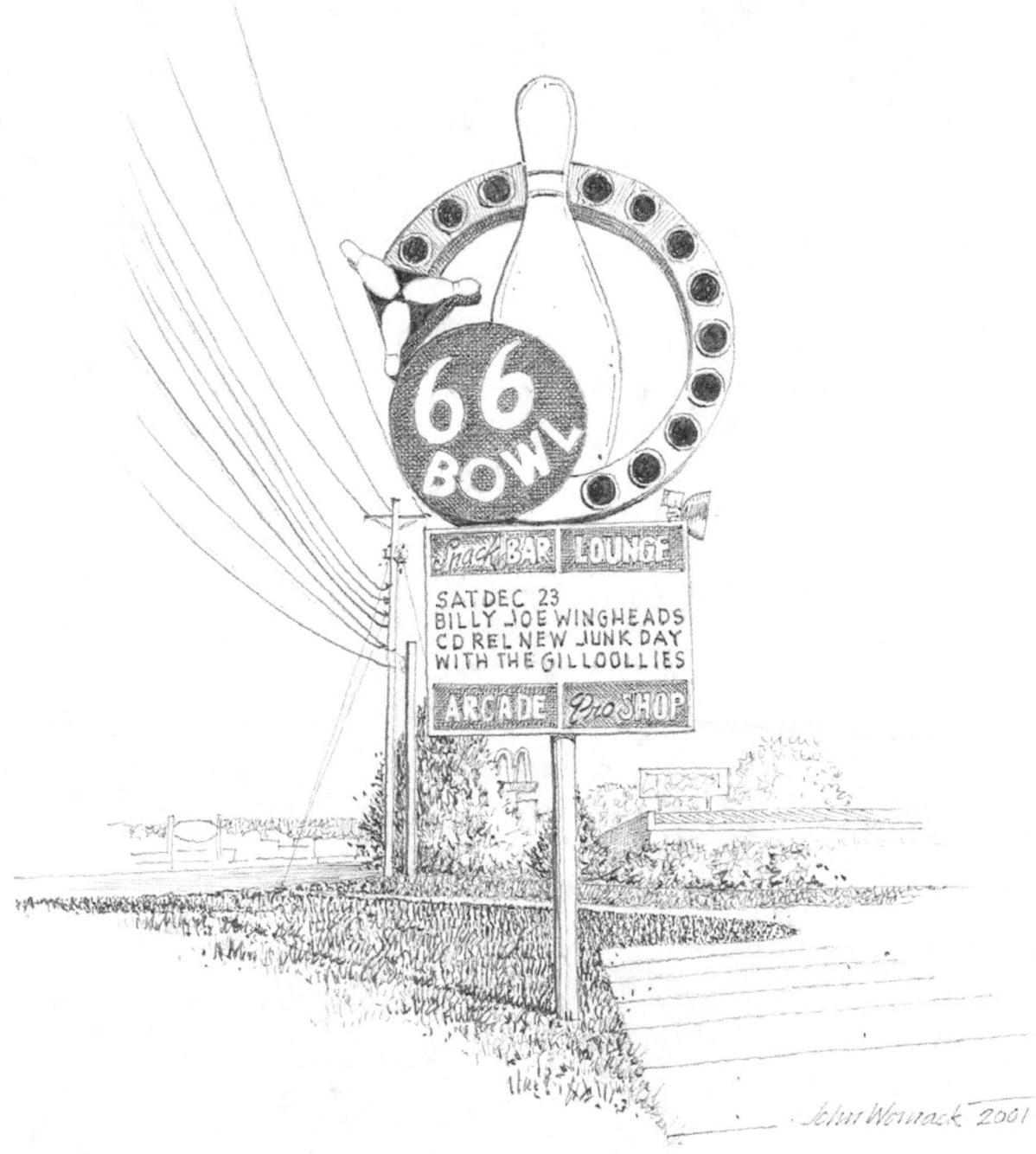

Sixty-Six Bowling Alley Sign, West Oklahoma City, Oklahoma

Signs along Route 66 are often exemplary examples of the sign maker's art—especially the neon lighted signs. This sign is particularly fun in how it depicts a bowling ball on a circular path. For sure, the lanes of this bowling alley were straight and true, but its circular sign offers a unique way of showing motion and the bowler's success by using sequential lighting that begins at the base of the bowling ball then spirals its way to where it knocks down the pins.

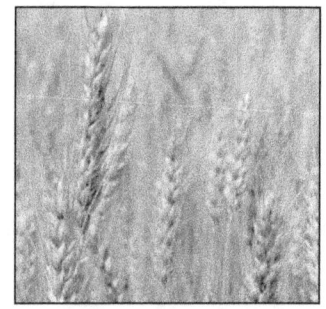

Oklahoma is a major wheat grower in the United States and grain storage silos are an integral part of the state's landscape.

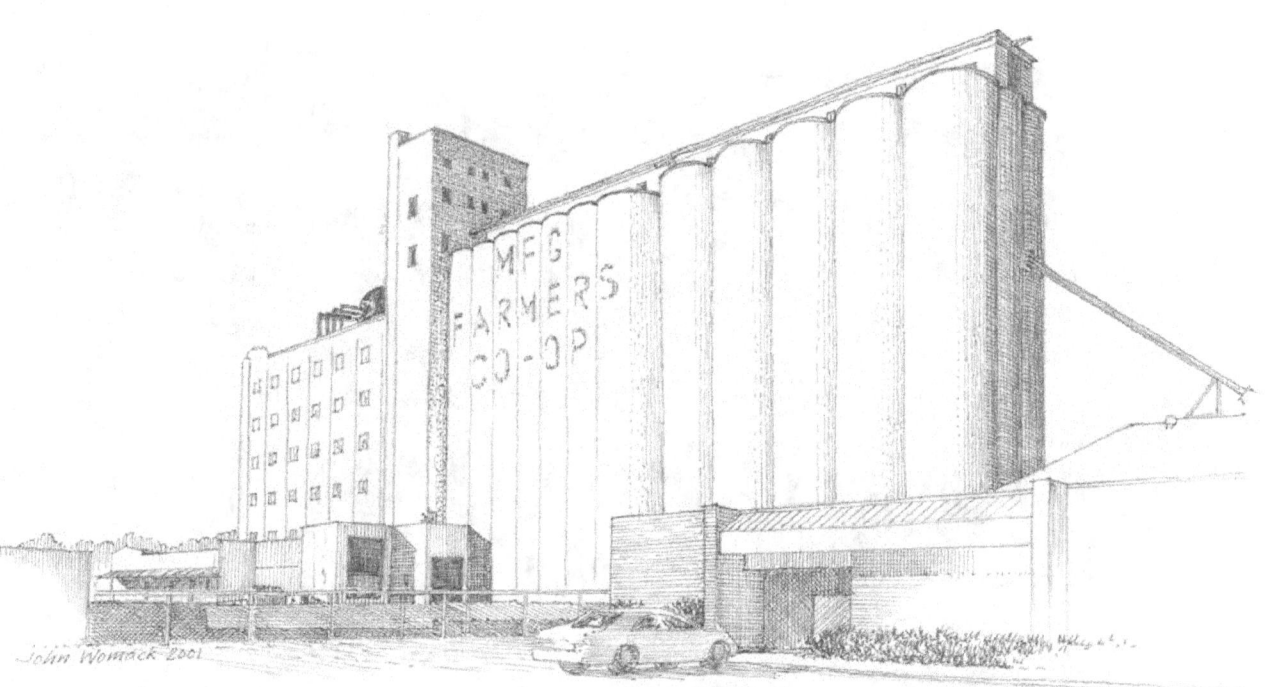

Grain Silo Elevator, Yukon, Oklahoma

Grain silos are immediate indicators that one is driving through agricultural land. This is one of two large grain elevators that flank Route 66 on the eastern edge of Yukon. The Swiss modernist architect, Le Corbusier, was greatly impressed by the grain silos he saw while touring the Midwestern regions of the United States. He saw them as true examples of how the functional resolution of specific problems can result in stunningly beautiful works of architecture.

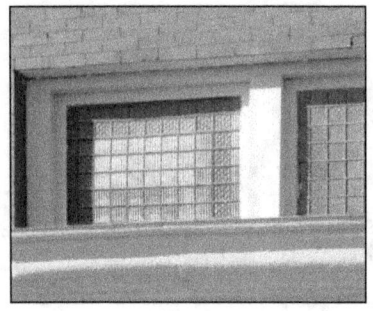

The ceilings of most of these early commercial buildings were originally covered in reflective metal panels. This surface would further amplify the light into the inner reaches of the store.

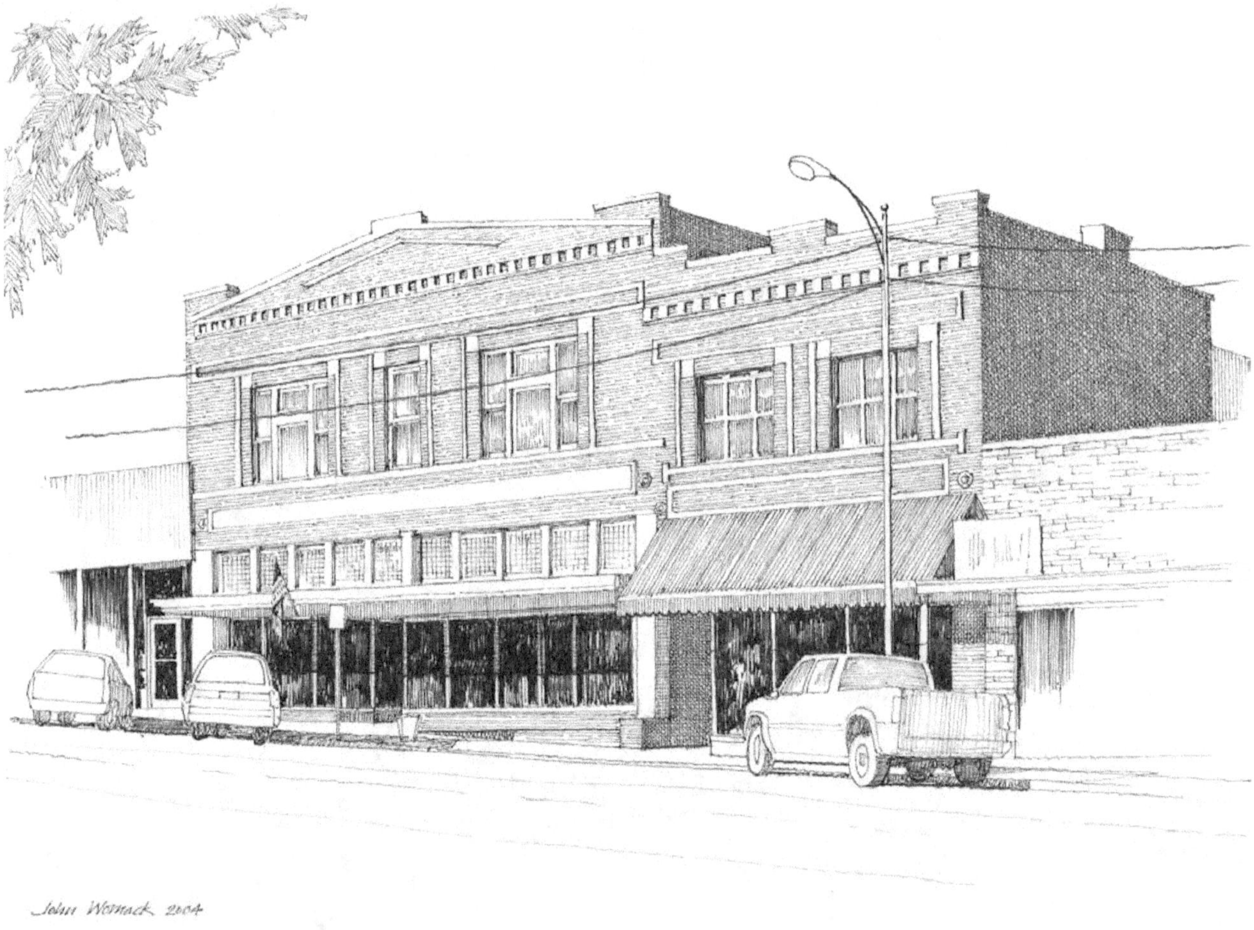

John Womack 2004

Downtown, Yukon, Oklahoma

Route 66 was often referred to as "America's Main Street," and in many Oklahoma towns the highway was, in fact, the town's main street. Yukon is one of these towns. This is a very well preserved commercial structure from the early 1900s. Still present in the transom above the display windows are the small, square, prismatic glass panels that brought natural light deep into the further recesses of the building. The brick detailing and construction is also exceptional.

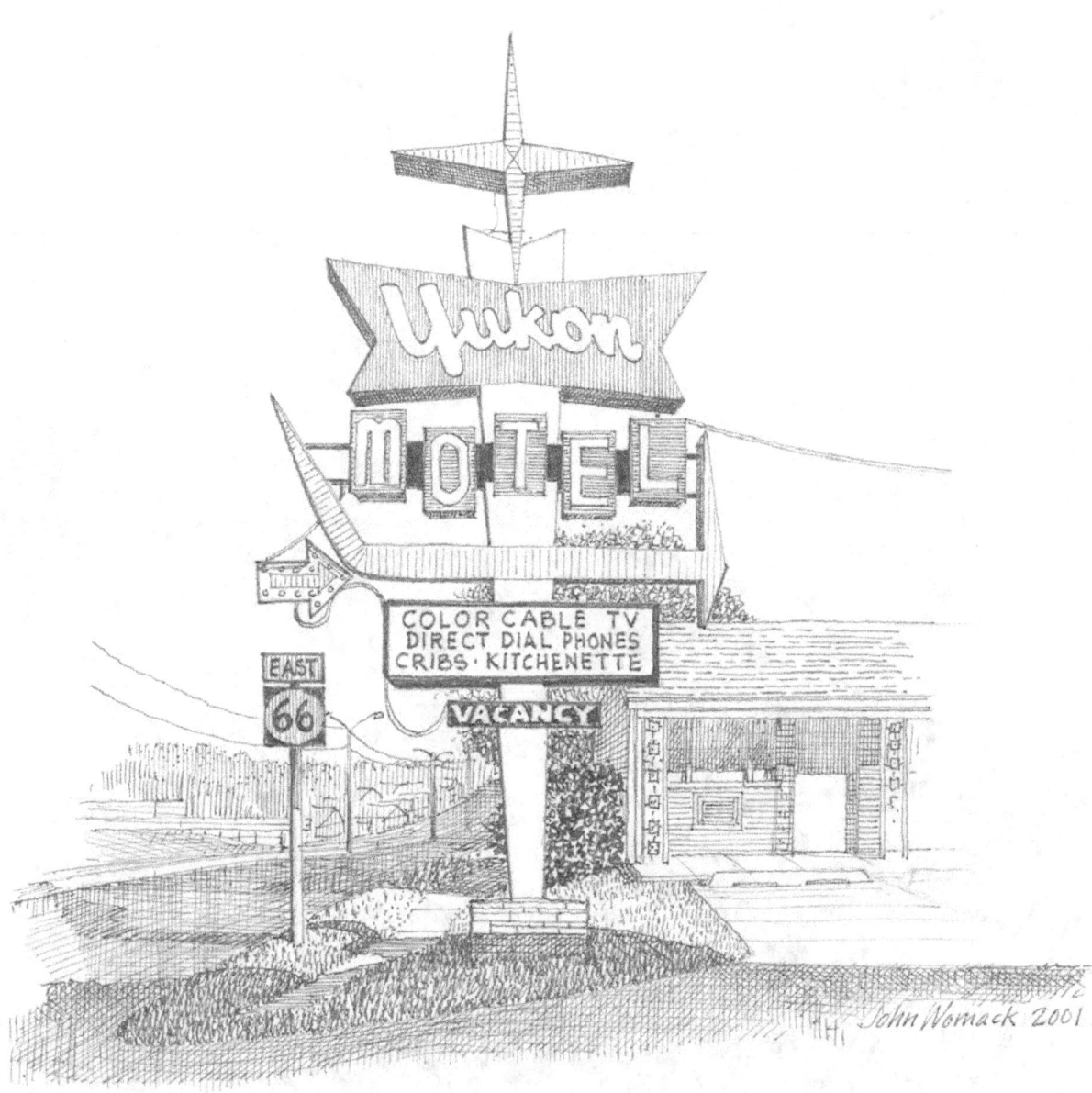

Yukon Motel Sign (removed), Yukon, Oklahoma

It is strange how fate sometimes seems to work opposite of one's desires, and this sign is a case in point. As mentioned in the introduction, this was one of my favorite signs on Route 66, but of all the signs I have studied, photographed, and sketched, this is the one sign that has been taken down and removed—and was replaced with a bland, generic sign of a national motel chain. It is rumored that the original sign was shipped to somewhere in Virginia.

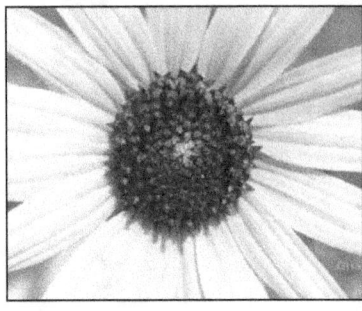

Sunflowers are so optimistic! They grow almost like a weed, often under harsh conditions. Their color and pattern continually reward our observation.

John Womack 2004

Barn, west of Yukon, Oklahoma

This is a classic prairie barn with fine lines and proportions. The barn began as a farm shelter, but in more recent times has contained several different businesses. At one time, windmills were a common sight along Route 66 as it ran through rural farming areas. Windmills began to die out in the 1950s with the availability of rural electric power. Today, with rising utility costs, windmills are making a comeback. Sunflowers are also a familiar western Oklahoma sight.

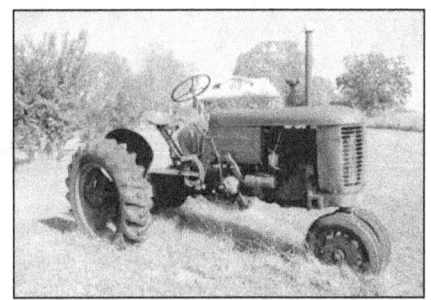

This old tractor, "put out to pasture," is like so many sights along Route 66—slowly rusting away, yet still provocative in form, color and history.

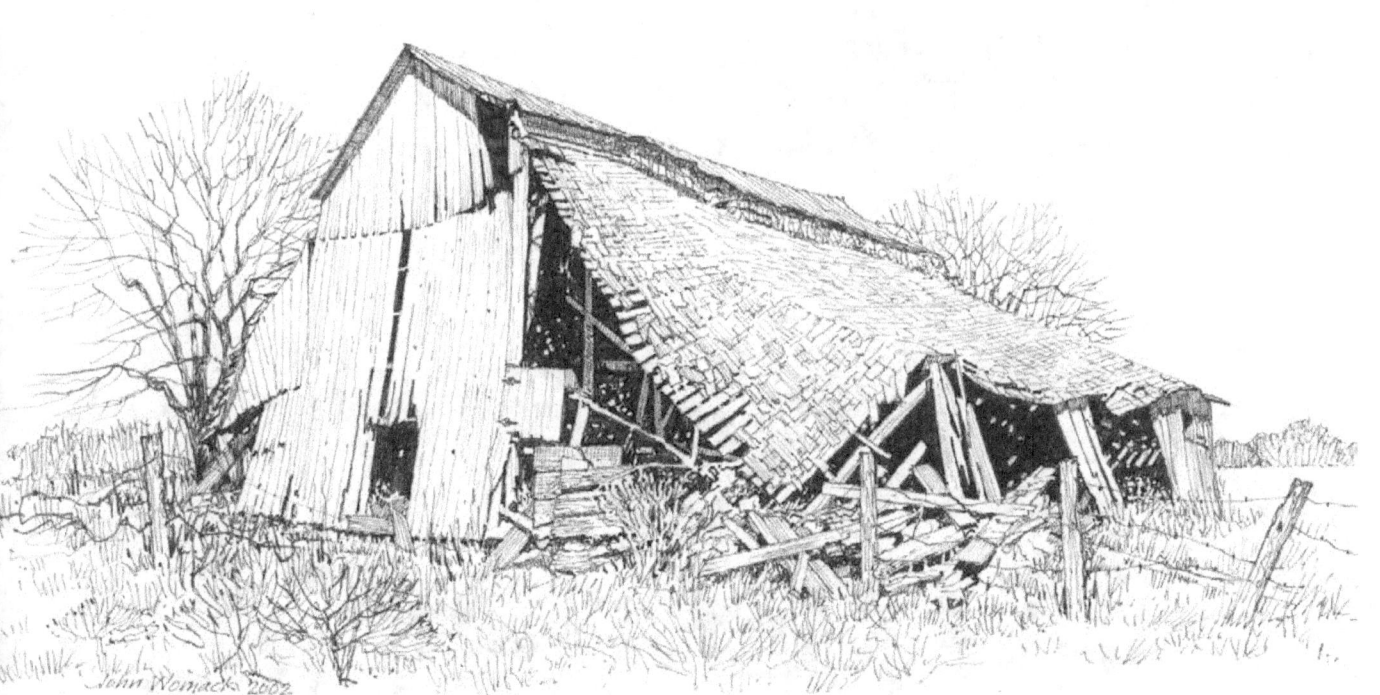

Decaying Barn (removed), east of El Reno, Oklahoma

A lot of people respond to old barns and can't help but admire their picturesque or nostalgic qualities. As barns slowly decay, they evoke a certain kind of mystery. Such ruins develop a marvelous patina of age and complex texture accented by grayed, broken-wood siding, scattered bits of yellowed stone masonry, bits and pieces of weathered wood shingles— all intermingled in twisted wire fencing, wild prairie weeds, and rich deep-green grasses.

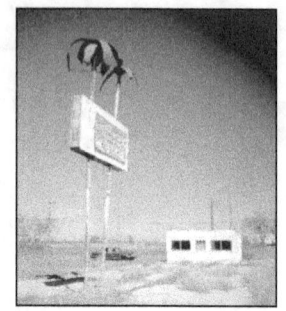

El Reno's old Oasis Drive-in Restaurant still sports its original palm leaf sign and the old food prep building. The sign was repainted in 2005.

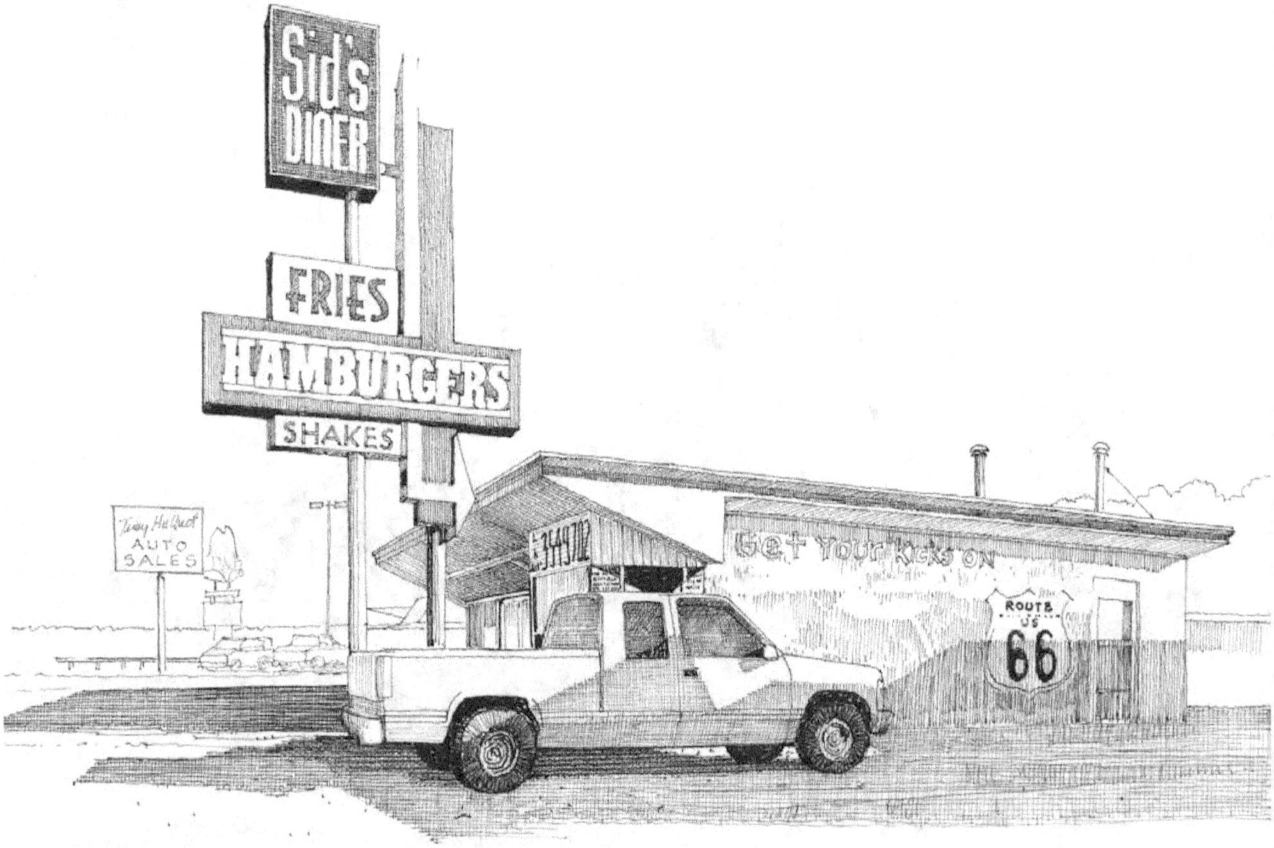

Sid's Diner, El Reno, Oklahoma

Following the establishment of Fort Reno in 1874, a town known as "Reno City" was started on the north bank of the North Canadian River. When the railroad decided to place its tracks on the south side of the river, the people of Reno City simply packed up, moved to the other side of the river, and named the town, El Reno. During this relocation, entire buildings (even a three-story hotel) were placed upon rollers and moved across the shallow river to the new town site.

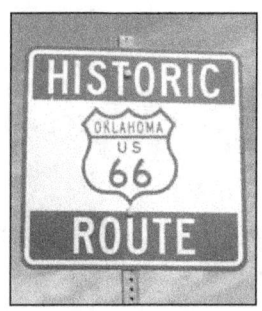

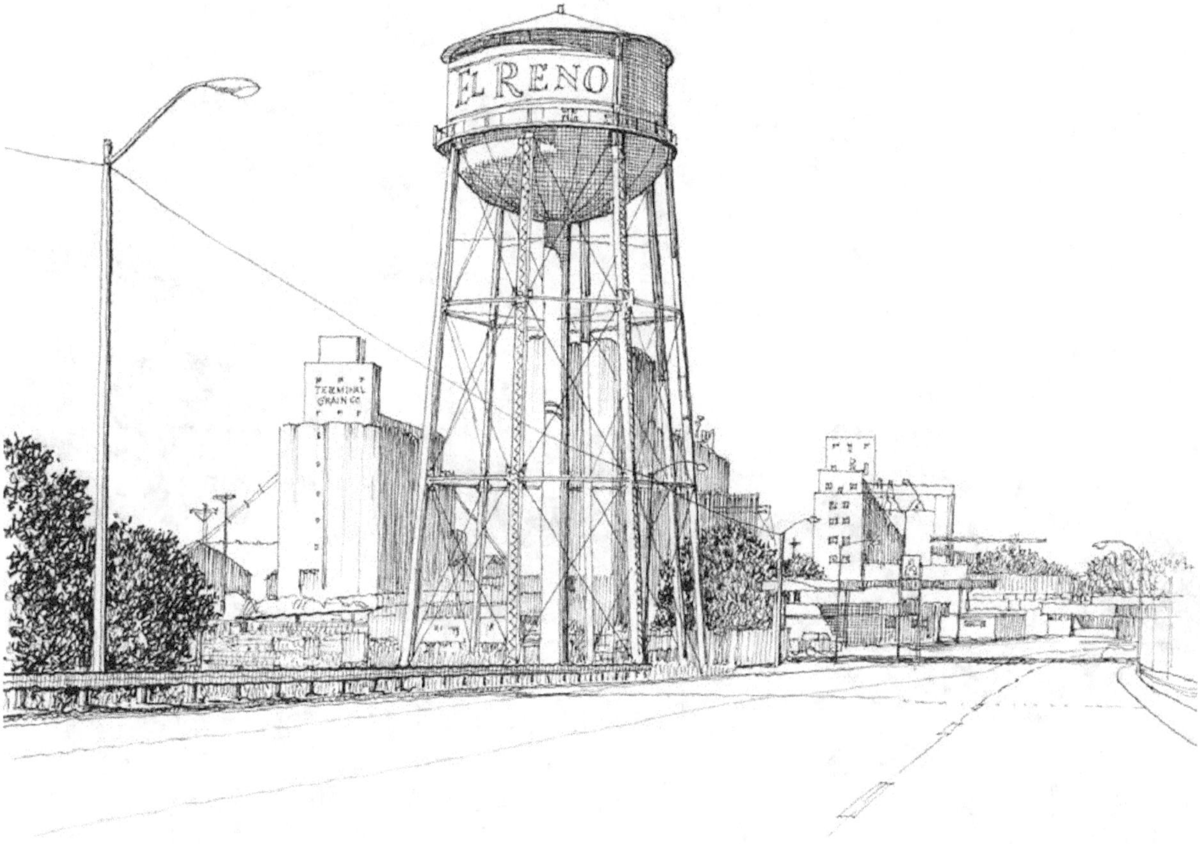

Water Tower, El Reno, Oklahoma

When entering El Reno, the highway traveler is presented with an impressive view of the water tower and several grain elevators, all painted white. Against a blue sky, the various structures glisten in the sunlight and give the impression of a modern metropolis in the making. The water tower, with its height, size, and closeness to the highway, creates a strong sense of entry into the city. Many water towers became prominent landmarks along Route 66.

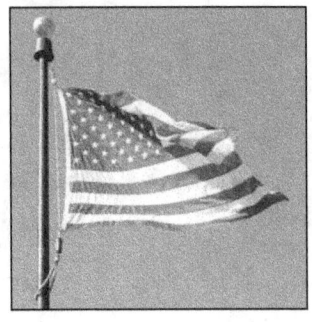

Flags have always fascinated me and none more so than "Old Glory." It is a beautiful design and represents profoundly the idea of a country that thrives in its peoples' diversity and the ideas they embrace.

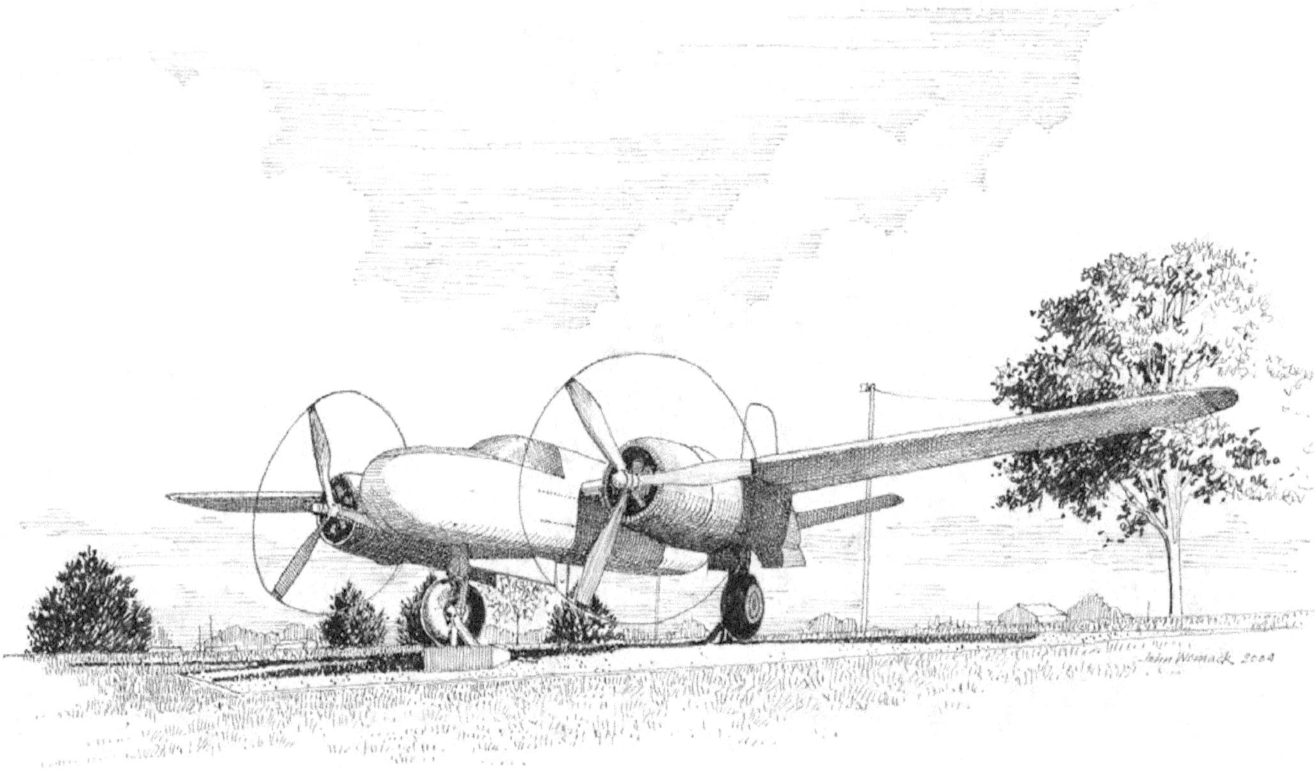

Douglas A-26 Invader, Veterans of Foreign Wars Hall, El Reno, Oklahoma

This relic from World War II (A-26s also flew in Korea and Vietnam) sits in front of the V.F.W. Hall on a rise of land above Route 66. I don't know how long it has been there, but it was 30 years ago when I first saw and admired it! Airplanes are fascinating—especially the war birds. To me, they evoke wonder in their design and engineering and also shear awe in the bravery and courage of the pilots and crew who flew them.

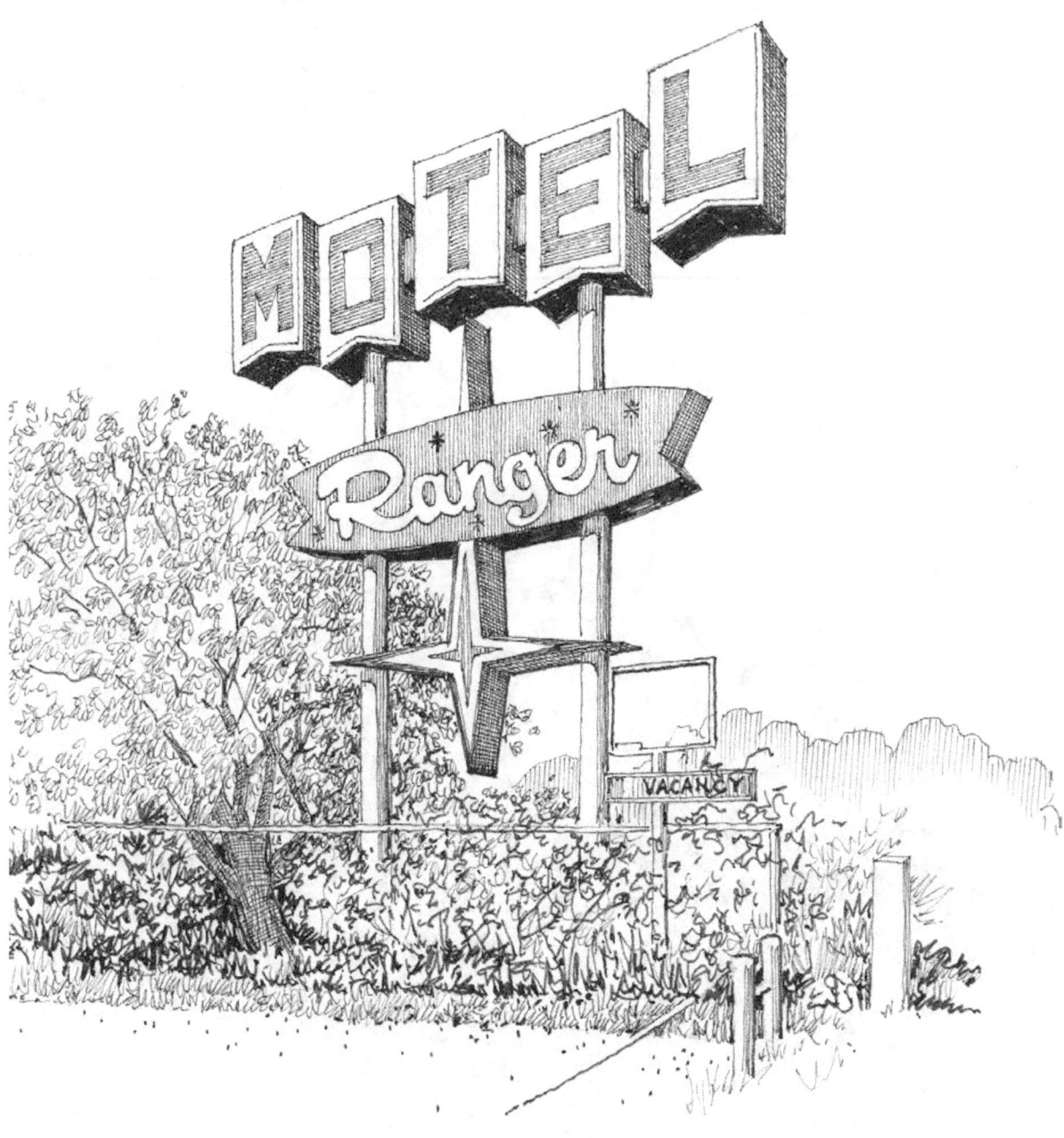

Ranger Motel sign, El Reno, Oklahoma

El Reno has many surviving Route 66 artifacts, though many are showing the effects of time. I suppose that is why so many scenes from this town appear in this study. There are multiple reasons why such sights survive. Ironically, survival is sometimes a simple case of forgetfulness. We can easily forget how important some things were in our past, especially if that past has somehow lost its viability. Sadly, we often rediscover the value of such things too late.

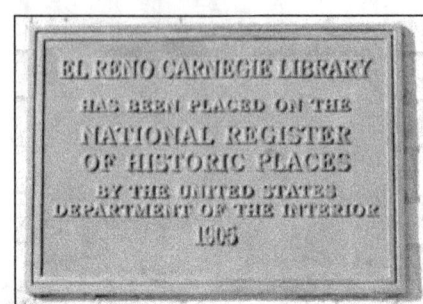

The El Reno-Carnegie Public Library is another building along Route 66 that has been named to the National Register of Historic Places.

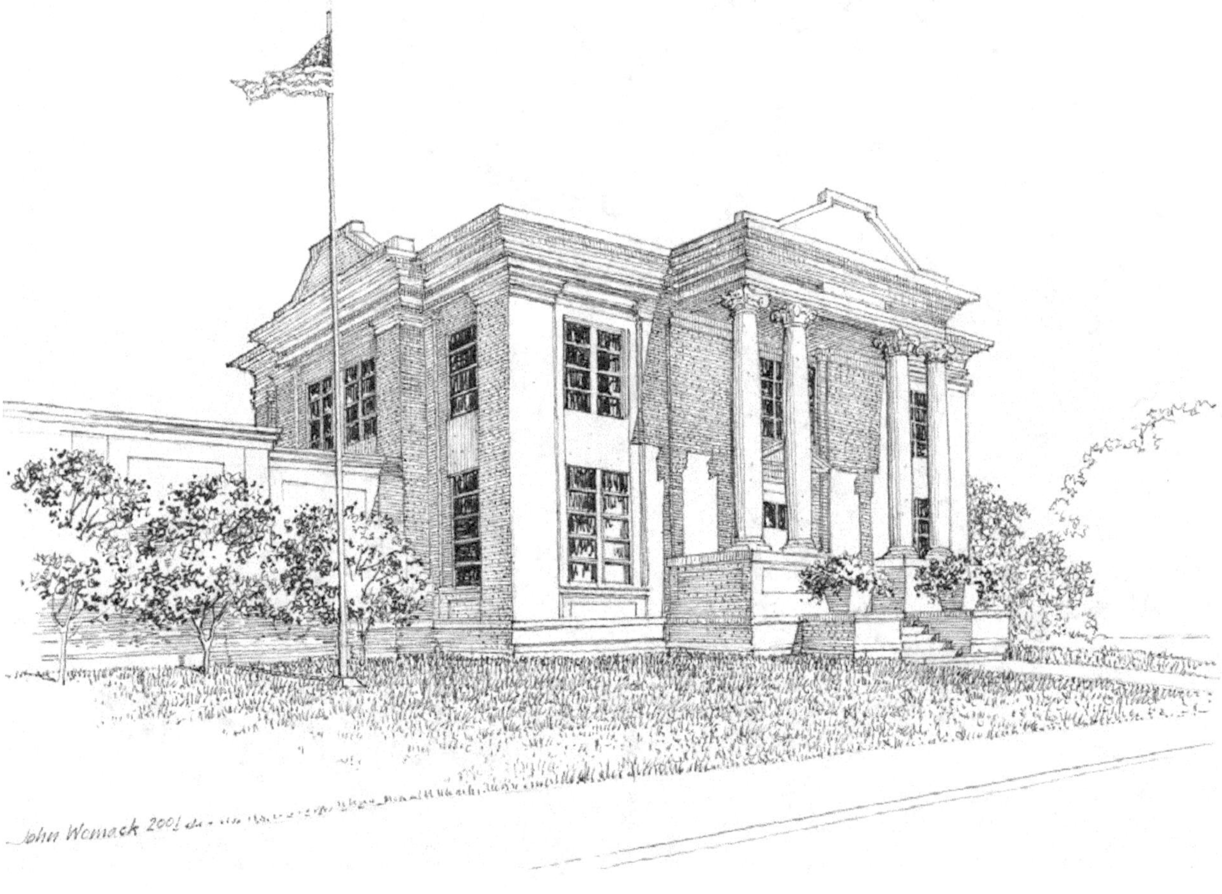

El Reno-Carnegie Public Library, El Reno, Oklahoma

No one can deny the appeal of such simple, refined elegance as displayed in this building. It is beautifully proportioned and beautifully crafted of fine yet humble materials. It is everything we might—or should—want in any building we might build, at any time in history. There is a saying, "We are what we build." We might also add to this, "We are what we preserve." Buildings speak directly, and openly, of our most important values and beliefs.

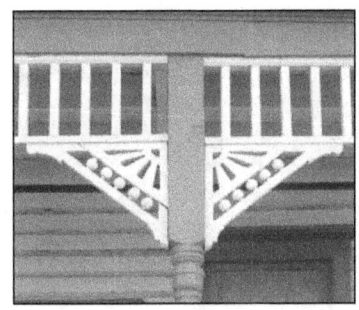

Detail of the intricate carving and detail work of a column capital on the El Reno Hotel.

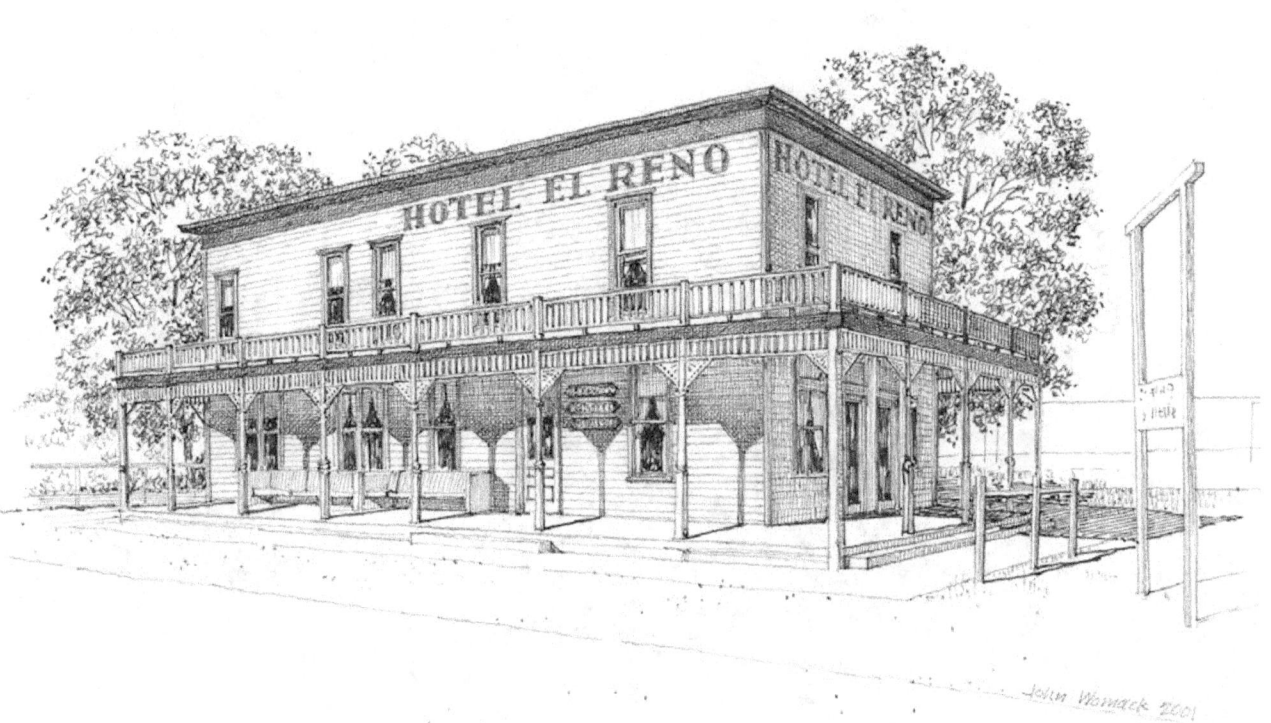

El Reno Hotel, El Reno, Oklahoma

El Reno has a fascinating history beginning with the founding of Fort Reno in 1874. The fort was established to protect the Cheyenne and Arapaho people from encroachment by unscrupulous white traders and advantage seekers. This hotel is an authentic remnant from those days of the Old West, and I find it compelling in its form, materials, and details of construction. The El Reno Hotel is located in the city's historical district near the original train station.

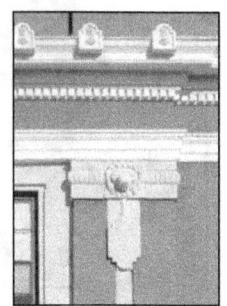

East of the boarding house below and the El Reno Hotel is a brick building that was also originally a hotel. It now houses El Reno's Senior Center. The building is beautifully detailed.

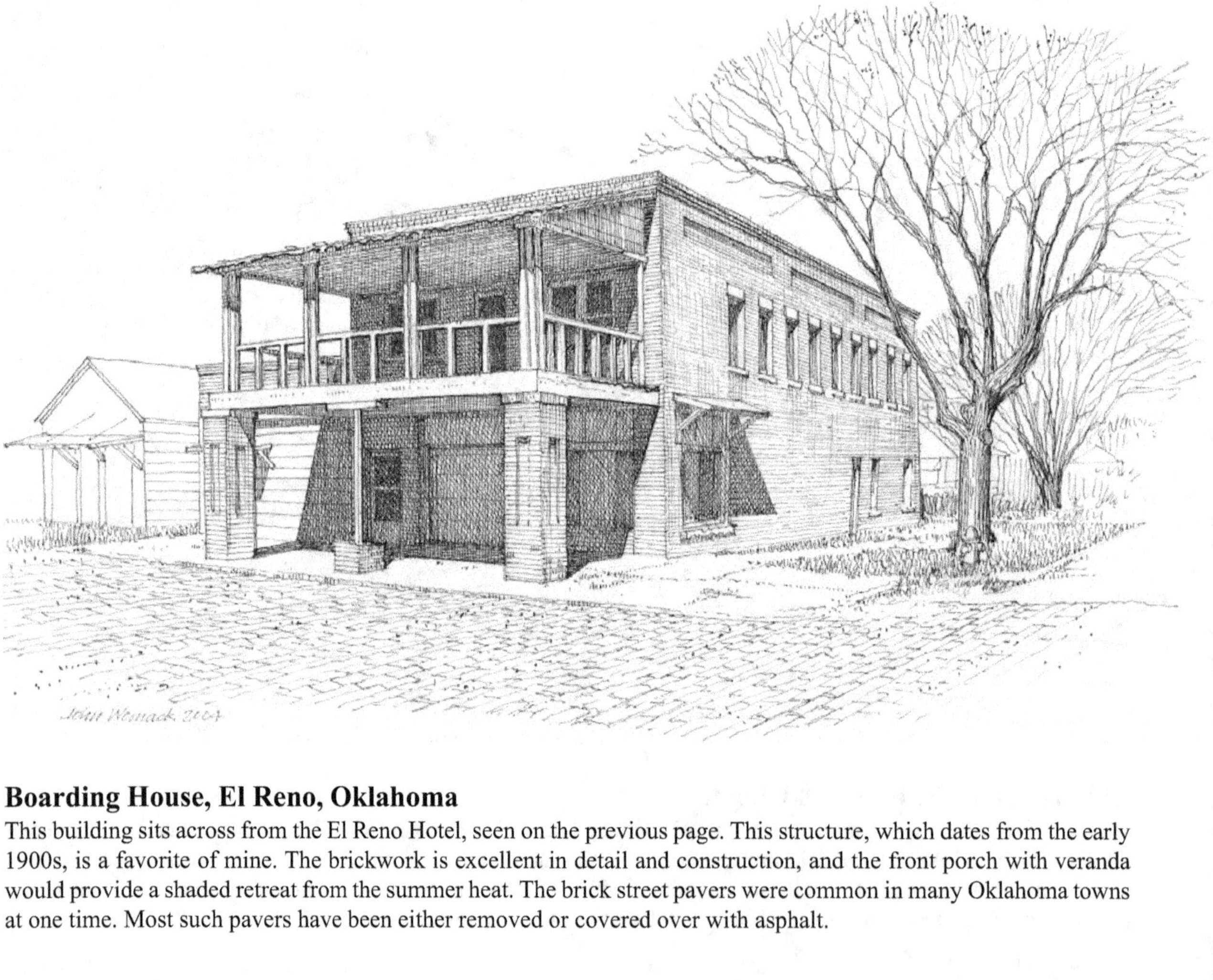

Boarding House, El Reno, Oklahoma

This building sits across from the El Reno Hotel, seen on the previous page. This structure, which dates from the early 1900s, is a favorite of mine. The brickwork is excellent in detail and construction, and the front porch with veranda would provide a shaded retreat from the summer heat. The brick street pavers were common in many Oklahoma towns at one time. Most such pavers have been either removed or covered over with asphalt.

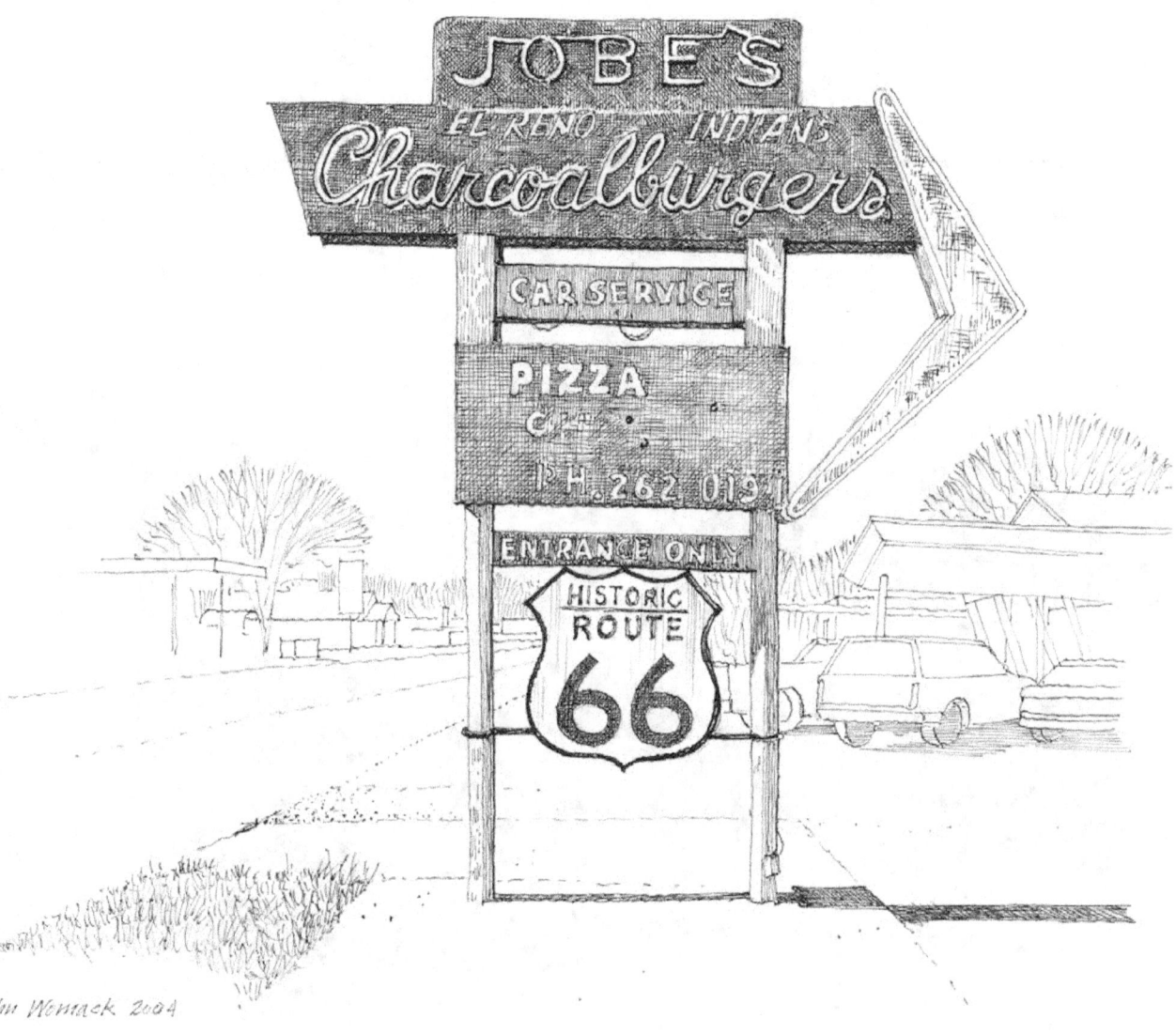

Jobe's Drive-in sign (now altered), El Reno, Oklahoma

After World War II, America quickly developed its love affair with the car. During the 1950s, drive-in restaurants became a staple in just about every American town and invariably, a hangout spot for young adults. Here, Jobe's sign works like a motel sign. Being located near the edge of the highway, oncoming travelers would get an early enticement to stop and eat. The original Jobe's sign, seen here, was removed in 2004 and replaced with a new similar sign.

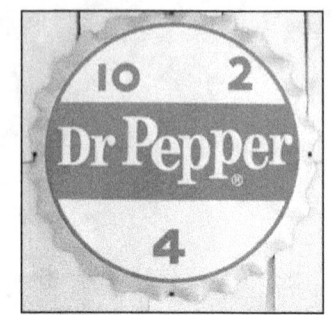

In 2005, the old drive-in restaurant was remodeled into a barber shop and now no longer resembles what is seen below.

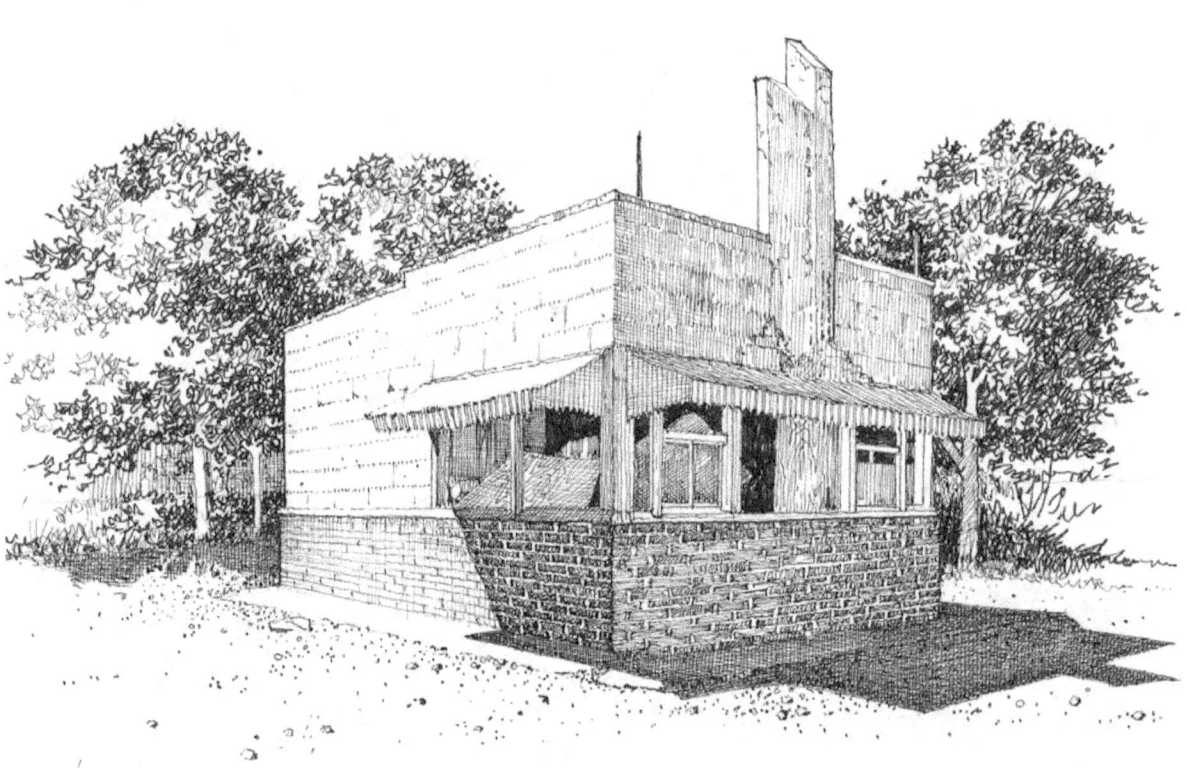

Deserted Drive-In Food Stand, El Reno, Oklahoma

When I was a kid, I called every drive-in, quick-serve hamburger joint a "Dairy Queen," maybe because the place my family frequented back then was indeed a Dairy Queen. There are no signs, or messages, on this building to identify what its name was originally. Such places as this have certainly gone by the wayside for the most part. Drive-in restaurants with push button order-coms are about the closest things to these places nowadays.

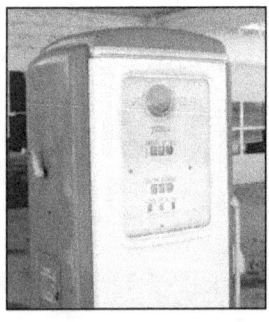

The old gas pumps are gradually disappearing except for those saved by collectors.

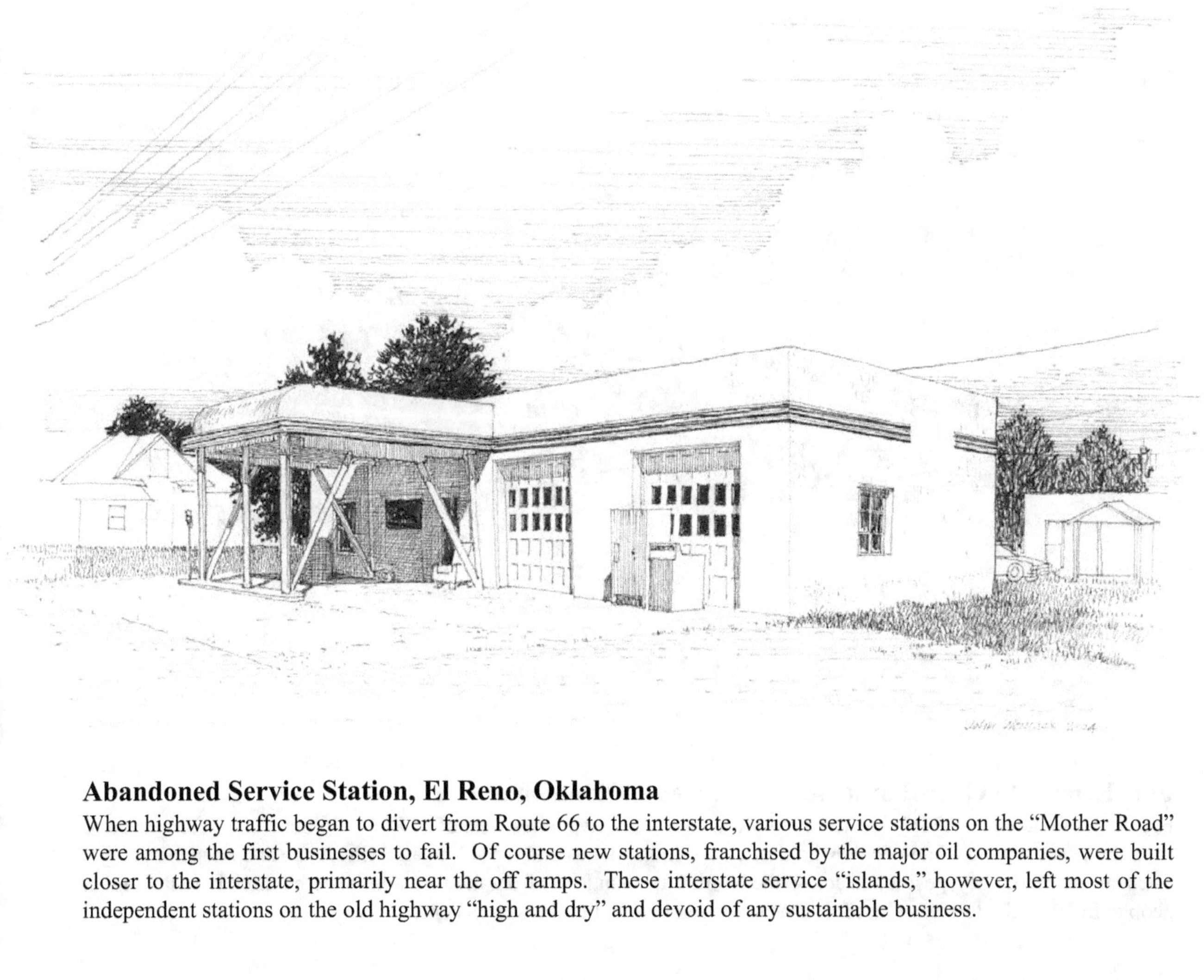

Abandoned Service Station, El Reno, Oklahoma

When highway traffic began to divert from Route 66 to the interstate, various service stations on the "Mother Road" were among the first businesses to fail. Of course new stations, franchised by the major oil companies, were built closer to the interstate, primarily near the off ramps. These interstate service "islands," however, left most of the independent stations on the old highway "high and dry" and devoid of any sustainable business.

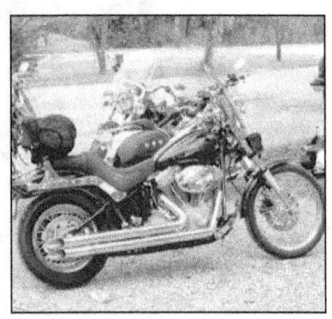

The strip of original concrete highway west of Fort Reno into Weatherford is a popular bike ride today.

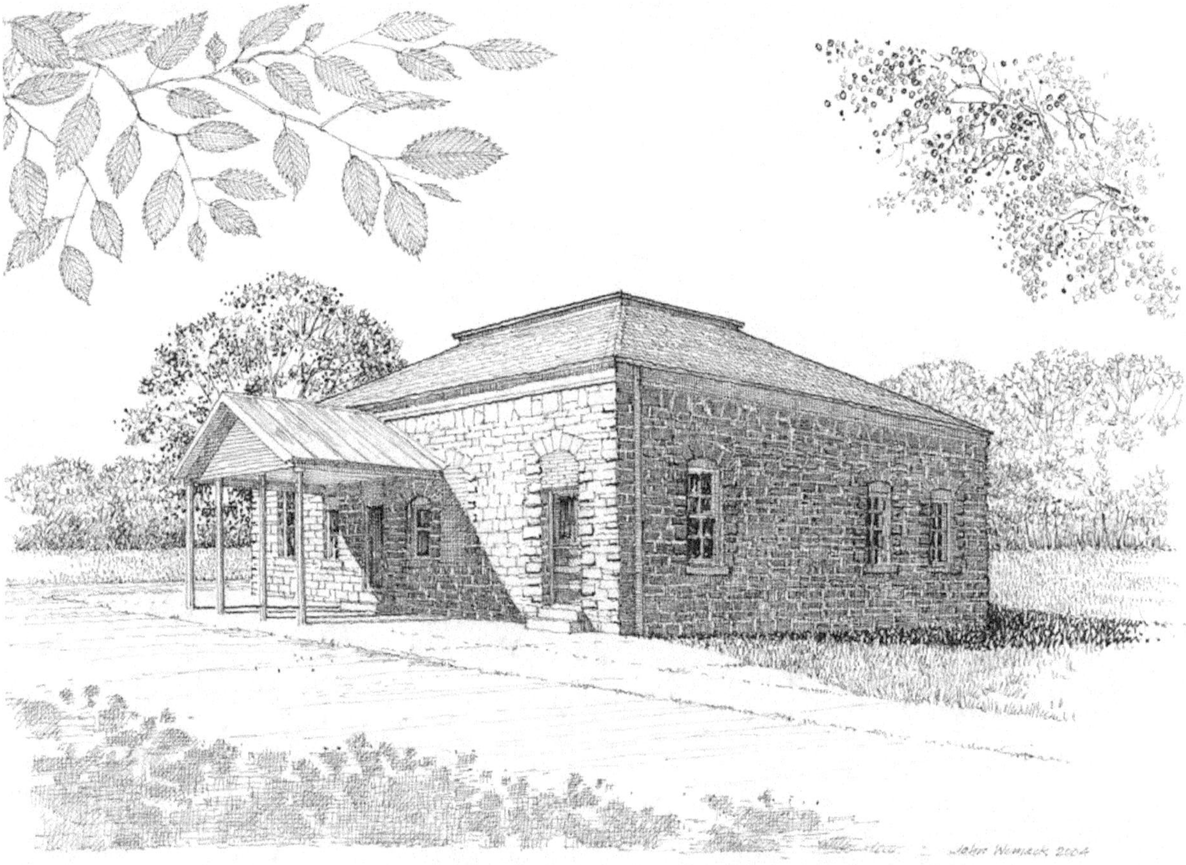

Fort Reno, Old Guardhouse, west of El Reno, Oklahoma

Fort Reno, founded in 1874, is located on old Route 66 about five miles west of El Reno. Soldiers at the fort served to keep the peace among white people who desired the Indian lands and the subjugated Cheyenne and Arapaho people. The Darlington Agency, positioned across the North Canadian River from the fort, administered directly to the Indian people. In 1908, the fort was closed. It is now a federal agricultural research center.

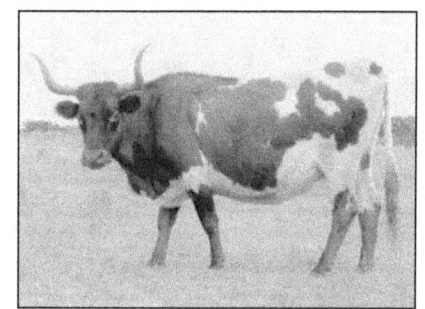

Like remnants from the old cattle drive days, longhorn cattle can still be seen along certain stretches of Route 66 in Oklahoma.

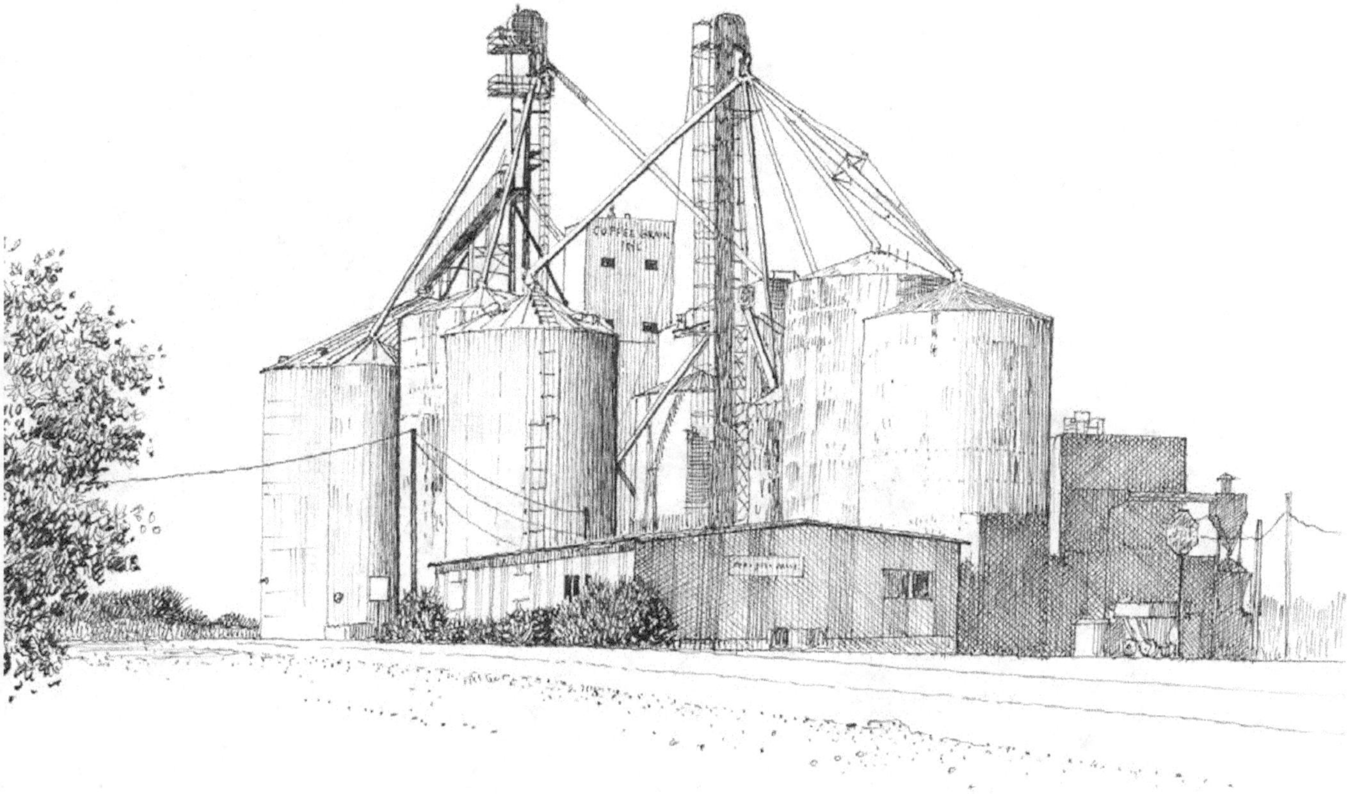

Coffey Grain Company, Calumet, Oklahoma

Route 66 and the town of Calumet had a relatively short life together—only seven years. In 1933, Calumet, Geary, and Bridgeport were bypassed in favor of a more direct route from El Reno to Weatherford. "Calumet" is a French word for the ceremonial pipes used for ages by various Native American peoples. Sometimes referred to as "peace pipes" by non-Indians, the calumet was a revered object that, when smoked, elicited the assistance of the spirit world.

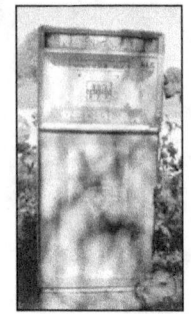

Old gas pumps have a certain poignancy about them. They date to a time when service attendants truly provided service—they filled the gas tank, checked the oil, and cleaned the windshield, just for starters!

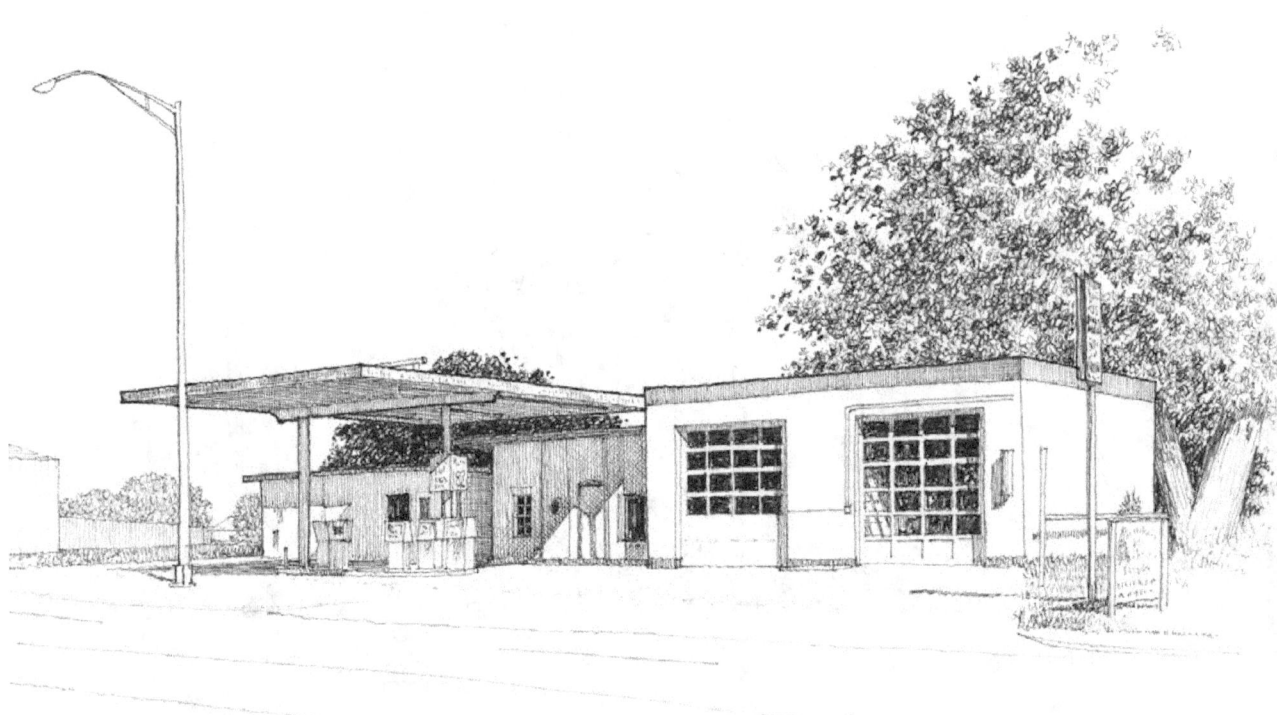

Service Station, Geary, Oklahoma

This station, still in operation in 2004, contains certain design details that indicate the station was originally one of the Phillips 66 cottage-style stations and probably dates to the early 1930s. The central section of building immediately to the left of the service garage is the original station. When Route 66 bypassed Geary, along with Calumet, in 1933, the chances were great that the two towns might not survive the times. But indeed they have survived.

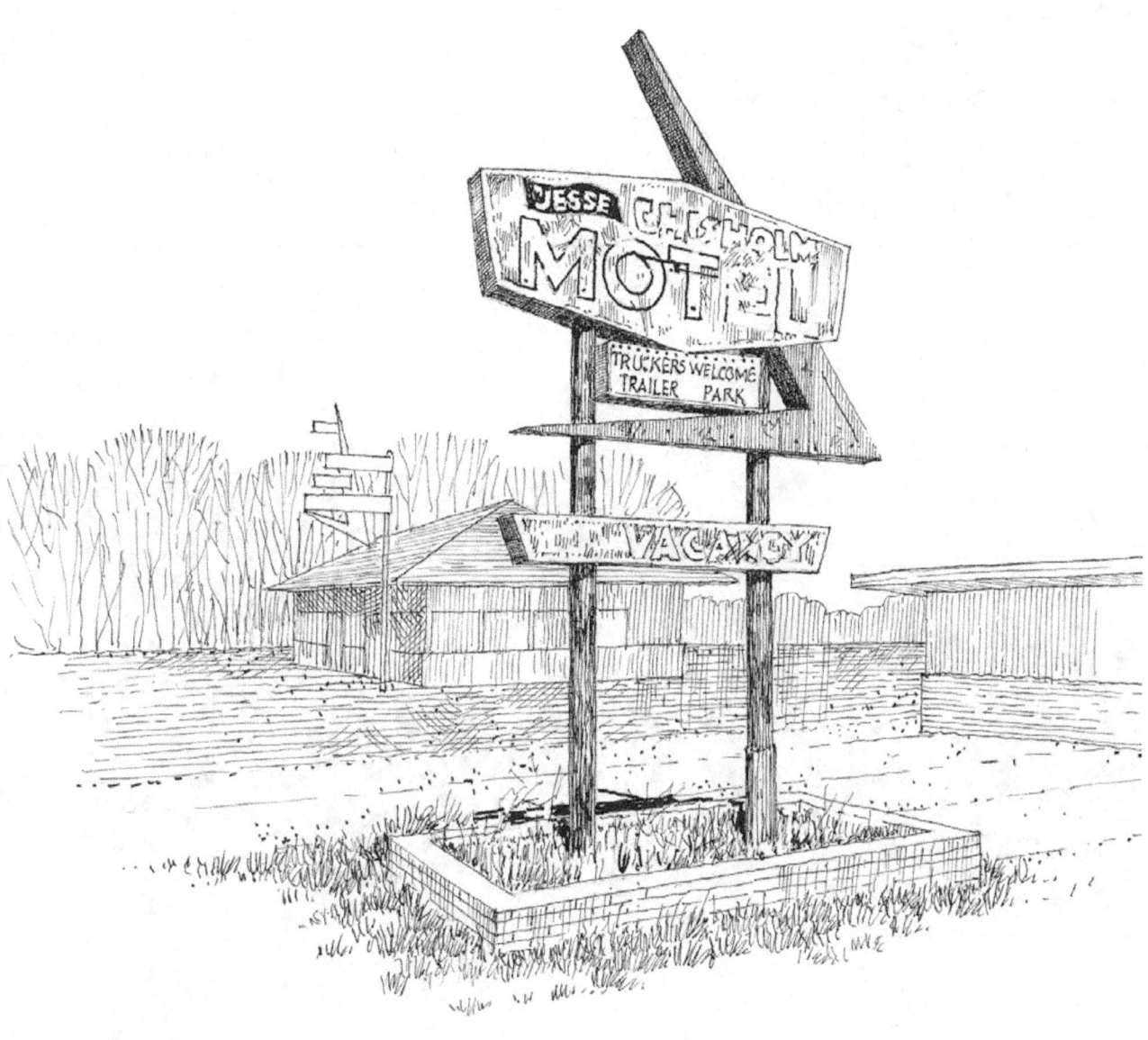

John Womack 2004

Jesse Chisolm Motel Sign, Geary, Oklahoma

Jesse Chisolm was a bona fide frontiersman and plainsman who changed the course of events in the West by establishing a trail from the Texas line through Oklahoma to Kansas. Chisolm was hauling trade goods, but the cattlemen in Texas saw something else in the trail—an "avenue" north with good water and grass along the way where their cattle could be driven to the railheads in Kansas. *Millions* of cattle were herded north along the Chisolm Trail from Texas.

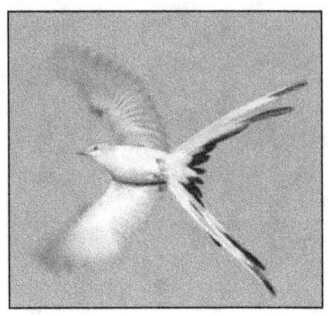

The scissortail flycatcher is Oklahoma's State Bird and is truly a beautiful bird. Their long forked, tail feathers and aerobatic flight gives them a most distinctive appearance. (Photo by Jim McCulloch)

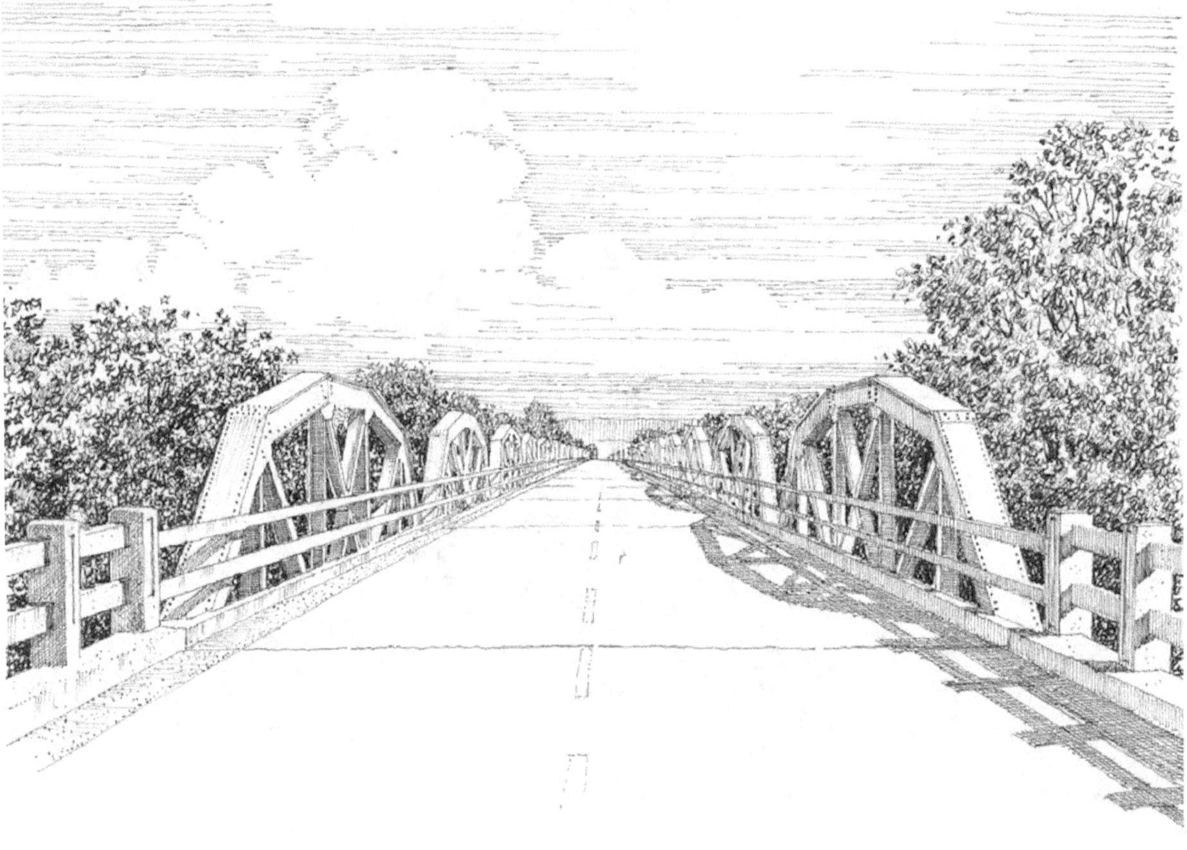

Pony Bridges, east of Hinton Junction, Oklahoma

Spanning the South Canadian River, this bridge is three quarters of a mile long and was built in 1933. In his *Oklahoma Route 66*, Jim Ross notes that from the western end of the Pony Bridge to the eastern edge of Weatherford lies the longest section of unaltered, first-generation paving still existing in Oklahoma—a distance of 18.3 miles. Officially, the bridge's name is the William H. Murray Bridge, named after "Alfalfa Bill Murray," governor of Oklahoma in 1933.

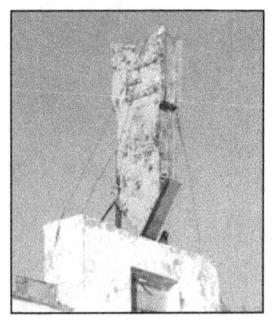

The old deserted diner at Hinton Junction still displays its classic, downward pointing "eat" arrow. Such arrows, often saying "Eat Here," were common along Route 66.

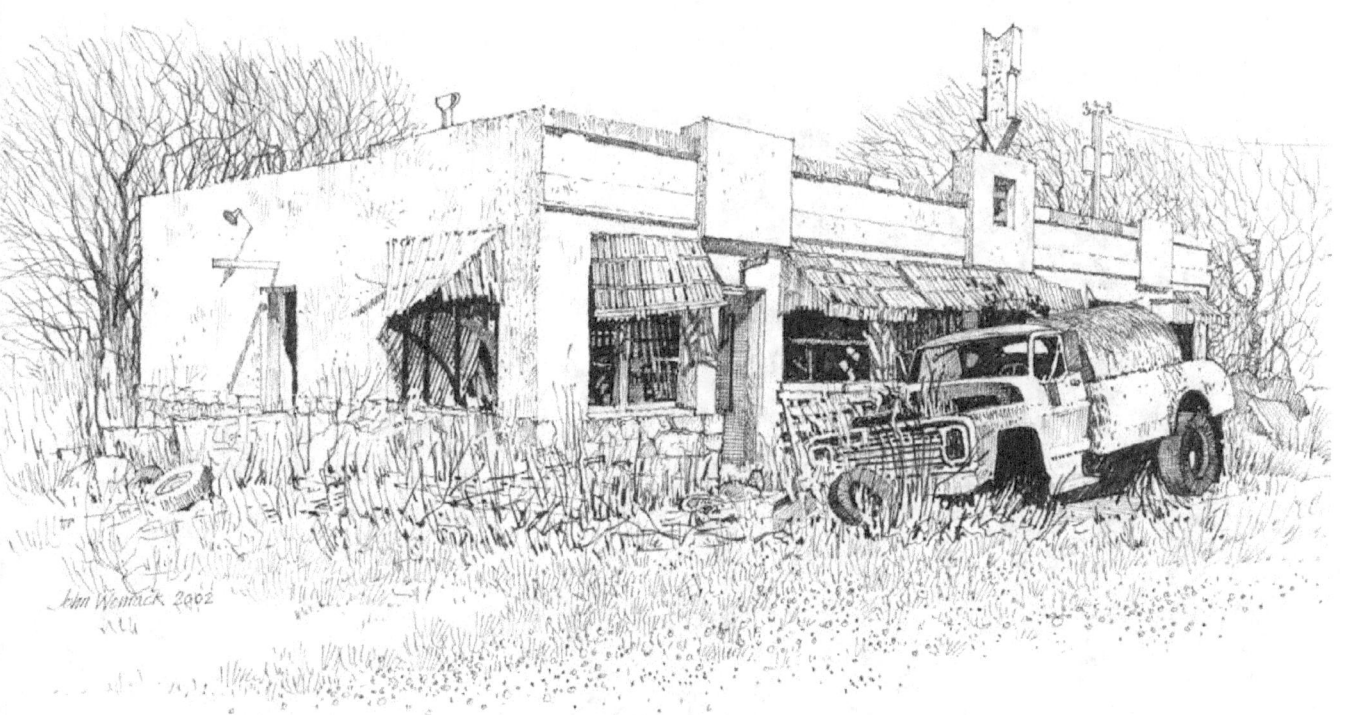

Hinton Station and Cafe, Hinton Junction, Oklahoma

This old derelict station is about all that is left of Hinton Junction. At one time, this dining and refueling spot was a thriving business and was owned by Leon Little, a local entrepreneur. Leon's house was located next door to the station, but the house has since vanished. Like the Avon Motel in Afton, this scene conveys an enormous sense of what the old highway was in its glory days and what it has become today.

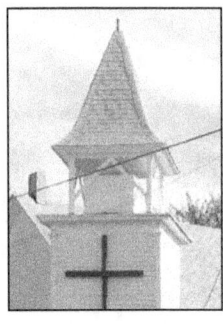

The church spire on the Methodist Church in Bridgeport is similar to many other church spires in other Oklahoma towns.

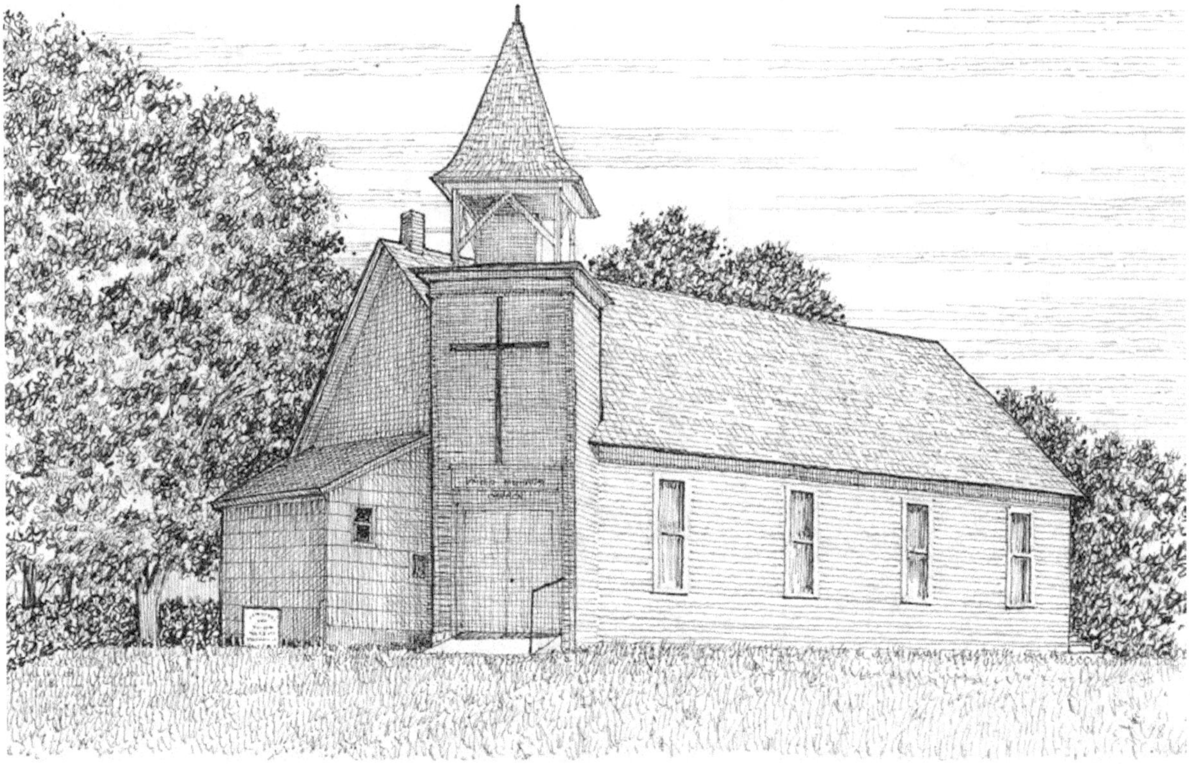

First Methodist Church, Bridgeport, Oklahoma

There is not much left in Bridgeport these days, but this little, white, wood-frame Methodist Church still shines in the sun. The road to Bridgeport is a little obscure. Travel east of Hinton Junction on old Route 66, and follow a thin strip of pavement that swings to the north; you will soon arrive in Bridgeport. This church is quite similar to the now torn down church that was once in Arcadia, Oklahoma.

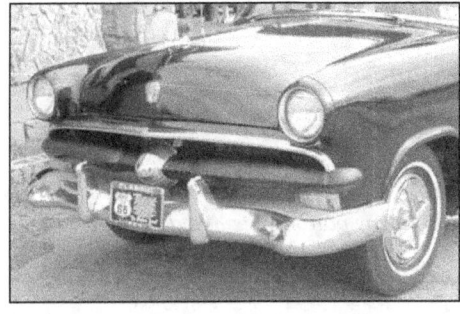

Driving the western portion of the original Route 66 surface is an enjoyable experience—especially in an antique car.

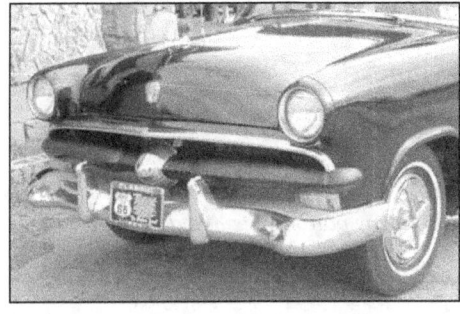

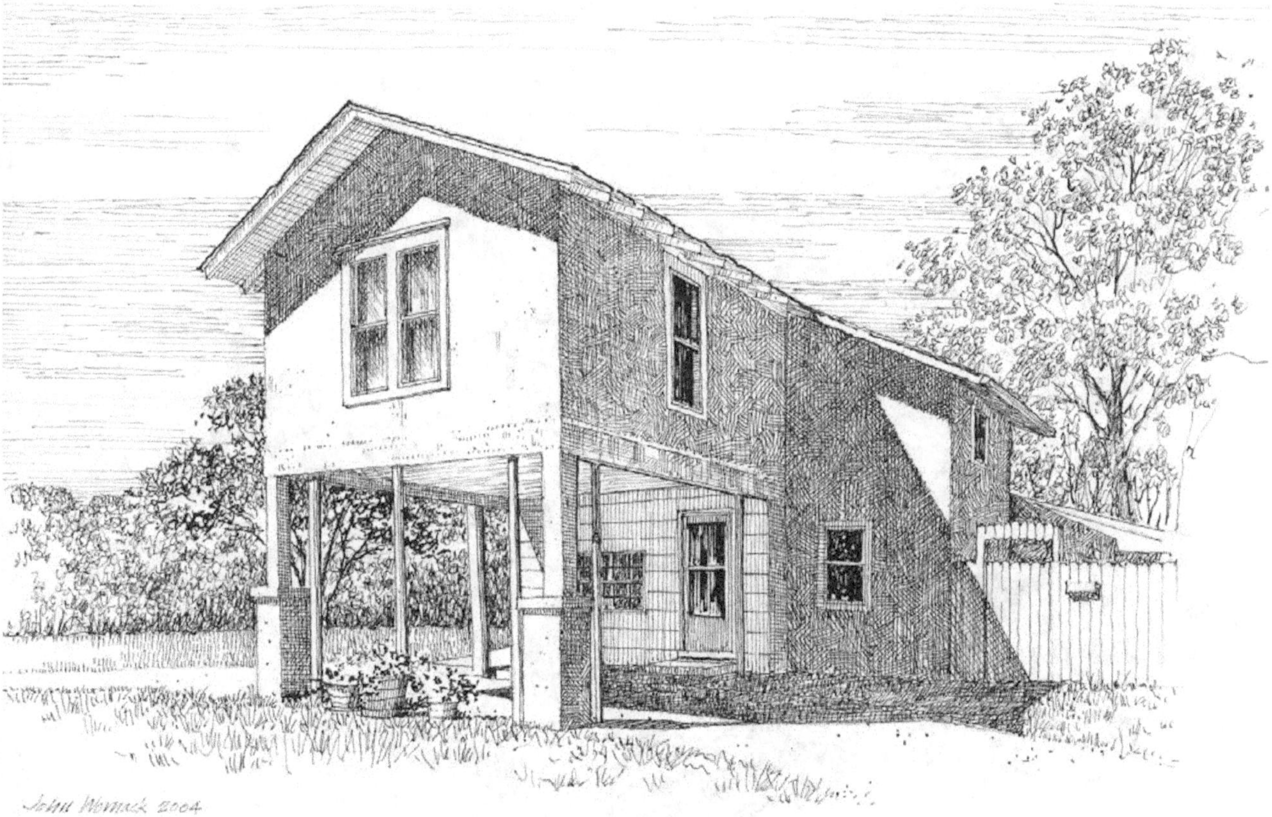

John Womack 2004

Former Service Station, east of Hydro, Oklahoma

This former gas station is now a residence and is of the same design as its more famous version, Lucille's, which is farther west on Route 66. Much of this structure has been covered in stucco and has undergone a few structural "enhancements." These stations so profoundly characterize the "mom and pop" type of businesses where people lived and worked in the same building. One moment the occupants might be pumping gas and the next, having a baby.

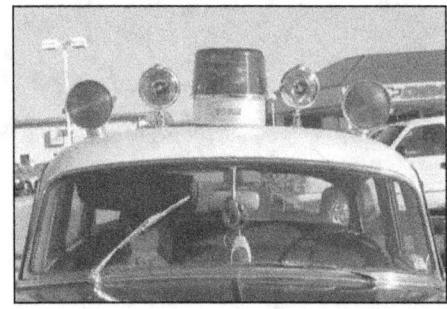

At one time, police cars and highway patrol units had a large rotating red light on top of the car that got everyone's attention when activated. Such lights were known as "cherry tops."

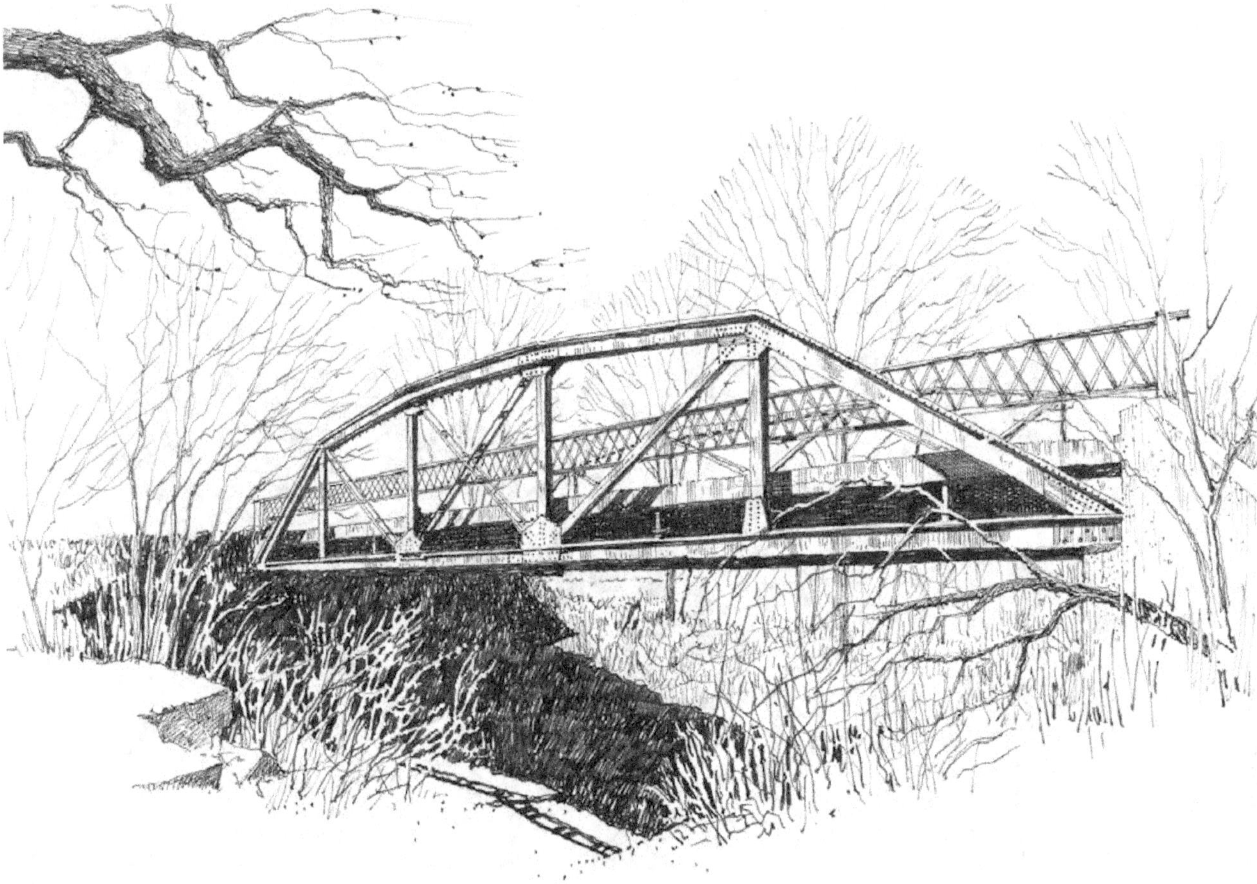

Bridge over Deer Creek, east of Hydro, Oklahoma

This early steel bridge is still in use today on Route 66. Though wider than the bridge over Salt Creek, this bridge is still narrow by modern standards. While visiting with some nearby residents, I learned that the night before my visit to the bridge a couple of men in a high speed chase from the police missed the bridge entirely and landed their car in the area to the left of this drawing. Both men survived the crash, but they were more than a bit bruised and battered.

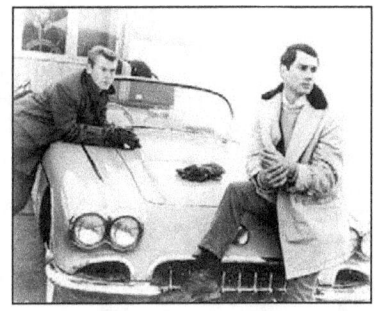

Route 66, *the TV show staring Martin Milner and George Maharis, forever linked the Chevrolet Corvette with the Mother Road.*

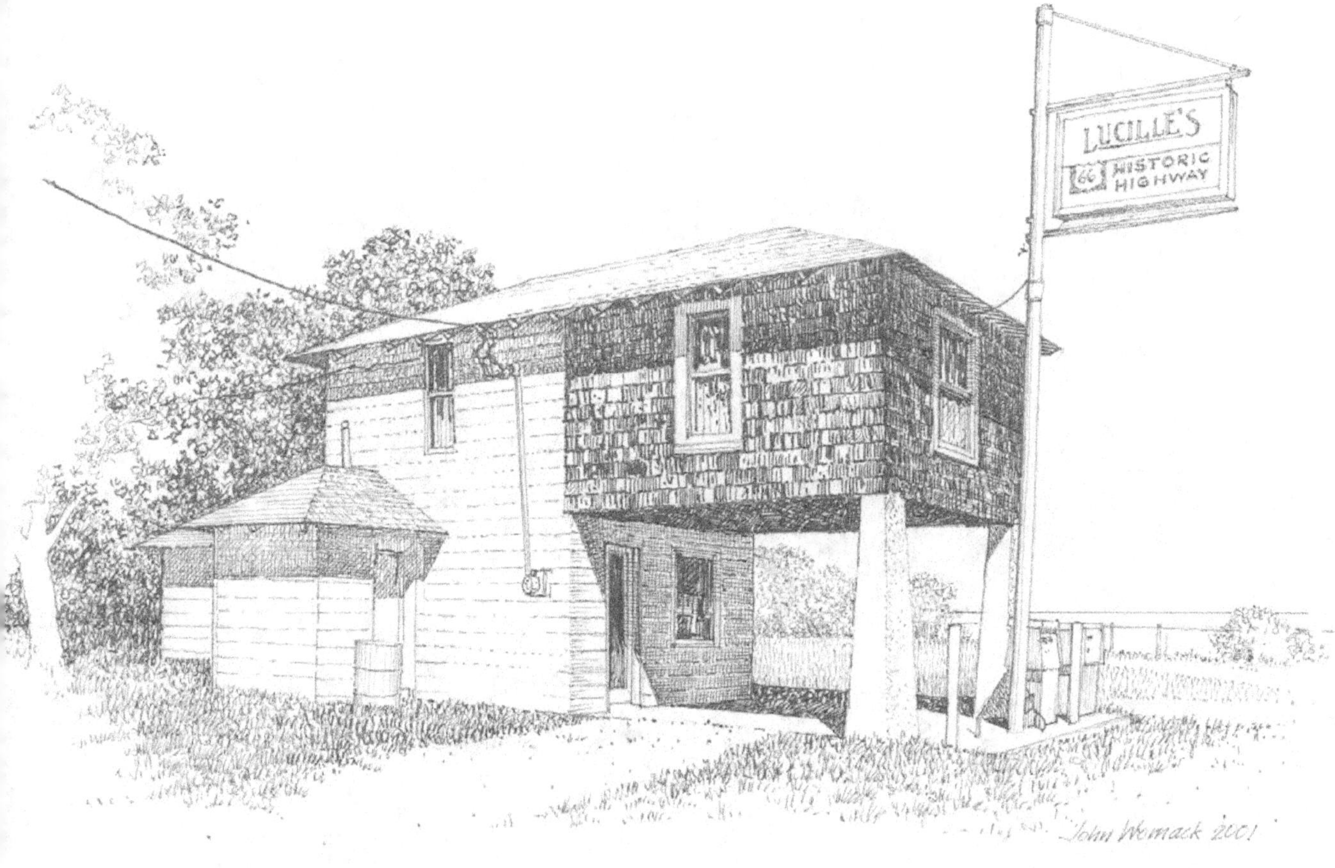

Lucille's Station, Hydro, Oklahoma

Lucille Hamon was one of the last of the Route 66 mom and pop businesses to survive (barely) the economic devastation brought on by the interstate highway system. Lucille is often referred to by Route 66 "road warriors" as the mother of the Mother Road, and her station seen here is one of the most well-known and photographed spots on the entire Route 66. The site was named to the National Register of Historic Places in 1997. Lucille died in 2000.

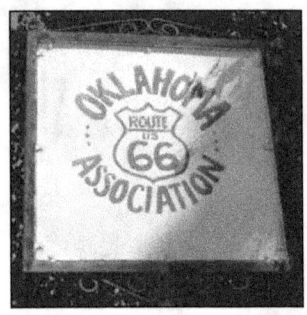

The Oklahoma Route 66 Association sponsors many road trips and get-togethers for its members. The Association also performs periodic cleanups and site repairs to various Route 66 places and artifacts.

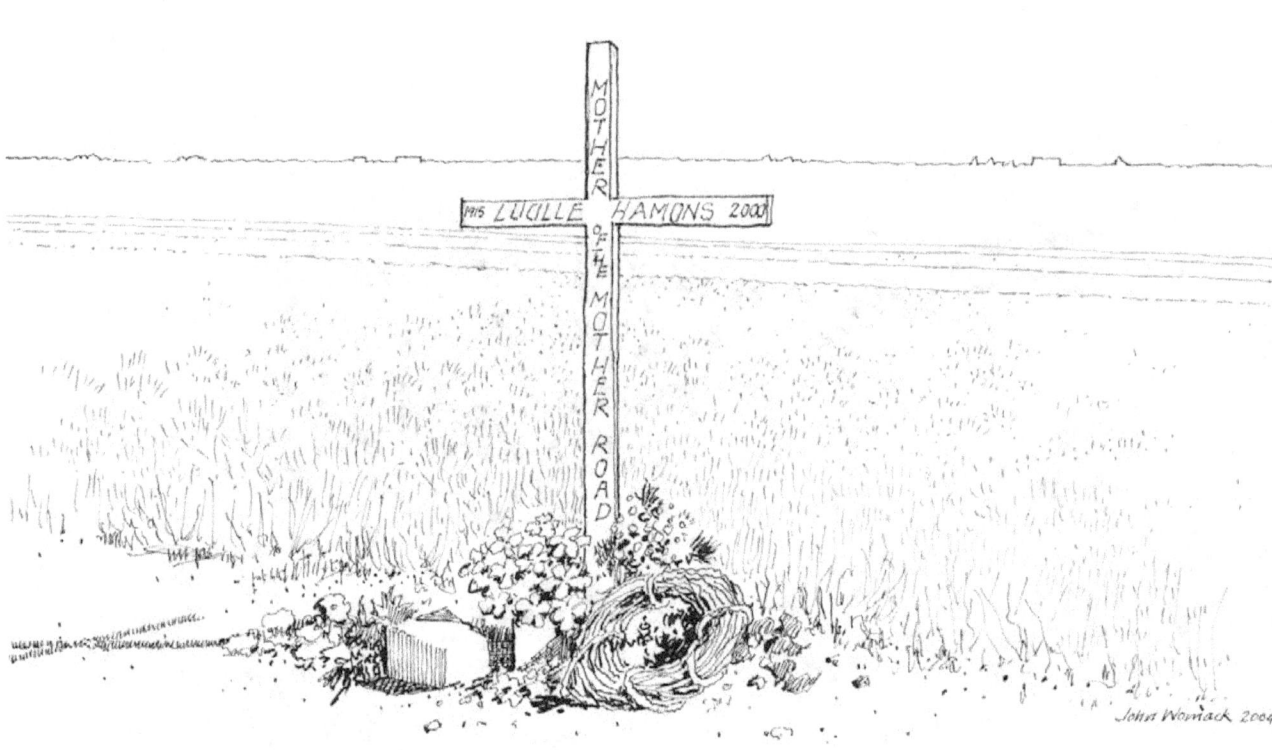

Roadside memorial for Lucille Hamon

Just when people began erecting roadside monuments for loved ones near the scene of their death, I don't know, but I seem to remember seeing one such memorial when I was a young lad. Roadside markers remind us of the possible danger when we go barreling down the highway at a high rate of speed. This marker is across from Lucille's station and though she was not the victim of a traffic accident, she was ultimately a victim of the highway and the interstate system.

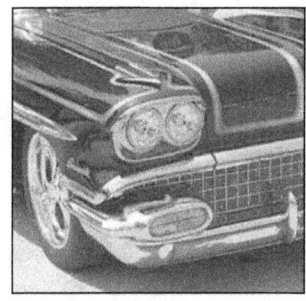

The American hot rod developed soon after the end of World War II. Customized cars, with stunning paint jobs and chrome plating soon followed. Route 66 has become a showplace for such cars.

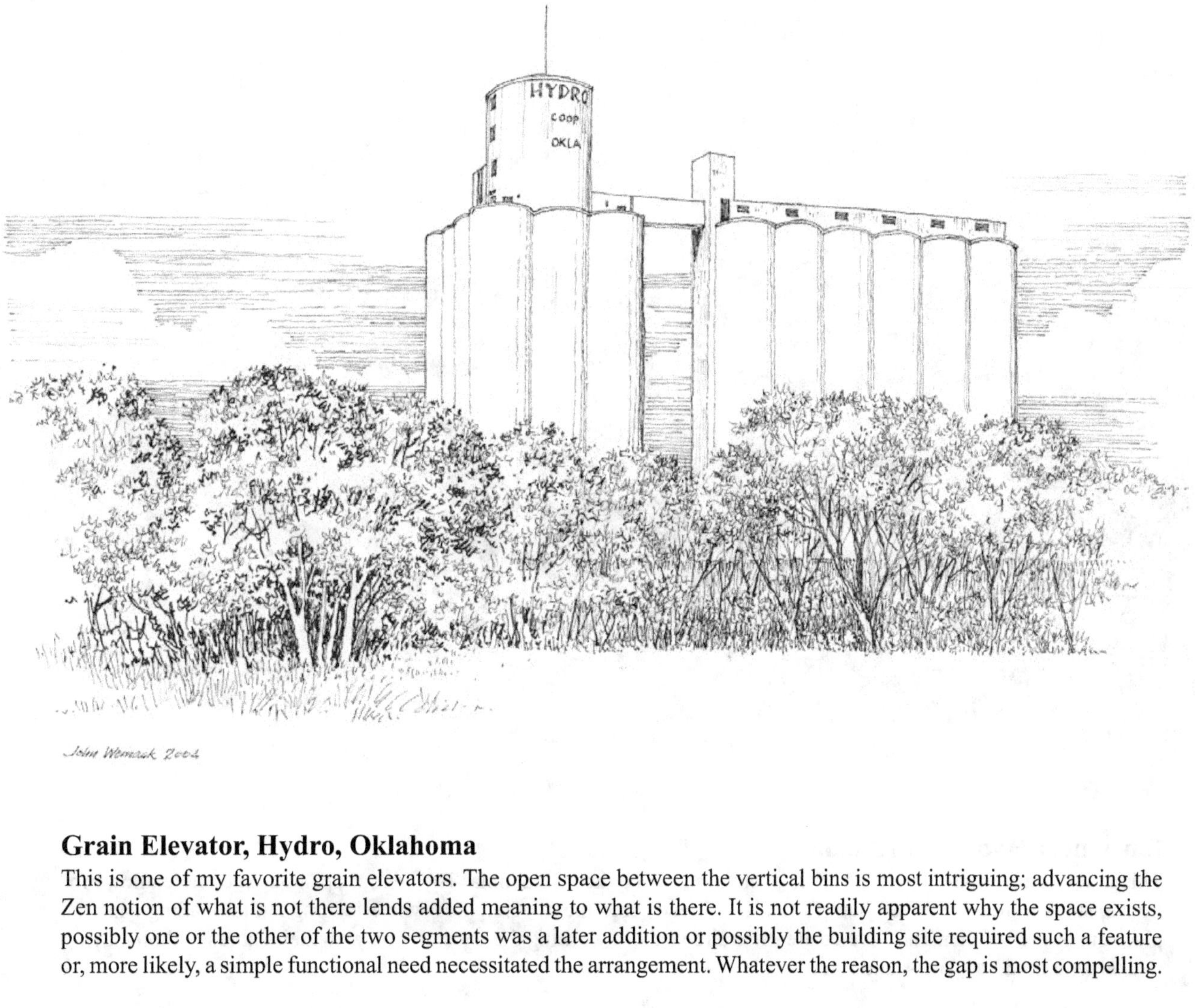

John Womack 2004

Grain Elevator, Hydro, Oklahoma

This is one of my favorite grain elevators. The open space between the vertical bins is most intriguing; advancing the Zen notion of what is not there lends added meaning to what is there. It is not readily apparent why the space exists, possibly one or the other of the two segments was a later addition or possibly the building site required such a feature or, more likely, a simple functional need necessitated the arrangement. Whatever the reason, the gap is most compelling.

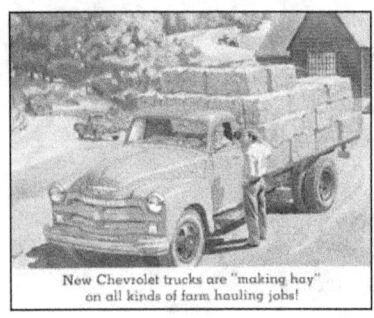

New Chevrolet trucks are "making hay" on all kinds of farm hauling jobs!

This Chevrolet truck advertisement points out that "making hay" means more than literally making hay.

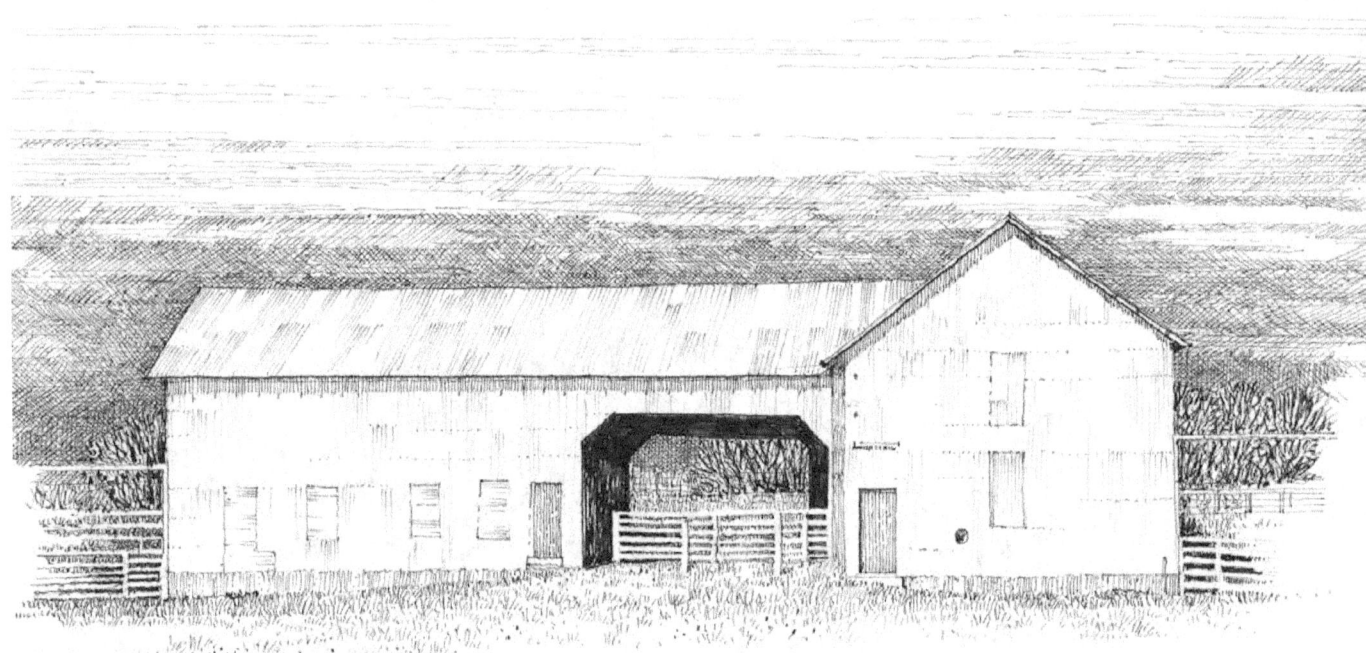

Barn, near Hydro, Oklahoma

This unique barn is part of a large cattle operation near Hydro, Oklahoma. The central open bay seen here allows for trucks, stock trailers, and feed haulers to drive directly into the covered area where loading and unloading can take place out of the weather. The covered area also allows those working there to carry on with their chores without having to deal with mud, ice, snow, and so on.

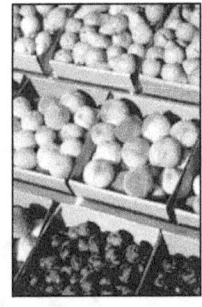

No doubt about it, fruit and vegetables grown on a nearby farm and delivered fresh to the vendor, taste better than "store-bought" produce.

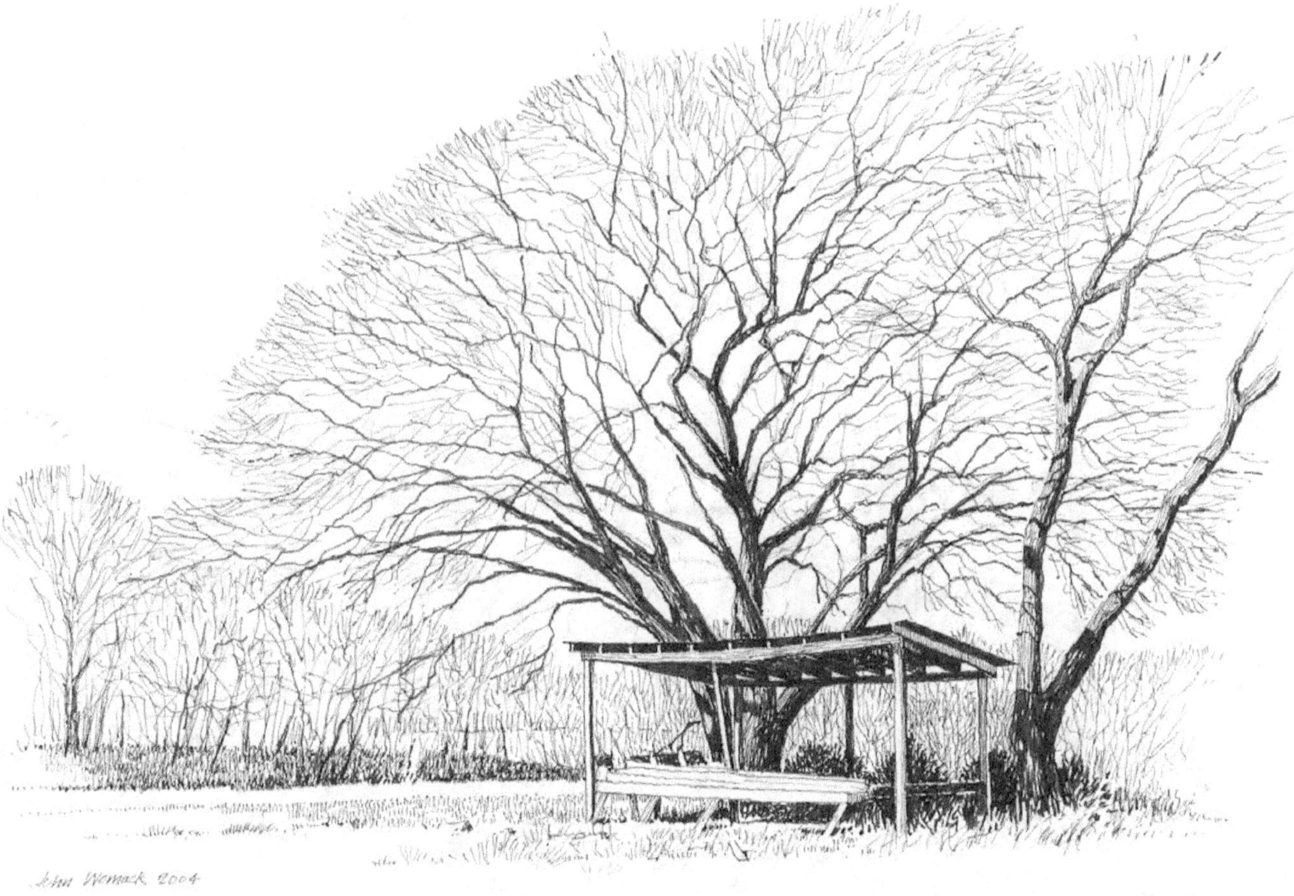

Produce Stand, east of Weatherford, Oklahoma

When speaking to various groups of people about Route 66, I typically start with this view, not because the old stand is a great piece of architecture, but because of its sense of place. When one considers the big elm tree behind the stand and the shade it provided, the various colors and smells of fruit and vegetables, people talking about the produce, the weather, birds in the trees, the breeze speaking in the leaves overhead—one begins to sense "the place."

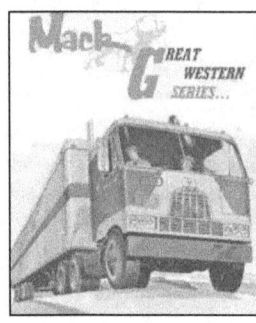

Route 66 carried multiple forms of vehicles: family cars, sports cars, motorcycles, buses, eighteen wheelers, military vehicles, and so on (from a 1950s Mack Truck poster).

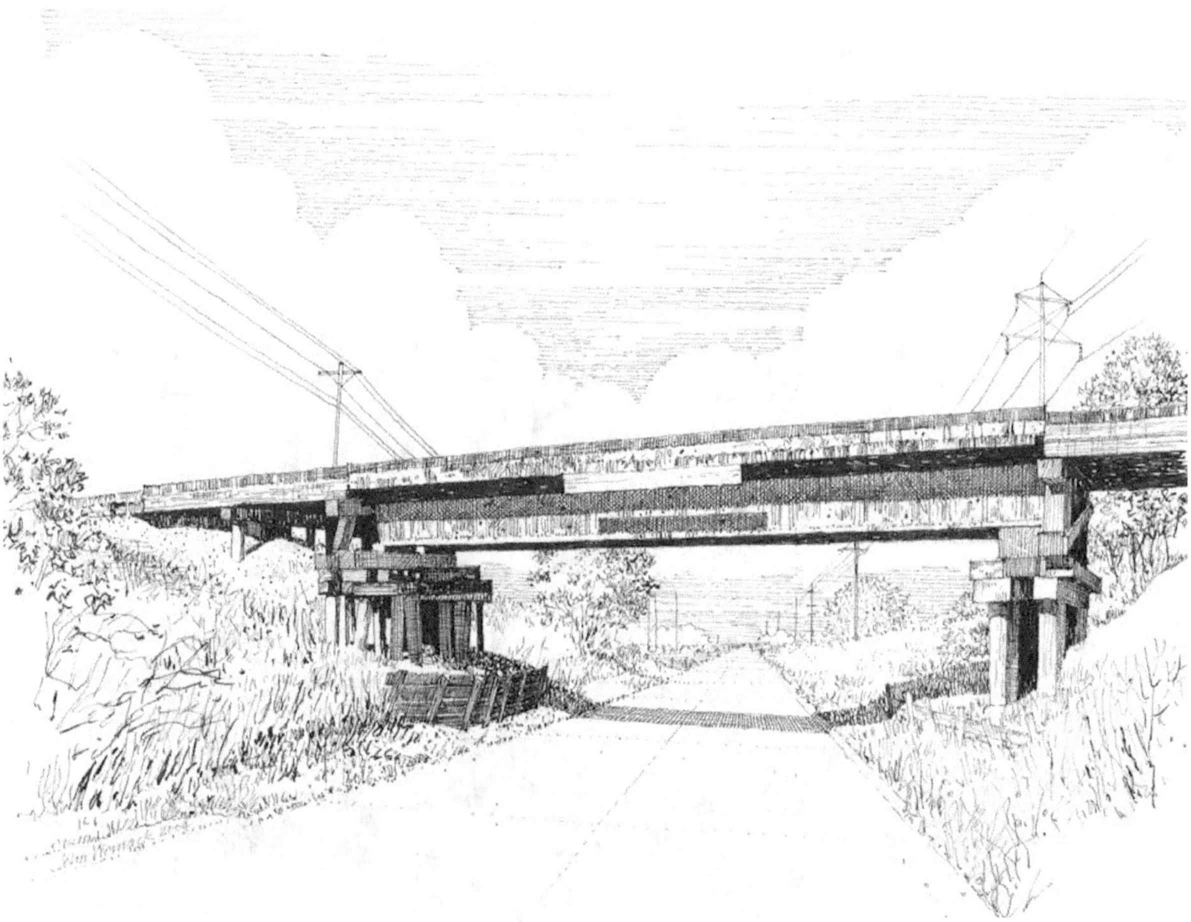

Railroad Trestle, east of Weatherford, Oklahoma

This railroad trestle dates to 1930 and still has the original Route 66 concrete pavement running below. The trestle's structural integrity appears a bit dubious to me. (It has been shored up with timbers and piles on both sides.) The concrete curb was noted for its tendency to act like a dam on each side of the road, and during a rainstorm, or soon after, water could pool on the road surface—a dangerous and unexpected hazard, especially when driving at night.

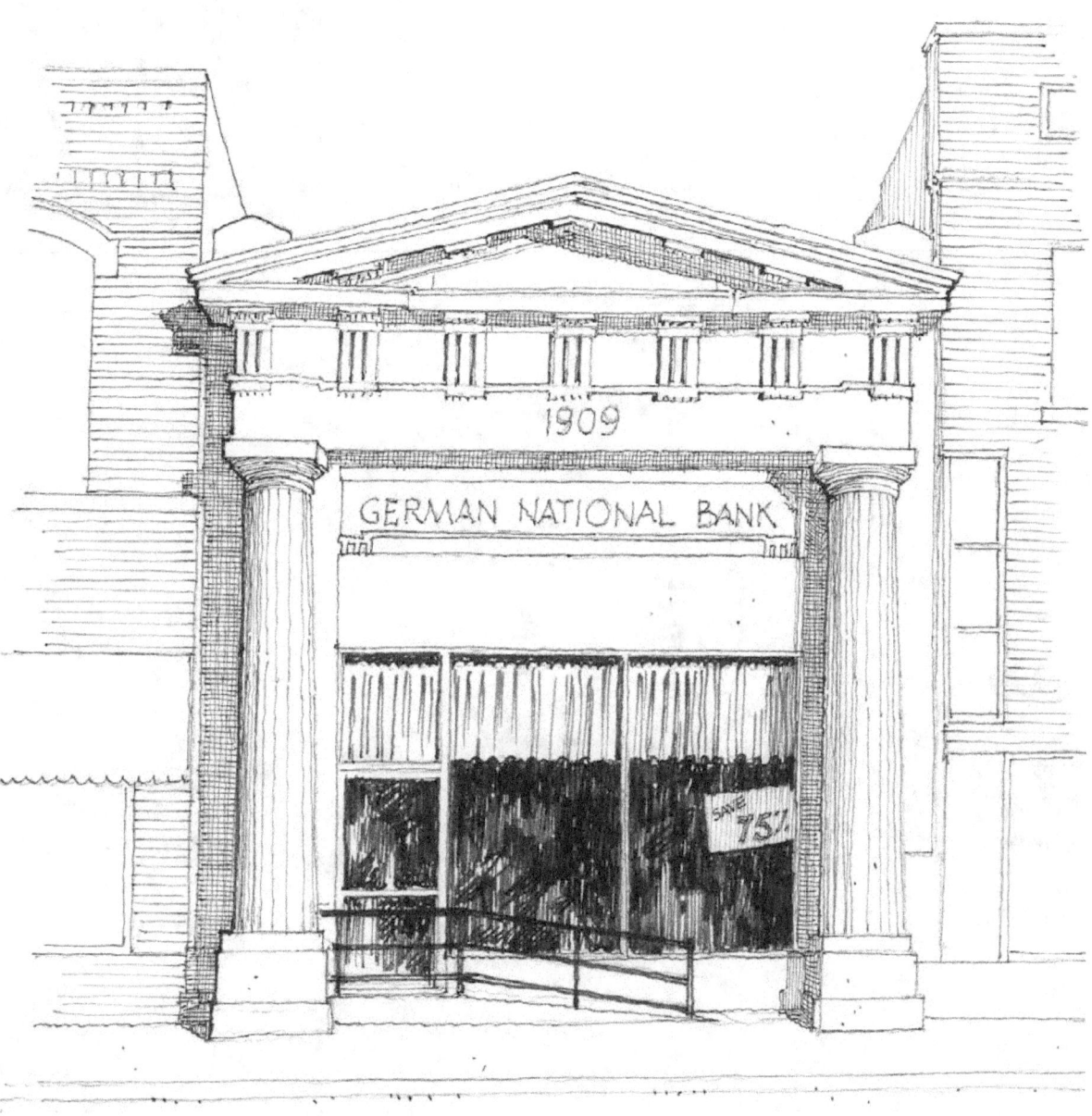

Former German National Bank, Weatherford, Oklahoma

During the 1890s, Weatherford was known as a "wild and wooly" place—saloons and dance halls outnumbered all other forms of business. With statehood in 1907, Oklahoma began to calm down a little. This former bank displays a dignified neo-Classical facade, something one might not anticipate in the Wild West. It seems probable that a large contingent of German immigrants in the area contributed to the need for a "German" bank.

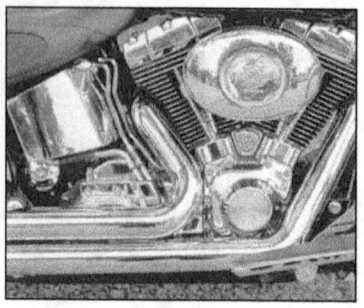

Chrome, steel and black leather have become an integral part of today's Route 66 "scene."

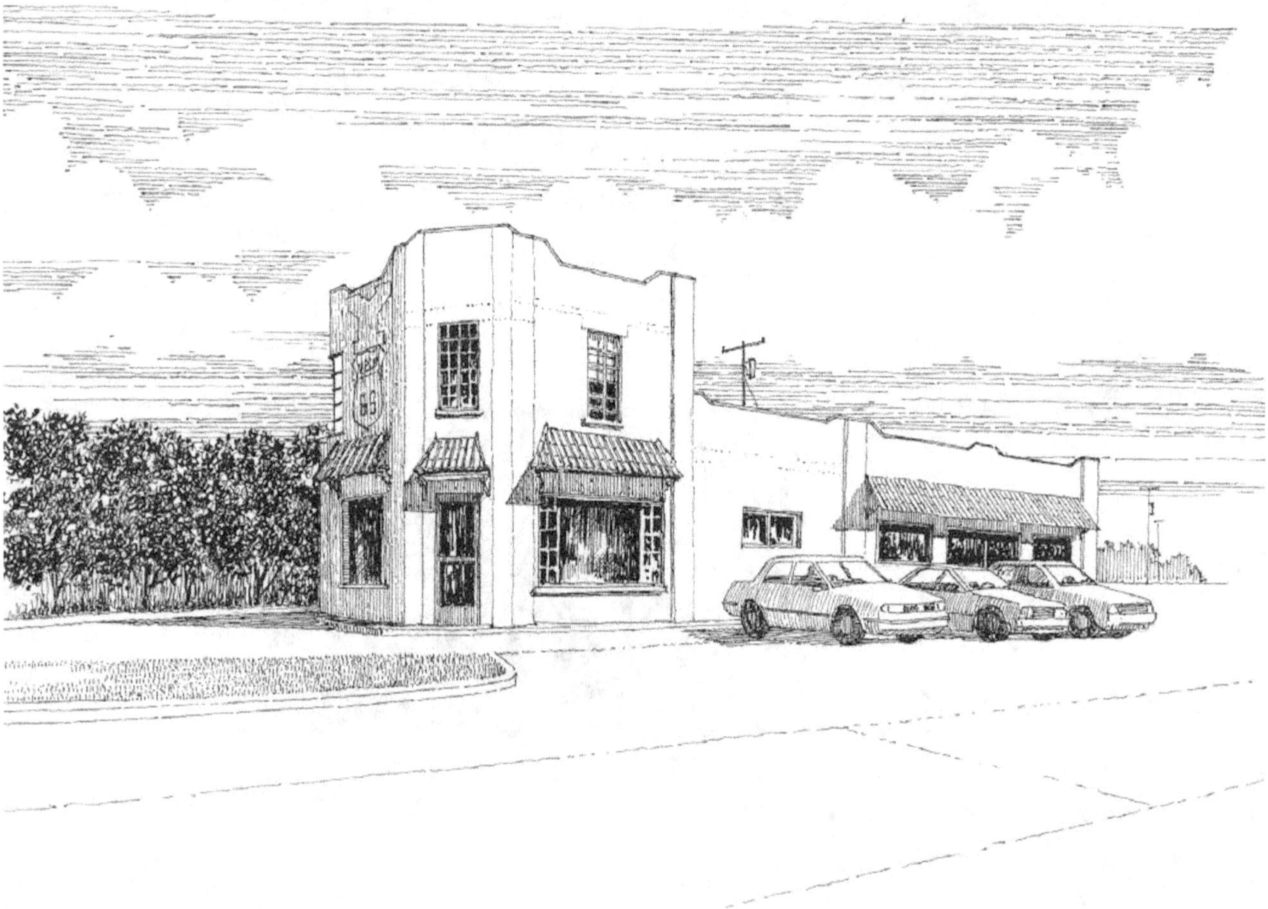

Former Roadhouse, Bessie "Y," near Clinton, Oklahoma

Roadhouses started appearing during the 1920s, were generally located on a "country" road, and were generally considered "rough" places to go. Drinking, dancing, gambling, you name it, and it probably went on in a roadhouse. I once asked a couple of Oklahoma Highway Patrol officers about the "Y," and they said you could still see bullet holes in the walls of the old place.

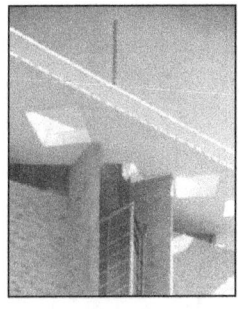

The contemporary detailing of horizontal white concrete slabs contrast with vertical brick walls and pilasters of the church.

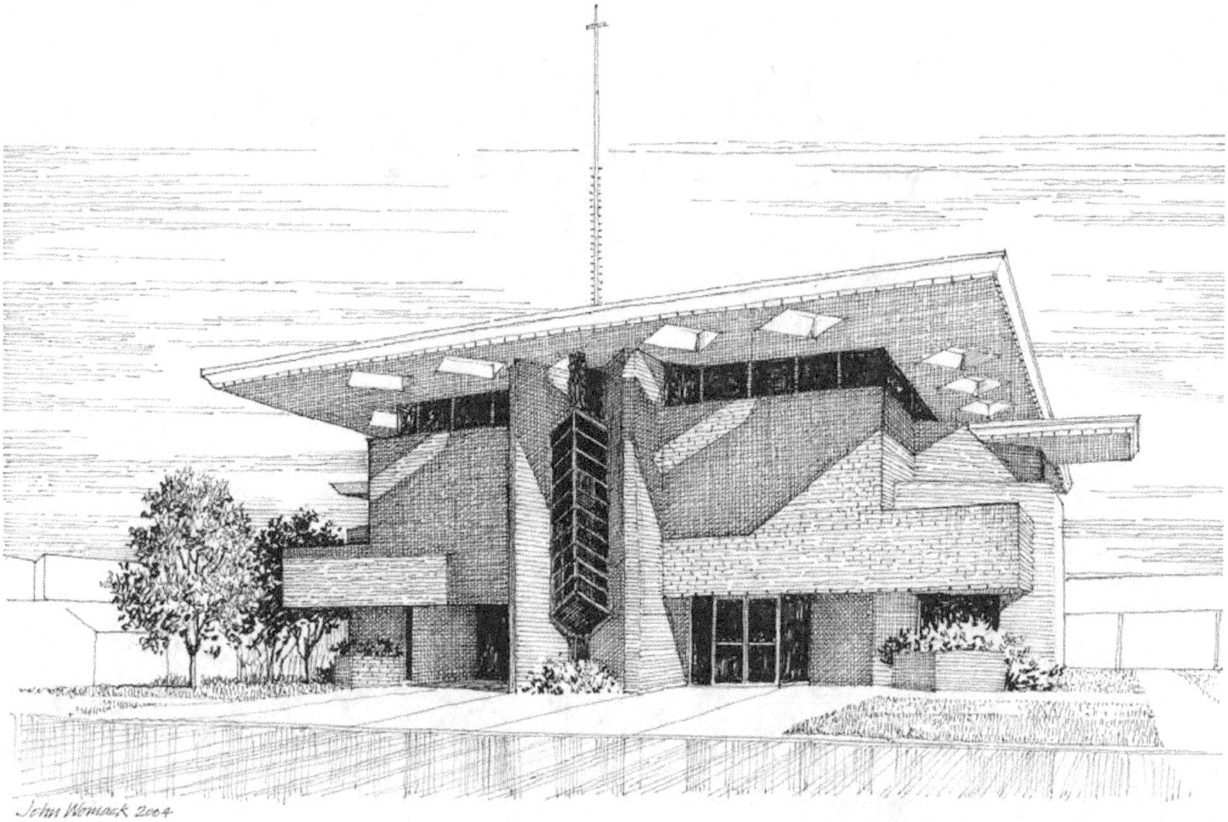

John Womack 2004

First United Methodist Church, Clinton, Oklahoma

The design of this church is influenced by the work of architect, Frank Lloyd Wright. It is interesting how different congregations of the same affiliation select different aesthetics to assist their worship. This can be seen quite readily by comparing the First United Methodist Church in Tulsa with the church seen here. One conveys a sense of the past, the other a sense of the future.

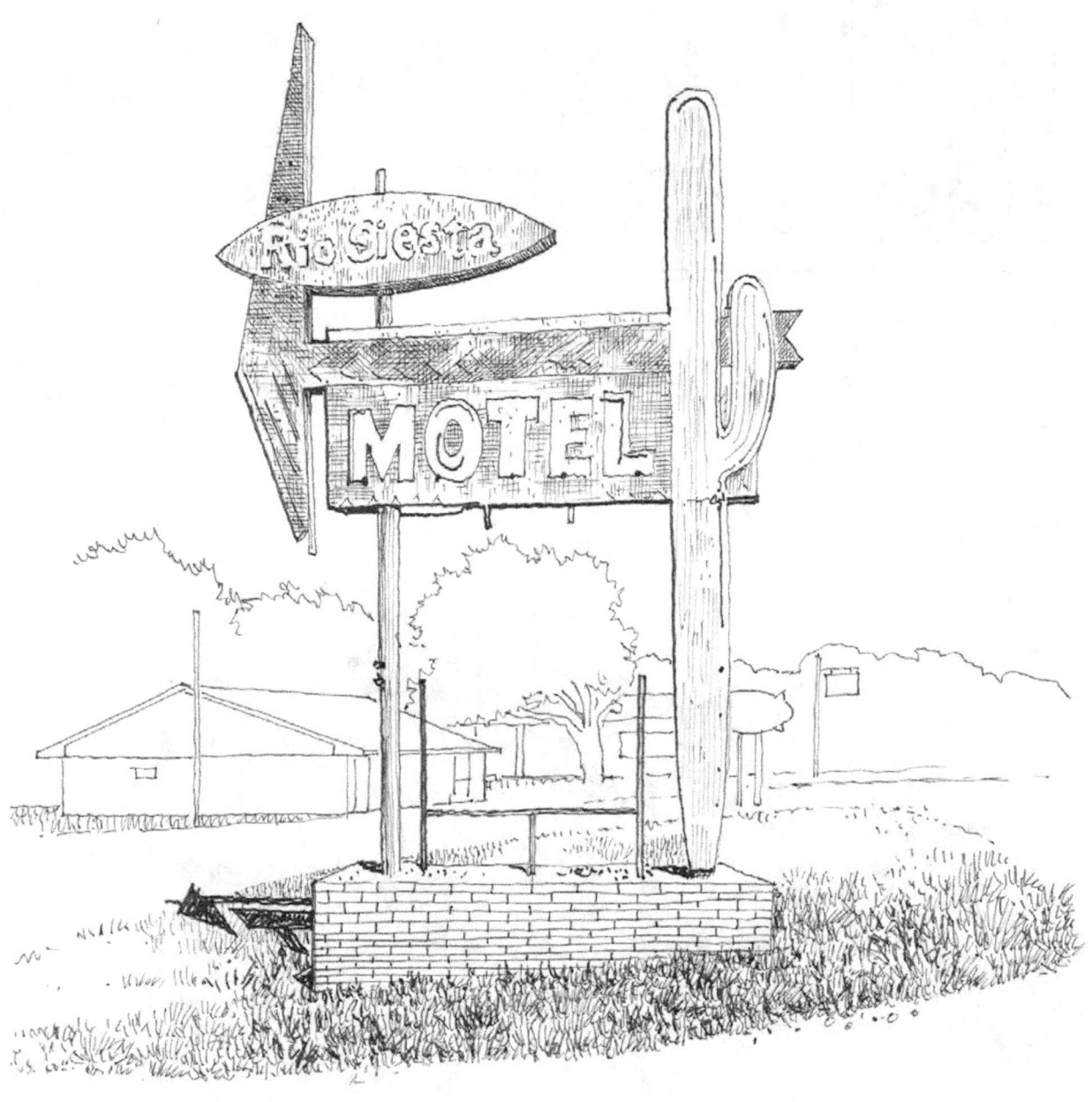

Rio Siesta Motel Sign, Clinton, Oklahoma

Clinton was founded in 1903 by Thomas J. Nance, a banker from a town just four miles north called Arapaho. The people in Arapaho had wanted the railroad junction in their town and leveled more than a few threats at Nance for creating his new town. Clinton won its place on the map and its railroad junction. Originally known as "Washita Junction," the town later changed its name to "Clinton" after a local federal judge, Clinton F. Irwin.

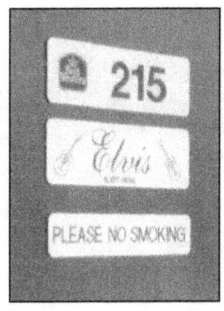

Across the highway from the Route 66 Museum in Clinton is the Trades Winds Motel, where Elvis stayed overnight on his cross country trips from Las Vegas to Memphis.

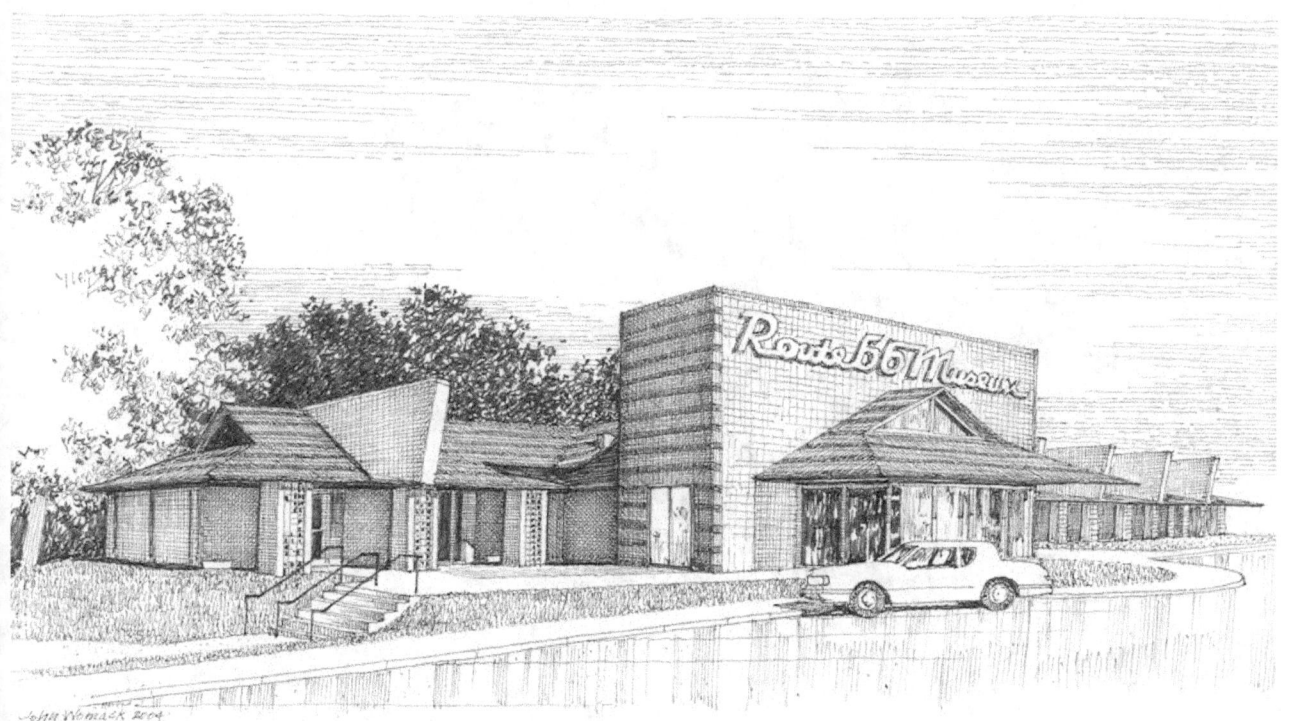

Oklahoma Route 66 Museum, Clinton, Oklahoma

This museum is a must stop if you are driving the Mother Road, or just visiting the area. The museum staff takes pride in providing unique displays for their visitors, and the museum shop has an incredible offering of books, maps, and other items pertaining to Route 66. If time allows, spend the night across the street in the Trade Winds Motel—in the very room that Elvis Presley occupied when passing through to and from Las Vegas.

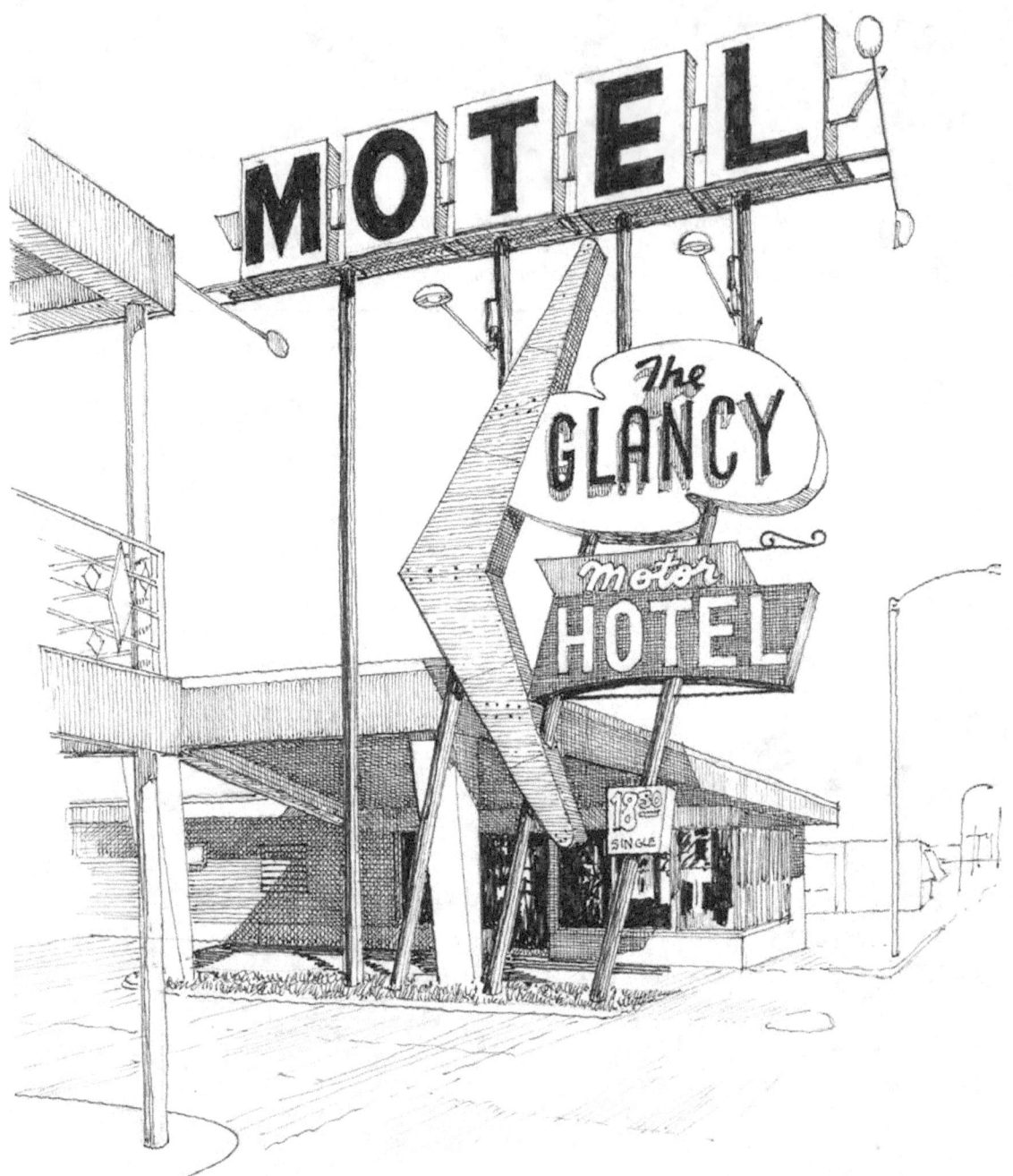

Glancy Motel Sign, Clinton, Oklahoma

The tallest part of the sign with the word "motel" appears to be a later addition to the leaning post sign proclaiming the place is a "motor hotel." Maybe a taller and bigger sign encouraged more people traveling the highway to stop and rest for the night? Next to the Glancy Motel stood Pop Hick's Restaurant. Pop Hicks was a popular eating stop for highway travelers and local people since its beginning in 1936. Unfortunately, the restaurant burned to the ground in 1999.

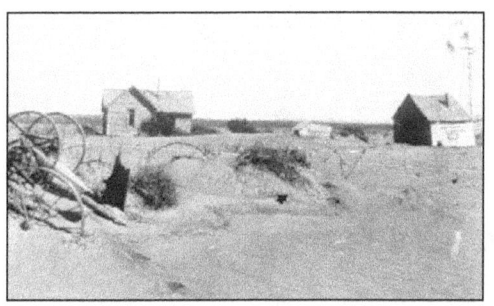

During the 1930s, the devastating effects of the Dust Bowl became more and more prevalent as one approached the western reaches of Oklahoma.

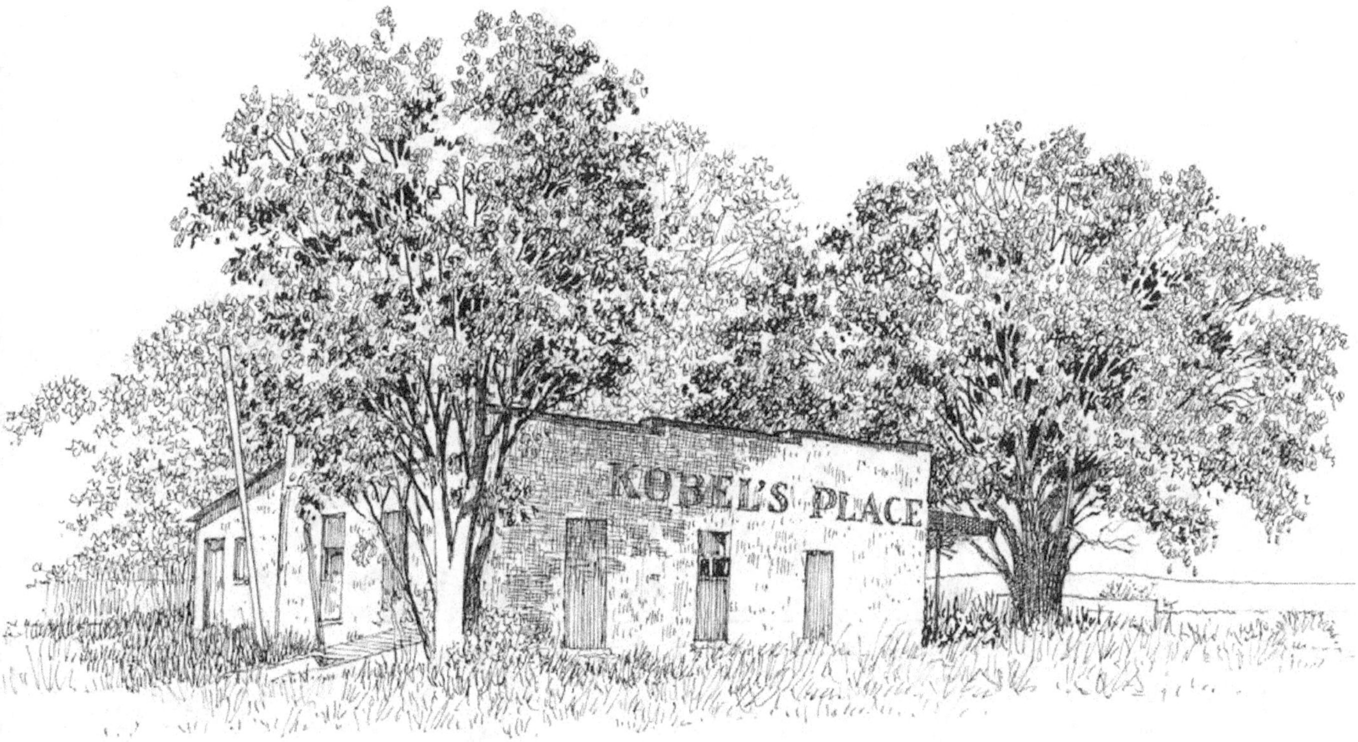

Kobel's Place, Foss, Oklahoma

The little town of Foss once had a bustling population of 1,000 people. Now there are only around 150 people living in Foss. The town was founded in the late 1890s when people found suitable well water at a depth of only 25 feet. The Great Depression and the Dust Bowl of the 1930s forced many of Foss' population to move on to other destinations. Kobel's Place served area inhabitants as a gas station, bus stop, and cafe. Kobel's is gradually returning to the landscape.

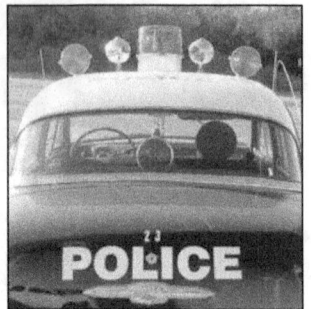

When the old "cherry top" started flashing one knew to pull over to the side of the road and let the police pass by, or maybe allow them to pull in behind you in order for them to "visit" with you (oops!).

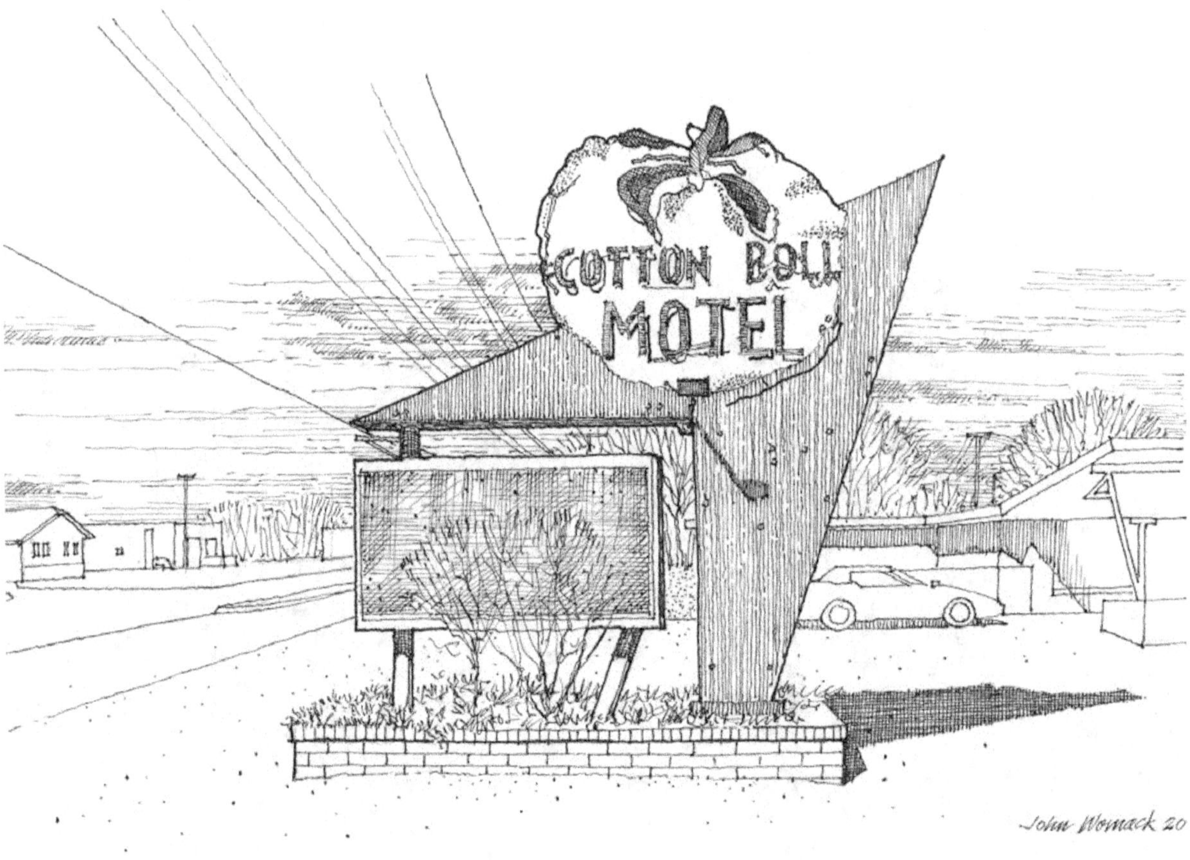

John Womack 20

Cotton Boll Motel Sign, Canute, Oklahoma

The name of this motel speaks of the region's cotton growing. Like many motels along Route 66, this motel is now a private residence. Canute was originally named "Oak" but was later changed to Canute in honor of the King of Denmark. Elsewhere I have mentioned motel signs and the various forms of arrows. The arrow seen here seems rather peculiar as to where it is pointing. Although it points in the general direction of the motel, it also seems to have "loftier" intentions.

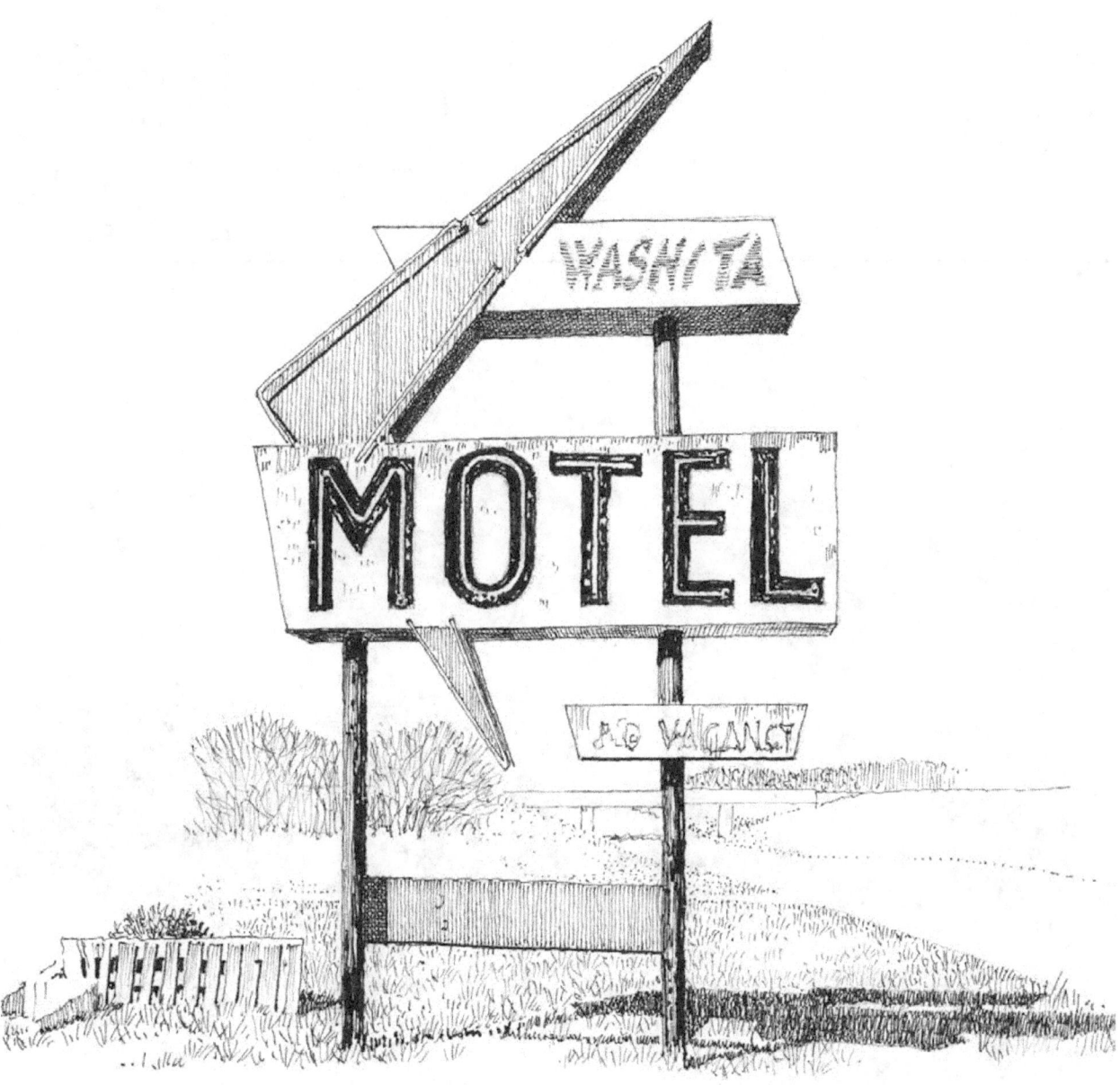

Washita Motel Sign, Canute, Oklahoma

The Washita River is one of the longest rivers in the state of Oklahoma. It is a little known fact that Oklahoma has more shoreline than any other state in the United States. Southern Cheyenne, Arapaho, Kiowa, Comanche, and Apache peoples frequented the rich buffalo country of western Oklahoma during the decades prior to their subjugation and placement on reservation lands. By 1890, the old, free life of the nomadic tribes of the West was over.

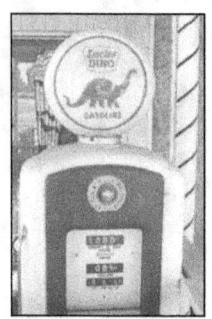

Sinclair Oil Company adopted the dinosaur logo in the early 1930s, and in time, the familiar brontosaurus became known as "Dino."

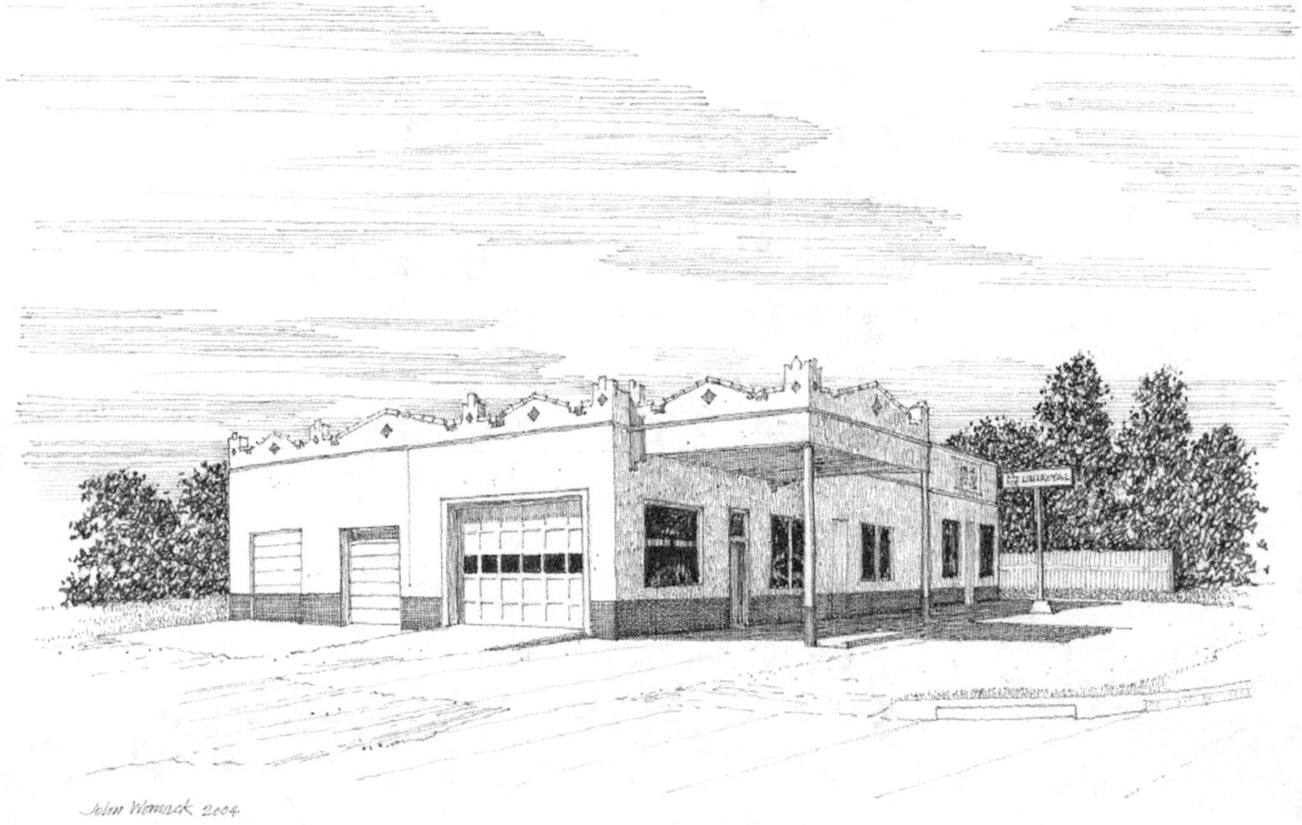

Former Service Station, Canute, Oklahoma

At one time, this former station housed a nightclub called the Tip Top Club. Later on, the nightclub became an ice cream and soda shop known as Thelma's Sundries. The upper wall edge, or cornice, seen here is rather elaborate in form and detail—something not often seen in service stations of the time. Sinclair Gasoline Company used a similar motif with its stations, and this may have been a Sinclair station.

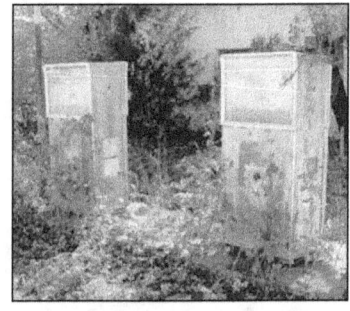

There were several gas pump manufacturers that brought the amber "go-juice" to vehicles. Wayne, Bennett, and Tokheim (which later became Wayne) pumps were among the most prevalent.

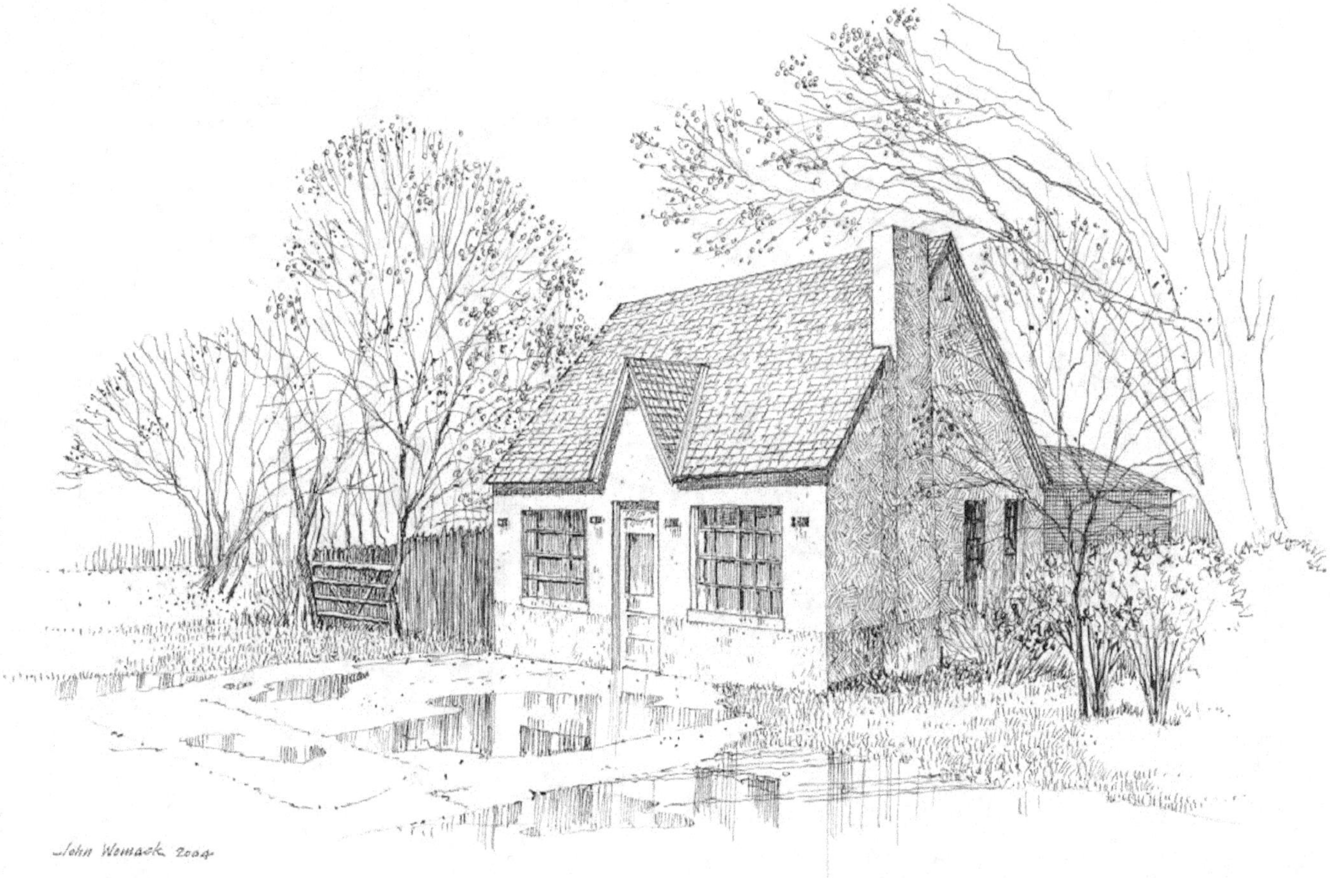

Cottage style station (Union Certified Gas Co.), Elk City, Oklahoma

Here is seen another variation of the cottage style station so closely associated with Route 66. This version is covered in stucco. Rain is greatly appreciated in western Oklahoma where the average rainfall is 24 inches per year. During the dry Dust Bowl years of 1934 through 1938, an estimated 300 million acres of topsoil were blown from Texas, Oklahoma, and Kansas. This, in combination with the Great Depression, had a devastating effect on many families.

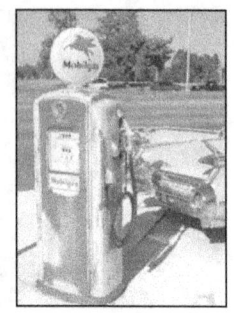

Mobil's winged horse, "Pegasus," dates to the late 1800s when the symbol was used by the original Standard Oil Trust. The name "Mobil" was adopted in 1954 by the Socony-Vacuum Corporation.

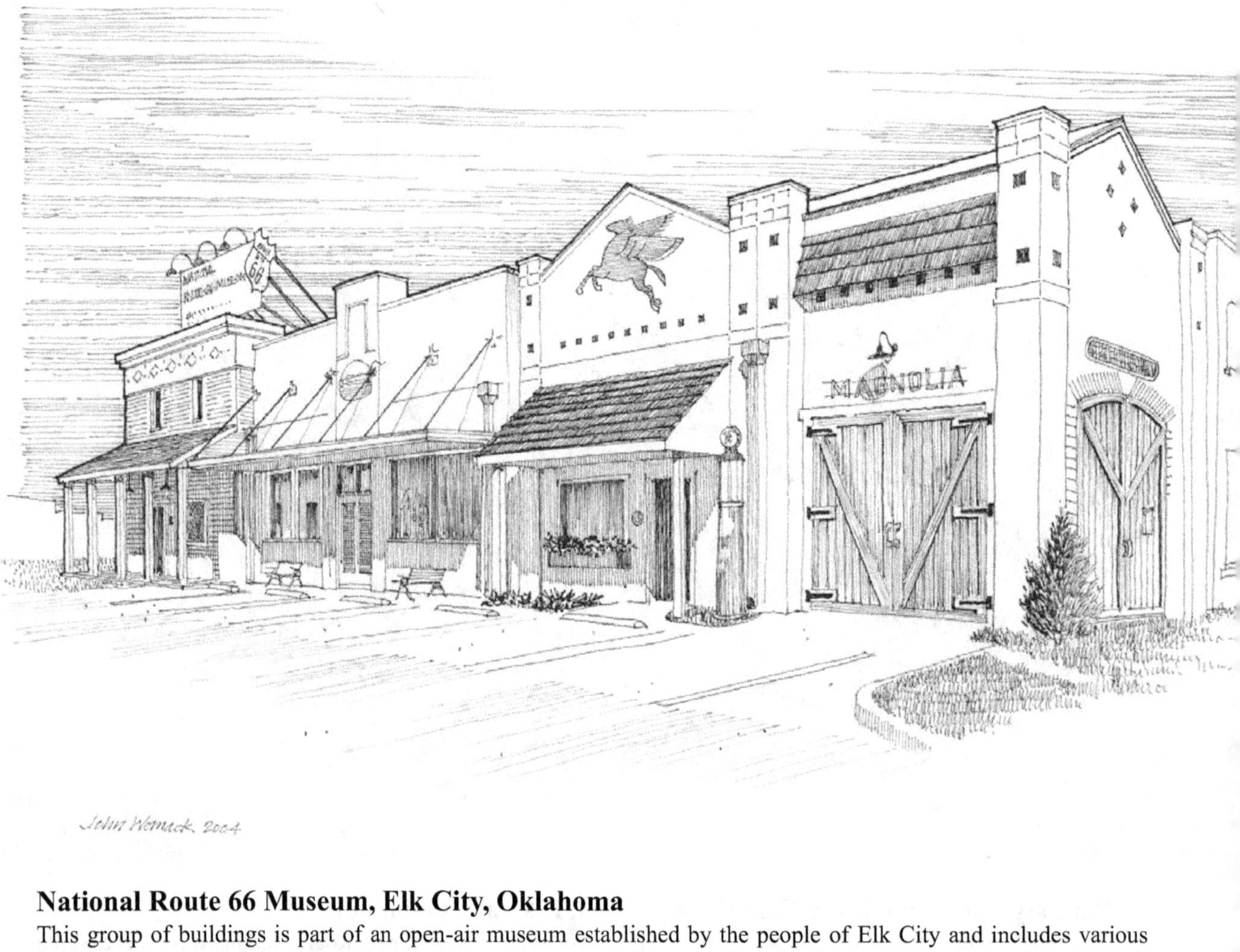

John Womack 2004

National Route 66 Museum, Elk City, Oklahoma

This group of buildings is part of an open-air museum established by the people of Elk City and includes various exhibits other than Route 66 material. The Route 66 museum offers excellent displays and has an extensive gift shop. The town was originally named "Busch" after Adolphus Busch of the Anheuser-Busch Brewery Company. Many early settlers objected to the name, especially women. In 1907, the town officially became "Elk City".

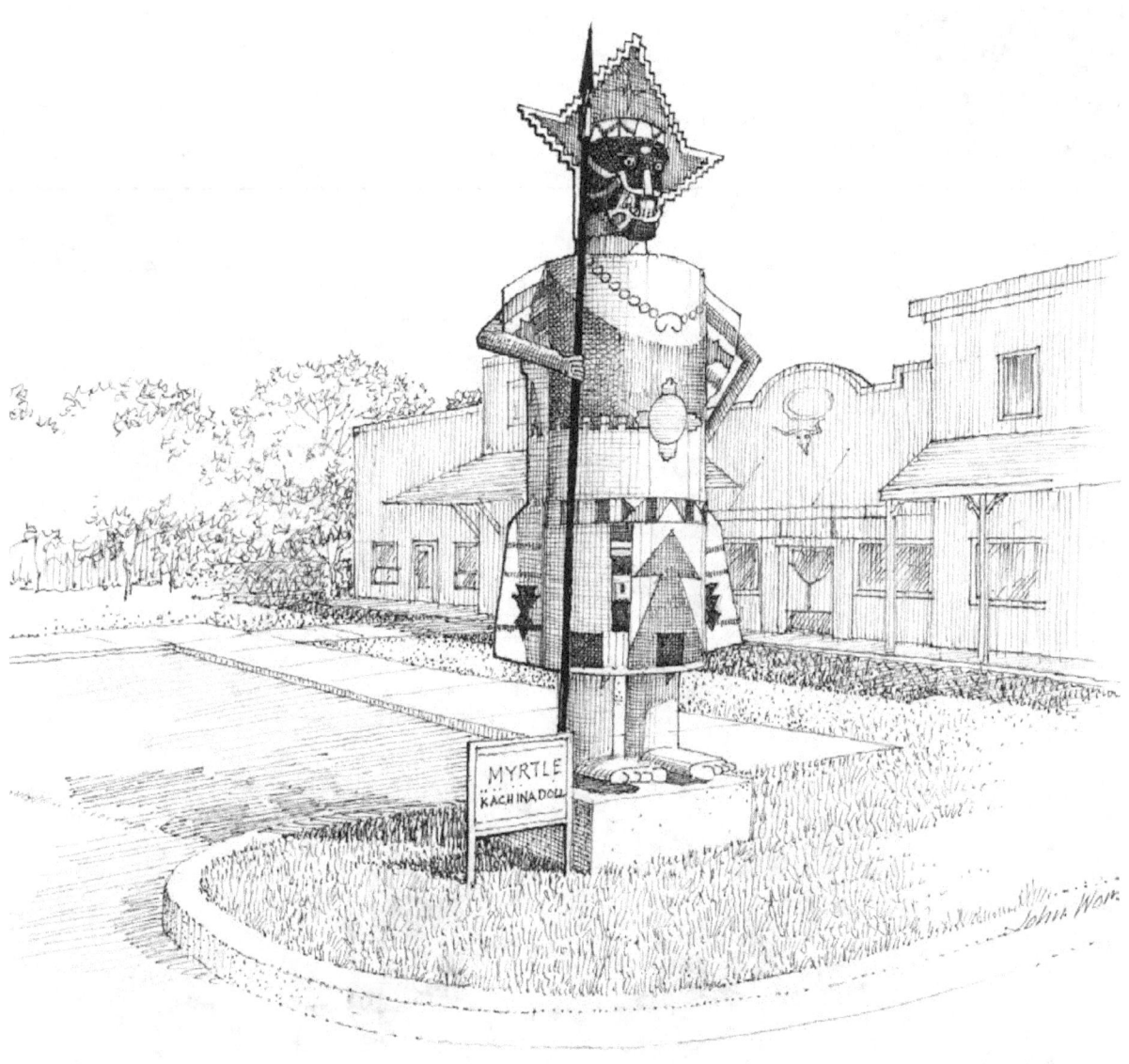

"Myrtle," National Route 66 Museum, Elk City, Oklahoma

This "kachina" sculpture, made from oil drums and other metal parts, was originally located west of Elk City at an Indian trading post named Queenan's. Now placed near the entrance to Elk City's Route 66 Museum, "Myrtle" typifies many such roadside tourist hooks that played upon a particular theme in an effort to entice highway travelers off the road and satisfy their curiosity—and hopefully spend a little money.

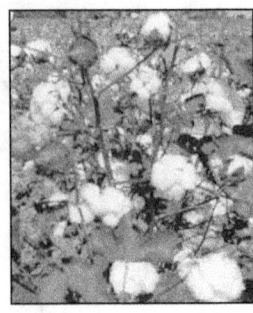

Cotton requires a warm-to-hot climate and some 180 frost-free days during the growing season.

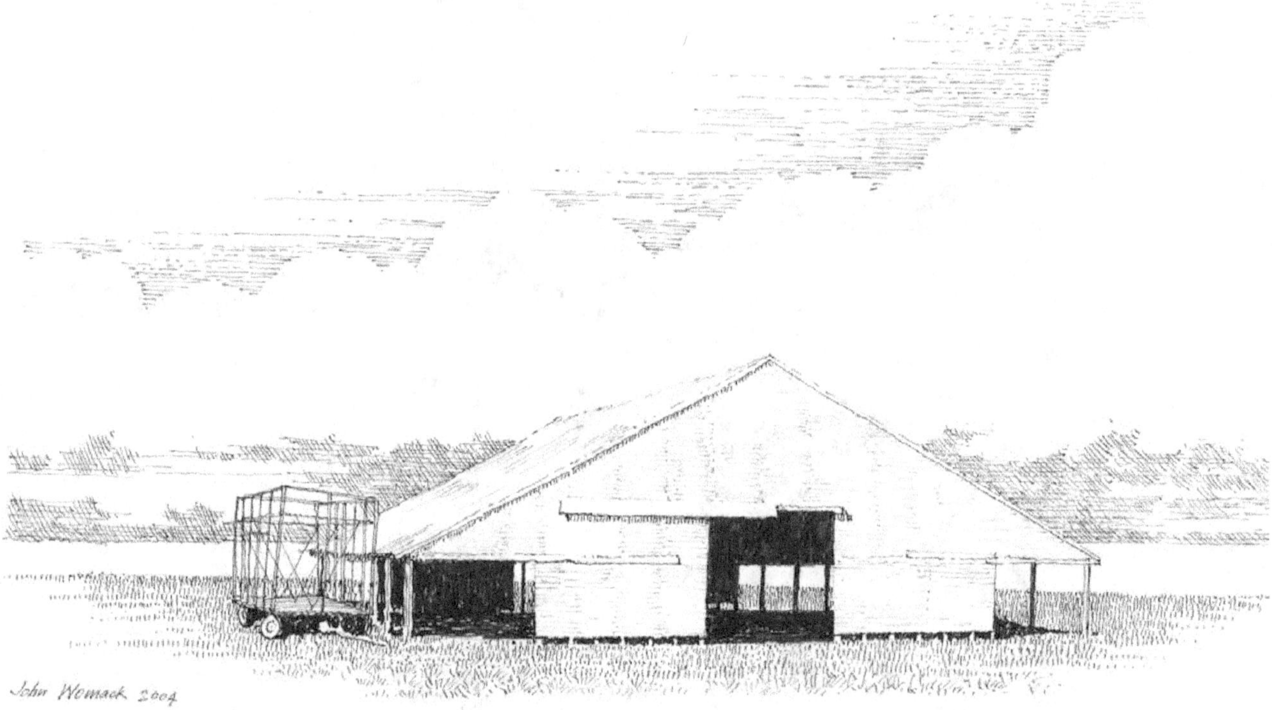

John Womack 2004

Cotton Barn, east of Sayre, Oklahoma

Cotton is a major agricultural crop in southwestern Oklahoma. Route 66 cuts through Beckham County before leaving the state and entering Texas. It is interesting to compare the barns of Oklahoma along Route 66 and how they change in form and material as their function and landscape vary. As seen here, the landscape is flat and almost featureless. The colors and shapes of many Oklahoma sunsets are simply awe-inspiring.

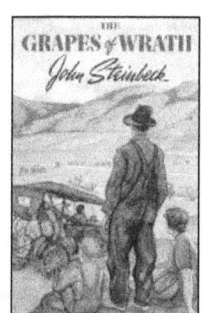

John Steinbeck gave Route 66 the name, "Mother Road," in his book, Grapes of Wrath. *Steinbeck's book brought a disturbing look into the lives of many Depression-deprived Americans of the 1930s.*

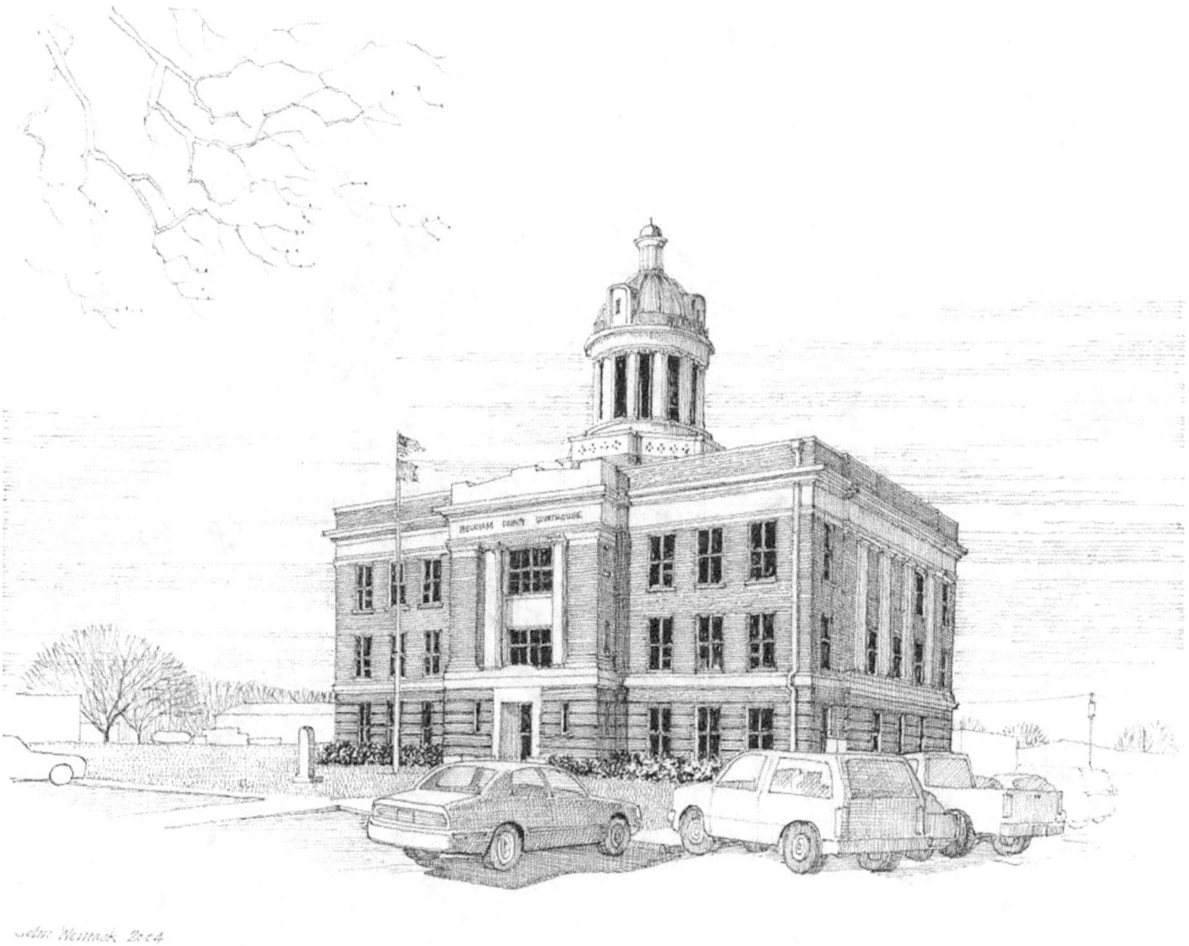

Beckham County Courthouse, Sayre, Oklahoma

This is an impressive courthouse that speaks directly to our sense of citizenship, law and order, and the notion of what democracy is all about. An interesting side note to this building, and its relationship to Route 66, is that it appeared in the 1940 movie, *The Grapes of Wrath*—John Steinbeck's story of a struggling Oklahoma family, traveling on Route 66 to California during the Great Depression.

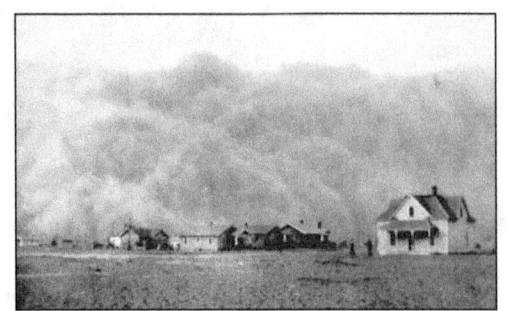

*Only photographs can begin to describe
the terrifying effect of a 1930s dust storm
(from a government file photo).*

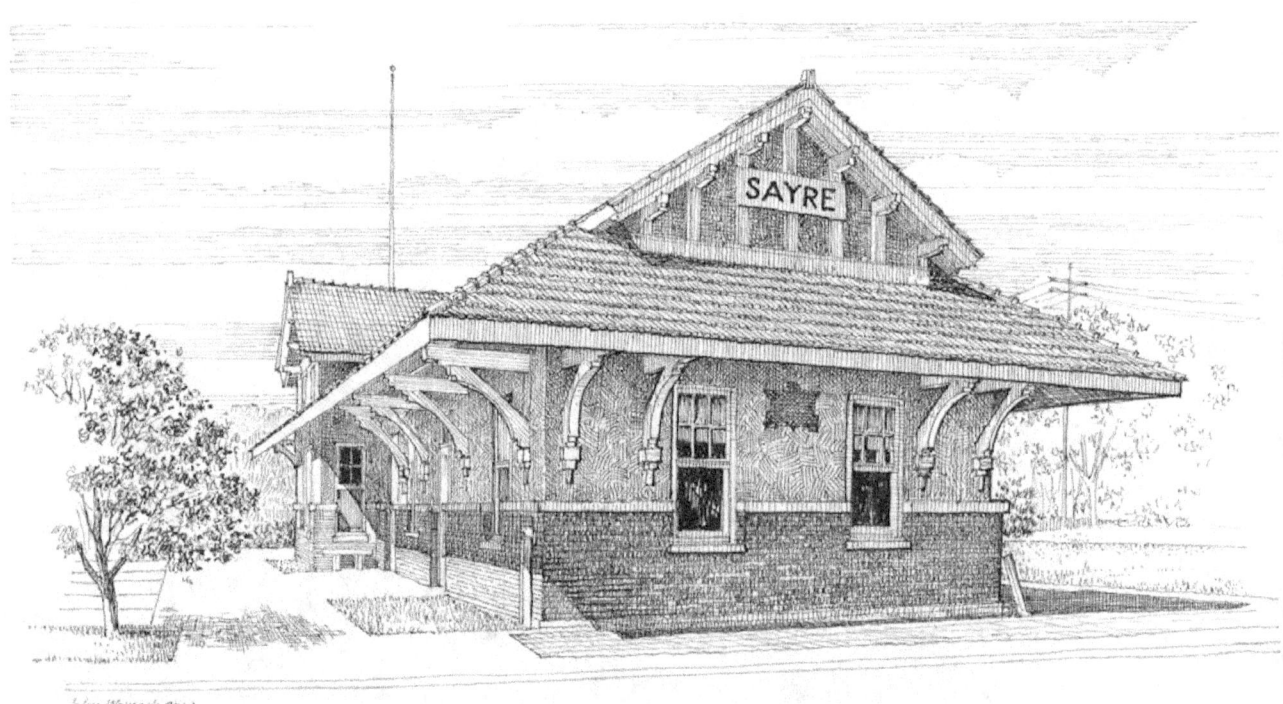

Rock Island Line Train Station and Depot, Sayre, Oklahoma

The old train station in Sayre is now home to the Short Grass Country Museum and Historical Society. Jesse Willard, Heavyweight Champion of the boxing world in 1915, brought a lot of attention to the town of Sayre. Following his retirement from boxing, Willard drove a freight wagon in and around town and also ran a boarding house in Sayre. The town received its name from Robert H. Sayre, a major stockholder in the railroad.

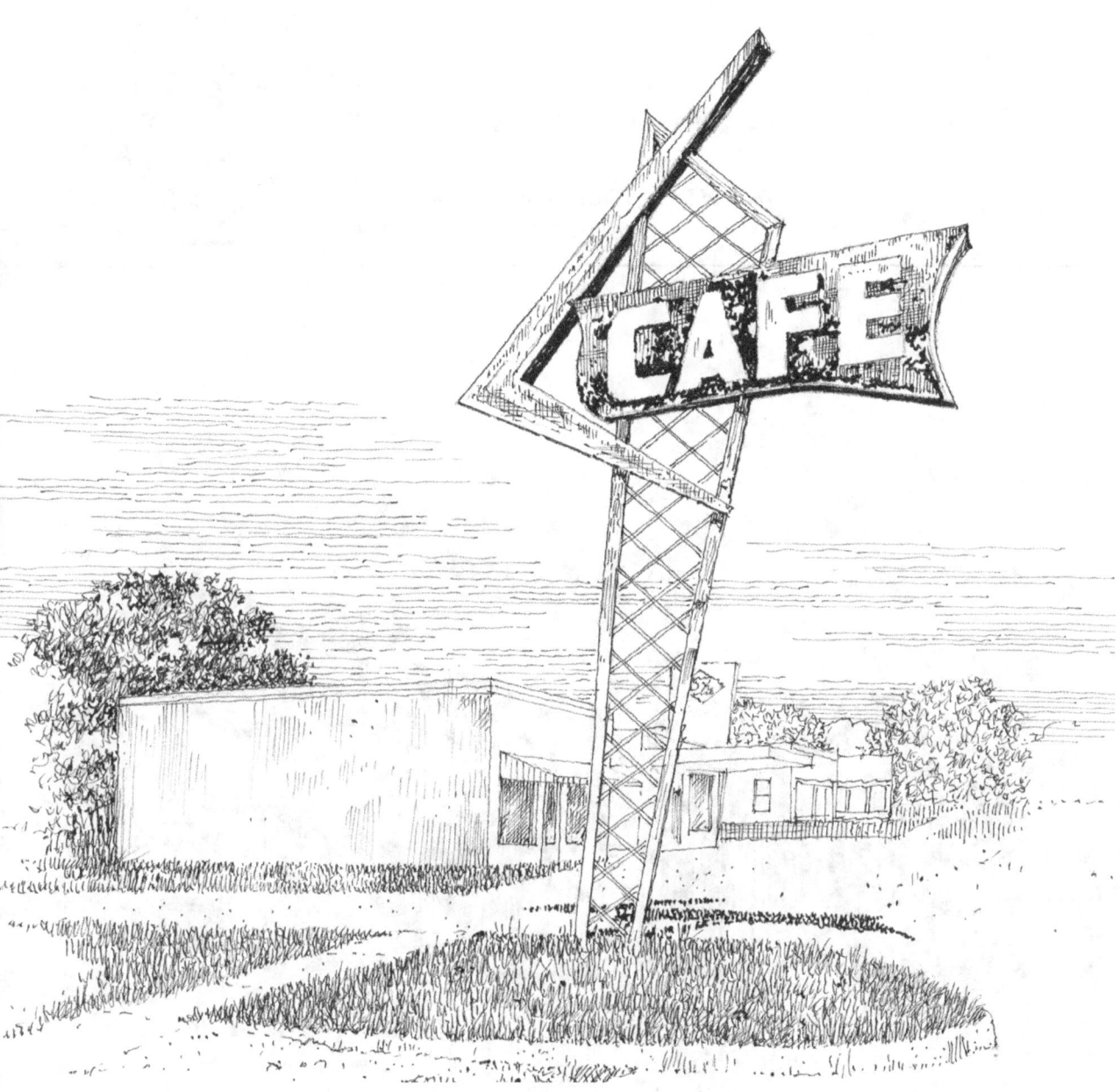

Cafe Sign, Sayre, Oklahoma

This deteriorating sign is emblematic of so many places along Route 66. Here the sign still points proudly to the cafe that, ironically, no longer exists. Approximately 20 miles north of Sayre is the Black Kettle Museum and site of the Washita Battlefield. On November 27, 1868, Lt. Col. George A. Custer's Seventh Cavalry attacked a sleeping village of Cheyenne and Arapaho people wintering along the Washita River. The "battle" remains controversial to this day.

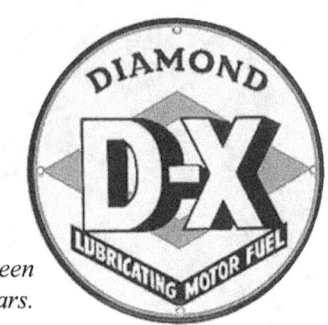

This old DX sign predates the newer station, seen below, by approximately twenty years.

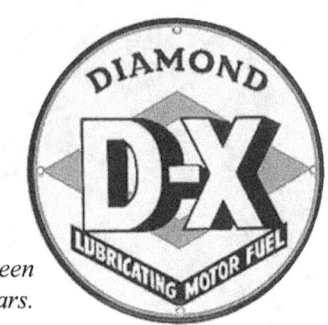

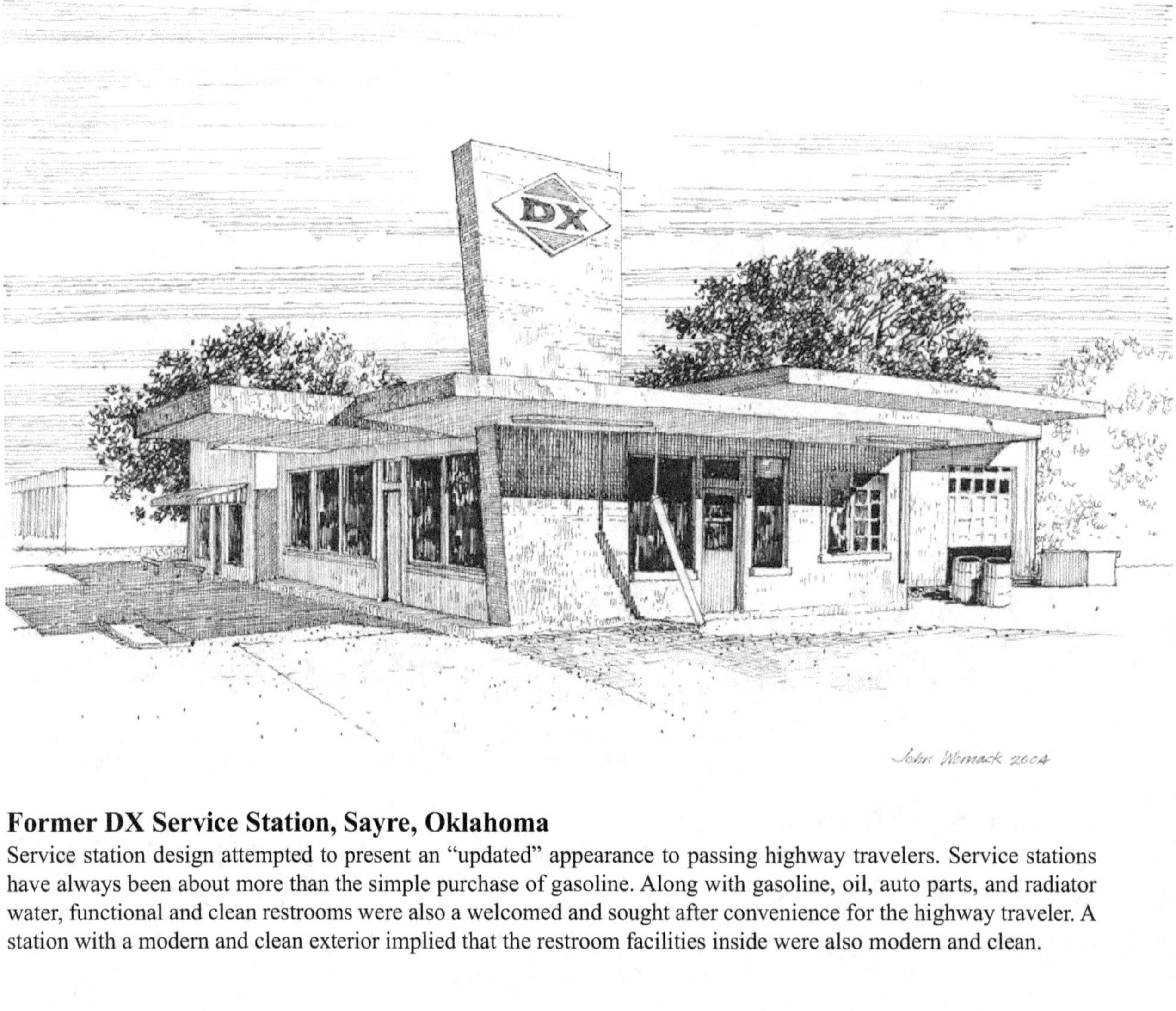

John Womack 2004

Former DX Service Station, Sayre, Oklahoma

Service station design attempted to present an "updated" appearance to passing highway travelers. Service stations have always been about more than the simple purchase of gasoline. Along with gasoline, oil, auto parts, and radiator water, functional and clean restrooms were also a welcomed and sought after convenience for the highway traveler. A station with a modern and clean exterior implied that the restroom facilities inside were also modern and clean.

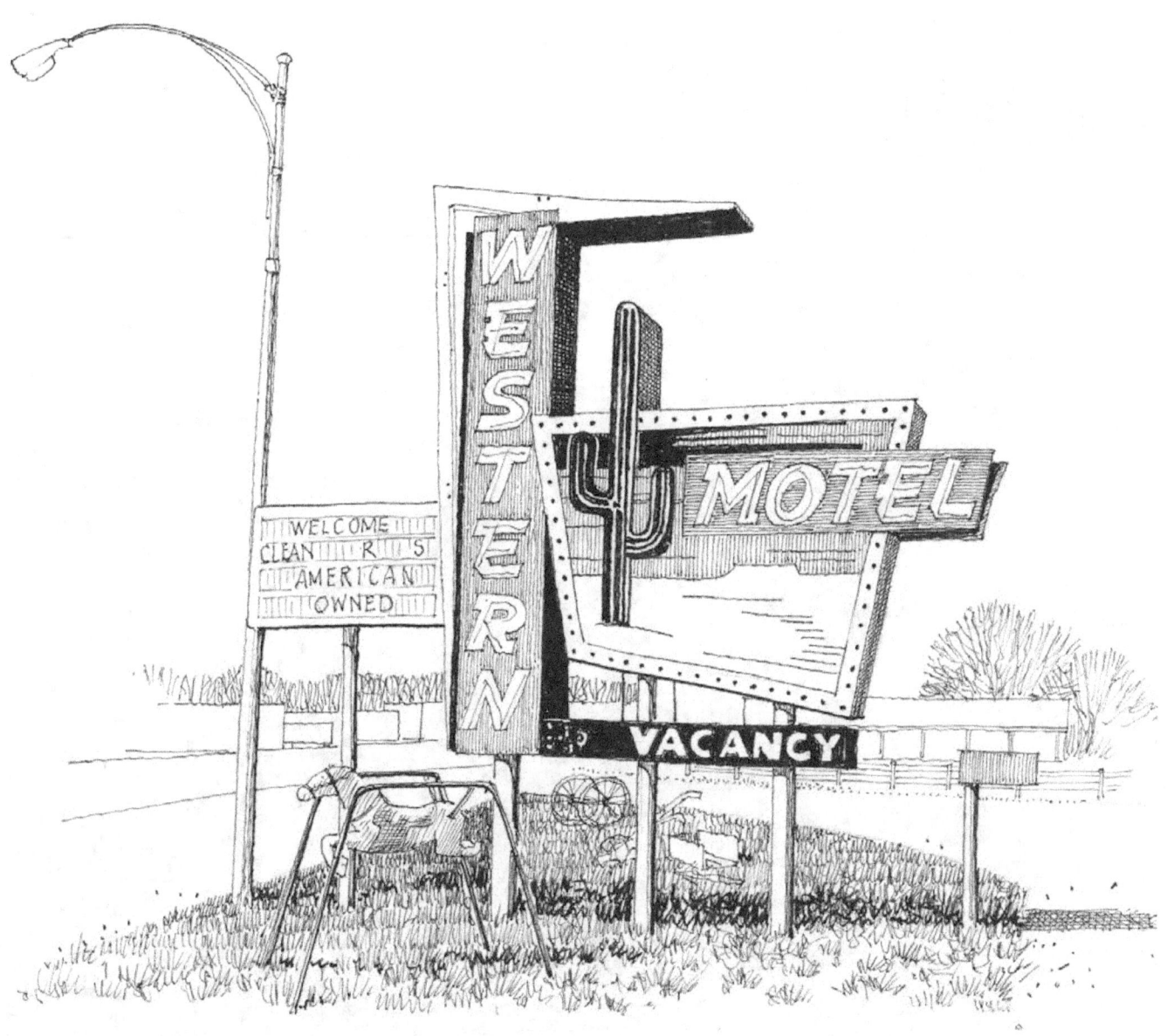

Western Motel Sign, Sayre, Oklahoma

Here is another sign with a cactus as part of its motif, and the arrow is also unique. The portion of the sign attached to the light pole appears to be a later addition. The message, "clean rooms" carries an obvious meaning; however, the other phrase, "American owned" is rather curious. The rocking horse in the foreground is a familiar toy to many of the baby boomer generation—I remember the one I rode when I was around four years old, and it looked like this one.

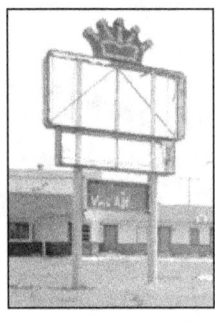

Signs of old abandoned motels still cast shadows upon the Mother Road in western Oklahoma.

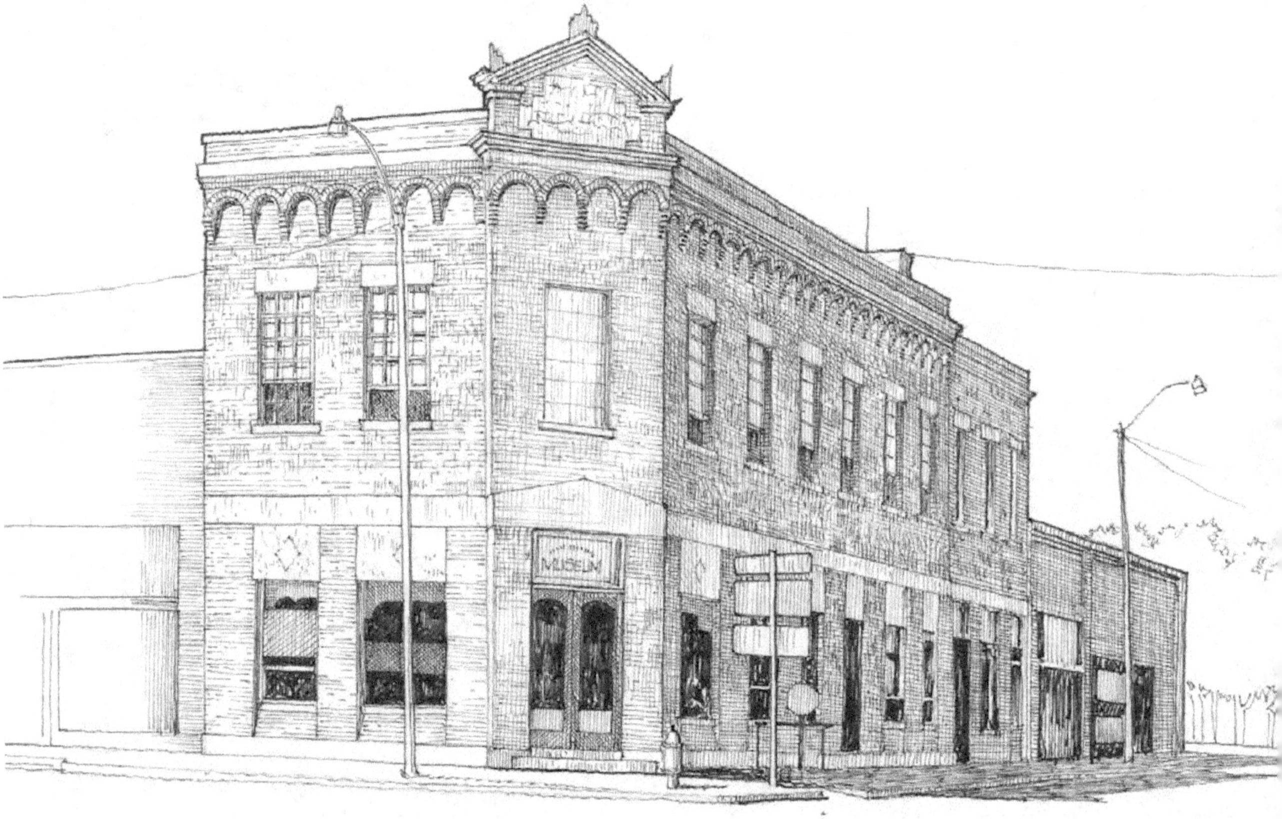

100th Meridian Museum, Erick, Oklahoma

This brick building, originally a bank, now houses a museum that tells the story of how the Texas and Oklahoma border was determined before accurate survey methods were developed. Erick was founded in 1901, and though deeply affected by hard times during the Depression, the town survived—due in large part to the presence of Route 66 and those that traveled the highway. Erick was home to country music greats Roger Miller and Sheb Wooley.

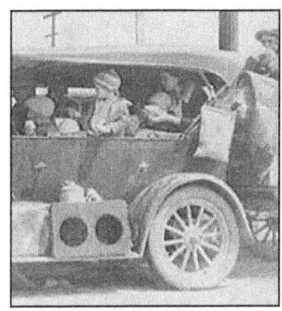

The Tulsa World *reported in 1936 that "one-fourth of homes in 45 counties most affected by dust storms had been abandoned in the previous three years."*

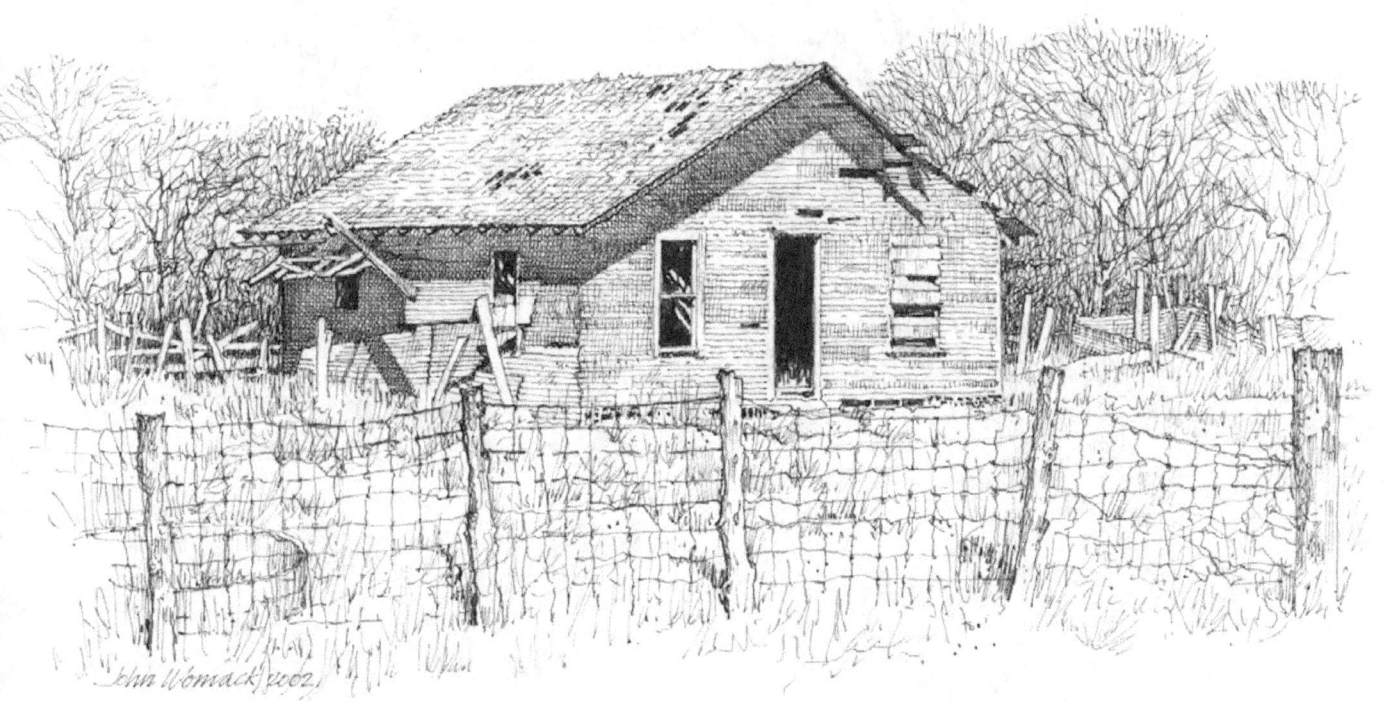

Abandoned Farm House, near Texola, Oklahoma

Again, another old farm house of unknown history but one that triggers my imagination. Extreme western Oklahoma suffered tremendously in the Dust Bowl of the 1930s. Thousands of Okies left the dried, parched soil of Oklahoma and traveled west on Route 66 in hopes of finding paying jobs in California and Arizona—like the Joad family in Steinbeck's novel, *Grapes of Wrath*.

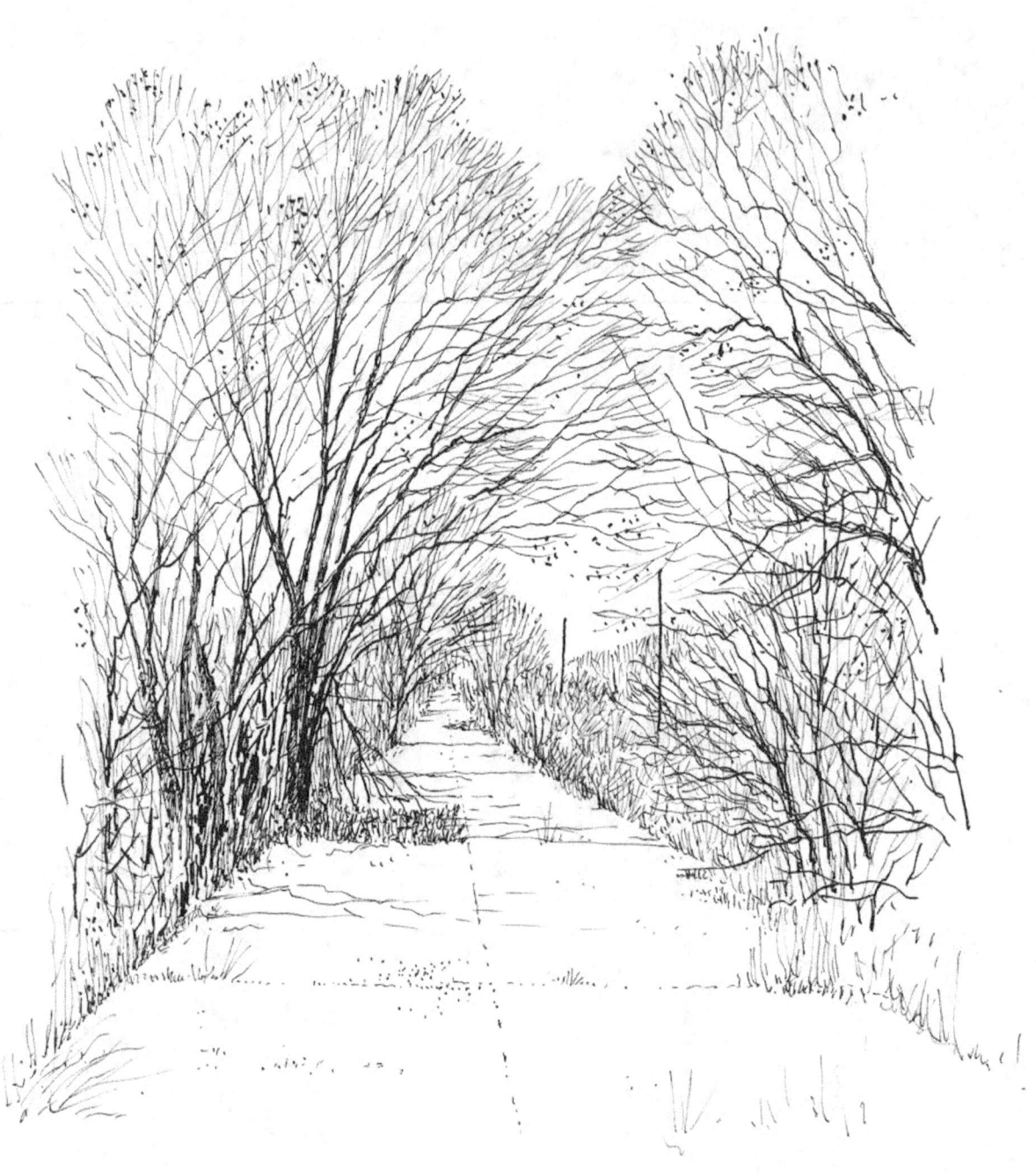

A deserted stretch of the original road, west of Sapulpa, Oklahoma

About the Artist and Author

John Calvin Womack is a native of Springdale, Arkansas, where he graduated from high school in 1968. Earning a Bachelors of Architecture degree and a Bachelor of Arts degree from the University of Arkansas in 1973, John entered the office of architect Euine Fay Jones in Fayetteville, Arkansas, where he worked for the next ten years. During his time with Fay Jones, he worked on many award-winning projects, two of which were the acclaimed Thorncrown Chapel and the Roy Reed Residence, both winners of National Honor Awards by the American Institute of Architects. Starting his own architectural practice in 1983, John continued designing projects in the organic tradition of Fay Jones and Frank Lloyd Wright. One of his first resi-dential designs appeared in *Fine Homebuilding's Special Issue on Houses* in 1988. His drawings and renderings have won awards in both architectural and art circles and have been published in various publications worldwide. In 1987, John began teaching in the University of Arkansas's School of Architecture as an adjunct professor. This exposure to teaching developed in him a passion for teaching and led to his obtaining a Masters of Architecture degree in 1994 from Oklahoma State University, which subsequently led to his joining the School of Architecture faculty at OSU in that same year. In the summer of 1994, John and his family moved from Fayetteville, Arkansas, to Stillwater, Oklahoma, where he continues to teach, draw, paint, and practice architecture.

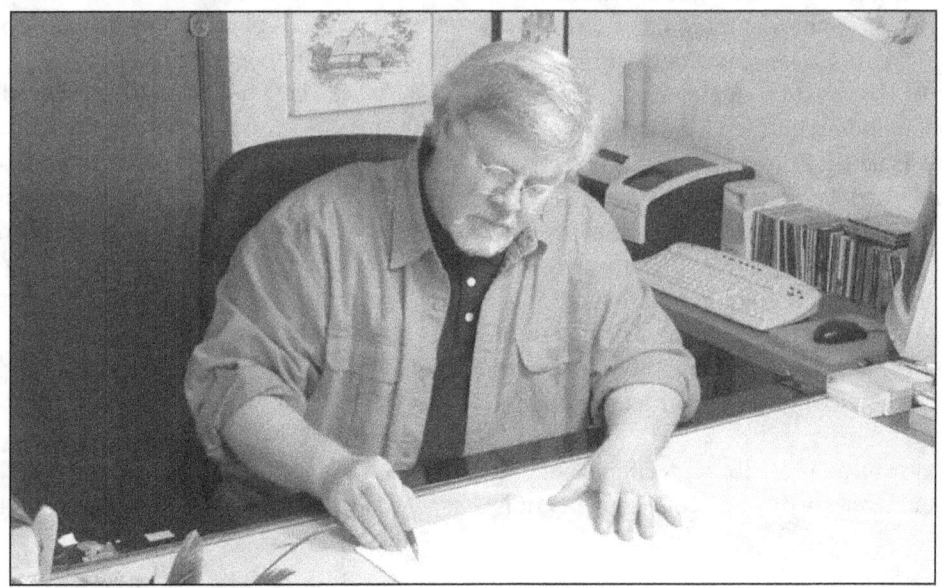

A Message from SHPO

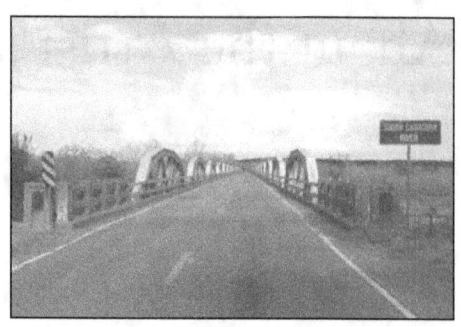

The William Murray Bridge, over the Canadian River. Photo by the State Historic Preservation Office, Oklahoma Historical Society.

Dear *Once Upon a Highway* Readers:

As part of its responsibilities under the National Historic Preservation Act, the State Historic Preservation Office (SHPO) carries out a statewide program to record archeological and historic resources and to nominate eligible properties to the National Register of Historic Places. These activities provide us the unique opportunity to study all aspects of Oklahoma's rich heritage and to work with the people concerned about protecting these important places. Of the dozens of survey and nomination projects we have completed, our studies of historic Route 66 are among the most interesting and rewarding. Gailard Sartain's eloquent introduction to *Once Upon a Highway* illustrates this point. There's just something about Route 66 that triggers memories and emotions.

We began our Route 66 survey initiative in 1984 in partnership with Oklahoma State University's Department of History and supplemented that early effort in cooperation with the U. S. Department of the Interior's Historic Route 66 Corridor Preservation Program. Roadbed segments, bridges, service stations, motels, and many other properties associated with travel on Route 66 were documented, and many of them are now listed on the National Register, a designation that signifies their worthiness of preservation. But, this special recognition does not guarantee that these buildings and structures will be preserved.

So, who is responsible for protecting Route 66 properties? As with any other piece of property, it is ultimately the owner's right to decide what happens to his property and his responsibility for whatever care it receives. However, each of us can play a role in the preservation of Route 66. The SHPO's programs provide tools for the property owner. For example, the National Register listing positions the owner to qualify for special tax incentives or grants for rehabilitation. Local organizations of all kinds sponsor events that focus on the historic highway, and these activities help keep the public aware of how important these historic properties are to the community and the tourists who visit them. Public awareness building is one of the best preservation strategies. As you leaf through the pages of this book, you see what John Womack has contributed to the Route 66 preservation effort; he has added to the documentation of these irreplaceable resources through his incredible drawings.

You can help too. Just drive the road, patronize the businesses working to keep the Route 66 spirit alive, and work as a local preservation advocate. With Route 66's recent designation as an Oklahoma Scenic Byway and the growing heritage tourism industry, there are bound to be ever-increasing visitors to the "Mother Road," and we will all benefit. So, get involved in protecting Route 66, and you are sure to have some fun along the way.

Melvena Heisch
Deputy SHPO
State Historic Preservation Office
Oklahoma Historical Society

www.ingramcontent.com/pod-product-compliance
Lightning Source LLC
Chambersburg PA
CBHW081124170526
45165CB00008B/2540